Environmental Economics: The Essentials

Environmental Economics: The Essentials offers a policy-oriented approach to the increasingly influential field of environmental economics that is based upon a solid foundation of economic theory and empirical research. Students will not only leave the course with a firm understanding of environmental economics, but they will also be exposed to a number of case studies showing how underlying economic principles provided the foundation for specific environmental and resource policies. This key text highlights what insights can be derived from the actual experience.

Key features include:

- Extensive coverage of the major issues including climate change, air and water pollution, sustainable development, and environmental justice;
- Introductions to the theory and method of environmental economics including externalities, experimental and behavioral economics, benefit-cost analysis, and methods for valuing the services provided by the environment;
- Boxed 'Examples' and 'Debates' throughout the text which highlight global examples and major talking points.

The text is fully supported with end-of-chapter summaries, discussion questions, and self-test exercises in the book, as well as with multiple-choice questions, simulations, references, slides, and an instructor's manual on the Companion Website. This text is adapted from the best-selling *Environmental and Natural Resource Economics*, 11th edition, by the same authors.

Tom Tietenberg is the Mitchell Family Professor of Economics, Emeritus at Colby College, Maine, USA.

Lynne Lewis is Elmer W. Campbell Professor of Economics at Bates College, Maine, USA.

Environmental Economics:
The Essentials

Tom Tietenberg and Lynne Lewis

Routledge
Taylor & Francis Group

NEW YORK AND LONDON

First published 2020
by Routledge
52 Vanderbilt Avenue, New York, NY 10017

and by Routledge
2 Park Square, Milton Park, Abingdon, Oxon, OX14 4RN

Routledge is an imprint of the Taylor & Francis Group, an informa business

Library of Congress Cataloging-in-Publication Data
A catalog record for this title has been requested

ISBN: 978-0-367-28037-6 (hbk)
ISBN: 978-0-367-28033-8 (pbk)
ISBN: 978-0-429-29929-2 (ebk)

Typeset in Sabon
by codeMantra
Printed and bound by CPI Group (UK) Ltd, Croydon, CR0 4YY

Visit the companion website: www.routledge.com/cw/Tietenberg

Contents in Brief

Preface   xvii

1 Visions of the Future   1

2 The Economic Approach: Property Rights, Externalities, and
   Environmental Problems   17

3 Evaluating Trade-Offs: Benefit-Cost Analysis and Other
   Decision-Making Metrics   45

4 Valuing the Environment: Methods   73

5 Economics of Pollution Control: An Overview   107

6 Stationary-Source Local and Regional Air Pollution   131

7 Mobile-Source Air Pollution   147

8 Climate Change   173

9 Water Pollution   195

10 Toxic Substances and Environmental Justice   227

11 The Quest for Sustainable Development   249

12 Visions of the Future Revisited   273

Answers to Self-Test Exercises   283
Glossary   291
Index   307

Contents in Full

Preface   **xvii**
    An Overview of the Book   **xvii**

1   **Visions of the Future**   **1**
   Introduction   **1**
     The Self-Extinction Premise   1
   Future Environmental Challenges   **2**
     Climate Change   2
       Example 1.1 *A Tale of Two Cultures*   3
     Water Accessibility   4
       Example 1.2 *Climate Change and Water Accessibility:*
       How Are these Challenges Linked?   5
   Meeting the Challenges   **5**
   How Will Societies Respond?   **6**
     The Role of Economics   7
       Debate 1.1 *Ecological Economics versus Environmental*
       Economics   7
     The Use of Models   8
   The Road Ahead   **9**
     The Underlying Questions   9
       Example 1.3 *Experimental Economics: Studying Human*
       Behavior in a Laboratory   10
       Debate 1.2 *What Does the Future Hold?*   11
     An Overview of the Book   12
   Summary   **13**
   Discussion Questions   **13**
   Self-Test Exercise   **14**
   Further Reading   **14**

2   **The Economic Approach: Property Rights, Externalities,**
   and Environmental Problems   **17**
   Introduction   **17**

The Human–Environment Relationship   **18**
The Environment as an Asset   18
The Economic Approach   19
Example 2.1 *Economic Impacts of Reducing Hazardous*
Pollutant Emissions from Iron and Steel Foundries   20
Environmental Problems and Economic Efficiency   **21**
Static Efficiency   21
Property Rights   **23**
Property Rights and Efficient Market Allocations   23
Efficient Property Rights Structures   23
Producer's Surplus, Scarcity Rent, and Long-Run Competitive
Equilibrium   24
Externalities as a Source of Market Failure   **25**
The Concept Introduced   25
Types of Externalities   26
Example 2.2 *Shrimp Farming Externalities in Thailand*   27
Perverse Incentives Arising from Some Property Right Structures   27
Public Goods   30
Imperfect Market Structures   31
Example 2.3 *Public Goods Privately Provided: The Nature*
Conservancy   33
Asymmetric Information   34
Government Failure   34
The Pursuit of Efficiency   **36**
Private Resolution through Negotiation—Property, Liability,
and the Coase Theorem   36
Legislative and Executive Regulation   39
An Efficient Role for Government   **40**
Example 2.4 *Can Eco-Certification Make a Difference?*
Organic Costa Rican Coffee   41
Summary   **42**
Discussion Questions   **42**
Self-Test Exercises   **43**
Further Reading   **44**

3   **Evaluating Trade-Offs: Benefit-Cost Analysis and Other**
Decision-Making Metrics   **45**
Introduction   **45**
Normative Criteria for Decision Making   **45**
Evaluating Predefined Options: Benefit-Cost Analysis   46
Finding the Optimal Outcome   47
Relating Optimality to Efficiency   48
Comparing Benefits and Costs across Time   49
Dynamic Efficiency   51

Applying the Concepts   **51**

Pollution Control   51

   Example 3.1 *Does Reducing Pollution Make Economic Sense?*
Evidence from the Clean Air Act   52

Estimating Benefits of Carbon Dioxide Emission Reductions   54

   Example 3.2 *Using the Social Cost of Carbon: The DOE*
Microwave Oven Rule   55

Issues in Benefit Estimation   56

   Debate 3.1 *What Is the Proper Geographic Scope for the*
Social Cost of Carbon?   57

Approaches to Cost Estimation   58

The Treatment of Risk   58

Distribution of Benefits and Costs   60

Choosing the Discount Rate   60

   Example 3.3 *The Importance of the Discount Rate*   61

   Debate 3.2 *Discounting over Long Time Horizons: Should*
Discount Rates Decline?   62

Divergence of Social and Private Discount Rates   **63**

A Critical Appraisal   64

   Example 3.4 *Is the Two for One Rule a Good Way to Manage*
Regulatory Overreach?   65

Other Decision-Making Metrics   **66**

Cost-Effectiveness Analysis   66

Impact Analysis   68

Summary   **68**

Discussion Questions   **69**

Self-Test Exercises   **70**

Further Reading   **71**

4   **Valuing the Environment: Methods**   **73**

Introduction   **73**

Why Value the Environment?   **74**

   Debate 4.1 *Should Humans Place an Economic Value on*
the Environment?   75

Valuation   **75**

Types of Values   77

Classifying Valuation Methods   78

Stated Preference Methods   78

Contingent Valuation Method   79

   Debate 4.2 *Willingness to Pay versus Willingness to Accept:*
Why So Different?   81

Choice Experiments   83

   Example 4.1 *Leave No Behavioral Trace: Using the Contingent*
Valuation Method to Measure Passive-Use Values   84

   Example 4.2 *The Value of US National Parks*   87

Revealed Preference Methods 89
   Example 4.3 *Using the Travel Cost Method to Estimate*
   Recreational Value: Beaches in Minorca, Spain 90
Benefit Transfer and Meta-Analysis 91
Using Geographic Information Systems to Enhance Valuation 92
Challenges 93
   Example 4.4 *Using GIS to Inform Hedonic Property Values:*
   Visualizing the Data 94
   Example 4.5 *Valuing the Reliability of Water Supplies: Coping*
   Expenditures in Kathmandu Valley, Nepal 95
   Debate 4.3 *Distance Decay in Willingness to Pay: When and*
   How Much Does Location Matter? 96
Valuing Human Life 97
   Debate 4.4 *What Is the Value of a Polar Bear?* 98
   Debate 4.5 *Is Valuing Human Life Immoral?* 100
Summary: Nonmarket Valuation Today 102
Discussion Question 103
Self-Test Exercises 103
Further Reading 104

5 Economics of Pollution Control: An Overview 107
Introduction 107
A Pollutant Taxonomy 108
Defining the Efficient Allocation of Pollution 109
Stock Pollutants 109
Fund Pollutants 110
Market Allocation of Pollution 112
Efficient Policy Responses 113
Cost-Effective Policies for Uniformly Mixed Fund Pollutants 114
Defining a Cost-Effective Allocation 114
Cost-Effective Pollution Control Policies 115
   Debate 5.1 *Should Developing Countries Rely on*
   Market-Based Instruments to Control Pollution? 120
Other Policy Dimensions 120
The Revenue Effect 121
   Example 5.1 *The Swedish Nitrogen Oxide Charge* 122
   Example 5.2 *RGGI Revenue: The Maine Example* 123
Responses to Changes in the Regulatory Environment 124
Instrument Choice under Uncertainty 124
Summary 125
Discussion Question 126
Self-Test Exercises 126
Further Reading 128
Appendix: The Simple Mathematics of Cost-Effective
Pollution Control 129

6   Stationary-Source Local and Regional Air Pollution   **131**
   Introduction   **131**
   Conventional Pollutants   **131**
      The Command-and-Control Policy Framework   132
      The Efficiency of the Command-and-Control Approach   133
         Debate 6.1 *Does Sound Policy Require Targeting New Sources*
         via the New Source Review?   133
         Debate 6.2 *The Particulate and Smog Ambient Standards*
         Controversy   135
      Cost-Effectiveness of the Command-and-Control Approach   136
         Example 6.1 *Controlling SO$_2$ Emissions by Command-and-*
         Control in Germany   137
      Air Quality   138
   Market-Based Approaches   **138**
      Emissions Charges   138
      Emissions Trading   139
         Example 6.2 *The Sulfur Allowance Program after 20 Years*   141
   Summary   **142**
         Example 6.3 *Technology Diffusion in the Chlorine-*
         Manufacturing Sector   143
   Discussion Questions   **144**
   Self-Test Exercises   **145**
   Further Reading   **145**

7   Mobile-Source Air Pollution   **147**
   Introduction   **147**
   Subsidies and Externalities   **149**
      Implicit Subsidies   149
      Externalities   149
      Consequences   151
   Policy toward Mobile Sources   **151**
      History of US Policy   151
      The US and EU Policy Approaches   152
         Example 7.1 *Monitoring and Enforcement:*
         The Volkswagen Experience   152
      Lead Phaseout Program   153
         Example 7.2 *Getting the Lead Out: The Lead Phaseout Program*   154
      Fuel Economy Standards—the US Approach   154
         Debate 7.1 *CAFE Standards or Fuel Taxes?*   155
         Example 7.3 *Fuel Economy Standards When Fuel Prices Are Falling* 156
      Gas Guzzler Tax   157
      Fuel Economy Standards in the European Union   157
         Example 7.4 *Car-Sharing: Better Use of Automotive Capital?*   158
      Fuel Economy Standards in Other Countries   159
      External Benefits of Fuel Economy Standards   159

Alternative Fuels and Vehicles   159
Transportation Pricing   161
　Example 7.5 *Zonal Mobile-Source Pollution-Control Strategies:*
　　Singapore   163
　Example 7.6 *Modifying Car Insurance as an Environmental*
　　Strategy   166
　Example 7.7 *The Cash-for-Clunkers Program:*
　　Did It Work?   167
　Example 7.8 *Counterproductive Policy Design*   168
Summary   **168**
Discussion Questions   170
Self-Test Exercises   170
Further Reading   171

8　Climate Change   **173**
Introduction   **173**
The Science of Climate Change   **174**
　Example 8.1 *Betting on Climate Science*   175
Negotiations over Climate Change Policy   **176**
　Characterizing the Broad Strategies   176
　Game Theory as a Window on Global Climate Negotiations   176
　　Debate 8.1 *Should Carbon Sequestration in the Terrestrial*
　　　Biosphere Be Credited?   177
The Precedent: Reducing Ozone-Depleting Gases   **180**
Economics and the Mitigation Policy Choice   **182**
　Providing Context: A Brief Look at Two Illustrative Carbon Pricing
　　Programs   182
　Carbon Markets and Taxes: How Have These Approaches Worked
　　in Practice?   183
　Three Carbon Pricing Program Design Issues: Using the Revenue,
　　Offsets, and Price Volatility   184
Controversy: The Morality of Emissions Trading   **187**
　Debate 8.2 *Is Global Greenhouse Gas Trading Immoral?*   187
Mitigation Policy: Timing   **188**
The Role of Adaptation Policy   **189**
Summary   **191**
Discussion Questions   192
Self-Test Exercises   192
Further Reading   193

9　Water Pollution   **195**
Introduction   **195**
Nature of Water Pollution Problems   **196**
　Types of Waste-Receiving Water   196
　Sources of Contamination   196
　Types of Pollutants   198

Debate 9.1 *Toxics in Fish Tissue: Do Fish Consumption Advisories Change Behavior?* 200

Traditional Water Pollution Control Policy 201

The US Experience 201

Early Legislation 201

Subsequent Legislation 202

The TMDL Program 204

The Safe Drinking Water Act 204

The Clean Water Rule 205

Ocean Pollution 205

Efficiency and Cost-Effectiveness 206

Ambient Standards and the Zero-Discharge Goal 206

National Effluent Standards 208

Municipal Wastewater Treatment Subsidies 208

Pretreatment Standards 209

Nonpoint Source Pollution 209

Watershed-Based Trading 210

Example 9.1 *Effluent Trading for Nitrogen in Long Island Sound* 211

Atmospheric Deposition of Pollution 215

The European Experience 215

Developing Country Experience 216

Example 9.2 *The Irish Bag Levy* 217

Example 9.3 *Economic Incentives for Water Pollution Control: The Case of Colombia* 218

Oil Spills—Tankers and Off-Shore Drilling 219

An Overall Assessment 220

Example 9.4 *Deepwater Horizon BP Oil Spill—Estimating the Damages* 221

Summary 223

Discussion Questions 223

Self-Test Exercises 224

Further Reading 225

10 Toxic Substances and Environmental Justice 227

Introduction 227

Nature of Toxic Substance Pollution 228

Health Effects 229

Policy Issues 229

Example 10.1 *The Arduous Path to Managing Toxic Risk: Bisphenol A* 230

Market Allocations and Toxic Substances 231

Occupational Hazards 231

Example 10.2 *Susceptible Populations in the Hazardous Workplace: An Historical Example* 234

Product Safety 235

Third Parties 235

The Incidence of Hazardous Waste Siting Decisions   **236**
  History   236
  Environmental Justice Research and the Emerging Role of GIS   237
  The Economics of Site Location   237
    Example 10.3 *Do New Polluting Facilities Affect Housing Values
      and Incomes? Evidence from New England*   238
    Example 10.4 *Which Came First—The Toxic Facility or the
      Minority Neighborhood?*   239
  The Policy Response   240
  The Toxic Release Inventory   242
    Debate 10.1 *Does Offering Compensation for Accepting an
      Environmental Risk Always Increase the Willingness to
      Accept the Risk?*   243
  Proposition 65   244
  International Agreements   244
    Example 10.5 *Regulating through Mandatory Disclosure:
      The Case of Lead*   245
Summary   **246**
Discussion Questions   **247**
Self-Test Exercises   **247**
Further Reading   **248**

11 The Quest for Sustainable Development   **249**
Introduction   **249**
Sustainability of Development   **250**
  Market Allocations   251
  Efficiency and Sustainability   252
  Trade and the Environment   254
    Debate 11.1 *Would the Protection of Elephant Populations
      Be Enhanced or Diminished By Allowing Limited
      International Trade in Ivory?*   255
    Example 11.1 *Has NAFTA Improved the Environment in Mexico?*   259
  Trade Rules under GATT and the WTO   259
    Debate 11.2 *Should an Importing Country Be Able to Use
      Trade Restrictions to Influence Harmful Fishing Practices
      in an Exporting Nation?*   260
  Natural Disasters   261
    Example 11.2 *Enhancing Resilience Against Natural Disasters
      with Flood Insurance*   262
  The Natural Resource Curse   263
    Example 11.3 *The "Natural Resource Curse" Hypothesis*   263
The Growth–Development Relationship   **264**
  Conventional Measures   264
  Alternative Measures   266

Summary   268
    Example 11.4 *Happiness Economics: Does Money Buy Happiness?*   269
Discussion Questions   270
Self-Test Exercises   270
Further Reading   271

12 Visions of the Future Revisited   273
Introduction   273
Addressing the Issues   273
  Conceptualizing the Problem   274
  Institutional Responses   275
    Example 12.1 *Private Incentives for Sustainable Development:*
    Can Adopting Sustainable Practices Be Profitable? 276
  Sustainable Development   278
    Example 12.2 *Public–Private Partnerships: The Kalundborg*
    Experience   279
A Concluding Comment   281
Discussion Questions   281
Further Reading   281

Answers to Self-Test Exercises   283
Glossary   291
Index   307

Preface

A glance at any newspaper will confirm that environmental economics is now a major player in environmental policy. Concepts such as cap-and-trade, carbon trading and carbon taxes, carbon offsets, sulfur allowance trading, gas guzzler taxes, tax credits of electric vehicles, pay-as-you-drive insurance, effluent trading, revenue-neutral taxes, oil-spill damage assessments, disclosure strategies for toxic substance control, extended producer responsibility, the social cost of carbon, the global commons, fuel economy savings, the Clean Development Mechanism, The United Nations Collaborative Program on Reducing Emissions from Deforestation and Forest Degradation in Developing Countries (REDD), congestion pricing, pollution havens, and sustainable development have moved from the textbook to the legislative hearing room. As the large number of current examples in *Environmental Economics: The Essentials* demonstrates, not only are ideas that were once restricted to academic discussions now part of the policy mix, but they are making a significant difference as well.

An Overview of the Book

Environmental Economics: The Essentials attempts to bring those who are beginning the study of environmental economics close to the frontiers of knowledge.

In this book we examine many of the newly popular market-based mechanisms within the context of both theory and practice. Environmental economics is a rapidly growing and changing field as many environmental issues become global in nature. In this text, we tackle some of the complex issues that face our globe and explore both the nature of the problems and how economics can provide potential solutions.

This book has a strong policy orientation. Although a great deal of theory and empirical evidence is discussed, their inclusion is motivated by the desire to increase understanding of intriguing market situations and policy problems. This explicit integration of research and policy within each chapter avoids a problem frequently encountered in applied economics textbooks—that is, in such texts the theory developed in earlier chapters is often only loosely connected to the rest of the book.

This is an economics book, but it goes beyond economics. Insights from the natural and physical sciences, literature, political science, and other disciplines are scattered liberally throughout the text. In some cases these references raise outstanding issues that economic analysis can help resolve, while in other cases they highlight important implications of the economic analysis or provide a contrasting point of view. They play an important role in overcoming the tendency to accept the material uncritically at a superficial level by highlighting those characteristics that make the economics approach unique.

Reflecting this new role of environmental economics in policy, a number of journals are now devoted either exclusively or mostly to the topics covered in this book. One journal, *Ecological Economics*, is dedicated to bringing economists and ecologists closer together in a common search for appropriate solutions for environmental challenges. Interested readers can also find advanced work in the field in *Land Economics, Journal of Environmental Economics and Management, Review of Environmental Economics and Policy, Environmental and Resource Economics*, and *International Review of Environmental and Environment and Development Economics*, among others.

A discussion list that involves material covered by this book is ResEcon. It is an academically inclined list focusing on problems related to environmental and natural resource management.

A very useful blog that deals with issues in environmental economics and their relationship to policy is located at www.env-econ.net.

Services on the Internet change so rapidly that some of this information may become obsolete. To keep updated on the various web options, visit the Companion Website of this text at www.routledge.com/cw/tietenberg. The site includes an online reference section with all the references cited in the book.

Supplements

For each chapter in the text, the *Online Instructor's Manual*, originally written by Lynne Lewis of Bates College, provides an overview, teaching objectives, a chapter outline with key terms, common student difficulties, and suggested classroom exercises. PowerPoint presentations, prepared by Hui Li of Eastern Illinois University, are available for instructors and include all art and figures from the text as well as lecture notes for each chapter. Professors can download the *Online Instructor's Manual* and the PowerPoint presentations at the Instructor Resource Center (www.routledge.com/cw/tietenberg).

The book's Companion Website (www.routledge.com/cw/tietenberg) features chapter-by-chapter web links to additional reading and economic data.

The Companion Website also provides self-study quizzes for each chapter. Written and updated by Elizabeth Wheaton of Southern Methodist University, each of these chapter quizzes contains multiple-choice questions for students to test what they have learned.

Acknowledgments

The most rewarding part of writing this book is that we have met so many thoughtful interesting people. We very much appreciate the faculty and students who pointed out areas of particular strength or areas where coverage could be expanded. Their support has been gratifying and energizing. One can begin to understand the magnitude of our debt to our colleagues by glancing at the several hundred names in the lists of references. Because their research contributions make this an exciting field, full of insights worthy of being shared, our task was easier and a lot more fun than it might otherwise have been.

We also owe a large debt of gratitude to the following group who provided detailed, helpful reviews of the text and supplied many useful ideas for this revision:

Massimiliano Mazzanti, Universita Bocconi, Italy
Richard Stahl, Louisiana State University, USA

Julia Swart, Utrecht University School of Economics, Netherlands
Beth Wheaton, Southern Methodist University, USA
Hermann Waibel, University of Hannover, Germany
Theocharis Grigoriadis, Freie Universitat Berlin, Germany
Jim Vincent, University of St. Thomas, USA
Viktoria Kahui, University of Otago, New Zealand
Joost Burmann, National University of Singapore, Malaysia
Wei Zhang, Connecticut College, USA
Dennis Guignet, American University, USA

Working with Routledge has been a delightful experience. Our commissioning editor, Andy Humphries, has been continually helpful since the initiation of this edition. We would also like to acknowledge Alaina Christensen and Kelly Cracknell, production editors, as well as Kate Reeves (copyeditor), Sarah Fish (copyeditor and proofreader), Hugh Jackson (proofreader), Linda Clark (indexer), Gareth Toye (cover designer), Keystroke (typesetting), and CodeMantra (typesetting), as well as those who managed the Companion Website content. Thanks to you all!

Lynne's most helpful research assistants for this edition were Amy Schmidt and Madeleine Shapiro.

Working with all of the fine young scholars who have assisted with our writing over the years has made it all the more obvious why teaching is the world's most satisfying profession. Finally, Tom would like to express publicly his deep appreciation to his wife, Gretchen, his daughter Heidi, and his son Eric for their love and support. Lynne would like to express her gratitude to Jack for his unwavering support, patience, and generosity. Thank you.

Tom Tietenberg
Lynne Lewis

Chapter 1

Visions of the Future

From the arch of the bridge to which his guide has carried him, Dante now sees the Diviners . . . coming slowly along the bottom of the fourth Chasm. By help of their incantations and evil agents, they had endeavored to pry into the future which belongs to the almighty alone, and now their faces are painfully twisted the contrary way; and being unable to look before them, they are forced to walk backwards.

—Dante Alighieri, *Divine Comedy: The Inferno*, translated by Carlyle (1867)

Introduction

The Self-Extinction Premise

About the time the American colonies won independence, Edward Gibbon completed his monumental *The History of the Decline and Fall of the Roman Empire*. In a particularly poignant passage that opens the last chapter of his opus, he re-creates a scene in which the learned Poggius, a friend, and two servants ascend the Capitoline Hill after the fall of Rome. They are awed by the contrast between what Rome once was and what Rome has become:

In the time of the poet it was crowned with the golden roofs of a temple; the temple is overthrown, the gold has been pillaged, the wheel of fortune has accomplished her revolution, and the sacred ground is again disfigured with thorns and brambles. . . . The forum of the Roman people, where they assembled to enact their laws and elect their magistrates, is now enclosed for the cultivation of potherbs, or thrown open for the reception of swine and buffaloes. The public and private edifices that were founded for eternity lie prostrate, naked, and broken, like the limbs of a mighty giant; and the ruin is the more visible, from the stupendous relics that have survived the injuries of time and fortune.

(Vol. 6, pp. 650–651)

What could cause the demise of such a grand and powerful society? Gibbon weaves a complex thesis to answer this question, suggesting ultimately that the seeds for Rome's destruction were sown by the Empire itself. Although Rome finally succumbed to such external forces as fires and invasions, its vulnerability was based upon internal weakness.

The premise that societies can germinate the seeds of their own destruction has long fascinated scholars. In 1798, Thomas Malthus published his classic *An Essay on the Principle of Population*, in which he foresaw a time when the urge to reproduce would cause population growth to exceed the land's potential to supply sufficient food, resulting in starvation and death. In his view, the most likely response to this crisis would involve rising death rates caused by environmental constraints, rather than a recognition of impending scarcity followed either by innovation or self-restraint.

Historically, our society has been remarkably robust, having survived wars and shortages, while dramatically increasing living standards and life expectancy. Yet, actual historical examples suggest that Malthus's self-extinction vision may sometimes have merit. Example 1.1 examines two specific cases: the Mayan civilization and Easter Island.

Future Environmental Challenges

Future societies will face challenges arising from resource scarcity and accumulating pollutants. Many specific examples of these broad categories of problems are discussed in detail in the following chapters. This section provides a flavor of what is to come by illustrating the challenges posed by one pollution problem (climate change) and one resource scarcity problem (water accessibility).

Climate Change

Energy from the sun drives the earth's weather and climate. Incoming rays heat the earth's surface, radiating heat energy back into space. Atmospheric "greenhouse" gases (water vapor, carbon dioxide, and other gases) trap some of the outgoing energy.

Without this natural "greenhouse effect," temperatures on the earth would be much lower than they are now and life as we know it would be impossible. It is possible, however, to have too much of a good thing. Problems arise when the concentration of greenhouse gases increases beyond normal levels, thus retaining excessive heat somewhat like a car with its windows closed in the summer.

Since the Industrial Revolution, greenhouse gas emissions have increased, considerably enhancing the heat-trapping capability of the earth's atmosphere. According to the US Global Change Research Program (USGCRP) (2014):[1]

> Evidence from the top of the atmosphere to the depths of the oceans, collected by scientists and engineers from around the world, tells an unambiguous story: the planet is warming, and over the last half century, this warming has been driven primarily by human activity—predominantly the burning of fossil fuels.

As the earth warms, the consequences are expected to affect both humans and ecosystems. Humans are susceptible to increased heat, as shown by the thousands of deaths in Europe in the summer of 2003 due to the abnormal heat waves. Human health can also be affected by diseases such as Lyme disease, which spread more widely as the earth warms. Rising sea levels (as warmer water expands and previously frozen glaciers melt), coupled with an increase in

EXAMPLE 1.1

A Tale of Two Cultures

The Mayan civilization, a vibrant and highly cultured society that occupied parts of Central America, did not survive. One of the major settlements, Copán, has been studied in sufficient detail to learn reasons for its collapse.

After AD 400 the population growth began to bump into an environmental constraint, specifically the agricultural carrying capacity of the land. The growing population depended heavily on a single, locally grown crop—maize—for food. By early in the sixth century, however, the carrying capacity of the most productive local lands was exceeded, and farmers began to depend upon more fragile parts of the ecosystem. Newly acquired climate data show that a two-century period with a favorable climate was followed by a general drying trend lasting four centuries that led to a series of major droughts. Food production failed to keep pace with the increasing population.

By the eighth and ninth centuries, the evidence reveals not only high levels of infant and adolescent mortality but also widespread malnutrition. The royal dynasty, an important source of leadership, collapsed rather abruptly sometime about AD 820–822.

The second case study, Easter Island, shares some remarkable similarities with both the Mayan case and the Malthusian vision. Easter Island lies some 2000 miles off the coast of Chile. Current visitors note that it is distinguished by two features: (1) its enormous statues carved from volcanic rock and (2) a surprisingly sparse vegetation, given the island's favorable climate and conditions. Both the existence of these imposing statues and the fact that they were erected at a considerable distance from the quarry suggests the presence of an advanced civilization, but current observers see no sign of it. What happened? According to scholars, the short answer is that a rising population, coupled with a heavy reliance on wood for housing, canoe building, and statue transportation, decimated the forest (Brander and Taylor, 1998). The loss of the forest contributed to soil erosion, declining soil productivity, and, ultimately, diminished food production. How did the community react to the impending scarcity? Apparently, the social response was war among the remaining island factions and, ultimately, cannibalism.

We would like to believe not only that in the face of impending scarcity societies would react by changing behavior to adapt to the diminishing resource supplies, but also that this benign response would follow automatically from a recognition of the problem. We even have a cliché to capture this sentiment: "necessity is the mother of invention." These stories do point out, however, that nothing is automatic about a problem-solving response. As we shall see as this book unfolds, sometimes societies not only fail to solve the problem but their reactions can actually intensify it.

Sources: Webster, D., Freter, A., & Golin, N. (2000). *Copan: The Rise and Fall of an Ancient Maya Kingdom.* Fort Worth, TX: Harcourt Brace Publishers; Brander, J. A., & Taylor, M. S. (1998). The simple economics of Easter Island: A Ricardo–Malthus model of renewable resource use. *The American Economic Review, 88*(1), 119–138; Turner, B. L., & Sabloff, J. A. (2012). Classic period collapse of the central Maya lowlands: Insights about human–environment relationships for sustainability. *Proceedings of the National Academy of Sciences, 109*(35), 13908–13914; Pringle, Heather. (2012). Climate change had political, human impact on ancient Maya. *Science* (November 9), 730–731.

storm intensity, are expected to flood coastal communities with greater frequency. Ecosystems will be subjected to unaccustomed temperatures; some species will adapt by migrating to new areas, but many others are not expected to be able to react in time. While these processes have already begun, they will intensify throughout the century.

Climate change also has an important moral dimension. Due to their more limited adaptation capabilities, many developing countries, which have produced relatively small amounts of greenhouse gases, are expected to be the hardest hit as the climate changes.

Dealing with climate change will require a coordinated international response. That is a significant challenge to a world system where the nation-state reigns supreme and international organizations are relatively weak.

Water Accessibility

Another class of threats is posed by the interaction of a rising demand for resources in the face of a finite supply. Water provides a particularly interesting example because it is so vital to life.

According to the United Nations, about 40 percent of the world's population lives in areas with moderate-to-high water stress. ("Moderate stress" is defined in the UN Assessment of Freshwater Resources as "human consumption of more than 20 percent of all accessible renewable freshwater resources," whereas "severe stress" denotes consumption greater than 40 percent.) By 2025, it is estimated that about two-thirds of the world's population—about 5.5 billion people—will live in areas facing either moderate or severe water stress.

This stress is not uniformly distributed around the globe. For example, in parts of the United States, Mexico, China, and India, groundwater is already being consumed faster than it is being replenished, and aquifer levels are steadily falling. Some rivers, such as the Colorado in the western United States and the Yellow in China, often run dry before they reach the sea. Formerly enormous bodies of water, such as the Aral Sea and Lake Chad, are now a fraction of their once-historic sizes. Glaciers that feed many Asian rivers are shrinking.

According to UN data, the continents most burdened by a lack of access to sufficient clean water are Africa and Asia. Up to 50 percent of Africa's urban residents and 75 percent of Asians are estimated to lack adequate access to a safe water supply.

The availability of potable water is further limited by human activities that contaminate the remaining supplies. According to the United Nations, 90 percent of sewage and 70 percent of industrial waste in developing countries are discharged without treatment. And climate change is expected to intensify both the frequency and duration of droughts, simultaneously increasing the demand for water and reducing its supply.

Some arid areas have compensated for their lack of water by importing it via aqueducts from more richly endowed regions or by building large reservoirs. This solution can, however, promote conflict when the water transfer or the relocation of people living in the area to be flooded by the reservoir produces a backlash. Additionally, aqueducts and dams may be geologically vulnerable. For example, in California, many of the aqueducts cross or lie on known earthquake-prone fault lines (Reisner, 2003). The reservoir behind the Three Gorges Dam in China is so vast that the pressure and weight from the stored water have caused tremors and landslides.

Furthermore, climate change and water accessibility are interdependent problems. Example 1.2 explores both their relationship and why it matters.

EXAMPLE 1.2

Climate Change and Water Accessibility: How Are these Challenges Linked?

From a policy analysis point of view, whether these challenges are interdependent matters. If they are linked, their interactions must be considered in the design of any polices created to meet the challenges. Otherwise the response may be neither efficient nor effective.

On May 3, 2016, the World Bank released a report that documents and analyzes the nature and economic implications of the linkages. It notes that climate change will exacerbate water scarcity even as demand for water increases, potentially leading to negative economic impacts and security challenges. According to the report:

Within the next 3 decades, the global food system will require between 40 to 50 percent more water; municipal and industrial water demand will increase by 50 to 70 percent; the energy sector will see water demand increase by 85 percent; and the environment, already the residual claimant, may receive even less.

The report further anticipates that in the Middle East and Africa conditions will worsen, costing these regions up to six percent of their GDP by 2050.

The report concludes:

While adopting policy reforms and investments will be demanding, the costs of inaction are far higher. The future will be thirsty and uncertain, but with the right reforms, governments can help ensure that people and ecosystems are not left vulnerable to the consequences of a world subject to more severe water-related shocks and adverse rainfall trends. (p. ix)

Source: World Bank. (2016). *High and Dry: Climate Change, Water, and the Economy.* Washington, DC: World Bank. License: Creative Commons Attribution CC BY 3.0 IGO.

Meeting the Challenges

As the scale of economic activity has proceeded steadily upward, the scope of environmental problems triggered by that activity has transcended both geographic and generational boundaries. When the environmental problems were smaller in scale, the nation-state used to be a sufficient form of political organization for resolving them, but is that still the case? Whereas each generation used to have the luxury of being able to satisfy its own needs without worrying about the needs of generations to come, intergenerational effects are now more prominent. Solving problems such as poverty, climate change, ozone depletion, and the loss of biodiversity requires international cooperation. Because future generations cannot speak for themselves, the current generation must speak for them. Current policies must incorporate our obligation to future generations, however difficult or imperfect that incorporation might prove to be.

International cooperation is by no means a foregone conclusion. Global environmental problems can result in very different effects on countries that will sit around the negotiating table. While low-lying countries could be completely submerged by the sea level rise predicted by some climate change models, arid nations could see their marginal agricultural lands succumb to desertification. Other nations may see agricultural productivity rise as warmer climates in traditionally intemperate regions support longer growing seasons.

Countries that unilaterally set out to improve the global environmental situation run the risk of making their businesses vulnerable to competition from less conscientious nations. Industrialized countries that undertake stringent environmental policies may not suffer much at the national level due to offsetting increases in income and employment in industries that supply renewable, cleaner energy and pollution control equipment. Some specific industries facing stringent environmental regulations, however, may well face higher costs than their competitors, and can be expected to lose market share accordingly. Declining market share and employment resulting from especially stringent regulations and the threat of out-sourced production are powerful influences. The search for solutions must accommodate these concerns.

The market system is remarkably resilient in how it responds to challenges. As we shall see, prices provide incentives not only for the wise use of current resources, but also for promoting innovations that can broaden the menu of future options.

Yet, as we shall also see, market incentives are not always consistent with promoting sustainable outcomes. Currently, many individuals and institutions have a large stake in maintaining the status quo, even when it poses an existential threat. Fishermen harvesting their catch from an overexploited fishery are loath to reduce harvests, even when the reduction may be necessary to conserve the stock and to return the population to a healthy level. Farmers who depend on fertilizer and pesticide subsidies will give them up reluctantly. Coal companies resist any attempt to reduce carbon emissions from coal-fired power plants.

How Will Societies Respond?

The fundamental question is how our society will respond to these challenges. One way to think systematically about this question involves feedback loops.

Positive feedback loops are those in which secondary effects tend to reinforce the basic trend. The process of capital accumulation illustrates one positive feedback loop. New investment generates greater output, which, when sold, generates profits. These profits can be used to fund additional new investments. Notice that with positive feedback loops, the process is self-reinforcing.

Positive feedback loops are also involved in climate change. Scientists believe, for example, that the relationship between emissions of methane and climate change may be described as a positive feedback loop. Because methane is a greenhouse gas, increases in methane emissions contribute to climate change. The rise of the planetary temperature, however, is triggering the release of extremely large quantities of additional methane that was previously trapped in the permafrost layer of the earth; the resulting larger methane emissions intensify the temperature increases, resulting in the release of more methane—a positive feedback.

Human behavior can also deepen environmental problems through positive feedback loops. When shortages of a commodity are imminent, for example, consumers typically begin to hoard the commodity. Hoarding intensifies the shortage. Similarly, people faced with shortages of food may be forced to eat the seed that is the key to more plentiful food in the future. Situations giving rise to this kind of downward spiral are particularly troublesome.

In contrast, a negative feedback loop is self-limiting rather than self-reinforcing. Perhaps the best-known planetary-scale example of a negative feedback loop is provided in a theory advanced by the English scientist James Lovelock. Called the *Gaia hypothesis*, after the Greek concept for Mother Earth, this view of the world suggests that the earth is a living organism with a complex feedback system that seeks an optimal physical and chemical environment. Deviations from this optimal environment trigger natural, nonhuman response mechanisms that restore the balance. In essence, according to the Gaia hypothesis, the planetary environment is characterized by negative feedback loops and, therefore, is, within limits, a self-limiting process.

As we proceed with our investigation, the degree to which our economic and political institutions serve to intensify or to limit emerging environmental problems will be a key focus of our analysis.

The Role of Economics

How societies respond to challenges will depend largely on the behavior of humans acting individually or collectively. Economic analysis provides an incredibly useful set of tools for anyone interested in understanding and/or modifying human behavior, particularly in the face of scarcity. In many cases, this analysis points out the sources of the market system's resilience as embodied in negative feedback loops. In others, it provides a basis not only for identifying the circumstances where markets fail, but also for clarifying how and why that specific set of circumstances supports degradation. This understanding can then be used as the basis for designing new incentives that restore a sense of harmony in the relationship between the economy and the environment for those cases where the market fails.

Over the years, two different, but related, economic approaches have been devised to address the challenges the future holds. Debate 1.1 explores the similarities and the differences of ecological economics and environmental economics and what they both can bring to the table.

DEBATE 1.1

Ecological Economics versus Environmental Economics

Over several decades or so, the community of scholars dealing with the role of the economy and the environment has settled into two camps: ecological economics (www.ecoeco.org/) and environmental economics (www.aere.org/). Although they share many similarities, ecological economics is consciously more methodologically pluralist, while environmental economics is based solidly on the standard paradigm of neoclassical economics. While neoclassical economics emphasizes maximizing human welfare and using economic incentives to modify destructive human behavior, ecological economics uses a variety of methodologies, including neoclassical economics, depending upon the purpose of the investigation.

While some observers see the two approaches as competitive (presenting an "either–or" choice), others, including the authors of this text, see them as complementary. Complementarity, of course, does not mean full acceptance. Significant differences exist not only between these two fields, but also within them over such topics as the valuation of environmental resources, the impact of trade on the environment, and the appropriate means for evaluating policy strategies for long-duration problems such as climate change. These differences arise not only over methodologies but also over the values that are brought to bear on the analysis.

This book draws from both fields. Although the basic foundation for the analysis is environmental economics, the chapters draw heavily from ecological economics to critique that view when it is controversial and to complement it with useful insights drawn from outside the neoclassical paradigm, when appropriate. Pragmatism is the reigning criterion. If a particular approach or study helps us to understand environmental problems and their resolution, it has been included in the text regardless of which field it came from.

The Use of Models

All of the topics covered in this book will be examined as part of the general focus on satisfying human wants and needs in light of limited environmental and natural resources. Because this subject is complex, it is better understood when broken into manageable portions. Once we master the components in individual chapters, we will be able to coalesce the individual insights into a more complete picture in the concluding chapter.

In economics, as in most other disciplines, we use models to investigate complex subjects such as relationships between the economy and the environment. Models are simplified characterizations of reality. Consider a familiar analog. Maps, by design, leave out much detail. They are, nonetheless, useful guides to reality. By showing how various locations relate to each other, maps give an overall perspective. Although they cannot capture all of the unique details that characterize particular locations, maps highlight those characteristics that are crucial for the purpose at hand.

The models in this text are similar. Through simplification, less detail is considered so that the main concepts and the relationships among them become more obvious.

Fortunately, models allow us to study rigorously issues that are interrelated and global in scale. Unfortunately, due to their selectivity, models may yield conclusions that are dead wrong. Details that are omitted may turn out, in retrospect, to be crucial in understanding a particular dimension. Therefore, models are useful abstractions, but the conclusions they yield depend on the structure of the model. As you shall see as you proceed though this book, change that structure and you are likely to change the conclusions. As a result, models should always be viewed with some caution.

Most people's views of the world are based on models, although frequently the assumptions and relationships involved may be implicit, perhaps even subconscious. In economics, the models are explicit; objectives, relationships, and assumptions are clearly specified so that the reader understands exactly how the conclusions are derived. The models are transparent.

The validity and reliability of economic models are tested by examining the degree to which they can explain actual behavior in markets or other settings. An empirical field known as *econometrics* uses statistical techniques, primarily regression analysis, to derive key economic functions. These data-derived functions, such as cost curves or demand functions, can then be used for such diverse purposes as testing hypotheses about the effects of various water policies or forecasting future prices of solar panels.

Examining human behavior in a non-laboratory setting, however, poses special challenges because it is nearly impossible to control completely for all the various factors that influence an outcome beyond those of primary interest. The search for more control over the circumstances that provide the data we use to understand human behavior has given rise to the use of another complementary analytical approach—*experimental economics* (see Example 1.3). Together, econometrics and experimental economics can provide different lenses to help us understand human behavior and its impact on the world around us.

The Road Ahead

Are current societies on a self-destructive path? In part, the answer depends on whether human behavior is perceived as a positive or a negative feedback loop. If increasing scarcity results in a behavioral response that involves a positive feedback loop (intensifies the pressure on the environment), pessimism is justified. If, on the other hand, human responses serve to reduce those pressures or could be reformed so as to reduce those pressures, optimism may be justified.

Not only does environmental and natural resource economics provide a firm basis for understanding the behavioral sources of environmental problems, but it also provides a firm foundation for crafting specific solutions to them. In subsequent chapters, for example, you will be exposed to how economic analysis can be (and has been) used to forge solutions to such diverse areas as climate change, toxic substance control, and environmental justice. Many of the solutions are quite novel.

Market forces are extremely powerful. Attempts to solve environmental problems that ignore these forces run a high risk of failure. Where normal market forces are compatible with efficient and sustainable outcomes, those outcomes can be supported and reinforced. Where normal market forces prove inefficient and/or unsustainable, they can be channeled into new directions that restore compatibility between outcomes and objectives. Environmental economics provides a specific set of directions for how this compatibility between goals and outcomes can be achieved.

The Underlying Questions

As we look to the future optimists see a continued prosperity based upon a market system that effectively responds to challenges, while pessimists see the challenges as sufficiently different in scope and scale as to raise doubts about our ability to deal with them in time. (Debate 1.2).

EXAMPLE 1.3

Experimental Economics: Studying Human Behavior in a Laboratory

The appeal of experimental economics is based upon its ability to study human behavior in a more controlled setting. During the mid-twentieth century economists began to design controlled laboratory experiments with human subjects. The experimental designs mimic decision situations in a variety of settings. Paid participants are informed of the rules of the experiment and asked to make choices. By varying the treatments faced by participants in these controlled settings experimenters can study how the treatments affect both choices and collective outcomes.

Consider one policy example of how these methods have been used in resource policy (Cummings et al., 2004). In April 2000, the Georgia legislature passed The Flint River Drought Protection Act, which required the state to hold an auction in drought years to pay some farmers to suspend irrigation. The purpose was to use a market mechanism to identify those farmers who could forego irrigation at the lowest cost and to fairly compensate them for their reduction in water use. With time running short to implement this act, state policymakers relied upon laboratory experiments designed by a team of economists, using local farmers as participants. The results were used to inform the process of choosing the specific auction design that was used to fulfill the requirements of this act.

To the extent that the results of experiments have proved to be replicable, they have created a deeper understanding about the effectiveness of markets, policies, and institutions. The large and growing literature on experimental economics has already shed light on such widely divergent topics as the effectiveness of alternative policies for controlling pollution and allocating water, how uncertainty affects choices, and how the nature of cooperative agreements affects the sustainability of shared natural resources.

While experiments have the advantage of being able to control the decision-making environment, the artificiality of the laboratory setting raises questions about the degree to which the results from laboratories can shed light on actual human behavior outside the lab. While the degree of artificiality can be controlled by careful research design, it cannot be completely eliminated. Over the years, however, this approach has provided valuable information that can complement what we have learned from observed behavior using econometrics.

Sources: Cummings, R. G., & Taylor, L. O. (2001/2002). Experimental economics in natural resource and environmental management. In H. Folmer and T. Tietenberg (Eds.), *The International Yearbook of Environmental and Natural Resource Economics*. Cheltenham, UK: Edward Elgar, 123–149; Smith, V. L. (1998). Experimental methods in economics. In J. Eatwell, M. Murray, & P. Newman (Eds.), *The New Palgrave Dictionary of Economics, Volume 2*. London: The Macmillan Press, 241–249; Cummings, Ronald G., Holt, Charles A., & Laury, Susan K. (2004). Using laboratory experiments for policymaking: An example from the Georgia irrigation reduction auction. *Journal of Policy Analysis and Management, 23*(2), 341–363.

DEBATE 1.2

What Does the Future Hold?

Is the economy on a collision course with the environment? Or has the process of reconciliation begun? One group, led most notably by Bjørn Lomborg, President of the Copenhagen Consensus Center, concludes that societies have resourcefully confronted environmental problems in the past and that environmentalist concerns to the contrary are excessively alarmist. As he states in his book, *The Skeptical Environmentalist*:

> The fact is, as we have seen, that this civilization over the last 400 years has brought us fantastic and continued progress. . . . And we ought to face the facts—that on the whole we have no reason to expect that this progress will not continue.

On the other end of the spectrum are the researchers at the Worldwatch Institute, who believe that current development paths and the attendant strain they place on the environment are unsustainable. As reported in that institute's State of the World 2012 report:

> In 1992, governments at the Rio Earth Summit made a historic commitment to sustainable development—an economic system that promotes the health of both people and ecosystems. Twenty years and several summits later, human civilization has never been closer to ecological collapse, one third of humanity lives in poverty, and another 2 billion people are projected to join the human race over the next 40 years.

These views not only interpret the available historical evidence differently, but also they imply very different strategies for the future.

Sources: Lomborg, B. (2001). *The Skeptical Environmentalist: Measuring the Real State of the World*. Cambridge: Cambridge University Press; The Worldwatch Institute. (2012). *The State of the World 2012*. Washington, DC: Island Press.

To act as if one vision is correct, when it is not, could prove to be a costly error. Thus, it is important to examine these two views (or some third view) as a basis for forging your own view. In order to assess the validity of these visions, we must address some basic issues:

- Is the problem correctly conceptualized as exponential growth with fixed, immutable resource limits? Does the earth have a finite carrying capacity? If so, how can the carrying-capacity concept be operationalized? Do current or forecasted levels of economic activity exceed the earth's carrying capacity?
- How does the economic system respond to scarcities? Is the process mainly characterized by positive or negative feedback loops? Do the responses intensify or ameliorate any initial scarcities? Does the answer depend upon the decision context?

- What is the role of the political system in controlling these problems? In what circumstances is government intervention necessary? What forms of intervention work best? Is government intervention uniformly benign, or can it make the situation worse? What specific roles are appropriate for the executive, legislative, and judicial branches?
- Many environmental problems are characterized by a considerable degree of uncertainty about the severity of the problem and the effectiveness of possible solutions. Can our economic and political institutions respond to this uncertainty in reasonable ways or does uncertainty become a paralyzing force?
- Can the economic and political systems work together to eradicate poverty and social injustice while respecting our obligations to future generations? Or do our obligations to future generations inevitably conflict with the desire to raise the living standards of those currently in absolute poverty or the desire to treat all people, especially the most vulnerable, with fairness? Can short- and long-term goals be harmonized? Is sustainable development feasible? If so, how can it be achieved? What does the need for sustainable outcomes imply about the future of economic activity in the industrialized nations? In the less-industrialized nations?

The rest of this book uses economic analysis and evidence to suggest answers to these complex questions.

An Overview of the Book

In the following chapters you will study the rich and rewarding field of environmental economics. The menu of topics is broad and varied. Economics provides a powerful analytical framework for examining the relationships between the environment, on one hand, and the economic and political systems, on the other. The study of economics can assist in identifying circumstances that give rise to environmental problems, in discovering causes of these problems, and in searching for solutions. Each chapter introduces a unique topic in environmental economics, while the overarching focus on development in an environment characterized by scarcity weaves these topics into a single theme.

We begin by comparing perspectives being brought to bear on these problems by economists and noneconomists. The manner in which scholars in various disciplines view problems and potential solutions depends on how they organize the available facts, how they interpret those facts, and what kinds of values they apply in translating these interpretations into policy. Before going into a detailed look at environmental problems, we shall compare the ideology of conventional economics to other prevailing ideologies in the natural and social sciences. This comparison not only explains why reasonable people may, upon examining the same set of facts, reach different conclusions, but also it conveys some sense of the strengths and weaknesses of economic analysis as it is applied to environmental problems.

Chapters 2 through 4 delve more deeply into the economic approach, highlighting many of the tools used by environmental economists including cost-benefit analysis, cost-effectiveness analysis, and methods available for monetizing nonmarket goods and services. Specific evaluation criteria are defined, and examples are developed to show how these criteria can be applied to current environmental problems.

Chapters 5 through 10 move on to an area of public policy—pollution control—that has come to rely much more heavily on the use of economic incentives to produce the desired response. The chapters in this section of the book reveal the unique aspects of local and regional air pollution, global problems such as climate change and ozone depletion, vehicle air pollution, water pollution, and toxic substances as well as the effectiveness of the various economic approaches used to control these pollutants.

Following this examination of the individual environmental problems and the successes and failures of policies that have been used to ameliorate these problems, we return to the big picture by assembling the bits and pieces of evidence accumulated in the preceding chapters and fusing them into an overall integrated response to the questions posed in the chapter. We also cover some of the major unresolved issues in environmental policy that are likely to be among those commanding center stage over the next several years if not decades.

Summary

Are our institutions so myopic that they have chosen a path that can only lead to the destruction of society as we now know it? We have briefly examined two points of view that provide different answers to that question. The Worldwatch Institute finds that the path is destructive, while Lomborg strikes a much more optimistic tone. The pessimistic view is based upon the inevitability of exceeding the carrying capacity of the planet as the population and the level of economic activity grow. The optimistic view sees initial scarcity triggering sufficiently powerful reductions in population growth and increases in technological progress bringing further abundance, not deepening scarcity.

Our examination of these different visions has revealed questions that can guide our assessment of what the future holds. Seeking the answers requires that we accumulate a much better understanding about how choices are made in economic and political systems and how those choices affect, and are affected by, the natural environment. We begin that process in Chapter 2, where the economic approach is developed in broad terms and is contrasted with other conventional approaches.

Discussion Questions

1. In his book *The Ultimate Resource*, economist Julian Simon makes the point that calling the resource base "finite" is misleading. To illustrate this point, he uses a yardstick, with its one-inch markings, as an analogy. The distance between two markings is finite— one inch—but an infinite number of points is contained within that finite space. Therefore, in one sense, what lies between the markings is finite, while in another, equally meaningful sense, it is infinite. Is the concept of a finite resource base useful or not? Why or why not?

2. This chapter contains two views of the future. Since the validity of these views cannot be completely tested until the time period covered by the forecast has passed (so that predictions can be matched against actual events), how can we ever hope to establish *in advance* which view is better? What criteria might be proposed for evaluating predictions?

3. Positive and negative feedback loops lie at the core of systematic thinking about the future. As you examine the key forces shaping the future, what examples of positive and negative feedback loops can you uncover?

4. Which point of view in Debate 1.2 do you find most compelling? Why? What logic or evidence do you find most supportive of that position?

5. How specifically might the interdependence of the water accessibility and climate change challenges affect the design of polices enacted to meet these challenges? Give some specific

examples of how well-designed policies might differ in the interdependence case compared to the independence case.

6. In his book *Thank You for Being Late: An Optimist's Guide to Thriving in the Age of Acclerations*, Thomas L. Friedman documents how the digital revolution is fundamentally changing life as we have known it. How do you think it will change the relationship between humans and the environment? Is this likely to be a force for renewed harmony or intensified disruption? Why? Do you have any specific examples to share that illustrate one outcome or the other?

Self-Test Exercise

1. Does the normal reaction of the price system to a resource shortage provide an example of a positive or a negative feedback loop? Why?

Note

1　See www.globalchange.gov/climate-change

Further Reading

Batabyal, A. A., & Nijkamp, P. (2011). Introduction to research tools in natural resource and environmental economics. In A. A. Batabyal & P. Nijkamp (Eds.), *Research Tools in Natural Resource and Environmental Economics*. Hackensack, NJ: World Scientific Publishing, 3–26. An introduction to the most frequently used theoretical, empirical, experimental, and interdisciplinary research tools in natural resource and environmental economics.

Delbeke, J., Klaassen, G., van Ierland, T., & Zapfel, P. (2009). The role of environmental economics in recent policy making at the European Commission. *Review of Environmental Economics and Policy*, 4, 24–43. This article examines how environmental economics has been used at the European Commission in climate change, energy, and air pollution policy.

Managi, Shunsuke (Ed.). (2015). *The Routledge Handbook of Environmental Economics in Asia*. New York: Routledge. An edited collection of essays that illustrates how the principles and methods of environmental economics can be applied to specific environmental and natural resource issues in Asia.

Motesharrei, Safa, Rivas, Jorge, & Kalnay, Eugenia. (2014). Human and nature dynamics (HANDY): Modeling inequality and use of resources in the collapse or sustainability of societies. *Ecological Economics*, 101 (May), 90–102. This paper discusses two mechanisms leading to two types of collapses and presents a dynamic model capable of reproducing the irreversible collapses found in history.

Noussair, Charles N. & van Soest, Daan P. (2014). Economic experiments and environmental policy. *Annual Review of Resource Economics*, 6, 319–337. This survey reviews the literature addressing whether government intervention is always necessary to protect the environment and whether it is always effective in doing so, and discusses the use of experimental laboratories to test market-based approaches to environmental policy.

Repetto, R. (Ed.). (2006). *Punctuated Equilibrium and the Dynamics of US Environmental Policy*. New Haven, CT: Yale University Press. A sophisticated discussion of how positive and negative feedback mechanisms can interact to produce environmental policy stalemates or breakthroughs.

Spash, Clive. (2017). *The Routledge Handbook of Ecological Economics*. New York: Routledge. Edited by a leading figure in the field, this handbook provides a current guide to the literature on ecological economics in an informative and easily accessible form.

Stavins, Robert N. (Ed.) (2019) Stavins, R. (Ed.) (2019) *Economics of the Environment: Selected Readings 7th Edition* (Cheltenham, UK: Edward Elgar Publishing Ltd). A compendium of significant articles in environmental economics, together with an original introductory chapter by the editor.

Additional references and historically significant references are available on this book's Companion Website: www.routledge.com/cw/Tietenberg

Chapter 2

The Economic Approach

Property Rights, Externalities, and Environmental Problems

The charming landscape which I saw this morning, is indubitably made up of some twenty or thirty farms. Miller owns this field, Locke that, and Manning the woodland beyond. But none of them owns the landscape. There is a property in the horizon which no man has but he whose eye can integrate all the parts, that is, the poet. This is the best part of these men's farms, yet to this their land deeds give them no title.

—Ralph Waldo Emerson, *Nature* (1836)

Introduction

Before examining specific environmental problems and the policy responses to them, it is important that we develop and clarify the economic approach, so that we have some sense of the forest before examining each of the trees. By having a feel for the conceptual framework, it becomes easier not only to deal with individual cases but also, perhaps more importantly, to see how they fit into a comprehensive approach.

In this chapter, we develop the general conceptual framework used in economics to approach environmental problems. We begin by examining the relationship between human actions, as manifested through the economic system, and the environmental consequences of those actions. We can then establish criteria for judging the desirability of the outcomes of this relationship. These criteria provide a basis for identifying the nature and severity of environmental problems, and a foundation for designing effective policies to deal with them.

Throughout this chapter, the economic point of view is contrasted with alternative points of view. These contrasts bring the economic approach into sharper focus and stimulate deeper and more critical thinking about all possible approaches.

The Human–Environment Relationship

The Environment as an Asset

In economics, the environment is viewed as a composite asset that provides a variety of services. It is a very special asset, to be sure, because it provides the life-support systems that sustain our very existence, but it is an asset nonetheless. As with other assets, we wish to enhance, or at least prevent undue depreciation of, the value of this asset so that it may continue to provide aesthetic and life-sustaining services.

The environment provides the economy with raw materials, which are transformed into consumer products by the production process, and energy, which fuels this transformation. Ultimately, these raw materials and energy return to the environment as waste products (see Figure 2.1).

The environment also provides goods and services directly to consumers. The air we breathe, the nourishment we receive from food and drink, and the protection we derive from shelter and clothing are all benefits we receive, either directly or indirectly, from the environment. One significant subclass of these, *ecosystem goods and services*, incorporates the benefits obtained directly from ecosystems, including biodiversity, breathable air, wetlands, water quality, carbon sequestration, and recreation. Anyone who has experienced the exhilaration of white-water rafting, the total serenity of a wilderness trek, or the breathtaking beauty of a

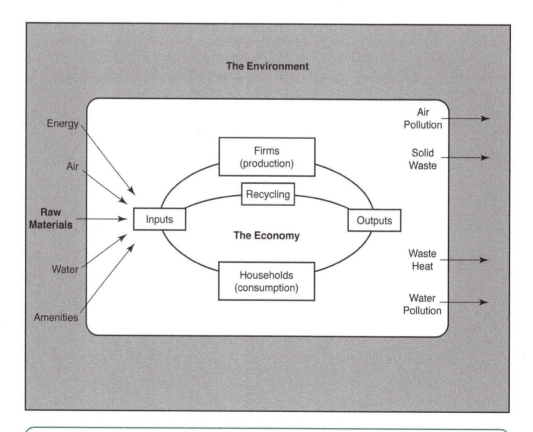

Figure 2.1 The Economic System and the Environment

sunset will readily recognize that ecosystems provide us with a variety of amenities for which no substitute exists.

If the environment is defined broadly enough, the relationship between the environment and the economic system can be considered a *closed system*. For our purposes, a closed system is one in which no inputs (energy or matter) are received from outside the system and no outputs are transferred outside the system. An *open system*, by contrast, is one in which the system imports or exports matter or energy.

If we restrict our conception of the relationship in Figure 2.1 to our planet and the atmosphere around it, then clearly we do not have a closed system. We derive most of our energy from the sun, either directly or indirectly. We have also sent spaceships well beyond the boundaries of our atmosphere. Nonetheless, historically speaking, for *material* inputs and outputs (not including energy), this system can be treated as a closed system because the amount of exports (such as abandoned space vehicles) and imports (e.g., moon rocks) are negligible. Whether the system remains closed depends on the degree to which space exploration opens up the rest of our solar system as a source of raw materials.

The treatment of our planet and its immediate environs as a closed system has an important implication that is summed up in the *first law of thermodynamics*—energy and matter can neither be created nor destroyed.[1] The law implies that the mass of materials flowing into the economic system from the environment has either to accumulate in the economic system or return to the environment as waste. When accumulation stops, the mass of materials flowing into the economic system is equal in magnitude to the mass of waste flowing into the environment.

Excessive wastes can, of course, depreciate the asset; when they exceed the absorptive capacity of nature, wastes reduce the services that the asset provides. Examples are easy to find: air pollution can cause respiratory problems, polluted drinking water can cause cancer, smog obliterates scenic vistas, climate change can lead to flooding of coastal areas.

The relationship of people to the environment is also conditioned by another physical law, the *second law of thermodynamics*. Known popularly as the *entropy law*, this law states that "entropy increases." *Entropy* is the amount of energy unavailable for work. Applied to energy processes, this law implies that no conversion from one form of energy to another is completely efficient and that the consumption of energy is an irreversible process. Some energy is always lost during conversion, and the rest, once used, is no longer available for further work. The second law also implies that, in the absence of new energy inputs, any closed system must eventually use up its available energy. Since energy is necessary for life, life ceases when useful energy flows cease.

We should remember that our planet is not even approximately a closed system with respect to energy; we gain energy from the sun. The entropy law does remind us, however, that the flow of solar energy establishes an upper limit on the flow of available energy that can be sustained. Once the stocks of stored energy (such as fossil fuels and nuclear energy) are gone, the amount of energy available for useful work will be determined solely by flow resources such as solar, wind, and hydro, and by the amount that can be stored (through dams, trees, and so on). Thus, in the very long run, the growth process will be limited by the availability of these flow resources and our ability to put them to work.

The Economic Approach

Two different types of economic analysis can be applied to increase our understanding of the relationship between the economic system and the environment: *Positive* economics attempts to describe *what is, what was,* or *what will be. Normative* economics, by contrast, deals with what *ought to be*. Disagreements within positive economics can usually be resolved by an appeal to the facts. Normative disagreements, however, involve value judgments.

Both branches are useful. Suppose, for example, we want to investigate the relationship between trade and the environment. Positive economics could be used to describe the kinds of impacts trade would have on the economy and the environment. It could not, however, provide any guidance on the question of whether trade was desirable. That judgment would have to come from normative economics, a topic we explore in the next section.

The fact that positive analysis does not, by itself, determine the desirability of some policy action does not mean that it is not useful in the policy process. Example 2.1 provides one example of the kinds of economic impact analyses that are used in the policy process.

EXAMPLE 2.1

Economic Impacts of Reducing Hazardous Pollutant Emissions from Iron and Steel Foundries

The US Environmental Protection Agency (EPA) was tasked with developing a "maximum achievable control technology standard" to reduce emissions of hazardous air pollutants from iron and steel foundries. As part of the rule-making process, the EPA conducted an *ex ante* economic impact analysis to assess the potential economic impacts of the proposed rule.

If implemented, the rule would require some iron and steel foundries to implement pollution control methods that would increase the production costs at affected facilities. The interesting question addressed by the analysis is how large those impacts would be.

The impact analysis estimated annual costs for existing sources to be $21.73 million. These cost increases were projected to result in small increases in output prices. Specifically, prices were projected to increase by only 0.1 percent for iron castings and 0.05 percent for steel castings. The impacts of these price increases were expected to be experienced largely by iron foundries using cupola furnaces as well as consumers of iron foundry products. Unaffected domestic foundries and foreign producers of coke were actually projected to earn slightly higher profits as a result of the rule.

This analysis helped in two ways. First, by showing that the impacts fell under the $100 million threshold that mandates review by the Office of Management and Budget, the analysis eliminated the need for a much more time- and resource-consuming analysis. Second, by showing how small the expected impacts would be, it served to lower the opposition that might have arisen from unfounded fears of much more severe impacts.

Source: Office of Air Quality Planning and Standards, United States Environmental Protection Agency. (November 2002). *Economic Impact Analysis of Proposed Iron and Steel Foundries*. NESHAP Final Report; National Emissions Standards for Hazardous Air Pollutants for Iron and Steel Foundries. (April 17, 2007). Proposed Rule. *Federal Register*, 72(73), 19150–19164.

A rather different context for normative economics can arise when the possibilities are more open-ended. For example, we might ask, how much should we control emissions of greenhouse gases (which contribute to climate change) and how should we achieve that degree of control? Or we might ask, how much forest of various types should be preserved? Answering these questions requires us to consider the entire range of possible outcomes and to select the best or optimal one. Although that is a much more difficult question to answer than one that asks us only to compare two predefined alternatives, the basic normative analysis framework is the same in both cases.

Environmental Problems and Economic Efficiency

Static Efficiency

The chief normative economic criterion for choosing among various outcomes occurring at the same point in time is called *static efficiency*, or merely *efficiency*. An allocation of resources is said to satisfy the static efficiency criterion if the economic surplus derived from those resources is maximized by that allocation. Economic surplus, in turn, is the sum of consumer's surplus and producer's surplus.

Consumer surplus is the value that consumers receive from an allocation minus what it costs them to obtain it. Consumer surplus is measured as the area under the demand curve minus the consumer's cost. This is the shaded triangle in Figure 2.2. The cost to the consumer is the area under the price line, bounded from the left by the vertical axis and the right by the quantity of the good. This rectangle, which captures price times quantity, represents consumer expenditure on this quantity of the good.

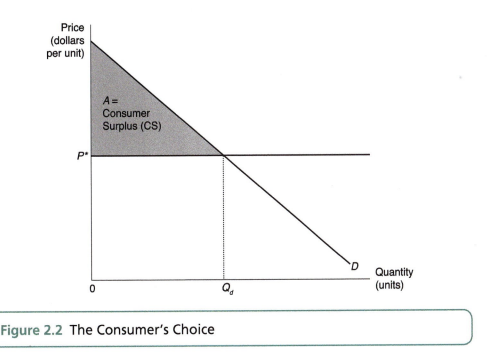

Figure 2.2 The Consumer's Choice

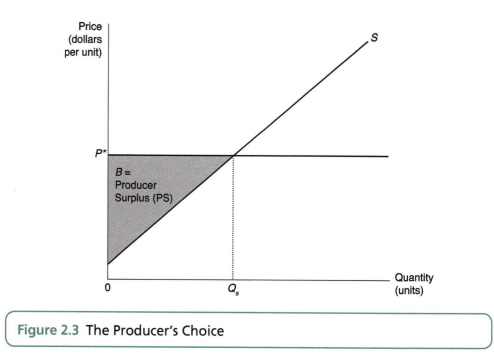

Figure 2.3 The Producer's Choice

Why is this area above the price line thought of as a surplus? For each quantity purchased, the corresponding point on the market demand curve represents the amount of money some person would have been willing to pay for the last unit of the good. The *total willingness to pay* for some quantity of this good—say, three units—is the sum of the willingness to pay for each of the three units. Thus, the total willingness to pay for three units would be measured by the sum of the willingness to pay for the first, second, and third units, respectively. It is now a simple extension to note that the total willingness to pay is the area under the continuous market demand curve to the left of the allocation in question. For example, in Figure 2.2 the total willingness to pay for Q_D units of the commodity is the total area under the demand curve up to Q_D. Thus it is the shaded triangle of consumer surplus plus the rectangle of cost. Total willingness to pay is the concept we shall use to define the total value a consumer would receive from the amount of the good they take delivery of. Thus, total value the consumer would receive is equal to the area under the market demand curve from the origin to the allocation of interest. Consumer surplus is thus the excess of total willingness to pay over the (lower) actual expenditure.

Meanwhile, sellers face a similar choice (see Figure 2.3). Given price P^*, the seller maximizes his or her own producer surplus by choosing to sell Q_s units. The *producer surplus* is designated by the shaded area B, the area under the price line that lies above the marginal cost curve (supply Curve S), bounded from the left by the vertical axis and the right by the quantity of the good. To calculate producer or consumer surplus, notice that as long as the functions are linear (as they are in the Figures), each area is represented as a right triangle. Remember that the area of a right triangle is calculated as 1/2 × the base of the triangle × the height of the triangle. Using this formula, try calculating these areas in the first self-test exercise at the end of this chapter.

Property Rights

Property Rights and Efficient Market Allocations

The manner in which producers and consumers use environmental resources depends on the property rights governing those resources. In economics, *property rights* refer to a bundle of entitlements defining the owner's rights, privileges, and limitations for use of the resource. By examining such entitlements and how they affect human behavior, we will better understand how environmental problems arise from government and market allocations.

These property rights can be vested either with individuals, groups, or with the state. How can we tell when the pursuit of profits is consistent with efficiency and when it is not?

Efficient Property Rights Structures

Let's begin by describing the structure of property rights that could produce efficient allocations in a well-functioning market economy. An efficient structure has three main characteristics:

1. *Exclusivity*—All benefits and costs accrued as a result of owning and using the resources should accrue to the owner, and only to the owner, either directly or indirectly by sale to others.
2. *Transferability*—All property rights should be transferable from one owner to another in a voluntary exchange.
3. *Enforceability*—Property rights should be secure from involuntary seizure or encroachment by others.

An owner of a resource with a well-defined property right (one exhibiting these three characteristics) has a powerful incentive to use that resource efficiently because a decline in the value of that resource represents a personal loss. Farmers who own the land have an incentive to fertilize and irrigate it because the resulting increased production raises income. Similarly, they have an incentive to rotate crops when that raises the productivity of their land.

When well-defined property rights are exchanged, as in a market economy, this exchange facilitates efficiency. We can illustrate this point by examining the incentives consumers and producers face when a well-defined system of property rights is in place. Because the seller has the right to prevent the consumer from consuming the product in the absence of payment, the consumer must pay to receive the product. Given a market price, the consumer decides how much to purchase by choosing the amount that maximizes his or her individual consumer surplus.

Is this allocation efficient? According to our definition of static efficiency, it is clear the answer is yes. The economic surplus is maximized by the market allocation and, as seen in Figure 2.4, it is equal to the sum of consumer and producer surpluses (areas $A + B$). Thus, we have not only established a procedure for measuring efficiency, but also a means of describing how the surplus is distributed between consumers and producers.

This distinction is crucially significant. Efficiency is *not* achieved because consumers and producers are seeking efficiency. They aren't! In a system with well-defined property rights and competitive markets in which to sell those rights, producers try to maximize their surplus and consumers try to maximize their surplus. The price system, then, induces those self-interested parties to make choices that also turn out to be efficient from the point of view of society as a whole. It channels the energy motivated by self-interest into socially productive paths.

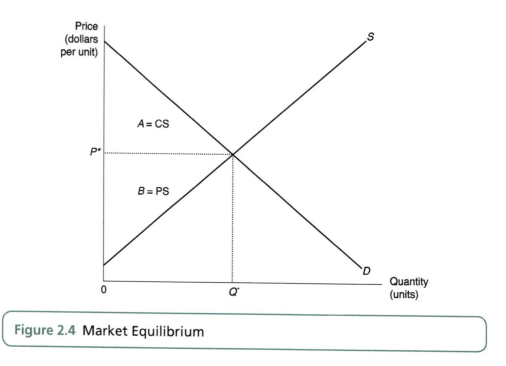

Figure 2.4 Market Equilibrium

Familiarity may have dulled our appreciation, but it is noteworthy that a system designed to produce a harmonious and congenial outcome could function effectively while allowing consumers and producers so much individual freedom in making choices. This is truly a remarkable accomplishment.

Producer's Surplus, Scarcity Rent, and Long-Run Competitive Equilibrium

Since the area under the price line is total revenue, and the area under the marginal cost (or supply) curve is total variable cost, producer's surplus is related to profits. In the short run when some costs are fixed, producer's surplus is equal to profits plus fixed cost. In the long run when all costs are variable, producer's surplus is equal to profits plus rent, the return to scarce inputs owned by the producer. As long as new firms can enter into profitable industries without raising the prices of purchased inputs, long-run profits and rent will equal zero.

Scarcity Rent. Most natural resource industries, however, do give rise to rent and, therefore, producer's surplus is not eliminated by competition, even with free entry. This producer's surplus, which persists in long-run competitive equilibrium, is called *scarcity rent*.

David Ricardo was the first economist to recognize the existence of scarcity rent. Ricardo suggested that the price of land was determined by the least fertile marginal unit of land. Since the price had to be sufficiently high to allow the poorer land to be brought into production, other, more fertile land could be farmed at an economic profit. Competition could not erode that profit because the amount of high-quality land was limited and lower prices would serve only to reduce the supply of land below demand. The only way to expand production would be to bring additional, less fertile land (more costly to farm) into production; consequently, additional production does not lower price, as it does in a constant-cost industry. As we shall see, other circumstances also give rise to scarcity rent for natural resources.

Externalities as a Source of Market Failure

The Concept Introduced

Exclusivity is one of the chief characteristics of an efficient property rights structure. This characteristic is frequently violated in practice. One broad class of violations occurs when an agent making a decision does not bear all of the consequences of his or her action.

Suppose two firms are located by a river. The first produces steel, while the second, somewhat downstream, operates a resort hotel. Both use the river, although in different ways. The steel firm uses it as a receptacle for its waste, while the hotel uses it to attract customers seeking water recreation. If these two facilities have different owners, an efficient use of the water is not likely to result. Because the steel plant does not bear the cost of reduced business at the resort resulting from waste being dumped into the river, it is not likely to be very sensitive to that cost in its decision making. As a result, it could be expected to dump too much waste into the river, and an efficient allocation of the river would not be attained.

This situation is called an externality. An *externality* exists whenever the welfare of some agent, either a firm or household, depends not only on his or her activities, but also on activities under the control of some other agent. In the example, the increased waste in the river imposed an external cost on the resort, a cost the steel firm could not be counted upon to consider appropriately in deciding the amount of waste to dump.

The effect of this external cost on the steel industry is illustrated in Figure 2.5, which shows the market for steel. Steel production inevitably involves producing pollution as well as steel. The demand for steel is shown by the demand curve D, and the private marginal cost of producing the steel (exclusive of pollution control and damage) is depicted as MC_p. Because society considers both the cost of pollution and the cost of producing the steel, the social marginal cost function (MC_s) includes both of these costs as well.

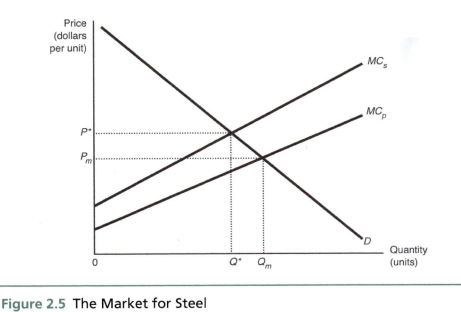

Figure 2.5 The Market for Steel

If the steel industry faced no outside control on its emission levels, it would seek to produce Q_m. That choice, in a competitive setting, would maximize its private producer surplus. But that is clearly not efficient, since the net benefit is maximized at Q^*, not Q_m. Can you see the deadweight loss? A deadweight loss arises whenever marginal social costs are not equal to marginal social benefits. In this case, at the market allocation, marginal social costs are higher than marginal benefits.

With the help of Figure 2.5, we can draw a number of conclusions about market allocations of commodities causing pollution externalities:

1. The output of the commodity is too large.
2. Too much pollution is produced.
3. The prices of products responsible for pollution are too low.
4. As long as the costs remain external, no incentives to search for ways to yield less pollution per unit of output are introduced by the market.
5. Recycling and reuse of the polluting substances are discouraged because release into the environment is so inefficiently cheap.

The effects of a market imperfection for one commodity end up affecting the demands for raw materials, labor, and so on. The ultimate effects are felt through the entire economy.

Types of Externalities

External effects, or externalities, can be positive or negative. Historically, the terms *external cost* (*external diseconomy*) and *external benefit* (*external economy*) have been used to refer, respectively, to circumstances in which the affected party is damaged by or benefits from the externality. Clearly, the water pollution example represents an external cost. External benefits are not hard to find, however. As noted in the opening quote to this chapter, private individuals who preserve a particularly scenic area provide an external benefit to all who pass. Generally, when external benefits are present, the market will undersupply the resources.

One other distinction is important. One class of externalities, known as *pecuniary externalities*, does not present the same kinds of problems as pollution does. Pecuniary externalities arise when the external effect is transmitted through altered prices. Suppose that a new firm moves into an area and drives up the rental price of land. That increase creates a negative effect on all those paying rent and, therefore, is an external diseconomy.

This pecuniary diseconomy, however, does not cause a market failure because the resulting higher rents are reflecting the true scarcity of land. The land market provides a mechanism by which the parties can bid for land; the resulting prices reflect the value of the land in its various uses. Without pecuniary externalities, the price signals would fail to sustain an efficient allocation.

The pollution example is *not* a pecuniary externality because the effect is not transmitted through prices. In this example, prices do not adjust to reflect the increasing waste load. The damage to the water resource is not reflected in the steel firm's costs. An essential feedback mechanism that is present for pecuniary externalities is not present for the pollution case.

The externalities concept is a broad one, covering a multitude of sources of market failure (Example 2.2 illustrates one). The next step is to investigate some specific circumstances that can give rise to externalities.

EXAMPLE 2.2

Shrimp Farming Externalities in Thailand

In the Tha Po village on the coast of Surat Thani Province in Thailand, more than half of the 1100 hectares of mangrove swamps have been cleared for commercial shrimp farms. Although harvesting shrimp is a lucrative undertaking, mangroves also serve as nurseries for fish and as barriers for storms and soil erosion. Following the destruction of the local mangroves, Tha Po villagers experienced a decline in fish catch and suffered storm damage and water pollution. Can market forces be trusted to strike the efficient balance between preservation and development for the remaining mangroves?

Calculations by economists Sathirathai and Barbier (2001) demonstrated that the value of the ecological services that would be lost from further destruction of the mangrove swamps exceeded the value of the shrimp farms that would take their place. Preservation of the remaining mangrove swamps would be the efficient choice.

Would a potential shrimp-farming entrepreneur make the efficient choice? Unfortunately, the answer is no. This study estimated the economic value of mangroves in terms of local use of forest resources, offshore fishery linkages, and coastal protection to be in the range of $27,264–$35,921 per hectare. In contrast, the economic returns to shrimp farming, once they are corrected for input subsidies and for the costs of water pollution, are only $194–$209 per hectare. However, as shrimp farmers are heavily subsidized and do not have to take into account the external costs of pollution, their financial returns are typically $7,706.95–$8,336.47 per hectare. In the absence of some sort of external control imposed by collective action, converting mangroves to shrimp farming would be the normal, if inefficient, result. The externalities associated with the ecological services provided by the mangroves support a biased decision that results in fewer social net benefits, but greater private net benefits.

Sources: Sathirathai, S., & Barbier, E. B. (April 2001). Valuing mangrove conservation in southern Thailand. *Contemporary Economic Policy*, 19(2). 109–122; Barbier, E. B., & Cox, M. (2004). An economic analysis of shrimp farm expansion and mangrove conversion in Thailand. *Land Economics*, 80(3), 389–407.

Perverse Incentives Arising from Some Property Right Structures

Private property is, of course, not the only possible way of defining entitlements to resource use. Other possibilities include:

- state-property regimes (the government owns and controls the property);
- common-property regimes (the property is jointly owned and managed by a specified group of co-owners); and
- *res nullius* or open-access regimes (in which no one owns or exercises control over the resources).

All of these create rather different incentives for resource use.

State-property regimes exist not only in former communist countries, but also to varying degrees in virtually all countries of the world. Parks and forests, for example, are frequently owned and managed by the government in capitalist as well as in socialist nations. Problems with both efficiency and sustainability can arise in state-property regimes when the incentives of bureaucrats, who implement and/or make the rules for resource use, diverge from collective interests.

Common-property resources are those shared resources that are managed in common rather than privately. Entitlements to use common-property resources may be formal, protected by specific legal rules, or they may be informal, protected by tradition or custom. Common-property regimes exhibit varying degrees of efficiency and sustainability, depending on the rules that emerge from collective decision making. While some very successful examples of common-property regimes exist, unsuccessful examples are even more common.

One successful example of a common-property regime involves the system of allocating grazing rights in Switzerland. Although agricultural land is normally treated as private property, in Switzerland grazing rights on the Alpine meadows have been treated as common property for centuries. Overgrazing is protected by specific rules, enacted by an association of users, which limit the amount of livestock permitted on the meadow. The families included on the membership list of the association have been stable over time as rights and responsibilities have passed from generation to generation. This stability has apparently facilitated reciprocity and trust, thereby providing a foundation for continued compliance with the rules.

Unfortunately, that kind of stability may be the exception rather than the rule, particularly in the face of heavy population pressure. The more common situation can be illustrated by the experience of Mawelle, a small fishing village in Sri Lanka. Initially, a complicated but effective rotating system of fishing rights was devised by villagers to assure equitable access to the best spots and best times while protecting the fish stocks. Over time, population pressure and the infusion of outsiders raised demand and undermined the collective cohesion sufficiently that the traditional rules became unenforceable, producing overexploitation of the resource and lower incomes for all the participants.

Res nullius property resources, the main focus of this section, can be exploited on a first-come, first-served basis because no individual or group has the legal power to restrict access. *Open-access resources*, as we shall henceforth call them, have given rise to what has become known popularly as the "tragedy of the commons."

The problems created by open-access resources can be illustrated by recalling the fate of the American bison. Bison are an example of "common-pool" resources. *Common-pool resources* are shared resources characterized by nonexclusivity and divisibility. *Nonexclusivity* implies that resources can be exploited by anyone, while *divisibility* means that the capture of part of the resource by one group subtracts it from the amount available to the other groups. (Note the contrast between common-pool resources and public goods, the subject of the next section.) In the early history of the United States, bison were plentiful; unrestricted hunting access was not a problem. Frontier people who needed hides or meat could easily get whatever they needed; the aggressiveness of any one hunter did not affect the time and effort expended by other hunters. In the absence of scarcity, efficiency was not threatened by open access.

As the years slipped by, however, the demand for bison increased and scarcity became a factor. As the number of hunters increased, eventually every additional unit of hunting activity increased the amount of time and effort required to produce an additional yield of bison.

Consider graphically how various property rights structures (and the resulting level of harvest) affect the scarcity rent (in this case, equivalent to the economic surplus received by consumers and producers), where the amount of rent is measured as the difference between the revenues received from the harvest minus the costs associated with producing that harvest. Figure 2.6 compares the revenue and costs for various levels of harvest. In the top panel the revenue is calculated by multiplying, for each level of hunting activity, the (assumed constant) price of bison by the amount harvested. The upward sloping total cost curve simply reflects that fact that increases in harvest effort result in higher total costs. (Marginal cost is assumed to be constant for this example.)

In terms of the top panel of Figure 2.6, the total surplus associated with any level of effort is measured as the vertical difference between the total revenue (benefits) curve and the total cost curve for that level of harvest.

In the bottom panel the marginal revenue curve is downward sloping (despite the constant price) because as the amount of hunting effort increases, the resulting bison population size decreases. Smaller populations support smaller harvests per unit of effort expended.

The efficient level of hunting activity in this model (E^*) maximizes the surplus. This can be seen graphically in two different ways. First, E^* maximizes the vertical difference between the total cost and total benefit (top panel). Second, in the bottom panel E^* is the level where the marginal revenue, which records the addition to the surplus from an additional unit of

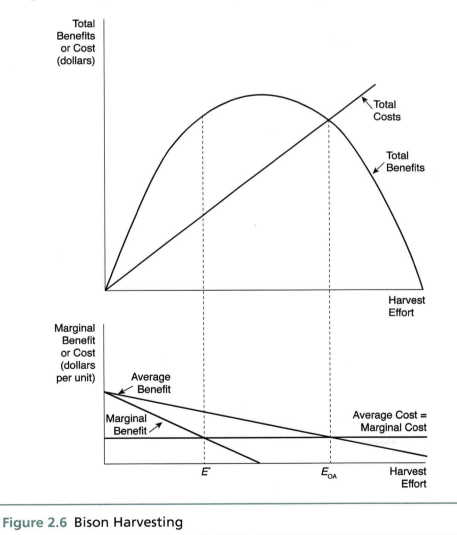

Figure 2.6 Bison Harvesting

effort, crosses the marginal cost curve, which measures the reduction in the surplus due to the additional cost of expending that last unit of effort. These two panels are simply two different (mathematically equivalent) ways to demonstrate the same outcome. (The curves in the bottom panel are derived from the curves in the top panel.)

With all hunters having completely unrestricted access to the bison, the resulting allocation would not be efficient. No individual hunter would have an incentive to protect scarcity rent by restricting hunting effort. Individual hunters, under this "open access" scenario (without exclusive rights), would exploit the resource until their total benefit equaled total cost, implying a level of effort equal to (E_{OA}). Excessive exploitation of the herd occurs because individual hunters cannot appropriate the scarcity rent; therefore, they ignore it. One of the losses from further exploitation that could be avoided by exclusive owners—the loss of scarcity rent due to overexploitation—is not part of the decision-making process of open-access hunters.

Two characteristics of this formulation of the open-access allocation are worth noting: (1) in the presence of sufficient demand, unrestricted access will cause resources to be overexploited; (2) the scarcity rent is dissipated—no one is able to appropriate the rent, so it is lost.

Why does this happen? Unlimited access destroys the incentive to conserve. A hunter who can preclude others from hunting his stock has an incentive to keep the herd at an efficient level. This restraint results in lower costs in the form of less time and effort expended to produce a given yield of bison. On the other hand, a hunter exploiting an open-access resource would not have an incentive to conserve because the potential additional economic surplus derived from self-restraint would, to some extent, be captured by other hunters who simply kept harvesting. Thus, unrestricted access to scarce resources promotes an inefficient allocation. As a result of excessive harvest and the loss of habitat as land was converted to farm and pasture, the Great Plains bison herds nearly became extinct (Lueck, 2002). Another example of open-access, fisheries, is covered in Chapter 12 of the companion book, *Natural Resource Economics*.

Public Goods

Public goods, defined as those that exhibit both consumption indivisibilities and nonexcludability, present a particularly complex category of environmental resources. *Nonexcludability* refers to a circumstance where, once the resource is provided, even those who fail to pay for it cannot be excluded from enjoying the benefits it confers. Consumption is said to be *indivisible* when one person's consumption of a good does not diminish the amount available for others. Several common environmental resources are public goods, including not only the "charming landscape" referred to by Emerson, but also clean air, clean water, and biological diversity.[2]

Biological diversity includes two related concepts: (1) the amount of genetic variability among individuals within a single species, and (2) the number of species within a community of organisms. *Genetic diversity*, critical to species survival in the natural world, has also proved to be important in the development of new crops and livestock. It enhances the opportunities for crossbreeding and, thus, the development of superior strains. The availability of different strains was the key, for example, in developing new, disease-resistant barley.

Because of the interdependence of species within ecological communities, any particular species may have a value to the community far beyond its intrinsic value. Certain species contribute balance and stability to their ecological communities by providing food sources or holding the population of the species in check.

The richness of diversity within and among species has provided new sources of food, energy, industrial chemicals, raw materials, and medicines. Yet, considerable evidence suggests that biological diversity is decreasing. Biodiversity is a valuable ecosystem service. Ecosystem services are covered in the companion to this book, *Natural Resource Economics*.

Can we rely solely on the private sector to produce the efficient amount of public goods, such as biological diversity? Unfortunately, the answer is no. Suppose that in response to diminishing ecological diversity we decide to take up a collection to provide some means of preserving endangered species. Would the collection yield sufficient revenue to pay for an efficient level of ecological diversity? The general answer is no. Let's see why.

In Figure 2.7, individual demand curves for preserving biodiversity have been presented for two consumers, A and B. The market demand curve is represented by the vertical summation of the two individual demand curves. A vertical summation is necessary because everyone can simultaneously consume the same amount of biological diversity. We are, therefore, able to determine the market demand by finding the sum of the amounts of money they would be willing to pay for that level of diversity.

What is the efficient level of diversity? It can be determined by a direct application of our definition of efficiency. The efficient allocation maximizes economic surplus, which is represented geometrically by the portion of the area under the market demand curve that lies above the constant marginal cost curve. The allocation that maximizes economic surplus is Q^*, the allocation where the demand curve crosses the marginal cost curve.

Why would a competitive market not be expected to supply the efficient level of this good? Since the two consumers have very different marginal willingness to pay from the efficient allocation of this good (OA versus OB), the efficient pricing system would require charging a different price to each consumer. Person A would pay OA and person B would pay OB. (Remember consumers tend to choose the level of the good that equates their marginal willingness to pay to the price they face.) Yet the producer would have no basis for figuring out how to differentiate the prices. In the absence of excludability, consumers are not likely to willingly reveal the strength of their preference for this commodity. All consumers have an incentive to understate the strength of their preferences to try to shift more of the cost burden to the other consumers.

Therefore, inefficiency results because each person is able to become a free rider on the other's contribution. A *free rider* is someone who derives the value from a commodity without paying an efficient amount for its supply. Because of the consumption indivisibility and nonexcludability properties of the public good, consumers receive the value of any diversity purchased by other people. When this happens it tends to diminish incentives to contribute, and the contributions are not sufficiently large to finance the efficient amount of the public good; it would be undersupplied. (In Chapter 8 we shall use the lens provided by game theory to show how the free rider effect helps to shape climate policy.)

The privately supplied amount may not be zero, however. Some diversity would be privately supplied. Indeed, as suggested by Example 2.3, the privately supplied amount may be considerable.

Imperfect Market Structures

Environmental problems also occur when one of the participants in an exchange of property rights is able to exercise an inordinate amount of power over the outcome. This can occur, for example, when a product is sold by a single seller, or *monopoly*.

It is easy to show that monopolies violate our definition of *efficiency* in the goods market (see Figure 2.8). According to our definition of *static efficiency*, the efficient allocation would result when OB is supplied. This would yield consumer surplus represented by triangle IGC *and* producer surplus denoted by triangle GCH. The monopoly, however, would produce and

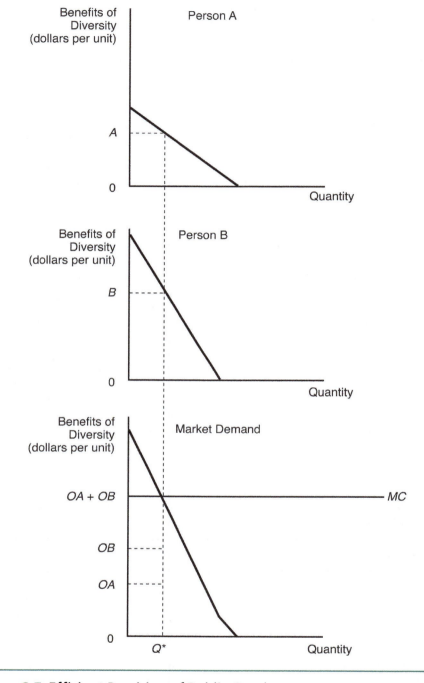

Figure 2.7 Efficient Provision of Public Goods

EXAMPLE 2.3

Public Goods Privately Provided: The Nature Conservancy

Can the demand for a public good such as biological diversity be observed in practice? Would the market respond to that demand? Apparently so, according to the existence of an organization called the Nature Conservancy.

The Nature Conservancy was born of an older organization called the Ecologist Union on September 11, 1950, for the purpose of establishing natural area reserves to aid in the preservation of areas, objects, and fauna and flora that have scientific, educational, or aesthetic significance. This organization purchases, or accepts as donations, land that has some unique ecological or aesthetic significance, to keep it from being used for other purposes. In so doing it preserves many species by preserving the habitat.

From humble beginnings, the Nature Conservancy has, as of 2017, been responsible for the preservation of 119 million acres of forests, marshes, prairies, mounds, and islands around the world. Additionally, the Nature Conservancy has protected 5000 miles of rivers and operates over 100 marine conservation projects. These areas serve as home to rare and endangered species of wildlife and plants. The Conservancy owns and manages the largest privately owned nature preserve system in the world.

This approach has considerable merit. A private organization can move more rapidly than the public sector. Because it has a limited budget, the Nature Conservancy sets priorities and concentrates on acquiring the most ecologically unique areas. Yet the theory of public goods reminds us that if this were to be the sole approach to the preservation of biological diversity, it would preserve a smaller-than-efficient amount.

Source: The Nature Conservancy, www.nature.org/about-us/vision-mission/index.htm?intc=nature.fnav.about

sell *OA*, where marginal revenue equals marginal cost, and would charge price *OF*. At this point, although the producer's surplus (*HFED*) is maximized, the sum of consumer and producer surplus is clearly not, because this choice causes society to lose economic surplus equal to triangle *EDC*.[3] Monopolies supply an inefficiently small amount of the good.

Imperfect markets clearly play some role in environmental problems. For example, the major oil-exporting countries have formed a cartel, resulting in higher-than-normal prices and lower-than-normal production. A *cartel* is a collusive agreement among producers to restrict production and raise prices. This collusive agreement allows the group to act as a monopolist. The inefficiency in the goods market would normally be offset to some degree by an associated reduction in social costs. The reduction in the combustion of oil would result in lower levels of pollution and, hence, the social cost associated with that pollution.

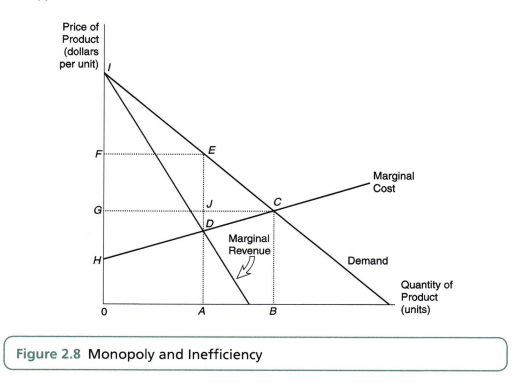

Figure 2.8 Monopoly and Inefficiency

Asymmetric Information

When all parties to a specific situation or transaction have access to the same amount of information about that situation, the information is said to be symmetrically distributed. If, however, one or more parties have more information than the others, the information distribution is said to be asymmetric.

Asymmetric information creates problems for the market when it results in a decision maker knowing too little to make an efficient choice. Suppose, for example, a consumer had a preference for organic food, but didn't know what food choices were truly organic. Since it would be relatively easy for producers to claim their produce was organically grown even if it were not, consumers who could not accurately distinguish truly organic produce from its fraudulent substitute would tend to be unwilling to pay a higher price for organic produce. As a result, both the profits and the output of organic farmers would be inefficiently low. If consumers do not have full information, negative externalities may result. (We shall encounter asymmetric information problems in several chapters, including energy, pollution control, toxic substances, and ecosystem services.)

Government Failure

Market processes are not the only sources of inefficiency. Political processes are fully as culpable. As will become clear in the chapters that follow, some environmental problems have arisen from a failure of political, rather than economic, institutions. To complete our study of the ability of institutions to allocate environmental resources, we must understand this source of inefficiency as well.

Government failure shares with market failure the characteristic that improper incentives are the root of the problem. Special interest groups use the political process to engage in what has become known as *rent seeking*. Rent seeking is the use of resources in lobbying and other activities directed at securing legislation that results in more profitable outcomes for those funding this activity. Successful rent-seeking activity will typically increase the net benefits going to the special interest group, but it will also frequently lower the surplus to society as a whole. In these instances, it is a classic case of the aggressive pursuit of a larger slice of the pie leading to a smaller pie.

Why don't the losers rise up to protect their interests? One main reason is voter ignorance. It is economically rational for voters to remain at least partially ignorant on many issues simply because of the high cost of keeping fully informed and the low probability that any single vote will be decisive. In addition, it is difficult for diffuse groups of individuals, each of whom is affected only to a small degree, to organize a coherent, unified opposition. Successful opposition is, in a sense, a public good, with its attendant tendency for free riding. Opposition to special interests would normally be underfunded, especially when the opposition is dispersed and the special interests are concentrated.

Rent seeking can take many forms. Producers can seek protection from competitive pressures brought by imports or can seek price floors to hold prices above their efficient levels. Consumer groups can seek price ceilings on goods or special subsidies to transfer part of their costs to the general body of taxpayers.

Rent seeking is not the only source of inefficient government policy. Sometimes governments act without full information and establish policies that are ultimately very inefficient. For example, some time ago, one technological strategy chosen by the government to control motor vehicle pollution involved adding a chemical substance (MTBE) to gasoline. Designed to promote cleaner combustion, this additive turned out to create a substantial water pollution problem.

Governments may also pursue social policy objectives that have the side effect of causing an environmental inefficiency. For example, looking back at Figure 2.5, suppose that the government, when pressured by lobbyists, decides to subsidize the production of steel. Figure 2.9 illustrates the outcome. The private marginal cost curve shifts down and to the right causing a further increase in production, lower prices, and even more pollution produced. Thus, the subsidy moves us even further away from where surplus is maximized at Q^*. The shaded triangle A shows the deadweight loss (inefficiency) without the subsidy. With the subsidy, the deadweight loss grows to areas $A + B + C$. This social policy has the side effect of increasing an environmental inefficiency.

This example provides a direct challenge to the presumption that more direct intervention by the government automatically leads to either greater efficiency or greater sustainability.

These cases illustrate the general economic premise that environmental problems arise because of a divergence between individual and collective objectives. This is a powerful explanatory device because not only does it suggest why these problems arise, but it also suggests how they might be resolved—by realigning individual incentives to make them compatible with collective objectives. As self-evident as this approach may be, it is controversial when people disagree about whether the problem is our improper values or the improper translation of our quite proper values into action.

Economists have always been reluctant to argue that values of consumers are warped, because that would necessitate dictating the "correct" set of values. Both capitalism and democracy are based on the presumption that the majority knows what it is doing, whether it is casting ballots for representatives or dollar votes for goods and services.

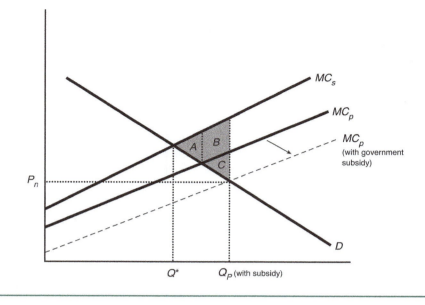

Figure 2.9 The Market for Steel Revisited

The Pursuit of Efficiency

We have seen that environmental problems can arise when property rights are ill defined, and when these rights are exchanged under something other than competitive conditions. We can now use our definition of efficiency to explore possible remedies, such as private negotiation, judicial remedies, and regulation by the legislative and executive branches of government.

Private Resolution through Negotiation—Property, Liability, and the Coase Theorem

The simplest means to restore efficiency occurs when the number of affected parties is small, making negotiation feasible. Suppose, for example, we return to the case used earlier in this chapter to illustrate an externality—the conflict between the polluting steel company and the downstream resort.

Figure 2.10 allows us to examine how this negotiation might take place. If the resort offers a payment of $C + D$ to the steel company, they would be better off if the steel firm responded by decreasing its production from Q_m to Q^*. Let's assume that the payment is equal to this amount. Would the steel company be willing to reduce production to the desired level? If they refused the compensation, their producer surplus would be $A + B + D$. If they accepted, their producer surplus would be $A + B$ plus the payment, so their total return would be $A + B + C + D$. Clearly, they are better off by C if they accept the payment. Society as a whole is better off by the amount C as well since the economic surplus from Q_m is $A - C$ and the economic surplus from Q^* is A.

Our discussion of individual negotiations raises two questions: (1) Should the property right always belong to the party who held it first (in this case the steel company)? (2) How can

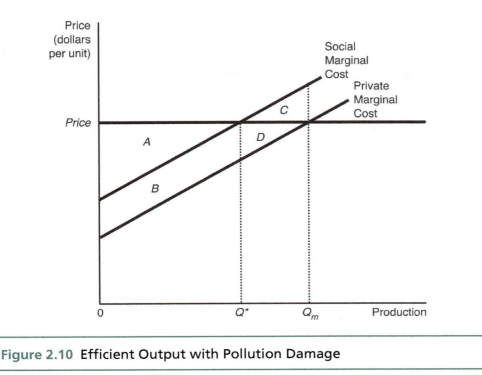

Figure 2.10 Efficient Output with Pollution Damage

environmental risks be handled when prior negotiation is clearly impractical? These questions are routinely answered by the court system.

The court system can respond to environmental conflicts by imposing either property rules or liability rules. Property rules specify the initial allocation of the entitlement or property right. The entitlements at conflict in our example are, on one hand, the right to add waste products to the river and, on the other, the right to an attractive river. In applying property rules, the court merely decides which right is preeminent and places an injunction against violating that right. The injunction is removed only upon obtaining the consent of the party whose right was violated. Consent is usually obtained in return for an out-of-court monetary settlement achieved via negotiation.

Note that, in the absence of a court decision, the entitlement is naturally allocated to the party that can most easily seize it. In our example, the natural allocation would give the entitlement to the steel company. The courts must decide whether to overturn this natural allocation.

How would they decide? And what difference would their decision make? The answers may surprise you.

In a classic article, economist Ronald Coase (1960) held that, as long as negotiation costs are negligible and affected consumers can negotiate freely with each other (when the number of affected parties is small), the court could allocate the entitlement to *either* party, and an efficient allocation would result. The only effect of the court's decision would be to change the distribution of surplus among the affected parties. This remarkable conclusion has come to be known as the *Coase theorem*.

Why is this so? In Figure 2.10, we showed that if the steel company has the property right, it is in the resort's interest to offer a payment that results in the desired level of output.

Suppose, now, that the resort has the property right instead. To pollute in this case, the steel company must pay the resort. Suppose it could pollute only if it compensated the resort for all damages. (In other words, it would agree to pay the difference between the two marginal cost curves up to the level of output actually chosen.) As long as this compensation was required, the steel company would choose to produce Q^* since that is the level at which its producer's surplus, given the compensation, is maximized. (Note that, due to the compensation, the curve the steel company uses to calculate its producer surplus is now the higher marginal cost curve.)

The difference between these different ways of allocating property rights lies in how the cost of obtaining the efficient level of output is shared between the parties. When the property right is assigned to the steel company, the cost is borne by the resort (part of the cost is the damage and part is the payment to reduce the level of damage). When the property right is assigned to the resort, the cost is borne by the steel company (it now must compensate for all damage). In either case, the efficient level of production results. The Coase theorem shows that the very existence of an inefficiency triggers pressures for improvements. Furthermore, the existence of this pressure does not depend on the assignment of property rights.

This is an important point, but the importance of this theorem should not be overstated. As we shall see, private efforts triggered by inefficiency can frequently prevent the worst excesses of environmental degradation. However, both theoretical and practical objections can be raised. The chief theoretical qualification concerns the assumption that wealth effects do not matter. The decision to confer the property right on a particular party results in a transfer of wealth to that party. This transfer might shift the demand curve for either steel or resorts out, as long as higher incomes result in greater demand. Whenever wealth effects are significant, the type of property rule issued by the court does affect the outcome.

Wealth effects normally are small, so the zero-wealth-effect assumption is probably not a fatal flaw. Some serious practical flaws, however, do mar the usefulness of the Coase theorem. The first involves the incentives for polluting that result when the property right is assigned to the polluter. Since pollution would become a profitable activity with this assignment, other polluters might be encouraged to increase production and pollution in order to earn the payments. That certainly would not be efficient.

Negotiation is also difficult to apply when the number of people affected by the pollution is large. You may have already noticed that in the presence of several affected parties, pollution reduction is a public good. The free-rider problem would make it difficult for the group to act cohesively and effectively for the restoration of efficiency.

When individual negotiation is not practical for one reason or another, the courts can turn to liability rules. These are rules that award monetary damages, after the fact, to the injured party. The amount of the award is designed to correspond to the amount of damage inflicted. Thus, returning to Figure 2.10, a liability rule would force the steel company to compensate the resort for all damages incurred. In this case, it could choose any production level it wanted, but it would have to pay the resort an amount of money equal to the area between the two marginal cost curves from the origin to the chosen level of output. In this case the steel plant would maximize its producer's surplus by choosing Q^*. (Why wouldn't the steel plant choose to produce more than that? Why wouldn't the steel plant choose to produce less than that?)

The moral of this story is that appropriately designed liability rules can also correct inefficiencies by forcing those who cause damage to bear the cost of that damage. Internalizing previously external costs causes profit-maximizing decisions to be compatible with efficiency.

As we shall see in subsequent chapters, this "internalizing externalities" principle plays a large role in the design of efficient policy in many areas of environmental policy.

Liability rules are interesting from an economics point of view because early decisions create precedents for later ones. Imagine, for example, how the incentives to prevent oil spills facing an oil company are transformed once it has a legal obligation to clean up after an oil spill and to compensate fishermen for reduced catches. It quickly becomes evident that in this situation, accident prevention can become cheaper than retrospectively dealing with the damage once it has occurred.

This approach, however, also has its limitations. It relies on a case-by-case determination based on the unique circumstances for each case. Administratively, such a determination is very expensive. Expenses, such as court time, lawyers' fees, and so on, fall into a category called *transaction costs* by economists. In the present context, these are the administrative costs incurred in attempting to correct the inefficiency. The Coase theorem relies on an assumption that transaction costs are low. In reality though, this is rarely the case. Transaction costs in many cases can be quite high. When the number of parties involved in a dispute is large and the circumstances are common, we are tempted to correct the inefficiency by statutes or regulations rather than court decisions.

Legislative and Executive Regulation

These remedies can take several forms. The legislature could dictate that no one produce more steel or pollution than Q^*. This dictum might then be backed up with sufficiently large jail sentences or fines to deter potential violators. Alternatively, the legislature could impose a tax on steel or on pollution. A per-unit tax equal to the vertical distance between the two marginal cost curves would work (see Figure 2.10).

Legislatures could also establish rules to permit greater flexibility and yet reduce damage. For example, zoning laws would establish separate areas for steel plants and resorts. This approach assumes that the damage can be substantially reduced by keeping nonconforming uses apart.

They could also require the installation of particular pollution control equipment (as when catalytic converters were required on automobiles), or deny the use of a particular production ingredient (as when lead was removed from gasoline). In other words, they can regulate outputs, inputs, production processes, emissions, and even the location of production in their attempt to produce an efficient outcome. In subsequent chapters, we shall examine the various options policymakers have not only to show how they can modify environmentally destructive behavior, but also to establish the degree to which they can promote efficiency.

Payments are, of course, not the only means victims have at their disposal for lowering pollution. When the victims also consume the products produced by the polluters, consumer boycotts are possible. When the victims are employed by the polluter, strikes or other forms of labor resistance are also possible.

Legislation and/or regulation can also help to resolve the asymmetric information problem. Because the fundamental problem is that one or more of the parties do not have sufficient crucial, trustworthy information, the obvious solution involves providing that information. How should that information be provided?

Labeling is one attempt to provide more information to consumers. Examples of labeling for food products include notifying consumers about products containing genetically modified organisms, and identifying organically grown crops and fair trade products.

A recent source of encouragement for organic farms has been the demonstrated willing-ness of consumers to pay a premium for organically grown fruits and vegetables. To allow consumers to discern which products are truly organic, growers need a reliable certification process. Additionally, fear of lost access to important foreign markets, such as the European Union, led to an industry-wide push in the United States for *mandatory* labeling standards that would provide the foundation for a national uniform seal. (*Voluntary* US certification programs had proved insufficient to assure access to European markets, since they were highly variable by state.)

In response to these pressures, the Organic Foods Production Act (OFPA) was enacted in the 1990 Farm Bill.[4] Title 21 of that law states the following objectives:

> (1) to establish national standards governing the marketing of certain agricultural products as organically produced; (2) to assure consumers that organically produced products meet a consistent standard; and (3) to facilitate interstate commerce in fresh and processed food that is organically produced.[5]

The USDA National Organic Program, established as part of this Act, is responsible for a mandatory certification program for organic production. The Act also established the National Organic Standards Board (NOSB) and charged it with defining the "organic" standards. The new rules, which took effect in October 2002, require certification by the USDA for labeling. Foods labeled as "100 percent organic" must contain only organic ingredients. Foods labeled as "organic" must contain at least 95 percent organic agricultural ingredients, excluding water and salt. Products labeled as "Made with Organic Ingredients" must contain at least 70 percent organic agricultural ingredients.

Certification allows socially conscious consumers to make a difference. As Example 2.4 demonstrates, eco-certification for coffee seems to be one such case.

An Efficient Role for Government

While the economic approach suggests that government action could well be used to restore efficiency, it also suggests that inefficiency is not a sufficient condition to justify government intervention. Any corrective mechanism involves transaction costs. If these transaction costs are high enough, and the surplus to be derived from correcting the inefficiency is small enough, then it is best simply to live with the inefficiency.

Consider, for example, the pollution problem. Wood-burning stoves, which were widely used for cooking and heat in the late 1800s in the United States, were sources of pollution, but because of the enormous capacity of the air to absorb the emissions, no regulation resulted. More recently, however, the resurgence of demand for wood-burning stoves in cold climates with nearby forests, precipitated in part by high oil prices, has resulted in strict regulations for wood-burning stove emissions because the population density is so much higher.

Over time, the scale of economic activity and the resulting emissions have increased. Cities are experiencing severe problems from air and water pollutants because of the clustering of activities. Both the increase in the number of emitters and their clustering have increased the amount of emissions per unit volume of air or water. As a result, pollutant concentrations have caused perceptible problems with human health, vegetation growth, and aesthetics.

Historically, as incomes have risen, the demand for leisure activities has also risen. Many of these leisure activities, such as canoeing and backpacking, take place in unique, pristine environmental areas. With the number of these areas declining as a result of conversion to other uses, the value of remaining areas has increased. Thus, the values derived from protecting

EXAMPLE 2.4

Can Eco-Certification Make a Difference? Organic Costa Rican Coffee

Environmental problems associated with agricultural production for export in developing countries can be difficult to tackle using conventional regulation because producers are typically so numerous and dispersed, while regulatory agencies are commonly inadequately funded and staffed. In principle, eco-certification of production could circumvent these problems by providing a means for the socially conscious consumer to identify environmentally superior products, thereby providing a basis for paying a price premium for them. These premiums, in turn, would create financial incentives for producers to meet the certification standards.

Do socially conscious buyers care enough to actually pay a price premium that is high enough to motivate changes in the way the products are produced? Apparently, for Costa Rican coffee at least, they do.

One study examined this question for certified organic coffee grown in Turrialba, Costa Rica, an agricultural region in the country's central valley, about 40 miles east of San José, the capital city. This is an interesting case because Costa Rican farmers face significant pressure from the noncertified market to lower their costs, a strategy that can have severe environmental consequences. In contrast, organic production typically not only involves higher labor costs, but the conversion from chemically based production can also reduce yields. In addition, the costs of initial certification and subsequent annual monitoring and reporting are significant.

The authors found that organic certification did improve coffee growers' environmental performance. Specifically, they found that certification significantly reduced the use of pesticides, chemical fertilizers, and herbicides, and increased the use of organic fertilizer. In general, their results suggest that organic certification has a stronger causal effect on preventing negative practices than on encouraging positive ones. The study notes that this finding is consistent with anecdotal evidence that local inspectors tend to enforce the certification standards prohibiting negative practices more vigorously than the standards requiring positive ones.

Source: Blackman, A., & Naranjo, M. A. (2012). Does eco-certification have environmental benefits? Organic coffee in Costa Rica. *Ecological Economics, 83*(November), 58–66.

some areas have risen over time until they have exceeded the transaction costs of protecting them from pollution and/or development.

The level and concentration of economic activity has increased pollution problems and driven up the demand for clean air and pristine areas. These changes have created the preconditions for government action. Can government respond efficiently or will rent seeking prevent efficient political solutions? We devote much of this book to pinning down the answer to that question.

Summary

How producers and consumers use the resources making up the environmental asset depends on the nature of the entitlements embodied in the property rights governing resource use. When property rights systems are exclusive, transferable, and enforceable, the owner of a resource has a powerful incentive to use that resource efficiently, since the failure to do so results in a personal loss.

The economic system will not always sustain efficient allocations, however. Specific circumstances that could lead to inefficient allocations include externalities, improperly defined property rights systems (such as open-access resources and public goods), imperfect markets for trading the property rights to the resources (monopoly), and asymmetric information. When these circumstances arise, market allocations typically do not maximize the surplus.

Due to rent-seeking behavior by special interest groups or the less-than-perfect implementation of efficient plans, the political system can produce inefficiencies as well. Voter ignorance on many issues, coupled with the public-good nature of any results of political activity, tends to create a situation in which maximizing an individual's private surplus (through lobbying, for example) can be at the expense of a lower economic surplus for all consumers and producers.

The efficiency criterion can be used to assist in the identification of circumstances in which our political and economic institutions lead us astray. It can also assist in the search for remedies by facilitating the design of regulatory, judicial, or legislative solutions.

Discussion Questions

1. In a well-known legal case, *Miller v. Schoene* (287 US 272), a classic conflict of property rights was featured. Red cedar trees, used only for ornamental purposes, carried a disease that could destroy apple orchards within a radius of 2 miles. There was no known way of curing the disease except by destroying the cedar trees or by ensuring that apple orchards were at least 2 miles away from the cedar trees. Apply the Coase theorem to this situation. Does it make any difference to the outcome whether the cedar tree owners are entitled to retain their trees or the apple growers are entitled to be free of them? Why or why not?

2. In primitive societies, the entitlements to use land were frequently possessory rights rather than ownership rights. Those on the land could use it as they wished, but they could not transfer it to anyone else. One could acquire a new plot by simply occupying and using it, leaving the old plot available for someone else. Would this type of entitlement system cause more or less incentive to conserve the land than an ownership entitlement? Why? Would a possessory entitlement system be more efficient in a modern society or a primitive society? Why?

3. In this chapter we have discussed how markets work. Recently some new markets have emerged that focus on sharing of durable goods among a wider circle of users. Examples include Airbnb and Uber. The rise of these sharing markets may well have an impact on the relationship between the economy and the environment.

   a. What are the market niches these firms have found? How is Airbnb different from Hilton? How is Uber different from Hertz or Yellow Cab? Is this a matter mainly of a different type of supply or is the demand side affected as well?

b. Why now? Markets for personal transportation and temporary housing have been around for a long time. How can these new companies find profitable opportunities in markets that have existed for some time? Is it evidence that the markets are not competitive? Or have the new opportunities been created by some changes in market conditions?

c. Are these new sharing markets likely on balance to be good for or harmful to the environment? Why?

Self-Test Exercises

1. Suppose the state is trying to decide how many miles of a very scenic river it should preserve. There are 100 people in the community, each of whom has an identical inverse demand function given by $P = 10 - 1.0q$, where q is the number of miles preserved and P is the per-mile price he or she is willing to pay for q miles of preserved river. (a) If the marginal cost of preservation is $500 per mile, how many miles would be preserved in an efficient allocation? (b) How large is the economic surplus?

2. Suppose the market demand function (expressed in dollars) for a normal product is $P = 80 - q$, and the marginal cost (in dollars) of producing it is $MC = 1q$, where P is the price of the product and q is the quantity demanded and/or supplied.

    a. How much would be supplied by a competitive market?
    b. Compute the consumer surplus and producer surplus. Show that their sum is maximized.
    c. Compute the consumer surplus and the producer surplus assuming this same product was supplied by a monopoly. (*Hint*: The marginal revenue curve has twice the slope of the demand curve.)
    d. Show that, when this market is controlled by a monopoly, producer surplus is larger, consumer surplus is smaller, and the sum of the two surpluses is smaller than when the market is controlled by competitive industry.

3. Suppose you were asked to comment on a proposed policy to control oil spills. Since the average cost of an oil spill has been computed as $X, the proposed policy would require any firm responsible for a spill immediately to pay the government $X. Is this likely to result in the efficient amount of precaution against oil spills? Why or why not?

4. "In environmental liability cases, courts have some discretion regarding the magnitude of compensation polluters should be forced to pay for the environmental incidents they cause. In general, however, the larger the required payments the better." Discuss.

5. Label each of the following propositions as descriptive or normative and defend your choice:

    a. Energy efficiency programs have created jobs.
    b. Money spent on protecting endangered species is wasted.
    c. Fisheries must be privatized to survive.
    d. Raising transport costs lower suburban land values.
    e. Birth control programs are counterproductive.

6. Identify whether each of the following resource categories is a public good, a common-pool resource, or neither and defend your answer:

    a. A pod of whales in the ocean to whale hunters.
    b. A pod of whales in the ocean to whale watchers.

c. The benefits from reductions of greenhouse gas emissions.

d. Water from a town well that excludes nonresidents.

e. Bottled water.

Notes

1   We know, however, from Einstein's famous equation ($E = mc^2$) that matter can be transformed into energy. This transformation is the source of energy in nuclear power.
2   Notice that public "bads," such as dirty air and dirty water, are also possible.
3   Producers would lose area *JDC* compared to the efficient allocation, but they would gain area *FEJG*, which is much larger. Meanwhile, consumers would be worse off, because they lose area *FECJG*. Of these, *FEJG* is merely a transfer to the monopoly, whereas *EJC* is a pure loss to society. The total pure loss (*EDC*) is called a *deadweight loss*.
4   The European Union has followed a similar, but not identical, policy.
5   Golan et al. (2001).

Further Reading

Lueck, D. (2002). The extermination and conservation of the American bison. *Journal of Legal Studies*, *31*(S$_2$), s609–s652. A fascinating look at the role property rights played in the fate of the American bison.

Mason, C. F. (2012). The economics of eco-labeling: Theory and empirical implications. *International Review of Environmental and Resource Economics*, *6*, 341–372. A survey of the growing literature on eco-labeling.

Ostrom, E. (1992). *Crafting Institutions for Self-Governing Irrigation Systems*. San Francisco, CA: ICS Press. A classic book by a Nobel Prize laureate that demonstrates that in favorable circumstances common-pool problems can sometimes be solved by voluntary organizations, rather than by a coercive state; among the cases considered are communal tenure in meadows and forests, irrigation communities, and fisheries.

Ostrom, E., Dietz, T., Dolsak, N., Stern, P., Stonich, S., & Weber, E. U. (Eds.). (2002). *The Drama of the Commons*. Washington, DC: National Academy Press. A compilation of articles and papers on common-pool resources.

Stavins, R. (2012). *The Economics of the Environment: Selected Readings*, 6th ed. New York: W. W. Norton and Company. A carefully selected collection of readings that would complement this text.

Additional references and historically significant references are available on this book's Companion Website: www.routledge.com/cw/Tietenberg

Chapter 3

Evaluating Trade-Offs

Benefit-Cost Analysis and Other Decision-Making Metrics

> No sensible decision can be made any longer without taking into account not only the world as it is, but the world as it will be.
> —Isaac Asimov, US science fiction novelist and scholar (1920–1992)

Introduction

In the last chapter we noted that economic analysis has both positive and normative dimensions. The normative dimension helps to separate the policies that make sense from those that don't. Since resources are limited, it is not possible to undertake all ventures that might appear desirable, so making choices is inevitable.

Normative analysis can be useful in public policy in several different situations. It might be used, for example, to evaluate the desirability of a proposed new pollution control regulation or a proposal to preserve an area currently scheduled for development. In these cases, the analysis helps to provide guidance on the desirability of a program before that program is put into place. In other contexts, it might be used to evaluate how an already-implemented program has worked out in practice. Here the relevant question is: Was this a wise use of resources? In this chapter, we present and demonstrate the use of several decision-making metrics that can assist us in evaluating options.

Normative Criteria for Decision Making

Normative choices can arise in two different contexts. In the first context, we need simply to choose among options that have been predefined, while in the second we try to find the optimal choice among all the possible options.

Evaluating Predefined Options: Benefit-Cost Analysis

If you were asked to evaluate the desirability of some proposed action, you would probably begin by attempting to identify both the gains and the losses from that action. If the gains exceed the losses, then it seems natural to support the action.

That simple framework provides the starting point for the normative approach to evaluating policy choices in economics. Economists suggest that actions have both benefits and costs. If the benefits exceed the costs, then the action is desirable. On the other hand, if the costs exceed the benefits, then the action is not desirable. (Comparing benefits and costs across time will be covered later in this chapter.)

We can formalize this in the following way. Let B be the benefits from a proposed action and C be the costs. Our decision rule would then be

if $B > C$, support the action.

Otherwise, oppose the action.[1]

As long as B and C are positive, a mathematically equivalent formulation would be

if $B/C > 1$, support the action.

Otherwise, oppose the action.

So far so good, but how do we measure benefits and costs? In economics, the system of measurement is anthropocentric, which simply means human centered. All benefits and costs are valued in terms of their effects (broadly defined) on humanity. As shall be pointed out later, that does *not* imply (as it might first appear) that ecosystem effects are ignored unless they *directly* affect humans. The fact that large numbers of humans contribute voluntarily to organizations that are dedicated to environmental protection provides ample evidence that humans place a value on environmental preservation that goes well beyond any direct use they might make of it. Nonetheless, the notion that humans are doing the valuing is a controversial point that will be revisited and discussed in Chapter 4, along with the specific techniques for valuing these effects.

In benefit-cost analysis, benefits are measured simply as the relevant area under the demand curve since the demand curve reflects consumers' willingness to pay. Total costs are measured by the relevant area under the marginal cost curve.

It is important to stress that environmental services have costs even though they are produced without any human input. All costs should be measured as opportunity costs. To firm up this notion of opportunity cost, consider an example. Suppose a particular stretch of river can be used either for white-water rafting or to generate electric power. Since the dam that generates the power would flood the rapids, the two uses are incompatible. The opportunity cost of producing power is the foregone net benefit that would have resulted from the white-water rafting. The *marginal opportunity cost curve* defines the additional cost of producing another unit of electricity resulting from the associated incremental loss of net benefits due to reduced opportunities for white-water rafting.

Since net benefit is defined as the excess of benefits over costs, it follows that net benefit is equal to that portion of the area under the demand curve that lies above the supply curve.

Consider Figure 3.1, which illustrates the net benefits from preserving a stretch of river. Suppose that we are considering preserving a 4-mile stretch of river and that the benefits and costs of that action are reflected in Figure 3.1. Should that stretch be preserved? Why or why not? Hold on to your answer because we will return to this example later.

Finding the Optimal Outcome

In the preceding section, we examined how benefit-cost analysis can be used to evaluate the desirability of specific actions. In this section, we want to examine how this approach can be used to identify "optimal," or best, approaches.

In subsequent chapters, which address individual environmental problems, the normative analysis will proceed in three steps. First, we will identify an optimal outcome. Second, we will attempt to discern the extent to which our institutions produce optimal outcomes and, where divergences occur between actual and optimal outcomes, to attempt to uncover the behavioral sources of the problems. Finally, we can use both our knowledge of the nature of the problems and their underlying behavioral causes as a basis for designing appropriate policy solutions. Although applying these three steps to each of the environmental problems must reflect the uniqueness of each situation, the overarching framework used to shape that analysis remains the same.

To provide some illustrations of how this approach is used in practice, consider two examples: one drawn from natural resource economics and another from environmental economics. These are meant to be illustrative and to convey a flavor of the argument; the details are left to upcoming chapters.

Consider the rising number of depleted ocean fisheries. Depleted fisheries, which involve fish populations that have fallen so low as to threaten their viability as commercial fisheries, not only jeopardize oceanic biodiversity, but also pose a threat to both the individuals who make their living from the sea and the communities that depend on fishing to support their local economies.

How would an economist attempt to understand and resolve this problem? The first step would involve defining the optimal stock or the optimal rate of harvest of the fishery. The second step would compare this level with the actual stock and harvest levels. Once this economic framework is applied, not only does it become clear that stocks are much lower than optimal for many fisheries, but also the reason for excessive exploitation becomes clear. Understanding

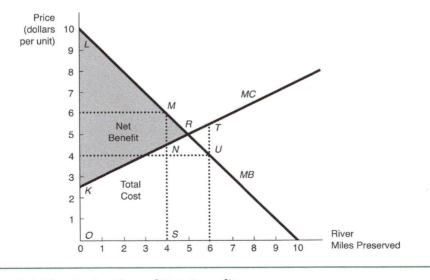

Figure 3.1 The Derivation of Net Benefits

the nature of the problem has led quite naturally to some solutions. Once implemented, these policies have allowed some fisheries to begin the process of renewal.

Another problem involves solid waste. As local communities run out of room for landfills in the face of an increasing generation of waste, what can be done?

Economists start by thinking about how one would define the optimal amount of waste. The definition necessarily incorporates waste reduction and recycling as aspects of the optimal outcome. The analysis not only reveals that current waste levels are excessive, but also suggests some specific behavioral sources of the problem. Based upon this understanding, specific economic solutions have been identified and implemented. Communities that have adopted these measures have generally experienced lower levels of waste and higher levels of recycling.

In the rest of the book, similar analysis is applied to energy, minerals, water, pollution, climate change, and a host of other topics. In each case, the economic analysis helps to point the way toward solutions. To initiate that process, we must begin by defining "optimal."

Relating Optimality to Efficiency

According to the normative choice criterion introduced earlier in this chapter, desirable outcomes are those where the benefits exceed the costs. It is therefore a logical next step to suggest that optimal polices are those that maximize net benefits (benefits minus costs). The concept of *static efficiency*, or merely *efficiency*, was introduced in Chapter 2. An allocation of resources is said to satisfy the static efficiency criterion if the economic surplus from the use of those resources is maximized by that allocation. Notice that the net benefits area to be maximized in an "optimal outcome" for public policy is identical to the "economic surplus" that is maximized in an efficient allocation. Hence, efficient outcomes are also optimal outcomes.

Let's take a moment to show how this concept can be applied. Previously, we asked whether an action that preserved 4 miles of river was worth doing (Figure 3.1). The answer is yes because the net benefits from that action are positive. (Can you see why?)

Static efficiency, however, requires us to ask a rather different question, namely, what is the optimal (or efficient) number of miles to be preserved? We know from the definition that the optimal amount of preservation would maximize net benefits. Does preserving 4 miles maximize net benefits? Is it the efficient outcome?

We can answer that question by establishing whether it is possible to increase the net benefit by preserving more or less of the river. If the net benefit can be increased by preserving more miles, clearly, preserving 4 miles could not have maximized the net benefit and, therefore, could not have been efficient.

Consider what would happen if society were to choose to preserve 5 miles instead of 4. Refer back to Figure 3.1. What happens to the net benefit? It increases by area *MNR*. Since we can find another allocation with greater net benefit, 4 miles of preservation could not have been efficient. Could 5? Yes. Let's see why.

We know that 5 miles of preservation convey more net benefits than 4. If this allocation is efficient, then it must also be true that the net benefit is smaller for levels of preservation higher than 5. Notice that the additional cost of preserving the sixth unit (the area under the marginal cost curve) is larger than the additional benefit received from preserving it (the corresponding area under the demand curve). Therefore, the triangle *RTU* represents the reduction in net benefit that occurs if 6 miles are preserved rather than 5.

Since the net benefit is reduced, both by preserving less than 5 miles and by preserving more than 5, we conclude that five units is the preservation level that maximizes net benefit (the shaded area). Therefore, from our definition, preserving 5 miles constitutes an efficient or optimal allocation.[2]

One implication of this example, which will be very useful in succeeding chapters, is what we shall call the "first equimarginal principle":

> First Equimarginal Principle (the "Efficiency Equimarginal Principle"): Social net benefits are maximized when the social marginal benefits from an allocation equal the social marginal costs.

The social marginal benefit is the increase in social benefits received from supplying one more unit of the good or service, while social marginal cost is the increase in cost incurred from supplying that additional unit of the good or service.

This criterion helps to minimize wasted resources, but is it fair? The ethical basis for this criterion is derived from a concept called *Pareto optimality*, named after the Italian-born Swiss economist Vilfredo Pareto, who first proposed it around the turn of the twentieth century.

> Allocations are said to be Pareto optimal if no other feasible allocation could benefit at least one person without any deleterious effects on some other person.

Allocations that do not satisfy this definition are suboptimal. Suboptimal allocations can always be rearranged so that some people can gain net benefits without the rearrangement causing anyone else to lose net benefits. Therefore, the gainers could use a portion of their gains to compensate the losers sufficiently to ensure they were at least as well off as they were prior to the reallocation.

Efficient allocations are Pareto optimal. Since net benefits are maximized by an efficient allocation, it is not possible to increase the net benefit by rearranging the allocation. Without an increase in the net benefit, it is impossible for the gainers to compensate the losers sufficiently; the gains to the gainers would necessarily be smaller than the losses to the losers.

Inefficient allocations are judged inferior because they do not maximize the size of the pie to be distributed. By failing to maximize net benefit, they are forgoing an opportunity to make some people better off without harming others.

Comparing Benefits and Costs across Time

The analysis we have covered so far is very useful for thinking about actions where time is not an important factor. Yet many of the decisions made now have consequences that persist well into the future. Time is a factor. Exhaustible energy resources, once used, are gone. Biological renewable resources (such as fisheries or forests) can be overharvested, leaving smaller and possibly weaker populations for future generations. Persistent pollutants can accumulate over time. How can we make choices when the benefits and costs occur at different points in time?

Incorporating time into the analysis requires an extension of the concepts we have already developed. This extension provides a way for thinking not only about the magnitude of benefits and costs, but also about their timing. In order to incorporate timing, the decision rule must provide a way to compare net benefits received in different time periods. The concept that allows this comparison is called *present value*. Before introducing this expanded decision rule, we must define present value.

Present value explicitly incorporates the time value of money. A dollar today invested at 10 percent interest yields $1.10 a year from now (the return of the $1 principal plus $0.10

interest). The present value of $1.10 received one year from now is therefore $1, because, given $1 now, you can turn it into $1.10 a year from now by investing it at 10 percent interest. We can find the present value of any amount of money (X) received one year from now by computing $X/(1 + r)$, where r is the appropriate interest rate (10 percent in our above example).

What could your dollar earn in 2 years at r percent interest? Because of compound interest, the amount would be $\$1(1 + r)(1 + r) = \$1(1 + r)^2$. It follows then that the present value of X received 2 years from now is $X/(1 + r)^2$. The present value of X received in three years is $X/(1+r)^3$.

By now the pattern should be clear. The present value of a *one-time* net benefit received n years from now is

$$PV[B_n] = \frac{B_n}{(1 + r)^n}$$

The present value of a stream of net benefits $\{B_0, \ldots, B_n\}$ received over a period of n years is computed as

$$PV[B_0, \ldots, B_n] = \sum_{i=0}^{n} \frac{B_i}{(1 + r)^i}$$

where r is the appropriate interest rate and B_0 is the amount of net benefits received immediately. The process of calculating the present value is called *discounting*, and the rate r is referred to as the discount rate.

The number resulting from a present-value calculation has a straightforward interpretation. Suppose you were investigating an allocation that would yield the following pattern of net benefits on the last day of each of the next 5 years: $3,000, $5,000, $6,000, $10,000, and $12,000. If you use an interest rate of 6 percent $(r = 0.06)$ and the above formula, you will discover that this stream has a present value of $29,205.92 (see Table 3.1). Notice how each amount is discounted back the appropriate number of years to the present and then these discounted values are summed.

What does that number mean? If you put $29,205.92 in a savings account earning 6 percent interest and wrote yourself checks, respectively, for $3,000, $5,000, $6,000, $10,000, and $12,000 on the last day of each of the next 5 years, your last check would just restore the account to a $0 balance (see Table 3.2). Thus, you should be indifferent about receiving $29,205.92 now or in the specific 5-year stream of benefits totaling $36,000; given one, you can get the other. Hence, the method is called present value because it translates everything back to its current worth.

It is now possible to show how this analysis can be used to evaluate actions. Calculate the present value of net benefits from the action. If the present value is greater than zero, the action can be supported. Otherwise it should not.

Table 3.1 Demonstrating Present Value Calculations

Year	1	2	3	4	5	Sum
Annual Amounts	$3,000	$5,000	$6,000	$10,000	$12,000	$36,000
Present Value $(r = 0.06)$	$2,830.19	$4,449.98	$5,037.72	$7,920.94	$8,967.10	$29,205.92

Table 3.2 Interpreting Present Value Calculations

Year	1	2	3	4	5	6
Balance at Beginning of Year	$29,205.92	$27,958.28	$24,635.77	$20,113.92	$11,320.75	$0.00
Year-End Fund Balance before Payment ($r = 0.06$)	$30,958.28	$29,635.77	$26,113.92	$21,320.75	$12,000.00	
Payment	$3,000	$5,000	$6,000	$10,000	$12,000	

Dynamic Efficiency

The static efficiency criterion is very useful for comparing resource allocations when time is not an important factor. How can we think about optimal choices when the benefits and costs occur at different points in time?

The traditional criterion used to find an optimal allocation when time is involved is called *dynamic efficiency*, a generalization of the static efficiency concept already developed. In this generalization, the present-value criterion provides a way for comparing the net benefits received in one period with the net benefits received in another.

An allocation of resources across *n* time periods satisfies the dynamic efficiency criterion if it maximizes the present value of net benefits that could be received from all the possible ways of allocating those resources over the *n* periods.

Applying the Concepts

Having now spent some time developing the concepts we need, let's take a moment to examine some actual studies in which they have been used.

Pollution Control

Benefit-cost analysis has been used to assess the desirability of efforts to control pollution. Pollution control certainly confers many benefits, but it also has costs. Do the benefits justify the costs? That was a question the US Congress wanted answered, so in Section 812 of the Clean Air Act Amendments of 1990, it required the US Environmental Protection Agency (EPA) to evaluate the benefits and costs of the US air pollution control policy initially over the 1970–1990 period and subsequently over the 1990–2020 time period (see Example 3.1).

In responding to this congressional mandate, the EPA set out to quantify and monetize the benefits and costs of achieving the emissions reductions required by US policy. Benefits quantified by this study included reduced death rates and lower incidences of chronic bronchitis, lead poisoning, strokes, respiratory diseases, and heart disease as well as the benefits of better visibility, reduced structural damages, and improved agricultural productivity.

We shall return to this study later in the book for a deeper look at how these estimates were derived, but a couple of comments are relevant now. First, despite the fact that this study did not attempt to value all pollution damage to ecosystems that was avoided by this policy, the net benefits are still strongly positive. While presumably the case for controlling pollution would have been even stronger had all such avoided damage been included, the desirability of this form of control is evident even with only a partial consideration of benefits. An inability to monetize *all* benefits and costs does not necessarily jeopardize the ability to reach sound policy conclusions.

Although these results justify the conclusion that pollution control made economic sense, they do not justify the stronger conclusion that the policy was efficient. To justify that conclusion, the study would have had to show that the present value of net benefits was maximized, not merely positive. In fact, this study did not attempt to calculate the maximum net benefits outcome, and if it had, it would have almost certainly discovered that the policy during this period was not optimal. As we shall see in Chapters 6 and 8, the costs of the chosen policy approach were higher than necessary to achieve the desired emissions reductions. With an optimal policy mix, the net benefits would have been even higher.

EXAMPLE 3.1

Does Reducing Pollution Make Economic Sense? Evidence from the Clean Air Act

In its 1997 report to Congress, the EPA presented the results of its attempt to discover whether the Clean Air Act had produced positive net benefits over the period 1970–1990. The results suggested that the present value of benefits (using a discount rate of 5 percent) was $22.2 trillion, while the costs were $0.523 trillion. Performing the necessary subtraction reveals that the net benefits were therefore equal to $21.7 trillion. According to this study, US air pollution control policy during this period made very good economic sense.

Soon after the period covered by this analysis, substantive changes were made in the Clean Air Act Amendments of 1990 (the details of those changes are covered in later chapters). Did those additions also make economic sense?

In August of 2010, the US EPA issued a report of the benefits and costs of the Clean Air Act from 1990 to 2020. This report suggests that the costs of meeting the 1990 Clean Air Act Amendment requirements are expected to rise to approximately $65 billion per year by 2020 (2006 dollars). Almost half of the compliance costs ($28 billion) arise from pollution controls placed on cars, trucks, and buses, while another $10 billion arises from reducing air pollution from electric utilities.

These actions are estimated to cause benefits (from reduced pollution damage) to rise from roughly $800 billion in 2000 to almost $1.3 trillion in 2010, ultimately reaching approximately $2 trillion per year (2006 dollars) by 2020! For persons living in the United States, a cost of approximately $200 per person by 2020 produces approximately a $6,000 gain in benefits per person from the improvement in air quality. Many of the estimated benefits come from reduced risk of early mortality due to exposure to fine particulate matter. Table 3.3 provides a summary of the costs and benefits and includes a calculation of the benefit/cost ratio.

Table 3.3 Summary Comparison of Benefits and Costs from the Clean Air Act 1990–2020 (Estimates in Million 2006$)

	Annual Estimates			Present Value Estimate
	2000	2010	2020	1990–2020
Monetized Direct Costs:				
Low[1]				
Central	$20,000	$53,000	$65,000	$380,000
High[1]				
Monetized Direct Benefits:				
Low[2]	$90,000	$160,000	$250,000	$1,400,000
Central	$770,000	$1,300,000	$2,000,000	$12,000,000
High[2]	$2,300,000	$3,800,000	$5,700,000	$35,000,000
Net Benefits:				
Low	$70,000	$110,000	$190,000	$1,000,000
Central	$750,000	$1,200,000	$1,900,000	$12,000,000
High	$2,300,000	$3,700,000	$5,600,000	$35,000,000
Benefit/Cost Ratio:				
Low[3]	5/1	3/1	4/1	4/1
Central	39/1	25/1	31/1	32/1
High[3]	115/1	72/1	88/1	92/1

Notes:

1 The cost estimates for this analysis are based on assumptions about future changes in factors such as consumption patterns, input costs, and technological innovation. We recognize that these assumptions introduce significant uncertainty into the cost results; however, the degree of uncertainty or bias associated with many of the key factors cannot be reliably quantified. Thus, we are unable to present specific low and high cost estimates.

2 Low and high benefit estimates are based on primary results and correspond to 5th and 95th percentile results from statistical uncertainty analysis, incorporating uncertainties in physical effects and valuation steps of benefits analysis. Other significant sources of uncertainty not reflected include the value of unquantified or unmonetized benefits that are not captured in the primary estimates and uncertainties in emissions and air quality modeling.

3 The low benefit/cost ratio reflects the ratio of the low benefits estimate to the central costs estimate, while the high ratio reflects the ratio of the high benefits estimate to the central costs estimate. Because we were unable to reliably quantify the uncertainty in cost estimates, we present the low estimate as "less than X" and the high estimate as "more than Y," where X and Y are the low and high benefit/cost ratios, respectively.

Sources: US Environmental Protection Agency. (1997). *The Benefits and Costs of the Clean Air Act, 1970 to 1990*. Washington, DC: Environmental Protection Agency, Table 18, p. 56; US Environmental Protection Agency Office of Air and Radiation, *The Benefits and Costs of the Clean Air Act, 1990 to 2020— Summary Report, 8/16/2010*. Full Report available at www.epa.gov/clean-air-act-overview/benefits-and-costs-clean-air-act-1990-2010-first-prospective-study (accessed January 14, 2018).

Estimating Benefits of Carbon Dioxide Emission Reductions

Benefit-cost analysis is frequently complicated by the estimation of benefits and costs that are difficult to quantify. (Chapter 4 takes up the topic of nonmarket valuation in detail.) One such value is the benefit of reductions in carbon emissions.

Executive Order 12866 requires government agencies "to assess both the costs and the benefits of the intended regulation and, recognizing that some costs and benefits are difficult to quantify, propose or adopt a regulation only upon a reasoned determination that the benefits of the intended regulation justify its costs."[3] In order to include benefits from reducing carbon dioxide emission, agencies use what is called the "social cost of carbon" to reflect what those damages would have been in the absence of the reductions. The social cost of carbon is the marginal increase in the present value (in dollars) of the economic damages (e.g., sea level rise, floods, changes in agricultural productivity, and altered ecosystem services) resulting from a small increase (usually 1 metric ton) in carbon dioxide emissions. Since the social cost of carbon is a present value calculation, both the timing of the emission reduction and the discount rate play an important role.

The Interagency Working Group on Social Cost of Carbon presented the first set of estimates for the social cost of carbon in 2010. In 2013, these estimates were revised upwards with the estimate for the social cost of carbon increasing from $22 to approximately $37 per ton of carbon (using a discount rate of 3 percent). In 2016, they were revised again. Table 3.4 illustrates the 2016 revised social cost of carbon dioxide using 2.5, 3, and 5 percent discount rates for selected years. The fourth column presents the extreme case (95th percentile) using a 3 percent discount rate. Notice the importance of the discount rate in determining what value is used. (Can you explain why?)

The social cost of carbon is useful in making sure that the calculated benefits of carbon reductions reflect the reduced damages that can be expected. Example 3.2 demonstrates one way the social cost of carbon has been used in policy.

How much difference has it made in general? One study examined all economically significant federal regulations since 2008 to see what difference using a social cost of carbon would make. When they compared the ranking of the proposed policy to the status quo, they

Table 3.4 Revised Social Cost of CO_2, 2015–2050 (in 2007 dollars per metric ton of CO_2)

Year	Discount	Rates		
	5% Avg	3% Avg	2.5% Avg	3% 95th
2015	$11	$36	$56	$105
2020	$12	$42	$62	$123
2025	$14	$46	$68	$138
2030	$16	$50	$73	$152
2035	$18	$55	$78	$168
2040	$21	$60	$84	$183
2045	$23	$64	$89	$197
2050	$26	$69	$95	$212

Source: https://19january2017snapshot.epa.gov/climatechange/social-cost-carbon_.html (accessed May 15, 2017).

found little evidence that use of the social cost of carbon to include carbon reduction benefits into the calculation affected US policy choices to date. The authors speculate that the absence of a discernible impact may be explained, in part, because US regulators have succeeded in selecting the "low-hanging fruit," where the net benefits of early policies that reduce carbon are the largest and therefore most likely to pass a benefit-cost test even without using the social cost of carbon.[4]

In 2017, with the election of President Donald Trump everything changed. Soon after taking office President Trump signed an Executive Order that calls on agencies to disband the Interagency Working Group on Social Cost of Greenhouse Gases and to withdraw the documents that are the basis for the current calculation of the social cost of carbon. That EPA website has now been removed, although scientists have preserved the material (it can be found at https://19january2017snapshot.epa.gov/climatechange/social-cost-carbon_.html).

While this order does not abandon the concept completely, it does signal a desire to use a new approach to measuring and using the concept. What will this mean for future policies? Stay tuned.

EXAMPLE 3.2

Using the Social Cost of Carbon: The DOE Microwave Oven Rule

In 2013, the Department of Energy (DOE) announced new rules for energy efficiency for microwave ovens in standby mode. By improving the energy efficiency of these ovens, this rule would reduce carbon emissions. In the regulatory impact analysis associated with this rule, it was necessary to value the reduced damages from this lower level of emissions. The social cost of carbon was used to provide this information.

Using the 2010 social cost of carbon produced a present value of net benefits for the microwave oven rule over the next 30 years of $4.2 billion. Since this value is positive, it means that implementing this rule would increase efficiency.

We know that using the revised 2013 number would increase the present value of net benefits, but by how much? According to the DOE, using the 2013 instead of the 2010 social cost of carbon increases the present value of net benefits to $4.6 billion. In this case the net benefits were large enough both before and after the new social cost of carbon (SCC) estimates to justify implementing the rule, but it is certainly possible that in other cases these new estimates would justify rules that prior to the change would not have been justified.

Note that microwave purchasers will bear the cost of this set of rules (as prices rise to reflect the higher production costs), but they will not receive all of the benefits (those reflecting a reduction in external costs). However, the DOE notes that due to the increased energy efficiency of the appliances subject to these rules (and the resulting lower energy costs for purchasers), the present value of savings to consumers is estimated to be $3.4 billion over the next 30 years (DOE 2013), an amount that is larger than the costs. In this case the rules represent a win for both microwave consumers and the planet.

Sources: http://energy.gov/articles/new-energy-efficiency-standards-microwave-ovens-save-consumers-energy-bills; *Technical Update of the Social Cost of Carbon for Regulatory Impact Analysis—Under Executive Order 12866*, https://obamawhitehouse.archives.gov/sites/default/files/omb/inforeg/scc-tsd-final-july-2015.pdf; DOE Microwave Rule (2013) 78 FR 36316 (June 17), https://www.federalregister.gov/documents/2013/06/17/2013-13535/ energy-conservation-program-energy-conservation-standards-for-standby-mode-and-off-mode-for

Issues in Benefit Estimation

The analyst charged with the responsibility for performing a benefit-cost analysis encounters many decision points requiring judgment. If we are to understand benefit-cost analysis, the nature of these judgments must be clear in our minds.

Primary versus Secondary Effects. Environmental projects usually trigger both primary and secondary consequences. For example, the primary effect of cleaning a lake will be an increase in recreational uses of the lake. This primary effect will cause a further ripple effect on services provided to the increased number of users of the lake. Are these secondary benefits to be counted?

The answer depends upon the employment conditions in the surrounding area. If this increase in demand results in employment of previously unused resources, such as labor, the value of the increased employment should be counted. If, on the other hand, the increase in demand is met by a shift in previously employed resources from one use to another, it is a different story. In general, secondary employment benefits should be counted in high unemployment areas or when the particular skills demanded are underemployed at the time the project is commenced. They should not be counted when the project simply results in a rearrangement of productively employed resources.

Accounting Stance. The accounting stance refers to the geographic scale or scope at which the benefits are measured. Scale matters because in a benefit-cost analysis only the benefits or costs affecting that specific geographic area are counted. Suppose, for example, that the federal government picks up many of the costs, but the benefits are received by only one region. Even if the benefit-cost analysis shows this to be a great project for the region, that will not necessarily be the case for the nation as a whole. Once the national costs are factored in, the national project benefits may not exceed the national project costs. Debate 3.1 examines this issue in relation to the social cost of carbon.

Aggregation. Related to accounting stance are challenges of aggregation. Estimates of benefits and costs must be aggregated in order to derive total benefits and total costs. How many people benefit and how many people incur costs are very important in any aggregation, but, additionally, *how* they benefit might impact that aggregation. Suppose, for example, those living closer to the project received more benefits per household than those living farther away. In this case these differences should be accounted for.

With and Without Principle. The "with and without" principle states that only those benefits that would result from the project should be counted, ignoring those that would have accrued anyway. Mistakenly including benefits that would have accrued anyway would overstate the benefits of the program.

Tangible versus Intangible Benefits. *Tangible benefits* are those that can reasonably be assigned a monetary value. *Intangible benefits* are those that cannot be assigned a monetary value, either because data are not available or reliable enough or because it is not clear how to measure the value even with data.[5] Quantification of intangible benefits is the primary topic of the next chapter.

How are intangible benefits to be handled? One answer is perfectly clear: they should not be ignored. To ignore intangible benefits is to bias the results. That benefits are intangible does not mean they are unimportant.

DEBATE 3.1

What Is the Proper Geographic Scope for the Social Cost of Carbon?

The Social Cost of Carbon is an estimate of the economic damages associated with a small increase in carbon dioxide (CO_2) emissions, conventionally 1 metric ton, in a given year. Any reduction in these damages resulting from a proposed regulation is used to estimate the climate benefits of US rulemakings.

Because climate change is a global public good, the efficient damage estimate must include all damages, not just damages to the United States. Some critics argue that, because it is used in US regulatory procedures, it should include only US damages; otherwise it might justify regulations that impose costs on US citizens for the purpose of producing benefits enjoyed by citizens of other countries who do not bear the cost.

Proponents of the global metric point out that the measure is designed to be a means of internalizing a marginal external cost and it cannot do that accurately and efficiently if it leaves out some of the costs. Calculating it only for US damages would create a biased measure that would underestimate the damages and raise the possibility of biased regulatory decisions based upon it.

Furthermore, they argue that the characterization of this measure as allowing benefits created by American citizens to be enjoyed by foreign citizens is a bit misleading. These benefits do not reflect goods and services purchased by US citizens that are enjoyed abroad. Rather they reflect a reduction in the damages that US citizens would otherwise be imposing on others. American law typically does not allow someone to inflict damage on neighbors simply because they are on the other side of some boundary. Reducing damages imposed on others has a different moral context than spillover benefits.

Some regulatory analysts have now suggested that the "US-only" measure should not replace the existing measure, but complement it. Both should be provided. What do you think?

Source: Dudley, Susan E., Fraas, Art, Gayer, Ted, Graham, John, Lutter, Randall, Shogren, Jason F., & Viscusi, W. Kip. (2016). How much will climate change rules benefit Americans? *Forbes* (February 9).

Intangible benefits should be quantified to the fullest extent possible. One frequently used technique is to conduct a sensitivity analysis of the estimated benefit values derived from less than perfectly reliable data. We can determine, for example, whether or not the outcome is sensitive, within wide ranges, to the value of this benefit. If not, then very little time has to be spent on the problem. If the outcome is sensitive, the person or persons making the decision bear the ultimate responsibility for weighing the importance of that benefit.

Approaches to Cost Estimation

Estimating costs is generally easier than estimating benefits, but it is not easy. One major problem for both derives from the fact that benefit-cost analysis is forward-looking and thus requires an estimate of what a particular strategy *will* cost, which is much more difficult than tracking down what an existing strategy *does* cost.

Two approaches have been developed to estimate these costs.

The Survey Approach. One way to discover the costs associated with a policy is to ask those who bear the costs, and presumably know the most about them, to reveal the magnitude of the costs to policymakers. Polluters, for example, could be asked to provide control-cost estimates to regulatory bodies. The problem with this approach is the strong incentive not to be truthful. An overestimate of the costs can trigger less stringent regulation; therefore, it is financially advantageous to provide overinflated estimates.

The Engineering Approach. The engineering approach bypasses the source being regulated by using general engineering information to catalog the possible technologies that could be used to meet the objective and to estimate the costs of purchasing and using those technologies. The final step in the engineering approach is to assume that the sources would use technologies that minimize cost. This produces a cost estimate for a "typical," well-informed firm.

The engineering approach has its own problems. These estimates may not approximate the actual cost of any particular firm. Unique circumstances may cause the costs of that firm to be higher, or lower, than estimated; the firm, in short, may not be typical.

The Combined Approach. To circumvent these problems, analysts frequently use a combination of survey and engineering approaches. The survey approach collects information on possible technologies, as well as special circumstances facing the firm. Engineering approaches are used to derive the actual costs of those technologies, given the special circumstances. This combined approach attempts to balance information best supplied by the source with that best derived independently.

In the cases described so far, the costs are relatively easy to quantify and the problem is simply finding a way to acquire the best information. This is not always the case, however. Some costs are not easy to quantify, although economists have developed some ingenious ways to secure monetary estimates even for those costs.

Take, for example, a policy designed to conserve energy by forcing more people to carpool. If the effect of this is simply to increase the average time of travel, how is this cost to be measured?

For some time, transportation analysts have recognized that people value their time, and a large amount of literature has now evolved to provide estimates of how valuable time savings or time increases would be. The basis for this valuation is opportunity cost—how the time might be used if it weren't being consumed in travel. Although the results of these studies depend on the amount of time involved, individual decisions seem to imply that travelers value their travel time at a rate not more than half their wage rates.

The Treatment of Risk

For many environmental problems, it is not possible to state with certainty what consequences a particular policy will have, because scientific estimates themselves often are imprecise. Determining the efficient exposure to potentially toxic substances requires obtaining results at high doses and extrapolating to low doses, as well as extrapolating from animal studies to humans. It also requires relying upon epidemiological studies that infer a pollution-induced adverse human health impact from correlations between indicators of health in human populations and recorded pollution levels.

For example, consider the potential damages from climate change. While scientists agree on most of the potential impacts of climate change, such as sea level rise and species losses, the timing and extent of those losses are not certain.

The treatment of risk in the policy process involves two major dimensions: (1) identifying and quantifying the risks, and (2) deciding how much risk is acceptable. The former is primarily scientific and descriptive, while the latter is more evaluative or normative.

Benefit-cost analysis grapples with the evaluation of risk in several ways. Suppose we have a range of policy options *A, B, C, D* and a range of possible outcomes *E, F, G* for each of these policies depending on how the economy evolves over the future. These outcomes, for example, might depend on whether the demand growth for the resource is low, medium, or high. Thus, if we choose policy *A*, we might end up with outcomes *AE, AF*, or *AG*. Each of the other policies has three possible outcomes as well, yielding a total of 12 possible outcomes.

We could conduct a separate benefit-cost analysis for each of the 12 possible outcomes. Unfortunately, the policy that maximizes net benefits for *E* may be different from that which maximizes net benefits for *F* or *G*. Thus, if we only knew which outcome would prevail, we could select the policy that maximized net benefits; the problem is that we do not. Furthermore, choosing the policy that is best if outcome *E* prevails may be disastrous if *G* results instead.

When a dominant policy emerges, this problem is avoided. A *dominant policy* is one that confers higher net benefits for every outcome. In this case, the existence of risk concerning the future is not relevant for the policy choice. This fortuitous circumstance is exceptional rather than common, but it can occur.

Other options exist even when dominant solutions do not emerge. Suppose, for example, that we were able to assess the likelihood that each of the three possible outcomes would occur. Thus, we might expect outcome *E* to occur with probability 0.5, *F* with probability 0.3, and *G* with probability 0.2. Armed with this information, we can estimate the expected present value of net benefits. The *expected present value of net benefits* for a particular policy is defined as the sum over outcomes of the present value of net benefits for that policy where each outcome is weighted by its probability of occurrence. Symbolically this is expressed as

$$EPVNB_j = \sum_{i=0}^{I} P_i PVNB_{ij}, \quad j = 1, \dots, J,$$

where

> $EPVNBj$ = expected present value of net benefits for policy *j*,
> Pi = probability of the *i*th outcome occurring,
> $PVNBij$ = present value of net benefits for policy *j* if outcome *i* prevails,
> J = number of policies being considered,
> I = number of outcomes being considered.

The final step is to select the policy with the highest expected present value of net benefits.

This approach has the substantial virtue that it weighs higher probability outcomes more heavily. It also, however, makes a specific assumption about society's preference for risk. This approach is appropriate if society is risk-neutral. *Risk-neutrality* can be defined most easily by the use of an example. Suppose you were to choose between being given a definite $50 or entering a lottery in which you had a 50 percent chance of winning $100 and a 50 percent chance of winning nothing. (Notice that the expected value of this lottery is $50 = 0.5($100) + 0.5($0).) You would be said to be risk-neutral if you would be indifferent between these two choices. If you view the lottery as more attractive, you would be exhibiting *risk-loving* behavior, while a preference for the definite $50 would suggest *risk-averse* behavior. Using the expected present value of net benefits approach implies that society is risk-neutral.

Is that a valid assumption? The evidence is mixed. The existence of gambling suggests that at least some members of society are risk-loving, while the existence of insurance suggests that, at least for some risks, others are risk-averse. Since the same people may gamble and own insurance policies, it is likely that the type of risk may be important.

Even if individuals were demonstrably risk-averse, this would not be a sufficient condition for the government to forsake risk-neutrality in evaluating public investments. One famous article (Arrow & Lind, 1970) argues that risk-neutrality is appropriate since "when the risks of a public investment are publicly borne, the total cost of risk-bearing is insignificant and, therefore, the government should ignore uncertainty in evaluating public investments." The logic behind this result suggests that as the number of risk bearers (and the degree of diversification of risks) increases, the amount of risk borne by any individual diminishes to zero.

When the decision is irreversible, as demonstrated by Arrow and Fisher (1974), considerably more caution is appropriate. Irreversible decisions may subsequently be regretted, but the option to change course will be lost forever. Extra caution also affords an opportunity to learn more about alternatives to this decision and its consequences before acting. Isn't it comforting to know that occasionally procrastination can be optimal?

There is a movement in national policy in both the courts and the legislature to search for imaginative ways to define acceptable risk. In general, the policy approaches reflect a case-by-case method. We shall see that current policy reflects a high degree of risk aversion toward a number of environmental problems.

Distribution of Benefits and Costs

Many agencies are now required to consider the distributional impacts of costs and benefits as part of any economic analysis. For example, the US EPA provides guidelines on distributional issues in its "Guidelines for Preparing Economic Analysis." According to the EPA, distributional analysis "assesses changes in social welfare by examining the effects of a regulation across different sub-populations and entities." Distributional analysis can take two forms: *economic impact analysis* and *equity analysis*. Economic impact analysis focuses on a broad characterization of who gains and who loses from a given policy. Equity analysis examines impacts on disadvantaged groups or sub-populations. The latter delves into the normative issue of equity or fairness in the distribution of costs and benefits. Loomis (2011) outlines several approaches for incorporating distribution and equity into benefit-cost analysis. Some issues of the distribution of benefits and costs related to energy efficiency rules for appliances were highlighted in Example 3.2.

Choosing the Discount Rate

Recall that discounting allows us to compare all costs and benefits in current dollars, regardless of when the benefits accrue or costs are charged. Suppose a project will impose an immediate cost of $4,000,000 (today's dollars), but the $5,500,000 benefits will not be earned until 5 years out. Is this project a good idea? On the surface it might seem like it is, but recall that $5,500,000 in 5 years is not the same as $5,500,000 today. At a discount rate of 5 percent, the present value of benefits minus the present value of costs is positive. However, at a 10 percent discount rate, this same calculation yields a negative value, since the present value of costs exceeds the benefits. Can you reproduce the calculations that yield these conclusions?

As Example 3.3 indicates, this has been, and continues to be, an important issue. When the public sector uses a discount rate lower than that in the private sector, the public sector

---

EXAMPLE 3.3

The Importance of the Discount Rate

Let's begin with an historical example. For years the United States and Canada had been discussing the possibility of constructing a tidal power project in the Passamaquoddy Bay between Maine and New Brunswick. This project would have heavy initial capital costs, but low operating costs that presumably would hold for a long time into the future. As part of their analysis of the situation, a complete inventory of costs and benefits was completed in 1959.

Using the same benefit and cost figures, Canada concluded that the project should not be built, while the United States concluded that it should. Because these conclusions were based on the same benefit-cost data, the differences can be attributed solely to the use of different discount rates. The United States used 2.5 percent while Canada used 4.125 percent. The higher discount rate makes the initial cost weigh much more heavily in the calculation, leading to the Canadian conclusion that the project would yield a negative net benefit. Since the lower discount rate weighs the lower future operating costs relatively more heavily, Americans saw the net benefit as positive.

In a more recent illustration of why the magnitude of the discount rate matters, on October 30, 2006, economist Nicholas Stern from the London School of Economics issued a report using a discount rate of 0.1 percent that concluded that the benefits of strong, early action on climate change would considerably outweigh the costs. Other economists, such as William Nordhaus of Yale University, who preferred a discount rate around 6 percent, found that optimal economic policies to slow climate change involve only modest rates of emissions reductions in the near term, followed by sharp reductions in the medium and long term.

In this debate, the desirability of strong current action is dependent (at least in part) on the size of the discount rate used in the analysis. Higher discount rates reduce the present value of future benefits from current investments in abatement, implying a smaller marginal benefit. Since the costs associated with those investments are not affected nearly as much by the choice of discount rate (remember that costs occurring in the near future are discounted less), a lower present value of marginal benefit translates into a lower optimal investment in abatement.

Far from being an esoteric subject, the choice of the discount rate is fundamentally important in defining the role of the public sector, the types of projects undertaken, and the allocation of resources across generations.

Sources: Stokey, E., & Zeckhauser, R. (1978). *A Primer for Policy Analysis.* New York: W. W. Norton, 164–165; Mikesell, R. (1977). *The Rate of Discount for Evaluating Public Projects.* Washington, DC: The American Enterprise Institute for Public Policy Research, 3–5; the Stern Report: http://webarchive. nationalarchives.gov.uk/20100407011151/http://www.hm-treasury.gov.uk/sternreview_index.htm; Nordhaus, W. (2007). A review of the Stern Review on the economics of climate change. *Journal of Economic Literature,* XLV (September), 686–702.

will find more projects with longer payoff periods worthy of authorization. And, as we have already seen, the discount rate is a major determinant of the allocation of resources among generations as well.

The discount rate can be defined conceptually as the social opportunity cost of capital. This cost of capital can be divided further into two components: (1) the riskless cost of capital, and (2) the risk premium. Traditionally, economists have used long-term interest rates on government bonds as one measure of the cost of capital, adjusted by a risk premium that would depend on the riskiness of the project considered. Unfortunately, the choice of how large an adjustment to make has been left to the discretion of the analysts. This ability to affect the desirability of a particular project or policy by the choice of discount rate led to a situation in which government agencies were using a variety of discount rates to justify programs or projects they supported. One set of hearings conducted by Congress during the 1960s discovered that, at one time, agencies were using discount rates ranging from 0 to 20 percent.

During the early 1970s, the Office of Management and Budget published a circular that required, with some exceptions, all government agencies to use a discount rate of 10 percent in their benefit-cost analysis. A revision issued in 1992 reduced the required discount rate to 7 percent. This circular also includes guidelines for benefit-cost analysis and specifies that certain rates will change annually.[6] This standardization reduces biases by eliminating the agency's ability to choose a discount rate that justifies a predetermined conclusion. It also allows a project to be considered independently of fluctuations in the true social cost of capital due to cycles in the behavior of the economy. On the other hand, when the social opportunity cost of capital differs from this administratively determined level, the benefit-cost analysis will not, in general, define the efficient allocation.

Example 3.3 highlights a different aspect of the choice of the discount rate for decisions involving long time horizons. It considers the question of whether or not discount rates should decline over time. Debate 3.2 explores this question.

DEBATE 3.2

Discounting over Long Time Horizons: Should Discount Rates Decline?

As you now recognize, the choice of the discount rate can significantly alter the outcome of a benefit-cost analysis. This effect is exacerbated over long time horizons and can become especially influential in decisions about spending now to mitigate damages from climate change, which may be uncertain in both magnitude and timing. What rate is appropriate? Recent literature and some evidence argue for declining rates of discount over long time horizons. Should a declining rate schedule be utilized? A blue-ribbon panel of experts recently gathered to debate this and related questions (Arrow et al., 2012).

An unresolved debate in the economics literature revolves around the question of whether discount rates should be positive ("descriptive"), reflecting actual market rates, or normative ("prescriptive"), reflecting ethical considerations. Those who argue for the descriptive approach prefer to use market rates of return since expenditures to mitigate climate change are investment expenditures. Those who argue for the alternative prescriptive approach argue for including judgments about intergenerational equity. These rates are usually lower than those found in actual markets (Griffiths et al. 2012).

In the United States, the Office of Management and Budget (OMB) currently recommends a constant rate of discount for project analysis. The recommendation is to use 3 percent and 7 percent real discount rates in sensitivity analysis (OMB, 2003) with options for lower rates if future generations are impacted. The United Kingdom and France utilize discount rate schedules that decline over time. Is one of these methods better than the other for discounting over long time horizons? If a declining rate is appropriate, how fast should that rate decline?

The blue-ribbon panel agreed that theory provides strong arguments for a "declining certainty-equivalent discount rate" (Arrow et al., 2012, p. 21). Although the empirical literature also supports a rate that is declining over time (especially in the presence of uncertainty about future costs and/or benefits), the results from the empirical literature vary widely depending on the model assumptions and underlying data. If a declining rate schedule were to be adopted in the United States, this group of experts recommends that the EPA's Science Advisory Board be asked to develop criteria that could be used as the common foundation for determining what the schedule should look like.

Sources: Arrow, K., Maureen, J., Cropper, L., Gollier, C., Groom, B., Heal, G. M., et al. (December 2012). How should benefits and costs be discounted in an intergenerational context: The views of an expert panel. *RFF DP 12–53*; Griffiths, C., Kopits, E., Marten, A., Moore, C., Newbold, S., & Wolverton, A. (2012). The social cost of carbon: Valuing carbon reductions in policy analysis. In R. A. de Mooij, M. Keen, & I. W. H. Parry (Eds.). *Fiscal Policy to Mitigate Climate Change: A Guide for Policy Makers*. Washington, DC: IMF, 69–87; OMB (Office of Management and Budget) (2003). Circular A-4: Regulatory Analysis. Washington, DC: Executive Office of the President. www.whitehouse.gov/omb/circulars_a004_a-4

Divergence of Social and Private Discount Rates

Earlier we concluded that producers, in their attempt to maximize producer surplus, also maximize the present value of net benefits under the "right" conditions, such as the absence of externalities, the presence of properly defined property rights, and the presence of competitive markets within which the property rights can be exchanged.

Now let's consider one more condition. If resources are to be allocated efficiently, firms must use the same rate to discount future net benefits as is appropriate for society at large. If firms were to use a higher rate, they would extract and sell resources faster than would be efficient. Conversely, if firms were to use a lower-than-appropriate discount rate, they would be excessively conservative.

Why might private and social rates differ? As noted above the social opportunity cost of capital can be separated into two components: the risk-free cost of capital and the risk premium. The *risk-free cost of capital* is the rate of return earned when there is absolutely no risk of earning more or less than the expected return. The *risk premium* is an additional cost of capital required to compensate the owners of this capital when the expected and actual returns may differ. Therefore, because of differences in the risk premium, the cost of capital is higher in risky industries than in no-risk industries.

Another difference between private and social discount rates may stem from a difference in social and private risk premiums. If the risk of certain private decisions is different from the risks faced by society as a whole, then the social and private risk premiums may differ. One obvious example is the risk *caused* by the government.

If the firm is afraid its assets will be confiscated by the government, it may choose a higher discount rate to make its profits before nationalization occurs. From the point of view of society—as represented by government—this is not a risk and, therefore, a lower discount rate is appropriate. When private rates exceed social rates, current production is higher than is desirable to maximize the net benefits to society. Both energy production and forestry have been subject to this source of inefficiency.

Another divergence in discount rates may stem from different underlying rates of time preference. Such a divergence in time preferences can cause not only a divergence between private and social discount rates (as when firms have a higher rate of time preference than the public sector), but even between otherwise similar analyses conducted in two different countries.

Time preferences would be expected to be higher, for example, in a cash-poor, developing country than in an industrialized country. Since the two benefit-cost analyses in these two countries would be based upon two different discount rates, they might come to quite different conclusions. What is right for the developing country may not be right for the industrialized country and vice versa.

Although private and social discount rates do not always diverge, they may. When those circumstances arise, market decisions are not efficient.

A Critical Appraisal

We have seen that it is sometimes, but not always, difficult to estimate benefits and costs. When this estimation is difficult or unreliable, it limits the value of a benefit-cost analysis. This problem would be particularly disturbing if biases tended to increase or decrease net benefits systematically. Do such biases exist?

In the early 1970s, Robert Haveman (1972) conducted a major study that continues to shed some light on this question. Focusing on Army Corps of Engineers water projects, such as flood control, navigation, and hydroelectric power generation, Haveman compared the *ex ante* (before the fact) estimate of benefits and costs with their *ex post* (after the fact) counterparts. Thus, he was able to address the issues of accuracy and bias. He concluded that:

> In the empirical case studies presented, ex post estimates often showed little relationship to their ex ante counterparts. On the basis of the few cases and the a priori analysis presented here, one could conclude that there is a serious bias incorporated into agency ex ante evaluation procedures, resulting in persistent overstatement of expected benefits. Similarly in the analysis of project construction costs, enormous variance was found among projects in the relationship between estimated and realized costs. Although no persistent bias in estimation was apparent, nearly 50 percent of the projects displayed realized costs that deviated by more than plus or minus 20 percent from ex ante projected costs.[7]

In the cases examined by Haveman, at least, the notion that benefit-cost analysis is purely a scientific exercise was clearly not consistent with the evidence; the biases of the analysts were merely translated into numbers.

Does their analysis mean that benefit-cost analysis is fatally flawed? Absolutely not! Valuation methods have improved considerably since the Haveman study, but problems remain. This study does, however, highlight the enduring importance of calculating an accurate value and of including all of the potential benefits and costs (e.g., nonmarket values). As elementary as it might seem including both the benefits and the costs is necessary. As Example 3.4 illustrates, that is not always the case in practice.

EXAMPLE 3.4

Is the Two for One Rule a Good Way to Manage Regulatory Overreach?

Environmental regulations can be costly, but they also produce economic benefits. Efficiency suggests that regulations whose benefits exceed their costs should be pursued and that is the path followed by previous Executive Orders (EOs) from Presidents Reagan (EO 12291), Clinton (EO 12866), and Obama (EO 13563).

In 2017, the Trump administration abandoned business as usual and issued EO 13771, mandating that for every new regulation issued, two must be thrown out.[8] What does economic analysis and, in particular, benefit-cost analysis have to say about this one-in, two-out prescription?

Executive Order 13771 reads, in part: "(c) . . . any new incremental costs associated with new regulations shall, to the extent permitted by law, be offset by the elimination of existing costs associated with at least two prior regulations."

In his attempt to reduce regulatory overreach President Trump's approach seems to suggest that only the costs are important when evaluating current and new regulations. Benefits don't matter. Since most of the current regulations were put into place based on benefits and costs, removing them based solely on costs would be a "blunt instrument"— one that is poorly targeted on making efficient choices.

Economist Robert Shiller further argues that regulation is in the public interest in many areas and "the world is far too complex to make it possible to count up regulations meaningfully and impose a two-for-one rule."

Alan Krupnick, economist at Resources for the Future, points out that even if a "cost-only" approach were justified, it would not be easy to implement. For example "what is a cost? Is it a projected cost in the rule or actual costs as implemented? Is it present discounted costs or something else to account for cost streams over time? Is it direct costs or do indirect costs (say, to consumers) count? Is it private costs or costs to society?"

Regardless of the answer to those questions, however, benefits do matter. As Krupnick notes, "How do we determine which regulations are ineffective and unnecessary without considering their benefits? The answer is simple—we cannot."

Imagine if we only saved endangered species that cost the least to save, or cleaned up only the least expensive oil spills. Making decisions based solely on costs is misguided economics.

Sources: www.rff.org/research/publications/trump-s-regulatory-reform-process-analytical-hurdles-and-missing-benefits; www.nytimes.com/2017/02/17/upshot/why-trumps-2-for-1-rule-on-regulations-is-no-quick-fix.html; www.env-econ.net/2017/02/two-for-one-too-blunt-an-instrument-for-good-governance.html

Haveman's analysis also serves to remind us that benefit-cost analysis is not a stand-alone technique. It should be used in conjunction with other available information. Economic analysis including benefit-cost analysis can provide useful information, but it should not be the only determinant for all decisions.

Benefit-cost analysis also limited in that it does not really address the question of who reaps the benefits and who pays the cost. It is quite possible for a particular course of action to yield high net benefits, but to have the benefits borne by one societal group and the costs borne by another. This scenario serves to illustrate a basic principle—ensuring that a particular policy is efficient provides an important, but not always the sole, basis for public policy. Other aspects, such as who reaps the benefit or bears the burden, are also important considerations. Distributional benefit-cost analysis can help illuminate potential inequities.

In summary, on the positive side, benefit-cost analysis is frequently a very useful part of the policy process. Even when the underlying data are not strictly reliable, the outcomes may not be sensitive to that unreliability. In other circumstances, the data may be reliable enough to give indications of the consequences of broad policy directions, even when they are not reliable enough to fine-tune those policies. Benefit-cost analysis, when done correctly, can provide a useful complement to the other influences on the political process by clarifying what choices yield the highest net benefits to society.

On the negative side, benefit-cost analysis has been attacked as seeming to promise more than can actually be delivered, particularly in the absence of solid benefit information. This concern has triggered two responses. First, regulatory processes have been developed that can be implemented with very little information and yet have desirable economic properties. The recent reforms in air pollution control, which we cover in Chapters 5 and 6, provide some powerful examples.

The second involves techniques that supply useful information to the policy process without relying on controversial techniques to monetize environmental services that are difficult to value. The rest of this chapter deals with the two most prominent of these—cost-effectiveness analysis and impact analysis.

Even when benefits are difficult or impossible to quantify, economic analysis has much to offer. Policymakers should know, for example, how much various policy actions will cost and what their impacts on society will be, even if the efficient policy choice cannot be identified with any certainty.

Other Decision-Making Metrics

Cost-Effectiveness Analysis

What can be done to guide policy when the requisite valuation for benefit-cost analysis is either unavailable or not sufficiently reliable? Without a good measure of benefits, making an efficient choice is no longer possible.

In such cases, however, it is often possible to set a policy target on some basis other than a strict comparison of benefits and costs. One example is pollution control. What level of pollution should be established as the maximum acceptable level? In many countries, studies of the effects of a particular pollutant on human health have been used as the basis for establishing that pollutant's maximum acceptable concentration. Researchers attempt to find a threshold level below which no damage seems to occur. That threshold is then further lowered to provide a margin of safety and that becomes the pollution target.

Approaches could also be based upon expert opinion. Ecologists, for example, could be enlisted to define the critical numbers of certain species or the specific critical wetlands resources that should be preserved.

Once the policy target is specified, however, economic analysis can have a great deal to say about the cost consequences of choosing a means of achieving that objective. The cost consequences are important not only because eliminating wasteful expenditures is an appropriate goal in its own right, but also to assure that they do not trigger a political backlash.

Typically, several means of achieving the specified objective are available; some will be relatively inexpensive, while others turn out to be very expensive. The problems are frequently complicated enough that identifying the cheapest means of achieving an objective cannot be accomplished without a rather detailed analysis of the choices.

Cost-effectiveness analysis frequently involves an *optimization procedure.* An optimization procedure, in this context, is merely a systematic method for finding the lowest-cost means of accomplishing the objective. This procedure does not, in general, produce an efficient allocation because the predetermined objective may not be efficient. All efficient policies are cost-effective, but not all cost-effective policies are efficient.

Earlier in this chapter we introduced the concept of the efficiency equimarginal principle. According to that principle, net benefits are maximized when the marginal benefit is equal to the marginal cost.

A similar, and equally important, equimarginal principle exists for cost-effectiveness:

> Second Equimarginal Principle (the Cost-Effectiveness Equimarginal Principle): The least-cost means of achieving an environmental target will have been achieved when the marginal costs of all possible means of achievement are equal.

Suppose we want to achieve a specific emissions reduction across a region, and several possible techniques exist for reducing emissions. How much of the control responsibility should each technique bear? The cost-effectiveness equimarginal principle suggests that the techniques should be used such that the desired reduction is achieved and the cost of achieving the last unit of emissions reduction (in other words, the marginal control cost) should be the same for all sources.

To demonstrate why this principle is valid, suppose that we have an allocation of control responsibility where marginal control costs are much higher for one set of techniques than for another. This cannot be the least-cost allocation since we could lower cost while retaining the same amount of emissions reduction. To be specific, costs could be lowered by allocating more control to the lower marginal cost sources and less to the high marginal cost sources. Since it is possible to find a way to lower cost while holding emissions constant, then clearly the initial allocation could not have minimized cost. Once marginal costs are equalized, it becomes impossible to find any lower-cost way of achieving the same degree of emissions reduction; therefore, that allocation must be the allocation that minimizes costs.

In our pollution control example, cost-effectiveness can be used to find the least-cost means of meeting a particular standard and its associated cost. Using this cost as a benchmark case, we can estimate how much costs could be expected to increase from this minimum level if policies that are not cost effective are implemented. Cost-effectiveness analysis can also be used to determine how much compliance costs can be expected to change if the EPA chooses a more stringent or less stringent standard. In Chapters 5 and 6, we shall examine in detail the current movement toward cost-effective polices, a movement that was triggered in part by studies showing that the cost reductions from reform could be substantial.

Impact Analysis

What can be done when the information needed to perform a benefit-cost analysis or a cost-effectiveness analysis is not available? The analytical technique designed to deal with this problem is called *impact analysis*. An impact analysis, regardless of whether it focuses on economic impact or environmental impact or both, attempts to quantify the consequences of various actions.

In contrast to benefit-cost analysis, a pure impact analysis makes no attempt to convert all these consequences into a one-dimensional measure, such as dollars, to ensure comparability. In contrast to cost-effectiveness analysis, impact analysis does not necessarily attempt to optimize. Impact analysis places a large amount of relatively undigested information at the disposal of the policymaker. It is up to the policymaker to assess the importance of the various predicted consequences and act accordingly.

On January 1, 1970, President Nixon signed the National Environmental Policy Act of 1969. This act, among other things, directed all agencies of the federal government to:

> include in every recommendation or report on proposals for legislation and other major Federal actions significantly affecting the quality of the human environment, a detailed statement by the responsible official on—
>
> i. the environmental impact of the proposed action;
> ii. any adverse environmental effects which cannot be avoided should the proposal be implemented;
> iii. alternatives to the proposed action;
> iv. the relationships between local short-term uses of man's environment and the maintenance and enhancement of long-term productivity; and
> v. any irreversible and irretrievable commitments of resources which would be involved in the proposed action should it be implemented.[9]

This was the beginning of the environmental impact statement, which is now a familiar, if controversial, part of environmental policy making.

Current environmental impact statements are more sophisticated than their early predecessors and may contain a benefit-cost analysis or a cost-effectiveness analysis in addition to other more traditional impact measurements. Historically, however, the tendency has been to issue huge environmental impact statements that are virtually impossible to comprehend in their entirety.

In response, the Council on Environmental Quality, which, by law, administers the environmental impact statement process, has set content standards that are now resulting in shorter, more concise statements. To the extent that they merely quantify consequences, statements can avoid the problem of "hidden value judgments" that sometimes plague benefit-cost analysis, but they do so only by bombarding the policymakers with masses of noncomparable information.

Summary

Finding a balance in the relationship between humanity and the environment requires many choices. Some basis for making rational choices is absolutely necessary. If not made by design, decisions will be made by default.

Normative economics uses benefit-cost analysis for judging the desirability of the level and composition of provided services. Cost-effectiveness analysis and impact analysis offer alternatives to benefit-cost analysis. All of these techniques offer valuable information for decision making and all have shortcomings.

A static efficient allocation is one that maximizes the net benefit over all possible uses of those resources. The dynamic efficiency criterion, which is appropriate when time is an important consideration, is satisfied when the outcome maximizes the present value of net benefits from all possible uses of the resources. Later chapters examine the degree to which our social institutions yield allocations that conform to these criteria.

Because benefit-cost analysis is both very powerful and very controversial, in 1996 a group of economists of quite different political persuasions got together to attempt to reach some consensus on its proper role in environmental decision making. Their conclusion is worth reproducing in its entirety:

> Benefit-cost analysis can play an important role in legislative and regulatory policy debates on protecting and improving health, safety, and the natural environment. Although formal benefit-cost analysis should not be viewed as either necessary or sufficient for designing sensible policy, it can provide an exceptionally useful framework for consistently organizing disparate information, and in this way, it can greatly improve the process and, hence, the outcome of policy analysis. If properly done, benefit-cost analysis can be of great help to agencies participating in the development of environmental, health and safety regulations, and it can likewise be useful in evaluating agency decision-making and in shaping statutes.[10]

Even when benefits are difficult to calculate, however, economic analysis in the form of cost-effectiveness can be valuable. This technique can establish the least expensive ways to accomplish predetermined policy goals and to assess the extra costs involved when policies other than the least-cost policy are chosen. What it cannot do is answer the question of whether those predetermined policy goals are efficient.

At the other end of the spectrum is impact analysis, which merely identifies and quantifies the impacts of particular policies without any pretense of optimality or even comparability of the information generated. Impact analysis does not guarantee an efficient outcome.

All three of the techniques discussed in this chapter are useful, but none of them can stake a claim as being universally the "best" approach. The nature of the information that is available and its reliability make a difference.

Discussion Questions

1. Is risk-neutrality an appropriate assumption for benefit-cost analysis? Why or why not? Does it seem more appropriate for some environmental problems than others? If so, which ones? If you were evaluating the desirability of locating a hazardous waste incinerator in a particular town, would the Arrow–Lind rationale for risk-neutrality be appropriate? Why or why not?
2. Was the executive order issued by President George W. Bush mandating a heavier use of benefit-cost analysis in regulatory rule making a step toward establishing a more rational regulatory structure, or was it a subversion of the environmental policy process? Why?

Self-Test Exercises

1. Suppose a proposed public policy could result in three possible outcomes: (1) present value of net benefits of $4,000,000, (2) present value of net benefits of $1,000,000, or (3) present value of net benefits of –$10,000,000 (i.e., a loss). Suppose society is risk-neutral and the probability of occurrence of each of these three outcomes are, respectively, 0.85, 0.10, and 0.05, should this policy be pursued or trashed? Why?

2. a. Suppose you want to remove ten fish of an exotic species that have illegally been introduced to a lake. You have three possible removal methods. Assume that q_1, q_2, and q_3 are, respectively, the amount of fish removed by each method that you choose to use so that the goal will be accomplished by any combination of methods such that $q_1 + q_2 + q_3 = 10$. If the marginal costs of each removal method are, respectively, $10q_1$, $5q_2$, and $2.5q_3$, how much of each method should you use to achieve the removal cost-effectively?

   b. Why isn't an exclusive use of method 3 cost-effective?

   c. Suppose that the three marginal costs were constant (not increasing as in the previous case) such that $MC_1 = \$10$, $MC_2 = \$5$, and $MC_3 = \$2.5$. What is the cost-effective outcome in that case?

3. Consider the role of discount rates in problems involving long time horizons such as climate change. Suppose that a particular emissions abatement strategy would result in a $500 billion reduction in damages 50 years into the future. How would the maximum amount spent now to eliminate those damages change if the discount rate is 2 percent, rather than 10 percent?

Notes

1 Actually if $B = C$, it wouldn't make any difference if the action occurs or not; the benefits and costs are a wash.

2 The monetary worth of the net benefit is the sum of two right triangles, and it equals $(1/2)(\$5)(5) + (1/2)(\$2.50)(5)$ or $18.75. Can you see why?

3 Interagency Working Group on the Social Cost of Carbon, August 2016. www.epa.gov/sites/production/files/2016-12/documents/sc_co2_tsd_august_2016.pdf (accessed November 18, 2017).

4 Hahn, Robert W., & and Ritz, Robert A. (2015). Does the social cost of carbon matter? Evidence from US policy. *The Journal of Legal Studies*, *44*(1) (January), 229–248.

5 The division between tangible and intangible benefits changes as our techniques improve. Recreation benefits were, until the advent of the travel-cost model, treated as intangible. The travel-cost model will be discussed in the next chapter.

6 Annual rates can be found at www.whitehouse.gov/omb/. 2010 rates can be found at www.whitehouse.gov/omb/circulars_a094/a94_appx-c

7 A more recent assessment of costs (Harrington et al., 1999) found evidence of both overestimation and underestimation, although overestimation was more common. The authors attributed the overestimation mainly to a failure to anticipate technical innovation.

8 Executive Order 13371, "Reducing Regulation and Controlling Regulatory Cost."

9 83 Stat. 853.

10 From Arrow, Kenneth, et al. (1996). Is there a role for benefit-cost analysis in environmental, health and safety regulation? *Science*, 272 (April 12), 221–222. Reprinted with permission from AAAS.

Further Reading

Freeman, A. Myrick III. (2003). *The Measurement of Environmental and Resource Values*, 2nd ed. Washington, DC: Resources for the Future. A comprehensive and analytically rigorous survey of the concepts and methods for environmental valuation.

Hanley, N., & Spash, C. L. (1994). *Cost-Benefit Analysis and the Environment.* Brookfield, VT: Edward Elgar. An account of the theory and practice of this form of analysis applied to environmental problems. Contains numerous specific case studies.

Norton, B., & Minteer, B. A. (2002). From environmental ethics to environmental public philosophy: Ethicists and economists: 1973–future. In T. Tietenberg and H. Folmer (Eds.), *The International Yearbook of Environmental and Resource Economics: 2002/2003.* Cheltenham, UK: Edward Elgar, 373–407. A review of the interaction between environmental ethics and economic valuation.

Scheraga, J. D., & Sussman, F. G. (1998). Discounting and environmental management. In T. Tietenberg and H. Folmer (Eds.), *The International Yearbook of Environmental and Resource Economics 1998–1999.* Cheltenham, UK: Edward Elgar, 1–32. A summary of the "state of the art" for the use of discounting in environmental management.

US Environmental Protection Agency (2010). *Guidelines for Preparing Economic Analyses* (Report # EPA 240-R-10-001). Downloadable at: www.epa.gov/environmental-economics/ guidelines-preparing-economic-analyses#download. The procedures prescribed by the USEPA for its analytical work.

Additional references and historically significant references are available on this book's Companion Website: www.routledge.com/cw/Tietenberg

Chapter 4

Valuing the Environment

Methods

For it so falls out / That what we have we prize not to the worth / Whiles we enjoy it, but being lack'd and lost / Why, then we rack the value, then we find / The virtue that possession would not show us / Whiles it was ours.

—William Shakespeare, *Much Ado About Nothing*

Introduction

Soon after the *Exxon Valdez* oil tanker ran aground on the Bligh Reef in Prince William Sound off the coast of Alaska on March 24, 1989, spilling approximately 11 million gallons of crude oil, the Exxon Corporation (now Exxon Mobil) accepted the liability for the damage caused by the leaking oil. This liability consisted of two parts: (1) the cost of cleaning up the spilled oil and restoring the site insofar as possible, and (2) compensation for the damage caused to the local ecology. Approximately $2.1 billion was spent in cleanup efforts and Exxon also spent approximately $303 million to compensate fishermen whose livelihoods were greatly damaged for the 5 years following the spill.[1] Litigation on environmental damages settled with Exxon agreeing to pay $900 million over 10 years. The punitive damages phase of this case began in May 1994. In January 2004, after many rounds of appeals, the US District Court for the State of Alaska awarded punitive damages to the plaintiffs in the amount of $4.5 billion.[2] This amount was later cut almost in half to $2.5 billion and in 2008 the Supreme Court ruled that even those punitive damages were excessive based on maritime law and further argued that the punitive damages should not exceed the $507 million in compensatory damages already paid.[3]

In the spring of 2010, the Deepwater Horizon, a BP well in the Gulf of Mexico, exploded and began spewing an *Exxon Valdez*-sized oil spill every 4 to 5 days. By the time the leaking well was capped in August 2010, an estimated 134 million gallons had been spread through the Gulf of Mexico, almost 20 times greater than the *Exxon Valdez* spill, and the largest maritime spill in US history. In 2016, a settlement was reached calling for total payments of $20.8 billion; $8.8 billion of this was for natural resource damages.[4] This amount is over and above the approximately $30 billion already spent on cleanup and other claims after the spill.[5] How can the economic damages from oil spills, like these that caused substantial economic and environmental harm, be calculated? Thousands of birds have been found dead in the Gulf since the BP spill, for example. What are they "worth"? Interestingly, the *Exxon Valdez* spill triggered pioneering work focused on providing monetary estimates of environmental damages, setting the stage for what is today considered standard practice for *nonmarket valuation*—the monetization of those goods and services without market prices.

In Chapter 3, we examined the basic concepts economists use to calculate these damages. Yet implementing these concepts is far from a trivial exercise. While the costs of cleanup are fairly transparent, estimating the damage is far more complex. For example, how were the $900 million in damages in the Exxon case and the $20 billion in the BP case determined?

In this chapter, we explore how we can move from the general concepts to the actual estimates of compensation required by the courts. A series of special techniques has been developed to value the benefits from environmental improvement or, conversely, to value the damage done by environmental degradation. Special techniques are necessary because most of the normal valuation techniques that have been used over the years cannot be applied to environmental resources. Benefit-cost analysis requires the monetization of all relevant benefits and costs of a proposed policy or project, not merely those where the values can be derived from market transactions As such, it is also important to monetize those environmental goods and services that are not traded in any market. Even more difficult to grapple with are those nonmarket benefits associated with values unrelated to use, topics explored below.

Why Value the Environment?

While it may prove difficult, if not impossible, to place a completely accurate value on certain environmental amenities, not making the attempt leaves us valuing them by default at $0. Will valuing them at $0 lead us to the best policy decisions? Probably not, but that does not prevent controversy from arising over attempts to replace $0 with a more appropriate value (Debate 4.1).

Many federal agencies depend on benefit-cost analyses for decision-making. Ideally, the goal is to choose the most economically desirable projects, given limited budgets. Estimation of benefits and costs is used for such diverse actions as follows:

● natural resources damage assessments, such as for oil spills (National Oceanic and Atmospheric Administration);
● the designation of critical habitat under the Endangered Species Act (US Fish and Wildlife Service);
● dam relicensing applications (The Federal Energy Regulatory Commission);
● estimating the costs and benefits of the Clean Air Act and the Clean Water Act.

These analyses, however, frequently fail to incorporate important nonmarket values. If the analysis does not include all the appropriate values, the results will be flawed. Is this exercise worth it?

DEBATE 4.1

Should Humans Place an Economic Value on the Environment?

Arne Naess, the late Norwegian philosopher, used the term *deep ecology* to refer to the view that the nonhuman environment has "intrinsic" value, a value that is independent of human interests. Intrinsic value is contrasted with "instrumental" value, in which the value of the environment is derived from its usefulness in satisfying human wants.

Two issues are raised by the Naess critique: (1) what is the basis for the valuing of the environment? and (2) how is the valuation accomplished? The belief that the environment may have a value that goes beyond its direct usefulness to humans is in fact quite consistent with modern economic valuation techniques. As we shall see in this chapter, economic valuation techniques now include the ability to quantify a wide range of "nonuse" values as well as the more traditional "use" values.

Controversies over how the values are derived are less easily resolved. As described in this chapter, economic valuation is based firmly upon human preferences. Proponents of deep ecology, on the other hand, would argue that allowing humans to determine the value of other species would have no more moral basis than allowing other species to determine the value of humans. Rather, deep ecologists argue, humans should only use environmental resources when necessary for survival; otherwise, nature should be left alone. And, because economic valuation is not helpful in determining survival necessity, deep ecologists argue that it contributes little to environmental management.

Those who oppose all economic valuation face a dilemma: when humans fail to value the environment, it may be assigned a default value of zero in calculations designed to guide policy. A value of zero, however derived, will tend to justify a great deal of environmental degradation that could not be justified with proper economic valuation. Support seems to be growing for the proposition that economic valuation can be a very useful means of demonstrating when environmental degradation is senseless, even when judged from a limited anthropomorphic perspective.

Sources: Costanza, R., et al. (1998). The value of ecosystem services: Putting the issues in perspective. *Ecological Economics*, *25*(1), 67–72; Daily, Gretchen, & Ellison, Katherine. (2003). *The New Economy of Nature: The Quest to Make Conservation Profitable*. Washington, DC: Island Press.

Valuation

While the valuation techniques we shall cover can be applied to both the damage caused by pollution and the services provided by the environment, each context offers its own unique aspects. We begin our investigation of valuation techniques by exposing some of the special challenges posed by the first of those contexts, pollution control.

In the United States, damage estimates are not only used in the design of policies, but, as indicated in the opening paragraphs of this chapter, they have also become important to the courts, who need some basis for deciding the magnitude of liability awards.[6]

The damage caused by pollution can take many different forms. The first, and probably most obvious, is the effect on human health. Polluted air and water can cause disease when ingested. Other forms of damage include loss of enjoyment from outdoor activities and damage to vegetation, animals, and materials.

Assessing the magnitude of this damage requires (1) identifying the affected categories, (2) estimating the physical relationship between the pollutant emissions (including natural sources) and the damage caused to the affected categories, (3) estimating responses by the affected parties toward mitigating some portion of the damage, and (4) placing a monetary value on the unmitigated physical damages. Each step is often difficult to accomplish.

Because the data used to track down causal relationships do not typically come from controlled experiments, identifying the affected categories is a complicated matter. Obviously, we cannot run large numbers of people through controlled experiments. If people were subjected to different levels of some pollutant, such as carbon monoxide, so that we could study the short-term and long-term effects, some might become ill and even die. Ethical concern precludes human experimentation of this type.

This leaves us essentially two choices. We can try to infer the impact on humans from controlled laboratory experiments on animals, or we can do statistical analysis of differences in mortality or disease rates for various human populations living in polluted environments to see the extent to which they are correlated with pollution concentrations. Neither approach is completely acceptable.

Animal experiments are expensive, and the extrapolation from effects on animals to effects on humans is tenuous at best. Many significant exposure effects do not appear for a long time. To determine these effects in a reasonable period of time, test animals are commonly subjected to large doses for relatively short periods. The researcher then extrapolates from the results of these high-dosage, short-duration experiments to estimate the effects of low-dose, long-duration exposure to pollution on a human population. Because these extrapolations move well beyond the range of experimental observations, many scientists disagree on how the extrapolations should be accomplished. Ethical concerns also arise with animal experiments.

Statistical studies, on the other hand, deal with human populations exposed to low doses for long periods, but, unfortunately, they have another set of problems—correlation does not imply causation. To illustrate, the fact that death rates are higher in cities with higher pollution levels does not prove that the higher pollution caused the higher death rates. Perhaps those same cities averaged older populations or perhaps they had more smokers. Existing studies have been sophisticated enough to account for many of these other possible influences but, because of the relative paucity of data, they have not been able to cover them all.

The problems discussed so far arise when identifying whether a particular observed effect results from pollution. The next step is to estimate how strong the relationship is between the effect and the pollution concentrations. In other words, it is necessary not only to discover *whether* pollution causes an increased incidence of respiratory disease, but also to estimate *how much* reduction in respiratory illness could be expected from a given reduction in pollution.

The nonexperimental nature of the data makes this a difficult task. It is not uncommon for different researchers analyzing the same data to come to remarkably different conclusions. Diagnostic problems are compounded when the effects are synergistic—that is, when the effect depends, in a nonadditive way, on contributing factors such as the victims' smoking habits or the presence of other harmful substances in the air or water.

Once physical damages have been identified, the next step is to place a monetary value on them. It is not difficult to see how complex an undertaking this is. Think about the difficulties in assigning a value to extending a human life by several years or to the pain, suffering, and grief borne by both a cancer victim and the victim's family.

How can these difficulties be overcome? What valuation techniques are available not only to value pollution damage, but also to value the large number of services that the environment provides?

Types of Values

Economists have decomposed the total economic value conferred by resources into three main components: (1) use value, (2) option value, and (3) nonuse or passive-use values. *Use value* reflects the direct use of the environmental resource. Examples include fish harvested from the sea, timber harvested from the forest, water extracted from a stream for irrigation, even the scenic beauty conferred by a natural vista. If you used one of your senses to experience the resource—sight, sound, touch, taste, or smell—then you have *used* the resource. Pollution can cause a loss of use value, such as when air pollution increases the vulnerability to illness, an oil spill adversely affects a fishery, or smog enshrouds a scenic vista.

Option value reflects the value people place on a future ability to use the environment. It reflects the willingness to pay to preserve the option to use the environment in the future even if one is not currently using it. Whereas use value reflects the value derived from current use, option value reflects the desire to preserve the potential for possible future use. Are you planning to go to Yellowstone National Park next summer? Perhaps not, but would you like to preserve the option to go someday?

Passive-use or *nonconsumptive use values* arise when the resource is not actually consumed in the process of experiencing it. These types of values reflect the common observation that people are more than willing to pay for improving or preserving resources that they will never use. One type of nonuse value is a *bequest value*. Bequest value is the willingness to pay to ensure a resource is available for your children and grandchildren. A second type of nonuse value, a pure nonuse value, is called *existence value*. Existence value is measured by the willingness to pay to ensure that a resource continues to exist in the absence of any interest in future use. The term existence value was coined by economist John Krutilla in his now-famous quote, "There are many persons who obtain satisfaction from mere knowledge that part of wilderness North America remains even though they would be appalled by the prospect of being exposed to it."[7] These values are "independent of any present or future use these people might make of those resources."[8]

When the Bureau of Reclamation began looking at sites for dams near the Grand Canyon, groups such as the Sierra Club rose up in protest of the potential loss of this unique resource. When Glen Canyon was flooded by Lake Powell, even those who never intended to visit recognized this potential loss. Because this value does not derive either from direct use or potential use, it represents a very different category of value.

These categories of value can be combined to produce the total willingness to pay (TWP):

TWP = Use Value + Option Value + Nonuse Value

Since nonuse or passive-use values are derived from motivations other than personal use, they are obviously less tangible than use values. Total willingness to pay estimated without nonuse values, however, will be less than the minimum amount that would be required to compensate individuals if they are deprived of this environmental asset. Furthermore, estimated nonuse values can be quite large. Therefore, it is not surprising that they are controversial. Indeed when the US Department of Interior drew up its regulations on the appropriate procedures for performing natural resource damage assessment, it prohibited the inclusion of nonuse values unless use values for the incident under consideration were zero. A subsequent 1989 decision by the District of Columbia Court of Appeals (880 F. 2nd 432) overruled this decision and allowed nonuse values to be included as long as they could be measured reliably.

Classifying Valuation Methods

Typically, the researcher's goal is to estimate the total willingness to pay for the good or service in question. This is the area under the demand curve up to the quantity consumed (recall discussion from Chapter 2). For a market good, this calculation is relatively straight-forward. However, nonmarket goods and services, the focus of this chapter, require the estimation of willingness to pay either through examining behavior, drawing inferences from the demand for related goods, or through responses to surveys. And, as highlighted above, capturing all components of value is challenging.

This section will provide a brief overview of some of the methods available to estimate these values and to convey some sense of the range of possibilities and how they are related. Subsequent sections will provide more specific information about how they are actually used.

Valuation methods can be separated into two broad categories: stated preference and revealed preference methods. Revealed preference methods are based on actual observable choices that allow resource values to be directly inferred from those choices. For example, in calculating how much local fishermen lost from the oil spill, the revealed preference method might calculate how much the catch declined and the resulting diminished value of the catch. In this case, prices are directly observable, and their use allows the direct calculation of the loss in value. Or, more indirectly, in calculating the value of an occupational environmental risk (such as some exposure to a substance that could pose some health risk), we might examine the differences in wages across industries in which workers take on different levels of risk.

Compare this with the direct stated preference method that can be used when the value is not directly observable, such as the value of preserving a species. Analysts derive this value by using a survey that attempts to elicit the respondents' willingness to pay (their "stated preference") for preserving that species.

Each of these broad categories of methods includes both indirect and direct techniques. The possibilities are presented in Table 4.1. We start with an examination of stated preference survey methods.

Stated Preference Methods

Stated preference methods use survey techniques to elicit willingness to pay for a marginal improvement or for avoiding a marginal loss. These methods are typically of two types, contingent valuation surveys and choice experiments. *Contingent valuation*, the most direct approach, provides a means of deriving values that cannot be obtained in more traditional ways. The simplest version of this approach merely asks respondents what they would be willing to pay for a change in environmental quality (such as an improvement in wetlands or reduced exposure to pollution) or on preserving the resource in its current state. Typically this question is framed as, "What is the maximum you are willing to pay for the change?"

Table 4.1 Economic Methods for Measuring Environmental and Resource Values

Methods	Revealed Preference	Stated Preference
Direct	Market Price Simulated Markets	Contingent Valuation
Indirect	Travel Cost Hedonic Property Values Hedonic Wage Values Avoidance Expenditures	Choice Experiments Conjoint Analysis Attribute-Based Models Contingent Ranking

Source: Modified by the authors from Mitchell and Carson, 1989.

Alternative versions ask a "yes" or "no" question, such as whether or not the respondent would pay $X to prevent the change or preserve the species. The answers reveal either an upper bound (in the case of a "no" answer) or a lower bound (in the case of a "yes" answer).

Choice experiments, on the other hand, present respondents with a set of options. Each set consists of various levels of attributes or characteristics of the good. One of the characteristics will be the "price" of that bundle of attributes. Each choice set typically includes the status quo bundle which includes a price of $0 since it represents no change. Respondents choose their preferred option.

Contingent Valuation Method

The contingent valuation survey approach creates a hypothetical market and asks respondents to consider a willingness-to-pay question *contingent* on the existence of this market. Contingent valuation questions come with their own set of challenges. The major concern with the use of the contingent valuation method has been the potential for survey respondents to give biased answers. Six types of potential bias have been the focus of a large amount of research: (1) strategic bias, (2) information bias, (3) starting-point bias, (4) hypothetical bias, (5) payment vehicle bias (protest bids), and (6) the observed discrepancy between willingness to pay (WTP) and willingness to accept (WTA).

Strategic bias arises when the respondent intentionally provides a biased answer in order to influence a particular outcome. If a decision to preserve a stretch of river for fishing, for example, depends on whether or not the survey produces a sufficiently large value for fishing, the respondents who enjoy fishing may be tempted to provide an answer that ensures a high value, rather than the lower value that reflects their true valuation. Another variation on strategic bias is social desirability bias, which occurs when respondents try to present themselves in a favorable light; one common example is when voters claim to have voted when they did not.

Information bias may arise whenever respondents are forced to value attributes with which they have little or no experience. For example, the valuation by a recreationist of a loss in water quality in one body of water may be based on the ease of substituting recreation on another body of water. If the respondent has no experience using the second body of water, the valuation could be based on an entirely false perception.

Visual aids have been shown to reduce uncertainty and unfamiliarity with the good or service being valued, but the nature of the visual aid may affect the response. Labao et al. (2008) found that colored photographs, as opposed to black-and-white photographs, influenced respondent willingness to pay for the Philippine Eagle. The colored photographs resulted in a higher willingness to pay than black-and-white photos. Why? The authors suggest that the higher willingness to pay could be explained by photographs in color simply providing more information or by "enhancing respondents' ability to assimilate information." In any case, the nature of the visual aide seems important for revealing preferences.

Starting-point bias may arise in those survey instruments in which a respondent is asked to check off their WTP from a predefined range of possibilities. How that range is defined by the designer of the survey may affect the resulting answers. A range of $0–$100 may produce a valuation by respondents different from, for example, a range of $10–$100, even if no responses are in the $0–$10 range. Ladenburg and Olsen (2008), in a study of willingness to pay to protect nature areas in Denmark from new highway development, found that the starting-point bias in their choice experiment was gender specific, with female respondents exhibiting the greatest sensitivity to the starting point.

Hypothetical bias can enter the picture because the respondent is being confronted by a contrived, rather than an actual, set of choices. Since he or she will not actually have to pay the estimated value, the respondent may treat the survey casually, providing ill-considered answers. One early survey (Hanemann, 1994) found ten studies that directly compared willingness-to-pay estimates derived from surveys with actual expenditures. Although some of the studies found that the willingness-to-pay estimates derived from surveys exceeded actual expenditures, the majority of those found that the differences were not statistically significant. Subsequently, Ehmke, Lusk, and List (2008) tested whether hypothetical bias depends on location and/or culture. In a study based on student experiments in China, France, Indiana, Kansas, and Niger, they found significant differences in bias across locations. Given that policymakers frequently rely on existing benefits estimates from other locations when making decisions, this finding should not be taken lightly. The strengths and weaknesses of using estimates derived in one setting to infer benefits in another, a technique known as *benefit transfer*, are discussed below.

Increasingly, environmental economists are using these types of experiments to try to determine the severity of some of these biases as well as to learn how to reduce bias. Some of these experiments are conducted in a laboratory setting, such as a computer lab or a classroom designed for this purpose. In one such experiment on voluntary provision of public goods (donations), Landry et al. (2006) found that for door-to-door interviews, an increase in physical attractiveness of the interviewer led to sizable increases in giving. Interestingly, physical attractiveness also led to increases in response rates, particularly by male households. Sometimes called *interviewer bias*, biases like these can be kept small through well-designed and pretested surveys.

Another challenge, *payment vehicle bias*, can arise when respondents react negatively to the choice of the payment vehicle. The payment vehicle represents how the stated WTP would be collected. Common choices include donations, taxes, or increases to utility bills. If a respondent is averse to taxes or has a negative perception of the agency collecting the (hypothetical) payment, they may state $0 for their willingness to pay. If their true willingness to pay is actually greater than zero, but they are "protesting" the question or payment vehicle, this zero must be excluded from the analysis. Determining which zero bids are valid and which are protests is important.

The final source of bias addresses observed gaps between two supposedly closely related concepts—willingness to pay (WTP) and willingness to accept (WTA) compensation. Respondents to contingent valuation surveys tend to report much higher values when asked for their willingness to accept compensation for a specified loss of some good or service than if asked for their willingness to pay for a specified increase of that same good or service. Economic theory suggests the two should be equal. Debate 4.2 explores some of the reasons offered for the difference.

Measuring willingness to pay or willingness to accept in the presence of price changes makes two new concepts relevant—compensating variation and equivalent variation. *Compensating variation* is the amount of money it would take to *compensate* for a price increase in order to make a consumer just as well off as she or he was before the price increase. How much the consumer was "hurt" by the price increase can be measured by the compensating variation. *Equivalent variation*, on the other hand, is the amount of money it would take to make a consumer indifferent (same income) between the money and the price increase. In other words, how much money would she or he pay to avoid the price increase?

If the compensating variation is greater than zero, that amount represents willingness to pay. If it is negative, it represents willingness to accept. In other words, for increases in environmental quality, compensating variation should be positive (WTP). For decreases in environmental quality, it should be negative (WTA). Equivalent variation is just the opposite— the amount of money the household would need to be given to be just as well off as before the environmental change. Equivalent variation will be positive for increases in environmental quality (WTA) and negative for decreases (WTP). In theory, in the absence of any income effects, these measures (along with consumer surplus) should be equivalent.

Much experimental work has been done on contingent valuation to determine how serious a problem biases may present. One early survey (Carson et al., 1994) uncovered 1,672 contingent valuation studies., A much more recent one gives annotations for more than 7,500 studies in 130 countries (Carson, 2011)! Are the results from these surveys reliable enough for the policy process?

DEBATE 4.2

Willingness to Pay versus Willingness to Accept: Why So Different?

Many contingent valuation studies have found that respondents tend to report much higher values for questions that ask what compensation the respondent would be willing to accept (WTA) to give something up than for questions that ask for the willingness to pay (WTP) for an incremental improvement in the same good or service. Economic theory suggests that differences between WTP and WTA should be small, but experimental findings both in environmental economics and in other microeconomic studies have found large differences. Why?

Some economists have attributed the discrepancy to a psychological endowment effect; the psychological value of something you own is greater than something you do not. In other words, you would require more compensation to be as well off without it than you would be willing to pay to get that same good, and as such, you would be less willing to give it up (WTA > WTP) (Kahneman, Knetsch, & Thaler, 1990). This is a form of what behavioral economists call loss aversion—the psychological premise that losses are more highly valued than gains.

Others have suggested that the difference may be explainable in terms of the market context. In the absence of good substitutes, large differences between WTA and WTP would be the expected outcome. In the presence of close substitutes, WTP and WTA should not be that different, but the divergence between the two measures should increase as the degree of substitution decreases (Hanemann, 1991; Shogren et al., 1994).

The characteristics of the good may matter as well. In their review of the evidence provided by experimental studies, Horowitz and McConnell (2002) find that for "ordinary goods" the ratio of WTA/WTP is smaller than the ratio of WTA/WTP for public and nonmarket goods. Their results support the notion that the nature of the property rights involved is not neutral.

The moral context of the valuation may matter as well. Croson et al. (Draft 2005) show that the amount of WTA compensation estimated in a damage case increases with the culpability of the party causing the damage as long as that party is also paying the damages. If, however, a third party is paying, WTA is insensitive to culpability. This difference suggests that the valuation implicitly includes an amount levied in punishment for the party who caused the damage (the valuation becomes the lost value plus a sanction).

It may also be the case that, in dynamic settings, respondents are uncertain about the value of the good. Zhao and Kling (2004) argue that in intertemporal settings, the equivalence of compensating variation/equivalent variation and WTP/WTA breaks down, in part because WTP and WTA have a behavioral component and the timing of a decision will be impacted by the consumer's rate of time preference and willingness to take risks. A buyer or seller, by committing to a purchase or sale, must forgo opportunities for additional information. These "commitment costs" reduce WTP and increase WTA. The larger the commitment costs, the larger is the divergence between the two measures.

Ultimately, the choice of which concept to use in environmental valuation comes down to how the associated property right is allocated. If someone owns the right to the resource, asking how much compensation they would require to give it up is the appropriate question. If the respondent does not have the right, using WTP to estimate the value of acquiring it is the right approach. However, as Horowitz and McConnell point out, since the holders and nonholders of "rights" value them differently, the initial allocation of property rights can have a strong influence on valuation decisions for environmental amenities. And, as Zhao and Kling note, the timing of the decision can also be an important factor.

Sources: Croson, R., Rachlinski, J. J., & Johnston, J. (Draft 2005). Culpability as an explanation of the WTA–WTP discrepancy in contingent valuation; Hanemann, W. M. (1991). Willingness to pay and willingness to accept: How much can they differ? *American Economic Review, 81*, 635–647; Horowitz, J. K., & McConnell, K. E. (2002). A review of WTA/WTP studies. *Journal of Environmental Economics and Management, 44*, 426–447; Kahneman, D., Knetsch, J., & Thaler, R. (1990). Experimental tests of the endowment effect and the Coase theorem. *Journal of Political Economy, 98*, 1325–1348; Shogren, J. F., Shin, Senung Y., Hayes, D. J., & Kliebenstein, J. B. (1994). Resolving differences in willingness to pay and willingness to accept. *American Economic Review, 84*(1), 255–270; Zhao, Jinhua, & Kling, Catherine. (2004). Willingness to pay, compensating variation, and the cost of commitment. *Economic Inquiry, 42*(3), 503–517.

Faced with the need to compute damages from oil spills, the National Oceanic and Atmospheric Administration (NOAA) convened a panel of independent economic experts (including two Nobel prize laureates) to evaluate the use of contingent valuation methods for determining lost passive-use or nonuse values. Their report, issued on January 15, 1993 (58 FR 4602), was cautiously supportive.

The committee made clear that it had several concerns with the technique. Among those concerns, the panel listed (1) the tendency for contingent valuation willingness-to-pay estimates to seem unreasonably large; (2) the difficulty in assuring the respondents have understood and absorbed the issues in the survey; and (3) the difficulty in assuring that respondents are responding to the specific issues in the survey rather than reflecting general warm feelings about public-spiritedness, known as the "warm glow" effect.[9]

But the panel also made clear its conclusion that suitably designed surveys could eliminate or reduce these biases to acceptable levels and it provided, in an appendix, specific guidelines for determining whether a particular study was suitably designed. The panel suggested that when practitioners follow these guidelines, they:

> can produce estimates reliable enough to be the starting point of a judicial process of damage assessment, including lost passive-use values. . . . [A well-constructed contingent valuation study] contains information that judges and juries will wish to use, in combination with other estimates, including the testimony of expert witnesses.

Specifically, they suggested the use of referendum-type (yes/no) willingness-to-pay questions, personal interviews when possible, clear scenario descriptions, and follow-up questions.

These guidelines have been influential in shaping subsequent studies. For example, Example 4.1 shares the results of a large contingent valuation survey, designed to estimate the value of preventing future spills. While influential, these guidelines have become dated, and, in 2017, new "contemporary guidelines" were published (Johnston et al., 2017). These guidelines provide best practice recommendations for both contingent valuation and choice experiments using what has been learned in the approximately 8000 stated preference studies published since the NOAA guidelines were first published. The authors offer 23 recommendations including designing a survey that clearly describes the status quo or baseline scenario, selecting a random sample of the affected population and choosing an appropriate survey mode. They also recommend pretesting of the survey instrument. They give extensive guidance on when to choose contingent valuation over a choice experiment and vice versa as well recommendations for reducing and addressing response bias.

Choice Experiments

Indirect hypothetical stated preference methods include several attribute-based methods. Attribute-based methods, such as choice experiments, are useful when project options have multiple levels of different attributes. Like contingent valuation, choice experiments are also survey based, but instead of asking respondents to state a willingness to pay, they are asked to choose among alternate bundles of goods. Each bundle has a set of attributes and the levels of each attribute vary across bundles. Since one of the attributes in each bundle is a price measure, willingness to pay can be identified.

Consider an example (Landry and Mires, 2017) that surveyed North Carolina residents on their preferences and willingness to pay for marine cultural heritage sites (e.g., shipwrecks). The choice experiment included five attributes including the preservation zone, the availability of public programs, and whether or not there was a walking, virtual, or diving trail. Table 4.2

EXAMPLE 4.1

Leave No Behavioral Trace: Using the Contingent Valuation Method to Measure Passive-Use Values

Until the *Exxon Valdez* tanker spilled 11 million gallons of crude oil into Prince William Sound in Alaska, the calculation of nonuse (or passive-use) values was not a widely researched topic. However, following the 1989 court ruling in *Ohio v. US Department of the Interior* that said lost passive-use values could now be compensated within natural resources damages assessments and the passage of the Oil Pollution Act of 1990, the estimation of nonuse and passive-use values became not only a topic of great debate, but also a rapidly growing research area within the economics community.

One study (Carson et al., 2003) discusses the design, implementation, and results of a large survey designed to estimate the passive-use values related to large oil spills. In particular, the survey asked respondents their willingness to pay to prevent a similar disaster in the future by funding an escort ship program that would help prevent and/or contain a future spill. The survey was conducted for the State of Alaska in preparation for litigation in the case against the *Exxon Valdez*.

The survey followed the recommendations made by the NOAA panel for conducting contingent valuation surveys and for ensuring reliable estimates. It relied upon face-to-face interviews and the sample was drawn from the national population. The study used a binary discrete-choice (yes/no) question where the respondent was asked whether he or she would be willing to pay a specific amount, with the amount varying across four versions of the survey. A one-time increase in taxes was the chosen method of payment. They also avoided potential embedding bias (where respondents may have difficulty valuing multiple goods) by using a survey that valued a single good. The survey contained pictures, maps, and background information to make sure the respondent was familiar with the good he/she was being asked to value.

Using the survey data, the researchers were able, statistically, to estimate a valuation function by relating the respondent's willingness to pay to respondent characteristics. After multiplying the estimate of the median willingness to pay by the population sampled, they reported aggregate lost passive-use values at $2.8 billion (in 1990 dollars). They point out that this number is a lower bound, not only because willingness to accept compensation would be a more appropriate measure of actual lost passive-use from the spill (see Debate 4.2), but also because their median willingness to pay was less than the mean.

The *Exxon Valdez* spill sparked a debate about the measurement of nonuse and passive-use values. Laws put into place after the spill now ensure that passive-use values will be included in natural resource damage assessments. Should other parts of the world follow suit?

Source: Carson, Richard T., Mitchell, Robert C., Hanemann, Michael, Kopp, Raymond J., Presser, Stanley, & Ruud, Paul A. (2003). Contingent valuation and lost passive use: Damages from the *Exxon Valdez* oil spill. *Environmental and Resource Economics, 25,* 257–286.

Table 4.2 Choice Experiment: Attributes and Levels

Attributes	Levels
Preservation Zone	• Status quo; 30 shipwrecks protected • 38 more shipwrecks (68 total; 127% increase); 2192 m² of bottomland • 56 more shipwrecks (124 total; 313% increase); 13,498 m² of bottomland
Public Programs	• No change • Increase museum exhibits and provide educational workshops • Increase museum exhibits and provide educational workshops, plus public television series about shipwrecks and creation of boating tours to shipwrecks
Walking Trail	• Yes/No
Virtual Trail	• Yes/No
Diving Trail	• Yes/No

reproduces the attributes and levels. With three attributes with three levels and two with two levels, there are 216 possible different profiles. Best practices suggests the use of a fractional factorial design and the authors chose eight versions with three choice sets per version of the survey, resulting in 24 choice sets.

Respondents were given a choice set of three different alternative management plans and the status quo (no purchase). Table 4.3 demonstrates a sample survey question. The researchers found a willingness to pay of $98 per household for a moderate level of public programs on Maritime Archeology and Shipwrecks; $90/household for the Walking Trails for *the Graveyard of the Atlantic*; and $84/household for Virtual Trails for *the Graveyard of the Atlantic*: (Landry and Mires 2017).

Choice experiments have evolved from both contingent valuation and marketing studies. This approach allows the respondent to make a familiar choice (choose a bundle) and allows the researcher to derive marginal willingness to pay for an attribute from that choice.

In another example, Haefele et al. (2016) present the results of a choice experiment in which they estimated the total economic value of US National Parks (Example 4.2). Including both visitation values and passive-use values for US residents, the total value of US National Parks and Programs more than pays for itself at $92 billion dollars. This estimate is considered a minimum bound since international visitation values were not included.

Contingent ranking, another survey method, also falls within this final category. Respondents are given a set of hypothetical situations that differ in terms of the environmental amenity available (instead of a bundle of attributes) and are asked to rank-order them. These rankings can then be compared to see the implicit tradeoffs between more of the environmental amenity and less of the other characteristics. When one or more of these characteristics is expressed in terms of a monetary value, it is possible to use this information and the rankings to impute a value to the environmental amenity.

Sometimes more than one of these techniques may be used simultaneously. In some cases, using multiple techniques is necessary to capture the total economic value; in other cases, it may be used to provide independent estimates of the value being sought as a check on the reliability of the estimate.

> Table 4.3 Sample Choice Experiment Question

I: Here is the first voting opportunity
(Please chose one of the four options below by putting an "X" in one of the empty boxes)

26.	Program 1	Program 2	Program 3	Status Quo
Preservation Zone	Yellow Zone	Yellow Zone	Red Zone	Red Zone
Public Programs	Large Investment	No Investment	Large Investment	No Investment
Walking Trails	Yes	No	No	No
Virtual Trails	No	Yes	Yes	No
SCUBA Diving Trails	Yes	No	No	No
One-time Tax	$12	$55	$145	$0
put an "X" in one of the boxes to the right	☐	☐	☐	☐

27. How confident are you about this choice from these options? (Please select one)
○ Very Certain ○ Somewhat Certain ○ Somewhat Uncertain ○ Very Uncertain ○ Don't Know

II: Now consider another voting opportunity with different choices
(Please choose one of the four options below by putting an "X" in one of the empty boxes)

28.	Program 4	Program 5	Program 6	Status Quo
Preservation Zone	Orange Zone	Orange Zone	Yellow Zone	Red Zone
Public Programs	Large Investment	No Investment	No Investment	No Investment
Walking Trails	No	Yes	No	No
Virtual Trails	No	Yes	No	No
SCUBA Diving Trails	Yes	No	Yes	No
One-time Tax	$145	$12	$55	$0
put on "X" in one of the boxes to the right	☐	☐	☐	☐

29. How confident are you about this choice from these options? (Please select one)
○ Very Certain ○ Somewhat Certain ○ Somewhat Uncertain ○ Very Uncertain ○ Don't Know

III: Finally, consider this third opportunity with different choices
(Please chose one of the four options below by putting an "X" in one of the empty boxes)

30.	Program 7	Program 8	Program 9	Status Quo
Preservation Zone	Red Zone	Red Zone	Yellow Zone	Red Zone
Public Programs	No Investment	Moderate Investment	Moderate Investment	No Investment
Walking Trails	Yes	No	Yes	No
Virtual Trails	Yes	No	Yes	No
SCUBA Diving Trails	No	Yes	No	No
One-time Tax	$12	$145	$55	$0
put on "X" in one of the boxes to the right	☐	☐	☐	☐

31. How confident are you about this choice from these options? (Please select one)
○ Very Certain ○ Somewhat Certain ○ Somewhat Uncertain ○ Very Uncertain ○ Don't Know

EXAMPLE 4.2

The Value of US National Parks

In 2016, the National Park Service in the United States turned 100 years old. As federal budget deficits loom, there has been some talk of selling off some of these sites. What is the value of the National Park lands, waters, and historic sites? According to the first ever comprehensive estimate, it is, at a minimum, valued at $92 billion.

Haefele et al. (2016a and b) present the results of a survey of American households focused on estimating the total economic value (TEV) of National Parks and Programs. Previous studies have focused on the value of specific National Park or monument sites, but none had attempted to estimate the value of all of these national treasures. The goal was to calculate total economic value; visitation values; and passive-use (or nonuse) values.

Using the population of all US households from which to draw a sample, researchers used a mixed mode approach that utilized both mail and internet surveys with phone call reminders. Two rounds of surveys were implemented between 2013 and 2015.

In the survey, participants were asked whether protecting National Parks was important to them. Nearly 95 percent of the sample said they were, even if they did not visit them. Moreover, 93.5 percent thought it was important to protect trails, parks, and open spaces for current and future generations whether they use them or not. The language in these questions suggests bequest and passive-use values. Only 6.2 percent thought the US should sell off some National Parks. The survey also included questions on respondents' political point of view. The sample of respondents leaned to the conservative side of the aisle.

The stated preference survey design was a choice experiment in which respondents chose among bundles that included the size of cuts to programs as well as the percentages of lands sold. Choice experiments typically allow respondents to choose a status quo bundle for which the price is $0. In order to minimize hypothetical bias (respondents stating a higher willingness to pay than they would actually pay), the choice question was followed by reminders to consider their budgets. This "cheap talk" technique has been shown to significantly reduce hypothetical bias.

Respondents were asked their willingness to pay a specific amount of money to pay for the National Park Service Programs. The payment vehicle utilized was an increase in federal income tax for each of the next 10 years. As we have discussed in this chapter, protest responses must be omitted from the data since those answers do not represent willingness to pay, instead representing a scenario (usually payment vehicle) protest. Since the payment vehicle chosen was federal income tax, there was some initial concern that protest zeros would be problematic, however, only 7.5 percent of the responses were considered to be protests.

Using econometric analysis, the marginal willingness to pay (or implicit price) for each type of National Park or National Park Service Program were estimated. These values are reproduced in Table 4.4.

> **Table 4.4** Per-household total economic value (TEV) for the National Park system and NPS Programs

National Parks	Estimated value
Nature-focused National Parks (79,096,632 acres)	$1,113.24
History-focused National Parks (226 sites)	$874.72
Water-focused National Parks (4,818,275 acres)	$977.93
Per household value for all National Park acres/sites	**$2,967.00**
NPS Programs	
Historic sites and buildings protected each year (2000)	$316.31
Acres transferred to communities each year (2700)	$98.41
National landmarks protected each year (114)	$347.98
Schoolchildren served by NPS educational programs (4.1 million)	$682.62
Per household value for all NPS programs	**$1,445.00**

Source: Table 4 in Haefele et al. (2016b)

These household values were then multiplied by the total number of households in the population to determine the total economic value. In order to present a minimum bound (or very conservative estimate), they assumed that households that did not return a survey were willing to pay $0.

The final tally of $92 billion includes both use values for visitors and passive-use or existence values, $62 billion of which (or two-thirds) is for the National Park Service lands and waters and historic sites, with $30 billion for programs. Of the $62 billion, the authors suggest that approximately half of that value is passive-use value. Of course, these values do not even include the willingness to pay of the millions of international tourists that visit US National Parks each year or those who hold passive-use values for these locations. Thus, the $92 billion TEV also represents "the minimum amount that US households are willing to pay to avoid the loss of the NPS and its programs" (Haefele et al., 2016a, p. 25).

According to one of the authors of the study, Linda Bilmes at Harvard University, the study shows that "Americans value the National Park Service at least 30 times more than the government spends on them." It is a happy 100th birthday indeed.

Sources: Haefele, Michelle, Loomis, John, & Bilmes, Linda. (2016a). Total economic valuation of the National Park Service Lands and Programs: Results of a survey of the American public. Faculty Research Working Paper Series. RWP16-024 (June); Haefele, Michelle, Loomis, John, & Bilmes, Linda. (2016b). Total economic valuation of US National Park Service estimated to be $92 billion: Implications for policy. *The George Wright Forum*, 33(3): 335–345; National Park Foundation Press Release. (June 30, 2016). National Park Foundation announces study determining value of America's National Parks to be $92 billion.

Revealed Preference Methods

Revealed preference methods are "observable" because they involve actual behavior and expenditures and "indirect" because they infer a value rather than estimate it directly. Suppose, for example, a particular sport fishery is being threatened by pollution, and one of the damages caused by that pollution is a reduction in sportfishing. How is this loss to be valued when access to the fishery is free?

Travel-Cost Method. One way to derive this loss is through *travel-cost* methods. Travel-cost methods may infer the value of a recreational resource (such as a sport fishery, a park, or a wildlife preserve where visitors hunt with a camera) by using information on how much visitors spend in getting to the site to construct a demand curve representing willingness to pay for a "visitor day."

Freeman et al. (2014) identify two variants of this approach. In the first, analysts examine the number of trips visitors make to a site. In the second, the analysts examine whether people decide to visit a site and, if so, which site. This second variant includes using a special class of models, known as random utility models, to value quality changes.

The first variant allows the construction of a travel cost demand function. The value of the flow of services from that site is the area under the estimated demand curve for those services or for access to the site, aggregated over all who visit the site. Using this variant, individual consumer surplus can be estimated. The area below the demand curve but above the travel cost (price) is the consumer surplus.

The second variant enables an analysis of how specific site characteristics influence choice and, therefore, indirectly how valuable those characteristics are. Knowledge of how the value of each site varies with respect to its characteristics allows the analyst to value how degradation of those characteristics (e.g., from pollution) would lower the value of the site.

Travel-cost models have been used to value National Parks, mountain climbing, recreational fishing, and beaches. Travel-cost models have also been used to value losses from events such as beach closures during oil spills, fish consumption advisories, and the cost of development that has eliminated a recreation area. The methodology for both variants is detailed in Parsons (2003).

In the random utility model, a person choosing a particular site takes into consideration site characteristics and its price (trip cost). Characteristics affecting the site choice include ease of access and environmental quality. Each site results in a unique level of utility and a person is assumed to choose the site giving the highest level of utility to that person. Welfare losses from an event such as an oil spill can then be measured by the resulting change in utility should the person have to choose an alternate, less desirable site.

Example 4.3 looks at the use of travel cost methods to estimate the economic impacts of beach closures due to oil spills in Minorca, Spain.

One interesting paradox that arises with the travel cost model is that those who live closest to the site, and may actually visit frequently, will have low travel costs. These users will appear to have a lower value for that site even if their (unmeasured) willingness to pay for the experience is very high. Another challenge in this model is how to incorporate the opportunity cost of time. Usually, this is represented by wages, but that approach is not universally accepted.

Hedonic Property Value and Hedonic Wage Methods. Two other revealed preference methods are the *hedonic property value* and *hedonic wage* methods. They share the characteristic that they use a statistical technique, known as multiple regression analysis, to

Using the Travel Cost Method to Estimate Recreational Value: Beaches in Minorca, Spain

Minorca, an island in the Mediterranean Sea, is a very popular tourist destination. Minorca's population doubles in the summer months from about 80,000 year-round residents to between 150,000 and 175,000 in the summer. The island's beaches are a major attraction.

Just how valuable are those beaches? To provide an estimate, researchers considered a hypothetical scenario in which an oil spill resulted in closure of certain beaches on the island. The analysis involved using a random utility model based upon survey data to estimate the economic impacts of these closures.

In 2008, 573 face-to-face individual surveys were conducted at 51 different beaches on the island using a discrete choice travel-cost survey. Respondents were asked some typical travel-cost survey questions such as where the trip originated, how they got to the site, how many people they were traveling with and their ages, and some questions to collect socio-economic demographics on the respondents. After being asked about their attitudes toward different beach attributes, they completed a questionnaire on the characteristics of the beach they were visiting. The characteristics included a measure of how urban the area was, the type of sand, how clean the beach was, how crowded it was, whether or not there was a toilet, presence of drink vendors, water temperature, calmness of the water, environmental quality, presence of a life guard, the direction the beach faced, and whether or not nudism was present on the beach. Travel costs included the cost of fuel and tolls plus travel time. Travel time varied by mode of transportation—using average walking and average driving speeds.

The random utility model allowed researchers to estimate the impacts on utility of the various beach characteristics identified by the surveys. Those characteristics positively affecting utility included north facing, presence of a life guard, presence of toilets and drink vendors, thin sand, presence of nudism, warm water temperatures, and good environmental quality. Characteristics negatively affecting utility included non-northern beaches, urban beaches, crowding, algae, and calm water.

Because some beach attributes were more highly valued than others, the range of estimates was dramatically affected by the details in the scenario. For example, for a closure affecting beaches on the west coast, the willingness to pay to avoid this loss was .24 euros (2008) per day per person with peak visitation of 25,000 visitors. Aggregating the per-visitor value across visitors produced a daily welfare loss from these closures of 6,000 euros. On the other extreme, a spill forcing closure of the more valuable northern beaches would cause the welfare loss to rise to 1.73 euros per day per person for a total of 43,250 euros during peak visitation.

It is easy to take highly enjoyable recreational sites for granted since they are freely provided by nature. As a result they may not be given their due when resources are allocated for their protection and enhancement. The travel-cost method can help to

Source: Pere, Riera, McConnell, Kenneth E., Giergiczny, Marek, & Mahieu, Pierre-Alexandre. (2011). Applying the travel-cost method to Minorca beaches: Some policy results. In Jeff Bennett (Ed.), *International Handbook on Non-Market Environmental Valuation.* Cheltenham, UK: Edward Elgar, 60–73.

inform policy not only by demonstrating how truly valuable they are, but also by allowing useful distinctions to be made among various recreation resources.

"tease out" the environmental component of value in a related market. For example, it is possible to discover that, all other things being equal, property values are lower in polluted neighborhoods than in clean neighborhoods. (Property values fall in polluted neighborhoods because they are less desirable places to live.)

Hedonic property value models use market data (house prices) and then break down the house sales price into its attributes, including the house characteristics (e.g., number of bedrooms, lot size, and features), the neighborhood characteristics (e.g., crime rates, school quality, and so on), and environmental characteristics (e.g., air quality, percentage of open space nearby, distance to a local landfill, etc.).

Hedonic models allow for the measurement of the marginal willingness to pay for discrete changes in an attribute. Numerous studies have utilized this approach to examine the effect on property value of things such as distance to a hazardous waste site (Michaels & Smith, 1990), large farm operations (Palmquist et al., 1997), open space and land use patterns (Bockstael, 1996; Geoghegan et al., 1997; Acharya & Bennett, 2001), dams and rivers (Bohlen & Lewis, 2009; Lewis and Landry, 2017), brownfields (Mihaescu & vom Hofe, 2012), and shale oil production facilities (Gopalakrishnan & Klaiber, 2013). This approach has become commonplace with the use of geographic information systems (discussed below).[10]

Hedonic wage approaches are similar except that they attempt to isolate the environmental risk component of wages, which serves to isolate the amount of compensation workers require in order to work in risky occupations. It is well known that workers in high-risk occupations demand higher wages in order to be induced to undertake the risks. When the risk is environmental (such as exposure to a toxic substance), the results of the multiple regression analysis can be used to construct a willingness to pay to avoid this kind of environmental risk. Additionally, the compensating wage differential can be used to calculate the value of a statistical life (Taylor, 2003). Techniques for valuing reductions in life-threatening risks will be discussed later in this chapter.

Benefit Transfer and Meta-Analysis

The NOAA panel report has created an interesting dilemma. Although it legitimized the use of contingent valuation for estimating passive-use (nonconsumptive use) and nonuse values, the panel has also set some rather rigid guidelines that reliable studies should follow. The cost of completing an "acceptable" contingent valuation study could well be so high that they will only be useful for large incidents, those for which the damages are high enough to justify their use. Yet, due to the paucity of other techniques, the failure to use contingent valuation may, by default, result in passive-use values of zero. That is not a very appealing alternative.[11]

One key to resolving the dilemma created by the possible expense of implementing the NOAA panel's recommendations may be provided by a technique called benefit transfer. Since original studies are time consuming and expensive, benefit transfer allows the estimates for the site of interest to be based upon estimates from other sites or from an earlier time period to provide the foundation for a current estimate.

Benefit transfer methods can take one of three forms: value transfers, benefit function transfers, or meta-analysis. Sometimes the actual benefit values derived from point estimates can simply be directly transferred from one context to another, usually adjusted for differences between the study site and the policy site. Function transfer involves using a previously estimated benefit function that relates site characteristics to site values. In this case, the differentiating characteristics of the site of interest are entered into the previously derived benefit function in order to derive newer, more site-specific values (Johnston et al., 2006).

Most recently, meta-analysis has been utilized. *Meta-analysis*, sometimes called the "analysis of analyses," takes empirical estimates from a sample of studies, statistically relates them to the characteristics of the studies, and calculates the degree to which the reported differences can be attributed to differences in location, subject matter, or methodology. For example, meta-analysis has been used with cross sections of contingent valuation studies as a basis for isolating and quantifying the determinants of nonuse value. Once these determinants have been isolated and related to specific policy contexts, it may be possible to transfer estimates from one context to another by finding the value consistent with the new context without incurring the time and expense of conducting new surveys each time.

Benefit transfer methods have been widely used in situations for which financial, time, or data constraints preclude original analysis. Policymakers frequently look to previously published studies for data that could inform a prospective decision. Benefit transfer has the advantage of being quick and inexpensive, but the accuracy of the estimates deteriorates as the new context tends to deviate (either temporally or spatially) the further it is from the context used to derive the estimates. Benefit transfer has not escaped controversy. Johnston and Rosenberger (2010) and Johnston et al. (2015) provide a comprehensive discussion of benefit transfer and outline some of the potential problems with the use of benefit transfer, including a lack of studies that are both of sufficiently high quality and policy relevant. Additionally, many of the published studies do not provide enough information on the attributes to allow an assessment of how they might have affected the derived value.

In response to some of these concerns, a valuation inventory database has emerged. The Environmental Valuation Reference Inventory (EVRI) is an online searchable database of over 4000 empirical studies on the economic value of environmental benefits and human health effects. It was specifically developed as a tool for use in benefit transfer.[12]

Benefit transfers are also subject to large errors. A few studies have tested the validity of environmental value transfer across sites. In those that have, the transfer errors have been sizable and wide ranging, sometimes over 100 percent for stated preference survey transfers (Brouwer, 2000, and Rosenberg and Stanley, 2006). Using meta-data from 31 empirical studies, Kaul et al. (2013) find a median transfer error of 39 percent. Lewis and Landry (2017) compare original hedonic property value model results to a test of transferring those results via benefit function transfer and find errors ranging from 29 percent to 1000 percent! These results suggest caution with the use of benefit transfer.

Using Geographic Information Systems to Enhance Valuation

Geographic information systems (GIS) are computerized mapping models and analysis tools. A GIS map is made up of layers such that many variables can be visualized simultaneously using overlays. GIS offers a powerful collection of tools for depicting and examining spatial relationships. Most simply, GIS can be used to produce compelling measurements and graphics that communicate the spatial structure of data and analytic results with a force and clarity otherwise impossible. But the technology's real value lies in the potential it brings to ask novel questions and enrich our understanding of social and economic processes by explicitly considering their spatial structure. Models that address environmental externalities have, almost by definition, a strong spatial component.[13]

Fundamentally spatial in nature, use of GIS in hedonic property models is a natural fit. Housing prices vary systematically and predictably from neighborhood to neighborhood. Spatial characteristics, from air quality to the availability of open space, can influence property values of entire neighborhoods; if one house enjoys abundant open space or especially good air quality, it is highly likely that its neighbors do as well.

In a 2008 paper, Lewis, Bohlen, and Wilson used GIS and statistical analysis to evaluate the impacts of dams and dam removal on local property values. In a unique "experiment," they collected data on property sales for 10 years before and after the Edwards Dam on the Kennebec River in Maine was removed. The Edwards Dam was the first federally licensed hydropower dam in the United States to be removed primarily for the purpose of river restoration. They also collected data on property sales approximately 20 miles upstream where two dams were still in place. GIS technology enhanced this study by facilitating the calculation of the distance from each home to both the river and the nearby dams. Lewis et al. (2008) found that homeowners pay a price penalty for living close to a dam. In other words, willingness to pay for identical housing is higher the further away from the dam the house is located. They also found that the penalty near the Edwards Dam site dropped to nearly zero after the dam was removed. Interestingly, the penalty upstream also dropped significantly. While a penalty for homes close to the dams upstream remains, it fell after the downstream dam was removed. Can you think of reasons why?[14]

Example 4.4 shows how the use of GIS can enable hedonic property value models to investigate how the view from a particular piece of property might affect its value.

Averting Expenditures. A final example of an indirect observable method involves examining "averting" or "avoidance" expenditures. Averting expenditures are those designed to reduce the damage caused by pollution by taking some kind of averting or defensive action. Examples include installing indoor air purifiers in response to an influx of polluted air or relying on bottled water as a response to the pollution of local drinking water supplies. Since people would not normally spend more to prevent a problem than would be caused by the problem itself, averting expenditures can provide a lower-bound estimate of the damage caused by pollution. They also cause a disproportionate hardship on poor households that cannot afford such coping expenditures. Dickie (2016) argues that ignoring averting expenditures or behavior may underestimate damages. He offers a simple example using contaminated drinking water. Suppose contaminated drinking water increases waterborne illness by 4 percent. If half the population avoids the contamination by some form of averting action such as using an alternate source of water, frequency of illness will drop to 2 percent. Only half the population is now exposed, thus reducing damages. However, the avoidance expenses must be included in the damage estimate. If they are not, the damages will be underestimated (Dickie, 2016). Example 4.5 illustrates the impact of coping or averting expenditures on residents of Kathmandu, Nepal.

Challenges

Aggregation. As you have probably figured out by now, nonmarket valuation faces several challenges. One challenge involves the aggregation of estimated values into a total value that can be used in benefit-cost analysis. How large is the relevant population? Do benefits change with distance to the resource in question? Debate 4.3 explores some of these challenging issues.

> ### EXAMPLE 4.4
>
> # Using GIS to Inform Hedonic Property Values: Visualizing the Data
>
> GIS offers economists and others powerful tools for analyzing spatial data and spatial relationships. For nonmarket valuation, GIS has proven to be especially helpful in enhancing hedonic property value models by incorporating both the proximity of environmental characteristics and their size or amount. GIS studies have also allowed for the incorporation of variables that reflect nearby types and diversity of land use.
>
> Geo-coding housing transactions assign a latitude and longitude coordinate to each sale. GIS allows other spatial data, such as land use, watercourses, and census data, to be "layered" on top of the map. By drawing a circle of the desired circumference around each house, GIS can help us to calculate the amount of each amenity that is in that circle as well as the density and types of people who live there. Numerous census data are available on variables such as income, age, education, crime rates, and commuting time. GIS also makes it relatively easy to calculate straight-line distances to desired (or undesired) locations, such as parks, lakes, schools, or landfills.
>
> In a 2002 paper entitled "Out of Sight, Out of Mind? Using GIS to Incorporate Visibility in Hedonic Property Value Models," Paterson and Boyle use GIS to measure the extent to which visibility measures affect house prices in Connecticut. In their study, visibility is measured as the percentage of land visible within one kilometer of the property, both in total and broken out for various land use categories. Finally, they added variables that measured the percentage of area in agriculture or in forest, or covered by water within one kilometer of each house.
>
> They find that visibility is indeed an important environmental variable in explaining property values, but the nature of the viewshed matters. While simply having a view is not a significant determinant of property values, viewing certain types of land uses is. Proximity to development reduces property values only if the development is visible, for example, suggesting that out of sight really does mean out of mind! They conclude that any analysis that omits variables that reflect nearby environmental conditions can lead to misleading or incorrect conclusions about the impacts of land use on property values. GIS is a powerful tool for helping a researcher include these important variables.
>
> *Source:* Paterson, Robert, & Boyle, Kevin. (2002). Out of sight, out of mind? Using GIS to incorporate visibility in hedonic property value models. *Land Economics, 78*(3), 417–425.

Partial Values. Another large challenge for nonmarket valuation is that most studies only capture a portion of the total value of an environmental good or service. For example, ecosystems are bundles of values, but the methods outlined in this chapter are only capable of capturing a portion of the value.

Figure 4.1 illustrates the different methods environmental economists use to capture different types of value. Each of these methods relies on different data and, many times, different experts. Rarely is the available time or money sufficient to apply all methods to a particular question.

Debate 4.4 illustrates the challenges and importance of attempts to capture the total economic value by examining a specific case study—polar bears in Canada.

EXAMPLE 4.5

Valuing the Reliability of Water Supplies: Coping Expenditures in Kathmandu Valley, Nepal

Nepal, like many other poor developing countries, experiences chronic shortages of safe drinking water. The Kathmandu Valley is no exception. The National Water Supply Corporation serves 70 percent of the population, but the public water supply is neither reliable nor safe. Shortages are frequent and the water quality is frequently contaminated with fecal coliform and nitrogen-ammonia (Pattanayak et al., 2005).

How much should be invested in improving water quality depends on how valuable clean water is to this population. Quantifying those benefits requires establishing how much residents would be willing to pay for cleaner water. One pathway for quantifying willingness to pay in this context can be found in analyzing how much households spend to cope with the unreliable water supply. It turns out they purchase water from water vendors, collect water from public taps, invest in wells or storage tanks, purchase filtration systems, and/or boil water. All of these coping mechanisms have both a financial cost and a cost associated with the time devoted to coping. Using coping costs as a proxy for willingness to pay can serve as the basis for constructing a lower-bound estimate of the demand curve for water provision in settings where other more direct valuation strategies are simply not practical to implement.

In a survey of 1500 households in five municipalities, researchers found that for households in the Kathmandu Valley, coping or averting behaviors cost the average household about 1 percent of monthly income, most of this attributed to the time spent collecting water. The authors note that these coping costs are almost twice as much as the current monthly bills paid to the water utility.

Some demographic factors were found to have influenced household coping expenditures.

- Wealthier households were found to have higher coping expenditures. As the authors note, this confirms the intuition that relatively rich households have more resources and therefore invest more in water treatment, storage, and purchases.
- More educated respondents also had higher coping costs, perhaps because these households better understood the risks of contaminated water.

If, as suggested by these two findings, the poor face higher financial and educational barriers in their quest for cleaner water, water policy in this region faces an environmental justice issue as well as an efficiency issue.

Even though averting expenditures represent only a lower bound of willingness to pay for water supply, they can provide valuable information for the estimation of benefits of water provision. In addition, these data imply that the common assertion that in poor countries the costs of supplying clean water are so high that they necessarily exceed the benefits received by water users may be a misconception—the value of water in this valley was found to be at least twice the current per unit charge even when the lower bound estimating technique was used.

Source: Pattanayak, Subhrendu K., Yang, Jui-Chen, Whittington, Dale, & Bal Kumar, K. C. (2005). Coping with unreliable public water supplies: Averting expenditures by households in Kathmandu, Nepal. *Water Resources Research, 41*(2), doi:10.1029/2003WR002443.

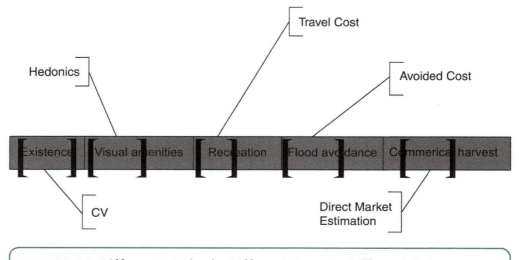

FIGURE 4.1 Different Methods, Different Experts, Different Data

Source: Courtesy of James Boyd, Resources for the Future

DEBATE 4.3

Distance Decay in Willingness to Pay: When and How Much Does Location Matter?

One challenge in performing benefit-cost analysis is accurately choosing the "extent of the market." The extent of the market refers to *who benefits* from the resource in question. Loomis (1996) argues that not accounting for the full extent of the market (i.e., including everyone who gains some benefit) can lead to **under**estimates of willingness to pay and aggregate value.

On the other hand, a more inclusive design might include respondents with vastly lower willingness to pay simply because of their location. For some resources, distant respondents have a lower willingness to pay for its improvement. It seems reasonable to expect, for example, that the benefits from a reduction in river pollution to an individual household would probably depend on its proximity to the river. Those closest to the river place the highest value on the improvement. In other words, since it seems reasonable to expect that some types of values do experience a "distance decay," in aggregating benefits this deterioration should certainly be taken into account.

Bateman et al. (2006) argue that not accounting for distance decay can lead to **over**estimates of willingness to pay. Those who are further away still benefit and should be counted, but at some kind of decreasing rate. Recently, the number of stated preference studies (contingent valuation and choice experiments) that focus on distance decay has increased so we have learned more about it.

What do these studies say about the circumstances that give rise to distance decay?

Interestingly, the empirical evidence suggests that both the type of value being measured (use or nonuse value) as well as the type of willingness to pay question (compensating versus equivalent variation) matter. Hanley et al. (2003) and Bateman et al. (2006) both find that distance decay does arise for use value, but very little or not at all for nonuse values. If, however, some of the current nonusers become users under the proposed scenario, their valuation would experience some distance decay. This result follows the intuition that if the willingness to pay question is framed as a marginal improvement in quality (compensating variation), then some of the nonusers might become users and that possibility would be reflected in their valuations. If the question is framed as equivalent variation (willingness to pay to avoid loss), nonuser valuations experience no distance decay, since they will remain nonusers.

These studies suggest that spatial patterns in nonmarket values have important implications not only for how benefit-cost analysis should be conducted and interpreted but also for how that analysis affects the policy evaluations. Different design choices as to the extent of the market and whether to aggregate across particular political or economic jurisdiction can lead to very different results. As Schaafsma et al. (2012) suggest, these spatial patterns should be taken into account both when drawing samples for willingness to pay surveys, and when aggregating the results.

Sources: Bateman, Ian, Day, Brett H., Georgiou, Stavros, & Lake, Ian. (September 2006). The aggregation of environmental benefit values: Welfare measures, distance decay and total WTP. Discussion paper; Hanley, Nick, Schlapfer, Felix, & Spurgeon, James. (2003). Aggregating the benefits of environmental improvements: Distance-decay functions for use and nonuse values. *Journal of Environmental Management, 68,* 297–304; Loomis, John B. (1996). How large is the extent of the market for public goods: Evidence from a nationwide contingent valuation survey. *Applied Economics, 28,* 779–782; Schaafsma, Marije, Brouwer, Roy, & Rose, John. (2012). Directional heterogeneity in WTP models for environmental valuation. *Ecological Economics, 79*(1), 21–31.

Valuing Human Life

One fascinating public policy area where these various approaches have been applied is in the valuation of human life. Many government programs, from those controlling hazardous pollutants in the workplace or in drinking water, to those improving nuclear power plant safety, are designed to save human life as well as to reduce illness. How resources should be allocated among these programs depends crucially on the value of human life. In order to answer this question, an estimate of the value of that life to society is necessary and federal regulations require such estimates for benefit-cost analysis. How is life to be valued?

DEBATE 4.4

What Is the Value of a Polar Bear?

Because polar bears are such a charismatic species, they have obviously attracted lots of popular support, but exactly how valuable are they? In 2011, the Canadian government issued a report in which it attempted to estimate the different socio-economic values of polar bears in Canada.

They commissioned the study in part to determine the economic impact of adding the polar bear to a list of at-risk species. This study represents one of the few studies to try to estimate the value of polar bears and the only one that tries to do it in a comprehensive fashion.

The authors tried to capture active use values (subsistence and sport hunting, polar bear viewing, and value in scientific research), as well as passive-use values (existence and bequest values). Multiple nonmarket valuation methods were used in this study including travel cost (viewing), market prices (hunting), meta-analysis, and benefit transfer (passive-use values). Time and budgetary constraints precluded the use of stated preference methods such as contingent valuation or choice experiments. The summary of their findings is reproduced in Figure 4.2. Note that the direct use values actually comprise a relatively small portion of the total value.

An effort to document the value of a species like this produces a value that is no doubt much closer to the truth than the default value of zero, but how close are these numbers to the true value? There are several caveats to consider:

- Consider the calculation for the value of polar bear meat. For this the cost, the next best substitute, which in this case was beef (for humans) and dog food was used. One could certainly argue for alternatives.
- Sport values were estimated using the benefit transfer method. Recall the challenges for using benefit transfer, in particular for a unique species like the polar bear. The study closest to this one was conducted in 1989 and focused on big game and grizzly bear hunting. For the polar bear study, the 1989 values were translated into 2009 dollars. The authors suggest their number might be an underestimate since hunting for a polar bear is such a unique experience. On the other hand, they also acknowledge that the number could just as easily be an overestimate if the charismatic image of the polar bear reduces willingness to pay for hunting.
- Finally, passive-use values were also calculated using benefit transfer. Since no study has been done on the preservation value of the polar bear in Canada, the researchers used a meta-analysis of species at risk (Richardson & Loomis, 2009). While that study calculated a total economic value, for the polar bear study the benefit transfer was specifically designed to capture only preservation value. It was relatively straightforward to remove direct uses (visitors) from the transferred value, but not the indirect use benefits such as scientific value.

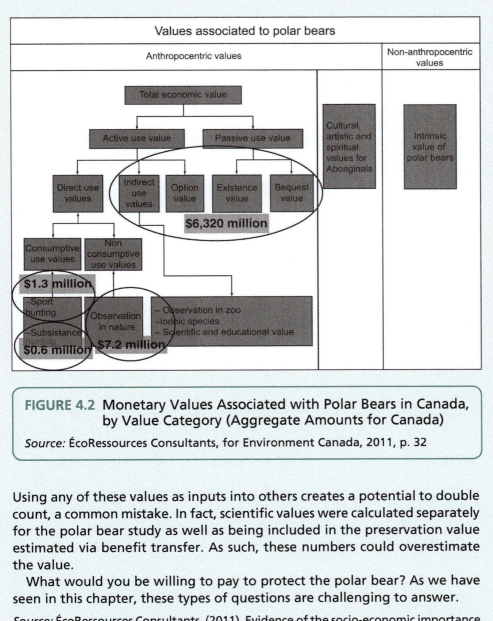

FIGURE 4.2 Monetary Values Associated with Polar Bears in Canada, by Value Category (Aggregate Amounts for Canada)

Source: ÉcoRessources Consultants, for Environment Canada, 2011, p. 32

Using any of these values as inputs into others creates a potential to double count, a common mistake. In fact, scientific values were calculated separately for the polar bear study as well as being included in the preservation value estimated via benefit transfer. As such, these numbers could overestimate the value.

What would you be willing to pay to protect the polar bear? As we have seen in this chapter, these types of questions are challenging to answer.

Source: ÉcoRessources Consultants. (2011). Evidence of the socio-economic importance of Polar bears for Canada. Report for Environment Canada. Full report is accessible at http://publications.gc.ca/site/archivee-archived.html?url=http://publications.gc.ca/collections/collection_2012/ec/CW66-291-2011-eng.pdf; Richardson, Leslie, & Loomis, John. (2009). Total economic valuation of endangered species: A summary and comparison of the United States and the rest of the world estimates. In K. N. Ninan (Ed.), *Conserving and Valuing Ecosystem Services and Biodiversity: Economic, Institutional and Social Challenges*. London: Earthscan, 25–46.

The simple answer, of course, is that life is priceless, but that turns out to be not very helpful. Because the resources used to prevent loss of life are scarce, choices must be made. The economic approach to valuing lifesaving reductions in environmental risk is to calculate the change in the probability of death resulting from the reduction in environmental risk and to place a value on the change. Thus, it is not life itself that is being valued, but rather a reduction in the probability that some segment of the population could be expected to die earlier than others. This *value of statistical life* (VSL) represents an individual's willingness to pay for small changes in mortality risks. It does not represent a willingness to pay to prevent certain death. It is measured as the "marginal rate of substitution between mortality risk and money (i.e., other goods and services)" (Cameron, 2010) and as such is also called *mortality risk valuation*. Debate 4.5 examines the controversy associated with valuing changes in these mortality risks.

DEBATE 4.5

Is Valuing Human Life Immoral?

In 2004, economist Frank Ackerman and lawyer Lisa Heinzerling teamed up to write a book that questions the morality of using benefit-cost analysis to evaluate regulations designed to protect human life. In *Priceless: On Knowing the Price of Everything and the Value of Nothing* (2004), they argue that benefit-cost analysis is immoral because it represents a retreat from the traditional standard that all citizens have an absolute right to be free from harm caused by pollution. When it justifies a regulation that will allow some pollution-induced deaths, benefit-cost analysis violates this absolute right.

Economist Maureen Cropper responds that it would be immoral not to consider the benefits of lifesaving measures. Resources are scarce and they must be allocated so as to produce the greatest good. If all pollution were reduced to zero, even if that were possible, the cost would be extremely high and the resources to cover that cost would have to be diverted from other beneficial uses. Professor Cropper also suggests that it would be immoral to impose costs on people about which they have no say—for example, the costs of additional pollution controls—without at least trying to consider what choices people would make themselves. Like it or not, hard choices must be made.

Cropper also points out that people are always making decisions that recognize a trade-off between the cost of more protection and the health consequences of not taking the protection. Thinking in terms of trade-offs should be a familiar concept. She points out that people drive faster to save time, thereby increasing their risk of dying. They also decide how much money to spend on medicines to lower their risk of disease or they may take jobs that pose morbidity or even mortality risks.

In her response to Ackerman and Heinzerling, Cropper acknowledges that benefit-cost analysis has its flaws and that it should never be the only decision-making guide. Nonetheless, she argues that it does add useful information to the process and throwing that information away could prove to be detrimental to the very people that Ackerman and Heinzerling seek to protect.

Sources: Ackerman, Frank, & Heinzerling, Lisa. (2004). *Priceless: On Knowing the Price of Everything and the Value of Nothing.* New York: The New Press; Ackerman, Frank. (2004). Morality, cost-benefit and the price of life. *Environmental Forum, 21*(5), 46–47; Cropper, Maureen. (2004). Immoral not to weigh benefits against costs. *Environmental Forum, 21*(5), 47–48.

It is possible to translate the value derived from this procedure into an "implied value of statistical life." This is accomplished by dividing the amount each individual is willing to pay for a specific reduction in the probability of death by the probability reduction. Suppose, for example, that a particular environmental policy could be expected to reduce the average concentration of a toxic substance to which 1 million people are exposed. Suppose further that this reduction in exposure could be expected to reduce the risk of death from 1 out of 100,000 to 1 out of 150,000. This implies that the number of expected deaths would fall from 10 to 6.67 in the exposed population as a result of this policy. If each of the 1 million persons exposed is willing to pay $5 for this risk reduction (for a total of $5 million), then the implied value of a statistical life is approximately $1.5 million ($5 million divided by 3.33). Alternatively, the VSL can be calculated using the change in WTP divided by the change in risk. For this example, that would be $5 divided by the change in risk of death (1/100,000–1/150,000), or $1.5 million. Thus, the VSL is capturing the rate of trade-off between money and a very small risk of death.

What actual values have been derived from these methods? One early survey (Viscusi, 1996) of a large number of studies examining reductions in a number of life-threatening risks found that most implied values for human life (in 1986 dollars) were between $3 million and $7 million. This same survey went on to suggest that the most appropriate estimates were probably closer to the $5 million estimate. In other words, all government programs resulting in risk reductions costing less than $5 million per life saved would be justified in benefit-cost terms. Those costing more might or might not be justified, depending on the appropriate value of a life saved in the particular risk context being examined.

In a meta-analysis, Mrozek and Taylor (2002) found much lower values for VSL. Using over 40 labor market studies, their research suggests that a range of $1.5 million to $2.5 million for VSL is more appropriate. What about age? Does the VSL change with age? Apparently so. Viscusi (2008) finds an inverted U-shape relationship between VSL and age. Specifically, using the hedonic wage model, they estimate a VSL of $3.7 million for persons ages 18–24, $9.7 million for persons ages 35–44, and $3.4 million for persons ages 55–62. According to their study, VSL rises with age, peaks, and then declines.

What about the value of statistical life across populations or countries with different incomes? Most agencies in the United States use VSLs between $5 million and $8 million.[15] These estimates are based largely on hedonic wage studies that have been conducted in the United States or in other high-income countries.[16] How might those results be translated into settings featuring populations with lower incomes?

Adjustments for income are typically derived using an estimate of the income elasticity of demand. Recall that income elasticity is the percent change in consumption given a 1 percent change in income. Hammitt and Robinson (2011) note that applying income elasticities, derived for countries like the United States, might result in nonsensical VSL estimates if blindly applied to lower-income countries. While US agencies typically assume a 0.4 to 0.6 percent change in VSL for a 1 percent change in real income over time, elasticities closer to 1.0 or higher are more realistic for transfers of these values between high- and low-income countries. Using the higher income elasticity number is merited since willingness to pay for mortality risk reduction as a percentage of income drops at very low incomes; what limited income is available in poorer households is reserved for basic needs.

Summary: Nonmarket Valuation Today

In this chapter, we have examined the most prominent, but certainly not the only, techniques available to supply policymakers with the information needed to implement efficient policy. Finding the total economic value of the service flows requires estimating three components of value: (1) use value, (2) option value, and (3) nonuse or passive-use values.

Our review of these various techniques included direct observation, contingent valuation, contingent choice experiments, travel cost, hedonic property and wage studies, and averting or defensive expenditures. When time or funding precludes original research, benefit transfer or meta-analysis provide alternate methods for the estimation of values. In January 2011, a panel of experts gathered at the annual meeting of the American Economics Association to reflect on nonmarket valuation 20 years after the *Exxon Valdez* spill and, unknown to any of them when the panelists were asked to participate, 8 months after the *Deepwater Horizon* spill. The panelists had all worked on estimation of damages from the *Exxon Valdez* spill. The consensus among panelists was that while many of the issues with bias have been addressed in the literature, many unanswered questions remain and some areas still need work. While they all agreed that it is "hard to underestimate the powerful need for values" (i.e., some number is definitely better than no number), and we now have in place methods that can be easily utilized by all researchers, they also emphasized several problem areas. First, the value of time in travel cost models has not been resolved. What is the opportunity cost of time if you are unemployed, for example?

Second, in discussing other revealed preference methods, they asked the question, "How do the recent numerous foreclosures in the real estate market affect hedonic property value model assumptions?"[17] Third, choice experiments do not resolve all of the potential problems with contingent valuation. While choice experiments do seem to better represent actual market choices, some of the issues that arise in contingent valuation, such as the choice of the payment vehicle, also arise with choice experiments. In addition, some new challenges, such as how the sequencing of choices in choice experiments might affect outcomes, arise. The panel highlighted how this area of research has been enhanced by the field of behavioral economics, an emerging research area that combines economics and psychology to examine human behavior. And finally, they suggested that the NOAA panel recommendations be updated to reflect the new body of research. In 2017, a new set of guidelines was published to do just that. The 23 recommendations in those guidelines address these questions regarding stated preference surveys and attempt to synthesize the now large body of research that informs nonmarket valuation (Johnston et al., 2017).

Some of these same experts, along with several others, implemented a nationwide survey following the BP spill to assess what US households would pay to avoid damages from another spill. Using state of the art techniques for stated preference surveys, they found that US households would be willing to pay $17.2 billion to avoid the damages from another spill (Bishop et al., 2017). One author claimed, "this is proof that our natural resources have an immense monetary value to citizens of the United States who visit the Gulf and to those who simply care that this valuable resource is not damaged."

Discussion Question

1. Certain environmental laws prohibit the EPA from considering the costs of meeting various standards when the levels of the standards are set. Is this a good example of appropriately prioritizing human health or simply an unjustifiable waste of resources? Why?

Self-Test Exercises

1. In Mark A. Cohen, "The Costs and Benefits of Oil Spill Prevention and Enforcement," *Journal of Environmental Economics and Management* Vol. 13 (June 1986), an attempt was made to quantify the marginal benefits and marginal costs of US Coast Guard enforcement activity in the area of oil spill prevention. His analysis suggests (p. 185) that the marginal per-gallon benefit from the current level of enforcement activity is $7.50, while the marginal per-gallon cost is $5.50. Assuming these numbers are correct, would you recommend that the Coast Guard increase, decrease, or hold at the current level their enforcement activity? Why?

2. Professor Kip Viscusi estimated that the cost per life saved by current government risk-reducing programs ranges from $100,000 for unvented space heaters to $72 billion for a proposed standard to reduce occupational exposure to formaldehyde.

    a. Assuming these values to be correct, how might efficiency be enhanced in these two programs?
    b. Should the government strive to equalize the marginal costs per life saved across all lifesaving programs?

3. a. Suppose that hedonic wage studies indicate a willingness to pay $50 per person for a reduction in the risk of a premature death from an environmental hazard of 1/100,000. If the exposed population is 4 million people, what is the implied value of a statistical life?
    b. Suppose that an impending environmental regulation to control that hazard is expected to reduce the risk of premature death from 6/100,000 to 2/100,000 per year in that exposed population of 4 million people. Your boss asks you to tell her what is the maximum this regulation could cost and still have the benefits be at least as large as the costs. What is your answer?

Notes

1 US District Court for the State of Alaska, Case Number A89-0095CV, January 28, 2004.
2 Ibid.
3 *Exxon Shipping Company v. Baker.*
4 Bishop et al. (2017).
5 In 2017, the United States Department of the Interior released the Deepwater Horizon Response and Restoration Administrative Record, which included an estimate of the total value of damages (see Example 9.4).
6 The rules for determining these damages are defined in Department of Interior regulations. See 40 Code of Federal Regulations 300:72–74.
7 Krutilla, John V. (1967). Conservation reconsidered. *American Economic Review*, 57(4), 777–786.
8 Ibid. p. 779.

9 A more detailed description of the methodological issues and concerns with contingent valuation with respect to the actual *Exxon Valdez* contingent valuation survey can be found in Mitchell (2002).

10 There are many examples in this category. These are just a few.

11 Whittington (2002) examines the reasons why so many contingent valuation studies in developing countries are unhelpful. Poorly designed or rapidly implemented surveys could result in costly policy mistakes on topics that are very important in the developing world. The current push for cheaper, quicker studies is risky and researchers need to be very cautious.

12 www.evri.ca

13 For examples see Bateman et al. (2002), who describe the contributions of GIS in incorporating spatial dimensions into economic analysis, including benefit-cost analysis; and Clapp et al. (1997), who discuss the potential contributions GIS can make for urban and real estate economics.

14 Interestingly, after this study was complete, one of the two upstream dams, the Fort Halifax Dam, was removed in July 2008 after years of litigation about its removal.

15 See, for example, www.epa.gov/environmental-economics/mortality-risk-valuation

16 Many labor market estimates of VSL average near $7 million (Viscusi, 2008).

17 This question was taken up by another panel of experts at the 2012 Association of Environmental and Resource Economics annual conference and later published by Boyle et al. (2012).

Further Reading

Bateman, Ian J., Lovett, Andrew A., & Brainard. Julii S. (2005). *Applied Environmental Economics: A GIS Approach to Cost-Benefit Analysis*. Cambridge: Cambridge University Press. Uses GIS to examine land use change and valuation.

Bennett, Jeff (Ed.). (2011). *The International Handbook on Non-Market Environmental Valuation*. Cheltenham, UK: Edward Elgar. An excellent compilation on nonmarket valuation.

Boardman, Anthony E., Greenberg, David H., Vining, Aidan R., & Weimer, David L. (2005). *Cost-Benefit Analysis: Concepts and Practice*, 3rd ed. Upper Saddle River, NJ: Prentice-Hall. An excellent basic text on the use of cost-benefit analysis.

Champ, Patricia A., Boyle, Kevin J., & Brown, T. C. (2016). *A Primer on Nonmarket Valuation*, 2nd ed. New York: Springer. A thorough overview of nonmarket valuation methods.

Costanza, R. et al. (1998). The value of the world's ecosystem services and natural capital. (Reprinted from *Nature*, 387, 253, 1997.) *Ecological Economics*, 25(1), 3–15. An ambitious, but ultimately flawed, attempt to place an economic value on ecosystem services. This issue of *Ecological Economics* also contains a number of articles that demonstrate some of the flaws.

Johnston, R. J., Rolfe, J., Rosenberger, R., & Brouwer, R. (Eds.). (2015). *Benefit Transfer of Environmental and Resource Values. A Guide for Researchers and Practitioners*. Dordrecht, the Netherlands: Springer. This article is a practical guide for the design and use of benefit transfer.

Johnston, Robert J., Boye, Kevin J., Adamowicz, Wiktor, Bennett, Jeff, Brouwer, Roy, Cameron, Trudy Ann, Hanemann, W. Michael, Hanley, Nick J., Ryan, Mandy, Scarpa, Riccardo, Tourangeau, Roger, & Vossler, Christian A. (2017). Contemporary guidance for stated preference studies. *JAERE*, 4(2). http://dx.doi.org/10.1086/691697. This issue includes an update to the NOAA guidelines for the use of contingent valuation. It also has recommendations for the use of choice experiments.

Mitchell, Robert Cameron, & Carson, Richard T. (1989). *Using Surveys to Value Public Goods: The Contingent Valuation Method*. Washington, DC: Resources for the Future.

A comprehensive examination of contingent valuation research with brief summaries of representative studies and recommendations for survey design.

Whitehead, John, Haab, Tim, & Huang, Ju-Chin (Eds.). (2011). *Preference Data for Environmental Valuation: Combining Revealed and Stated Approaches*. London: Routledge. A compilation of articles that use more than one valuation method or novel applications of data combinations written by nonmarket valuation economists.

Additional references and historically significant references are available on this book's Companion Website: www.routledge.com/cw/Tietenberg

Chapter 5

Economics of Pollution Control

An Overview

> Democracy is not a matter of sentiment, but of foresight. Any system that doesn't take the long run into account will burn itself out in the short run.
> —Charles Yost, *The Age of Triumph and Frustration* (1964)

Introduction

In Chapter 2 we introduced a schematic describing the relationship between the natural and economic systems. One side depicted the flow of mass and energy to the economic system, while the other depicted the flow of waste products back to the environment. Now we turn to examining how a balance can be achieved in the reverse flow of waste products back to the environment. Because the waste flows are inexorably intertwined with the flow of mass and energy into the economy, establishing a balance for waste flows will have feedback effects on the input flows as well.

Two questions must be addressed: (1) what is the appropriate level of flow of pollution? and (2) how should the responsibility for achieving this flow level be allocated among the various sources of the pollutant when reductions are needed?

In this chapter we lay the foundation for understanding the policy approach to controlling the flow of these waste products by developing a general framework for analyzing pollution control. This framework allows us to define efficient and cost-effective allocations for a variety of pollutant types, to compare these allocations to market allocations, and to demonstrate how efficiency and cost-effectiveness can be used to formulate desirable policy responses. This overview is then followed by a series of chapters that apply these principles by examining the policy approaches that have been adopted in the United States and in the rest of the world to establish control over waste flows.

A Pollutant Taxonomy

The amount of waste products emitted determines the load upon the environment. The damage done by this load depends on the capacity of the environment to assimilate the waste products (see Figure 5.1). We call this ability of the environment to absorb pollutants its *absorptive capacity*. If the emissions load exceeds the absorptive capacity, then the pollutant accumulates in the environment.

Pollutants for which the environment has little or no absorptive capacity are called *stock pollutants*. Stock pollutants accumulate over time as emissions enter the environment. Examples of stock pollutants include nonbiodegradable bottles tossed by the roadside; heavy metals, such as lead, that accumulate in the soils near the emissions source; and persistent synthetic chemicals, such as dioxin and PCBs (polychlorinated biphenyls).

Pollutants for which the environment has some absorptive capacity are called *fund pollutants*. For these pollutants, as long as the emissions rate does not exceed the absorptive capacity of the environment, the pollutants do not accumulate. Examples of fund pollutants are easy to find. Many organic pollutants injected into an oxygen-rich stream will be transformed by the resident bacteria into less-harmful inorganic matter. Carbon dioxide is absorbed by plant life and the oceans.

The point is *not* that the mass is destroyed; the law of conservation of mass suggests this cannot be the case. Rather, when fund pollutants are injected into the air or water, they may be transformed into substances that are not considered harmful to people or to the ecological system, or they may be so diluted or dispersed that the resulting concentrations are not harmful.

Pollutants can also be classified by their zone of influence, defined both horizontally and vertically. The horizontal dimension deals with the spatial domain over which damage from an emitted pollutant is experienced. The damage caused by *local* pollutants is experienced near the source of emission, while the damage from *regional* pollutants is experienced at greater distances from the source of emission. The limiting case is a *global* pollutant, where the damage affects the entire planet. The categories are not mutually exclusive; it is possible for a pollutant to be in more than one category. Sulfur oxides and nitrogen oxides, for example, are both local and regional pollutants.

The vertical zone of influence describes whether the damage is caused mainly by ground-level concentrations of an air pollutant or by concentrations in the upper atmosphere. For some pollutants, such as lead or particulates, the damage is determined mainly by concentrations

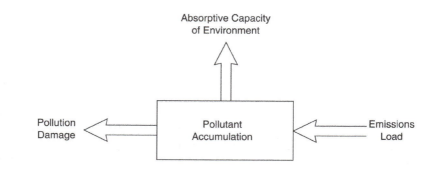

Figure 5.1 Relationship between Emissions and Pollution Damage

of the pollutant near the earth's surface. For others, such as ozone-depleting substances or greenhouse gases (described in Chapter 8), the damage is related more to their concentrations in the upper atmosphere. This taxonomy will prove useful in designing policy responses to these various types of pollution problems. Each type of pollutant requires a unique policy response. The failure to recognize these distinctions leads to counterproductive policy.

Defining the Efficient Allocation of Pollution

Pollutants are the residuals of production and consumption. These residuals must eventually be recycled or returned to the environment in one form or another. Since their presence in the environment may depreciate the service flows received, an efficient allocation of resources must take this cost into account. What is meant by the efficient allocation of pollution depends on the nature of the pollutant.

Stock Pollutants

The efficient allocation of a stock pollutant must take into account the fact that the pollutant accumulates in the environment over time and that the damage caused by its presence increases and persists as the pollutant accumulates. By their very nature, stock pollutants create an interdependency between the present and the future, since the damage imposed in the future depends on current actions.

The damage caused by pollution can take many forms. At high enough exposures to certain pollutants, human health can be adversely impacted, possibly even leading to death. Other living organisms, such as trees or fish, can be harmed as well. Damage can even occur to inanimate objects, as when acid rain causes sculptures to deteriorate or when particulates cause structures to discolor.

It is not hard to establish what is meant by an efficient allocation in these circumstances using the intuition we gained from the discussion of depletable resource models. Suppose, for example, that we consider the allocation of a commodity that we refer to as X. Suppose further that the production of X involves the generation of a proportional amount of a stock pollutant. The amount of this pollution can be reduced, but that takes resources away from the production of X. The damage caused by the presence of this pollutant in the environment is further assumed to be proportional to the size of the accumulated stock. As long as the stock of pollutants remains in the environment, the damage persists.

The dynamic efficient allocation, by definition, is the one that maximizes the present value of the net benefit. In this case the net benefit at any point in time, t, is equal to the benefit received from the consumption of X minus the cost of the damage caused by the presence of the stock pollutant in the environment.

This damage is a cost that society must bear, and in terms of its effect on the efficient allocation, this cost is not unlike that associated with extracting minerals or fuels. While for minerals the extraction cost rises with the cumulative amount of the depletable resource extracted, the damage cost associated with a stock pollutant rises with the cumulative amount deposited in the environment. The accretion of the stock pollutant is proportional to the production of X, which creates the same kind of linkage between the production of X and this pollution cost as exists between the extraction cost and the production of a mineral. They both rise over time with the cumulative amount produced. The one major difference is that the extraction cost is borne only at the time of extraction, while damage persists as long as the stock pollutant remains in the environment.

Exactly the same pattern would emerge for a commodity that is produced jointly with a stock pollutant. The efficient quantity of X (and therefore, the addition to the accumulation of this pollutant in the environment) would decline over time as the marginal cost of the damage rises. The price of X would rise over time, reflecting the rising social cost of production. To cope with the increasing marginal damage, the amount of resources committed to controlling the pollutant would increase over time. Ultimately, a steady state would be reached where additions to the amount of the pollutant in the environment would cease and the size of the pollutant stock would stabilize. At this point, all further emission of the pollutant created by the production of X would be controlled (perhaps through recycling). The price of X and the quantity consumed would remain constant. The damage caused by the stock pollutant would persist.

Technological progress could modify this efficient allocation. Specifically, technological progress could reduce the amount of pollutant generated per unit of X produced; it could create ways to recycle the stock pollutant rather than injecting it into the environment; or it could develop ways of rendering the pollutant less harmful. All of these responses would lower the marginal damage cost associated with a given level of production of X. Therefore, more of X could be produced with technological progress than without it.

Stock pollutants are, in a sense, the other side of the intergenerational equity coin from depletable resources. With depletable resources, it is possible for current generations to create a burden for future generations by using up resources, thereby diminishing the remaining endowment. Stock pollutants can create a burden for future generations by passing on damages that persist well after the benefits received from incurring the damages have been forgotten. Though neither of these situations automatically violates the weak sustainability criterion, they don't automatically satisfy it either.

Fund Pollutants

To the extent that the emission of fund pollutants exceeds the assimilative capacity of the environment, they accumulate and share some of the characteristics of stock pollutants. When the emissions rate is low enough, however, the discharges can be assimilated by the environment, with the result that the link between present emissions and future damage may be broken.

When this happens, current emissions cause current damage, and future emissions cause future damage, but the level of future damage is independent of current emissions. This independence of allocations among time periods allows us to explore the efficient allocation of fund pollutants using the concept of static, rather than dynamic, efficiency. Because the static concept is simpler, this affords us the opportunity to incorporate more dimensions of the problem without unnecessarily complicating the analysis.

The normal starting point for the analysis would be to maximize the net benefit from the waste flows. However, pollution is more easily understood if we deal with a mathematically equivalent formulation involving the minimization of two rather different types of costs: damage costs and control or avoidance costs.

To examine the efficient allocation graphically, we need to know something about how control costs vary with the degree of control and how the damages vary with the amount of pollution emitted. Though our knowledge in these areas is far from complete, economists normally agree on the shapes of these relationships.

Generally, the marginal damage caused by a unit of pollution increases with the amount emitted. When small amounts of the pollutant are emitted, the incremental damage is quite small. However, when large amounts are emitted, the marginal unit can cause significantly more damage. It is not hard to understand why. Small amounts of pollution are easily diluted in the environment, and the body can tolerate small quantities of substances. However, as the amount in the atmosphere increases, dilution is less effective and the body is less tolerant.

Marginal control costs commonly increase with the amount controlled. For example, suppose a source of pollution tries to cut down on its particulate emissions by purchasing an electrostatic precipitator that captures 80 percent of the particulates as they flow past in the stack. If the source wants further control, it can purchase another precipitator and place it in the stack above the first one. This second precipitator captures 80 percent of the remaining 20 percent, or 16 percent of the uncontrolled emissions. Thus, the first precipitator would achieve an 80 percent reduction from uncontrolled emissions, while the second precipitator, which costs the same as the first, would achieve only a further 16 percent reduction. Obviously each unit of emissions reduction by the second precipitator costs more than by the first.

In Figure 5.2 we use these two pieces of information on the shapes of the relevant curves to derive the efficient allocation. A movement from right to left refers to greater control and less pollution emitted. The efficient allocation is represented by Q^*, the point at which the damage caused by the marginal unit of pollution is exactly equal to the marginal cost of avoiding it.[1]

Greater degrees of control (points to the left of Q^*) are inefficient because the further increase in avoidance costs would exceed the reduction in damages. Hence, total costs would rise. Similarly, levels of control lower than Q^* would result in a lower cost of control but the increase in damage costs would be even larger, yielding an increase in total cost. Increasing or decreasing the amount controlled causes an increase in total costs. Hence, Q^* must be efficient.

The diagram suggests that under the conditions presented, the optimal level of pollution is not zero. If you find this disturbing, remember that we confront this principle every day. Take the damage caused by automobile accidents, for example. Obviously, a considerable

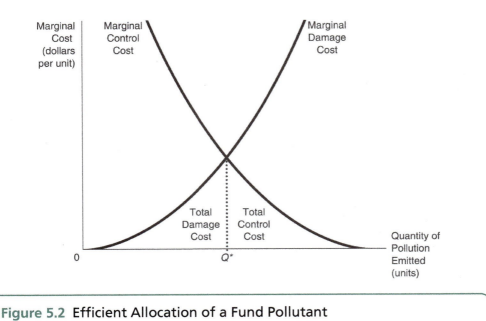

Figure 5.2 Efficient Allocation of a Fund Pollutant

amount of damage is caused by automobile accidents, yet we do not reduce that damage to zero because the cost of doing so would be too high.

The point is *not* that we do not know how to stop automobile accidents. All we would have to do is eliminate automobiles! Rather, the point is that since we value the benefits of automobiles, we take steps to reduce accidents (such as using speed limits) only to the extent that the costs of accident reduction are commensurate with the damage reduction achieved. The efficient level of automobile accidents is not zero.

The second point is that in some circumstances the optimal level of pollution *may* be zero, or close to it. This situation occurs when the damage caused by even the first unit of pollution is so severe that it is higher than the marginal cost of controlling it. This would be reflected in Figure 5.2 as a leftward shift of the damage cost curve of sufficient magnitude that its intersection with the vertical axis would lie above the point where the marginal cost curve intersects the vertical axis. This circumstance seems to characterize the treatment of highly dangerous radioactive pollutants such as plutonium.

Additional insights are easily derived from our characterization of the efficient allocation. For example, it should be clear from Figure 5.2 that the optimal level of pollution generally is not the same for all parts of the country. Areas that have higher population levels or are particularly sensitive to pollution would have a marginal damage cost curve that intersected the marginal control cost curve close to the vertical axis. Efficiency would imply lower levels of pollution for those areas. Areas that have lower population levels or are less sensitive should have higher efficient levels of pollution.

Examples of ecological sensitivity are not hard to find. For instance, some areas are less sensitive to acid rain than others because the local geological strata neutralize moderate amounts of the acid. Thus, the marginal damage caused by a unit of acid rain is lower in those fortunate regions than in other, less tolerant regions. It can also be argued that pollutants affecting visibility are more damaging in national parks and other areas where visibility is an important part of the aesthetic experience than in other more industrial areas.

Market Allocation of Pollution

Since air and water are treated in our legal system as common-pool resources, at this point in the book it should surprise no one that the market misallocates them. Our previously derived conclusion that free-access resources are overexploited certainly also applies here. Air and water resources have been overexploited as waste repositories. However, this conclusion only scratches the surface; much more can be learned about market allocations of pollution.

When firms create products, rarely does the process of converting raw material into outputs use 100 percent of the mass. The typical firm has several alternatives to control the amount of the residual. It can use inputs more completely so that less is left over. It can also produce less output, so that smaller amounts of the residual are generated. Recycling the residual is sometimes a viable option, as is removing the most damaging components of the waste stream and disposing of the rest.

Pollutant damages are commonly externalities to the firms that produce them.[2] When pollutants are injected into water bodies or the atmosphere, they cause damages to those firms and consumers (as well as to flora and fauna) downstream or downwind of the source, not to the source itself. These costs are typically *not* borne by the emitting source and hence not considered by it, although they certainly are borne by society at large.[3] As with other services that are systematically undervalued, the disposal of wastes into the air or water becomes inefficiently attractive. In this case the firm minimizes its costs when it chooses not to abate anything, since the only costs it bears are the control costs. What is cheapest for the firm is not cheapest for society.

In the case of stock pollutants, the problem is particularly severe. Uncontrolled markets would lead to an excessive production of the product that generates the pollution, too few resources committed to pollution control, and an inefficiently large amount of the stock pollutant in the environment. Thus, the burden on future generations caused by the presence of this pollutant would be inefficiently large.

The inefficiencies associated with pollution control and the previously discussed inefficiencies associated with the extraction or production of minerals, energy, and food exhibit some rather important differences. For private property resources, the market forces provide automatic signals of impending scarcity. These forces may be understated (as when the vulnerability of imports is ignored), but they operate in the correct direction. Even when some resources are treated as open-access (fisheries), the possibility for a private property alternative (fish farming) is enhanced. When private property and open-access resources sell in the same market, the private property owner tends to ameliorate the excesses of those who exploit open-access properties. Efficient firms are rewarded with higher profits.

With pollution, no comparable automatic amelioration mechanism is evident.[4] Because this cost is borne partially by innocent victims rather than producers, it does not find its way into product prices. Firms that attempt unilaterally to control their pollution are placed at a competitive disadvantage; due to the added expense, their costs of production are higher than those of their less conscientious competitors. Not only does the unimpeded market fail to generate the efficient level of pollution control, but also it penalizes those firms that might attempt to control an efficient amount. Hence, the case for some sort of government intervention is particularly strong for pollution control.

Efficient Policy Responses

Our use of the efficiency criterion has helped demonstrate why markets fail to produce an efficient level of pollution control as well as trace out the effects of this less-than-optimal degree of control on the markets for related commodities. It can also be used to define efficient policy responses.

In Figure 5.2 we demonstrated that, for a market as a whole, efficiency is achieved when the marginal cost of control is equal to the marginal damage caused by the pollution. This same principle applies to each emitter. Each emitter should control its pollution until the marginal cost of controlling the last unit is equal to the marginal damage it causes. One way to achieve this outcome would be to impose a legal limit on the amount of pollution allowed by each emitter. If the limit were chosen precisely at the level of emission where marginal control cost equaled the marginal damage, efficiency would have been achieved for that emitter.

An alternative approach would be to internalize the marginal damage caused by each unit of emissions by means of a tax or charge on each unit of emissions. Either this per-unit charge could increase with the level of pollution (following the marginal damage curve for each succeeding unit of emission) or the tax rate could be constant as long as the rate were equal to the marginal social damage at the point where the marginal social damage and marginal control costs cross (see Figure 5.2). Since the emitter is paying the marginal social damage when confronted by these fees, pollution costs would be internalized. The efficient choice would also be the cost-minimizing choice for the emitter.[5]

While the efficient levels of these policy instruments can be easily defined in principle, they are very difficult to implement in practice. To implement either of these policy instruments, we must know the level of emissions at which the two marginal cost curves cross for every emitter. That is a tall order, one that imposes an unrealistically high information burden on control authorities. Control authorities typically have very poor information on control costs and little reliable information on marginal damage functions.

How can environmental authorities allocate pollution control responsibility in a reasonable manner when the information burdens are apparently so unrealistically large? One approach, the choice of several countries including the United States, is to select specific legal levels of pollution based on some other criterion, such as providing adequate margins of safety for human or ecological health. Once these thresholds have been established by whatever means, only half of the problem has been resolved. The other half deals with deciding how to allocate the responsibility for meeting predetermined pollution levels among the large numbers of emitters.

This is precisely where the cost-effectiveness criterion comes in. Once the objective is stated in terms of meeting the predetermined pollution level at minimum cost, it is possible to derive the conditions that any cost-effective allocation of the responsibility must satisfy. These conditions can then be used as a basis for choosing among various kinds of policy instruments that impose more reasonable information burdens on control authorities.

Cost-Effective Policies for Uniformly Mixed Fund Pollutants

Defining a Cost-Effective Allocation

We begin our analysis with uniformly mixed fund pollutants, which analytically are the easiest to deal with. The damage caused by these pollutants depends simply on the amount entering the atmosphere. Thus, the policy can focus simply on controlling the total amount of emissions in a manner that minimizes the cost of control. What can we say about the cost-effective allocation of control responsibility for uniformly mixed fund pollutants?

Consider a simple example. Assume that two emissions sources are currently emitting 15 units each for a total 30 units. Assume further that the control authority determines that the environment can assimilate 15 units in total, so that a reduction of 15 units is necessary. How should this 15-unit reduction be allocated between the two sources in order to minimize the total cost of the reduction?

We can demonstrate the answer with the aid of Figure 5.3, which is drawn by measuring the marginal cost of control for the first source from the left-hand axis (MC_1) and the marginal cost of control for the second source from the right-hand axis (MC_2). Note that a total 15-unit reduction is achieved for every point on this graph; each point represents some different combination of reduction by the two sources that sums to 15. Drawn in this manner, the diagram represents all possible allocations of the 15-unit reduction between the two sources. The left-hand axis, for example, represents an allocation of the entire reduction to the second source, while the right-hand axis represents a situation in which the first source bears the entire responsibility. All points in between represent different degrees of shared responsibility. What allocation minimizes the cost of control?

In the cost-effective allocation, the first source cleans up ten units, while the second source cleans up five units. The total variable cost of control for this particular assignment of the responsibility for the reduction is represented by area A plus area B. Area A is the cost of control for the first source; area B is the cost of control for the second. Any other allocation would result in a higher total control cost. (Convince yourself that this is true.)

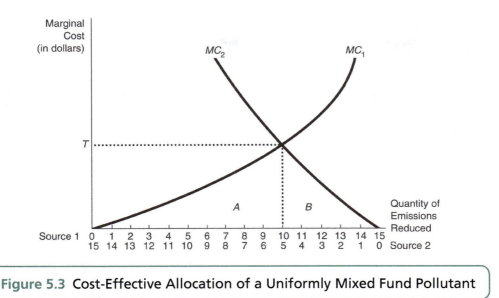

Figure 5.3 Cost-Effective Allocation of a Uniformly Mixed Fund Pollutant

Figure 5.3 also demonstrates the cost-effectiveness equimarginal principle introduced in Chapter 3. *The cost of achieving a given reduction in emissions will be minimized if and only if the marginal costs of control are equalized for all emitters.*[6] This is demonstrated by the fact that the marginal cost curves cross at the cost-effective allocation.

Cost-Effective Pollution Control Policies

This proposition can be used as a basis for choosing among the various policy instruments that the control authority might use to achieve this allocation. Sources have a large menu of options for controlling the amount of pollution they inject into the environment. The cheapest method of control will differ widely not only among industries but also among plants in the same industry. The selection of the cheapest method requires detailed information on the possible control techniques and their associated costs.

Generally, plant managers are able to acquire this information for their plants when it is in their interest to do so. However, the government authorities responsible for meeting pollution targets are not likely to have this information. Since the degree to which these plants would be regulated depends on cost information, it is unrealistic to expect these plant managers to transfer unbiased information to the government. Plant managers would have a strong incentive to overstate control costs in hopes of reducing their ultimate control burden.

This situation poses a difficult dilemma for control authorities. The cost of incorrectly assigning the control responsibility among various polluters is likely to be large. Yet the control authorities do not have sufficient information at their disposal to make a correct allocation. Those who have the information—the plant managers—are not inclined to share it. Can the cost-effective allocation be found? The answer depends on the approach taken by the control authority.

Emissions Standards. We start our investigation of this question by supposing that the control authority pursues a traditional legal approach by imposing a separate emissions limit on each source. In the economics literature this approach is referred to as the "command-and-control" approach. An *emissions standard* is a legal limit on the amount of the pollutant an individual source is allowed to emit. In our example it is clear that the two standards should add up to the allowable 15 units, but it is not clear how, in the absence of information on control costs, these 15 units are to be allocated between the two sources.

The easiest method of resolving this dilemma—and the one chosen in the earliest days of pollution control—would be simply to allocate each source an equal reduction. As is clear from Figure 5.3, this strategy would not be cost-effective. While the first source would have lower costs compared to the cost-effective allocation, this cost reduction would be substantially smaller than the cost increase faced by the second source. Compared to a cost-effective allocation, total costs would increase if both sources were forced to clean up the same amount.

When emissions standards are the policy of choice, there is no reason to believe that the authority will assign the responsibility for emissions reduction in a cost-minimizing way. This is probably not surprising. Who would have believed otherwise?

Surprisingly enough, however, some policy instruments do allow the authority to allocate the emissions reduction in a cost-effective manner even when it has no information on the magnitude of control costs. These policy approaches rely on economic incentives to produce the desired outcome. The two most common approaches are known as emissions charges and emissions trading.

Emissions Charges. An *emissions charge* is a fee, collected by the government, levied on each unit of pollutant emitted into the air or water. The total payment any source would make to the government could be found by multiplying the fee times the amount of pollution emitted. Emissions charges reduce pollution because paying the fees costs the firm money. To save money, the source seeks ways to reduce its pollution.

How much pollution control would the firm choose? A profit-maximizing firm would control, rather than emit, pollution whenever it proved cheaper to do so. We can illustrate the firm's decision with Figure 5.4. The level of uncontrolled emission is 15 units and the emissions charge is *T*. Thus, if the firm were to decide against controlling any emissions, it would have to pay *T* times 15, represented by area 0*TBC*.

Is this the best the firm can do? Obviously not, since it can control some pollution at a lower cost than paying the emissions charge. It would pay the firm to reduce emissions until the marginal cost of reduction is equal to the emissions charge. After that point it is cheaper

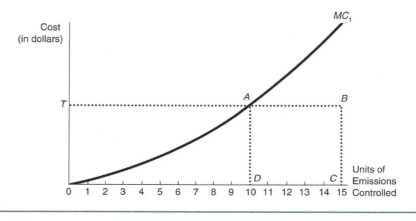

Figure 5.4 Cost-Minimizing Control of Pollution with an Emissions Charge

for the firm to pay the tax since the marginal cost curve rises above the tax. The firm would minimize its cost by choosing to clean up ten units of pollution and to emit five units. At this allocation the firm would pay control costs equal to area $0AD$ and total emissions charge payments equal to area $ABCD$ for a total cost of $0ABC$. This is clearly less than $0TBC$, the amount the firm would pay if it chose not to clean up any pollution.

Let's carry this one step further. Suppose that we levied the same emissions charge on both sources discussed in Figure 5.3. Each source would then control its emissions until its marginal control cost equaled the emissions charge. (Faced with an emissions charge T, the second source would clean up five units.) Since they both face the same emissions charge, they will *independently* choose levels of control consistent with equal marginal control costs. This is precisely the condition that yields a cost-minimizing allocation.

This is a remarkable finding. We have shown that as long as the control authority imposes the same emissions charge on all sources, the resulting incentives are *automatically* compatible with minimizing the costs of achieving that level of control. This is true in spite of the fact that the control authority may not have sufficient knowledge of control costs.

However, we have not yet dealt with the issue of how the appropriate level of the emissions charge is determined. Each level of a charge will result in *some* level of emissions reduction. Furthermore, as long as each firm minimizes its own costs, the responsibility for meeting that reduction will be allocated in a manner that minimizes control costs for all firms. How high should the charge be set to ensure that the resulting emissions reduction is the *desired* level of emissions reduction?

Without having the requisite information on control costs, the control authority cannot establish the correct tax rate on the first try. It is possible, however, to develop an iterative, trial-and-error process to find the appropriate charge rate. This process is initiated by choosing an arbitrary charge rate and observing the amount of reduction that occurs when that charge is imposed. If the observed reduction is larger than desired, it means the charge should be lowered; if the reduction is smaller, the charge should be raised. The new reduction that results from the adjusted charge can then be observed and compared with the desired reduction. Further adjustments in the charge can be made as needed. This process can be repeated until the actual and desired reductions are equal. At that point the correct emissions charge would have been found.

The charge system not only causes cost-minimizing sources to choose a cost-effective allocation of the control responsibility, it also stimulates the development of newer, cheaper means of controlling emissions, as well as promoting technological progress. This is illustrated in Figure 5.5.

The reason for this is rather straightforward. Control authorities base the emissions standards on specific technologies. As new technologies are discovered by the control authority, the standards are tightened. These stricter standards force firms to bear higher costs. Therefore, with emissions standards, firms have an incentive to hide technological changes from the control authority.

With an emissions charge system, the firm saves money by adopting cheaper new technologies. As long as the firm can reduce its pollution at a marginal cost lower than T, it pays to adopt the new technology. In Figure 5.5 MC^0 represents the MC before the new technology is adopted and MC^1 is the new lower marginal cost with the adoption of the new technology. The firm saves A and B by adopting the new technology and voluntarily increases its emissions reduction from Q^0 to Q^1.

With an emissions charge, the minimum cost allocation of meeting a predetermined emissions reduction can be found by a control authority even when it has insufficient information on control costs. An emissions charge also stimulates technological advances in

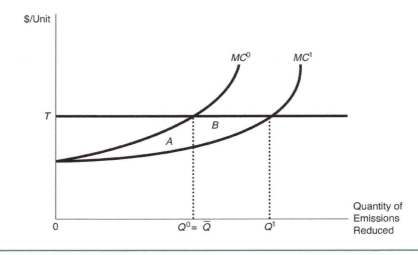

Figure 5.5 Cost Savings from Technological Change: Charges versus Standards

emissions reduction. Unfortunately, the process for finding the appropriate rate takes some experimenting. During the trial-and-error period of finding the appropriate rate, sources would be faced with a volatile emissions charge. Emissions charges that kept changing in the search for the right level would make planning for the future difficult for the firms subject to that charge. Investments that would make sense under a high emissions charge might not make sense when it falls. From either a policymaker's or business manager's perspective, this process leaves much to be desired.

Cap-and-Trade. Is it possible for the control authority to find the cost-minimizing allocation without going through a trial-and-error process? It is possible if cap-and-trade (a form of emissions trading) is the chosen policy. Under this system, all sources face a collective limit on their emissions (the cap) and they are allocated (or sold) allowances to emit. Each allowance authorizes a specific amount of emissions (commonly 1 ton). The control authority issues exactly the total number of allowances needed to produce the desired emissions level. These can be distributed among the firms either by auctioning them off to the highest bidder or by granting them directly to firms free of charge (an allocation referred to as "gifting"). However they are acquired, the allowances are freely transferable; they can be bought and sold. Firms emitting more than their holdings would buy additional allowances from firms who are emitting less than authorized. Any emissions by a source in excess of those allowed by its allowance holdings at the end of the year would cause the source to face severe monetary sanctions.

Why this system automatically leads to a cost-effective allocation can be seen in Figure 5.6. This figure treats the same set of circumstances as in Figure 5.3. Consider first the gifting alternative. Suppose that the first source was allocated seven allowances (each corresponds to one emission unit). Because it has 15 units of uncontrolled emissions, this would mean it must control eight units. Similarly, suppose that the second source was granted the remaining eight allowances. It would have to clean up seven units. Notice that both firms have an incentive to trade. The marginal cost of control for the second source (*C*) is substantially higher than

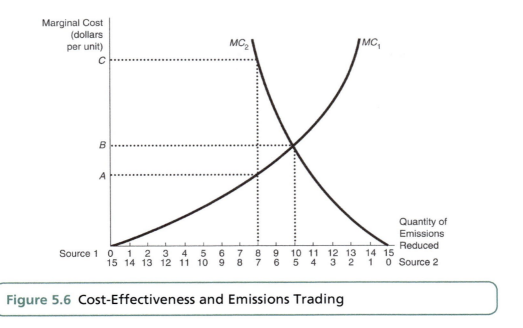

Figure 5.6 Cost-Effectiveness and Emissions Trading

that for the first (A). The second source could lower its cost if it could buy an allowance from the first source at a price lower than C. Meanwhile, the first source would be better off if it could sell an allowance for a price higher than A. Because C is greater than A, grounds for trade certainly exist.

A transfer of allowances would take place until the first source had only five allowances left (and controlled ten units), while the second source had ten allowances (and controlled five units). At this point, the allowance price would equal B, because that is the marginal value of that allowance to both sources, and neither source would have any incentive to trade further. The allowance market would be in equilibrium.

Notice that the market equilibrium for an emission-allowance system is the cost-effective allocation! Simply by issuing the appropriate number of allowances (15) and letting the market do the rest, the control authority can achieve a cost-effective allocation without having even the slightest knowledge about control costs. This system allows the government to meet its policy objective, while allowing greater flexibility in how that objective is met.

How would this equilibrium change if the allowances were auctioned off? Interestingly, it wouldn't; both allocation methods lead to the same result. With an auction, the allowance price that clears demand and supply is B, and we have already demonstrated that B supports a cost-effective equilibrium.

The incentives created by this system ensure that sources use this flexibility to achieve the objective at the lowest possible cost. As we shall see in the next two chapters, this remarkable property has been responsible for the prominence of this type of approach in current attempts to reform the regulatory process.

How far can the reforms go? Can developing countries use the experience of the industrialized countries to move directly into using these market-based instruments to control pollution?

As Debate 5.1 points out, that may be easier said than done.

DEBATE 5.1

Should Developing Countries Rely on Market-Based Instruments to Control Pollution?

Since the case for using market-based instruments seems so strong in principle, some observers have suggested that developing countries should capitalize on the experience of the industrialized countries to move directly to market-based instruments (such as emissions charges or cap-and-trade) to control pollution. The desirability of this strategy is seen as flowing from the level of poverty in developing countries; abating pollution in the least expensive manner would seem especially important to poorer nations. Furthermore, since developing countries are frequently also starved for revenue, revenue-generating instruments (such as emissions charges or auctioned allowances) would seem especially useful. Proponents also point out that a number of developing countries already use market-based instruments.

Another school of thought suggests that the differences in infrastructure between the developing and industrialized countries make the transfer of lessons from one context to another fraught with peril. To illustrate their more general point, they note that the effectiveness of market-based instruments presumes an effective monitoring and enforcement system, something that is frequently not present in developing countries. In its absence, the superiority of market-based instruments is much less obvious.

Some middle ground is clearly emerging. Those who are skeptical do not argue that market-based instruments should never be used in developing countries, but rather that they may not be as universally appropriate as the most enthusiastic proponents seem to suggest. They see themselves as telling a cautionary tale. And proponents are certainly beginning to see the crucial importance of infrastructure. Recognizing that some developing countries may be much better suited (by virtue of their infrastructure) to implement market-based systems than others, proponents are beginning to see capacity building as a logical prior step for those countries that need it.

For market-based instruments, as well as for other aspects of life, if it looks too good to be true, it probably is.

Sources: World Bank. (2000). *Greening Industry: New Roles for Communities, Markets and Governments.* Washington, DC: World Bank and Oxford University Press; Russell, C. S., & Vaughan, W. J. (2003). The choice of pollution control policy instruments in developing countries: Arguments, evidence and suggestions. In H. Folmer & T. Tietenberg (Eds.), *The International Yearbook of Environmental and Resource Economics 2003/2004.* Cheltenham, UK: Edward Elgar, 331–371.

Other Policy Dimensions

Two main pollution control policy instruments rely on economic incentives—charges and cap-and-trade. Both of these allow the control authority to distribute the responsibility for control in a cost-effective manner. The major difference between them we have discussed so far is that the appropriate charge can be determined only by an iterative trial-and-error process over time, whereas for the cap-and-trade approach the allowance price can be determined immediately by the market. Can other differences be identified? As it turns out, yes.

The Revenue Effect

One of the differentiating characteristics of these instruments is their ability to raise revenue. Environmental taxes and auctioned allowances raise revenue, but cap-and-trade programs that gift the allowances to users free of charge do not. Does this difference matter?

It does, for at least two reasons.[7] First, a number of authors (Parry & Bento, 2000; Bovenberg & Goulder, 1996; Goulder, 1997; Parry, 1995) have noted that the revenue from environmental taxes or auctioned transferable allowances could be substituted for the revenue from distortionary taxes, thereby reducing those taxes and their associated distortions. When this substitution is made, the calculations indicate that it allows an increase in the present value of net benefits from the application of this instrument, an effect that has been called the "double dividend." This effect creates a preference for instruments that can raise revenue as long as both the implementation of a revenue-raising instrument and the use of this revenue to reduce distortionary taxes are politically feasible.

The second important consideration is that the revenue from taxes or auctions could be used to reduce the burden on low-income households. The empirical evidence suggests that gifting allowances produces a regressive distribution of the control burden. (A regressive distribution is one that places a higher relative cost burden on low-income households or individuals as a percentage of their income.) That same evidence has also demonstrated that when the revenue from auctions or taxes is targeted appropriately, the regressiveness of the policy can be eliminated.

A final consequence of raising revenues involves their political feasibility. It seems quite clear that, until 2008, using a free-distribution ("gifting") approach for the initial allocation of allowances was a necessary ingredient to build the necessary political support for cap-and-trade legislation to be implemented (Raymond, 2003). Existing users frequently have the power to block implementation, while potential future users do not. This made it politically expedient to allocate a substantial part of the economic rent from these resources to existing users as the price of securing their support, sometimes in creative ways (see Example 5.1).

While this strategy reduces the adjustment costs to existing users, generally it raises them for new users. Interestingly in the climate change case, the empirical evidence suggests that only a small fraction of the total revenue would be needed to assure that the profits of carbon suppliers would be unchanged by a switch to a revenue raising approach (Bovenberg & Goulder, 2002). Gifting all allowances therefore may not be inevitable in principle, even if political feasibility considerations affect the design.

While the earliest programs gifted the allowances to large emitters, later programs have tended to rely more on auctions. On January 1, 2009, the historic tendency to "gift" allowances changed with the implementation of the Regional Greenhouse Gas Initiative (RGGI) in nine Northeastern states, from Maryland to Maine. This cap-and-trade program covers CO_2 emissions from large fossil fuel-fired electricity-generating plants.

A number of RGGI states have chosen to auction nearly 100 percent of these allowances, using a sealed-bid system, with the revenue returned to the states. Most states have chosen to use the revenue to promote energy efficiency (see Example 5.2), although two states—New York and New Hampshire—chose to siphon off some of the money for budget relief. New Jersey also pursued this latter option and subsequently dropped out of RGGI.

EXAMPLE 5.1

The Swedish Nitrogen Oxide Charge

One of the dilemmas facing those who wish to use charges to control pollution is that the amounts of revenue extracted from those subject to the tax can be considerable and that additional expense can produce a lot of political resistance to the policy. This resistance can be lowered if the revenue is rebated to those who pay it. However if all firms know they are getting their money back, the economic incentive to limit emissions is lost. Is it possible to design a system of rebates that will promote political feasibility without undermining abatement incentives?

The Swedish nitrogen oxide charge was designed specifically to resolve this dilemma. It was first imposed in 1992 on large energy sources. Some 120 heating plants and industrial facilities with about 180 boilers were subject to the tax.

It was intended from the beginning to have a significant incentive effect, not to raise revenue. Although the charge rate is high by international standards (thereby producing an effective economic incentive), the revenue from this tax is not retained by the government, but rather is rebated to the emitting sources (thereby lowering resistance to the policy by the regulated sources).

It is the form of this rebate that makes this an interesting scheme. While the tax is collected on the basis of *emissions*, it is rebated on the basis of *energy production*. In effect, this system rewards plants that emit little nitrogen oxide per unit of energy and penalizes plants that emit more per unit of energy. Designed in this way it provides incentives to reduce emissions per unit of energy produced.

As expected, emissions per unit of energy produced fell rather dramatically. Over the period from 1992 to 2007, the plants were able to reduce the amount of emissions per unit of input energy by 67 percent. According to one study (OECD, 2010) there were three main explanations for this:

- Cumulative energy output produced by the plants increased by 74 percent over the period. The expansion in output mostly took place in plants that were relatively emission-efficient.
- Regulated plants invested in NOx mitigation and were therefore able to produce more energy output with fewer emissions.
- Innovations in mitigation technology made it possible to reach even lower emission intensity levels for the same output level.

Note, however, that rebating the revenue means that this tax cannot produce a double dividend.

Sources: Organisation for Economic Co-operation and Development. (2013). The Swedish tax on nitrogen oxide emissions: Lessons in environmental policy reform. OECD Environment Policy Paper No. 2; OECD. (2010). *Innovation Impacts of the Swedish NOx Charge*. Paris: OECD. Available at www.oecd.org/greengrowth/consumption-innovation/43211635.pdf.

Using the revenue from auctions to promote investment in energy efficiency reduces the cost of meeting the carbon targets. Costs are reduced not only because less energy is used (and hence less carbon emitted), but also because the lower demand for energy lowers the price not only of the allowances, but of electricity too. (Can you see why?)

It would be hard to overemphasize what a departure from the previous norm this venture into auctioning represents. Allowing emitters to pollute up to the emissions standard without paying for the right to pollute (the traditional approach) implies that emitters have an implicit property right to pollute already; they don't have to buy it.

A cap-and-trade program with allowance auctions implies, in contrast, that the atmosphere is held in trust for the community. Institutions that use the atmosphere for emissions must therefore pay to acquire that scarce right. Notice that this understanding of who actually holds the property right to the atmosphere completely changes the lens through which this regulation is viewed.

EXAMPLE 5.2

RGGI Revenue: The Maine Example

The revenue received by Maine from the quarterly RGGI auctions is received by Efficiency Maine (EM), a specially created, quasi-independent organization. The enabling statute requires EM to spend most of the RGGI funds on energy efficiency measures such as more efficient lighting, motors, heating, and air conditioning, as well as on building weatherization.

For large customers such as paper mills, the money is allocated in response to applications from the large customers for specific projects. These are evaluated on the basis of the amount of kilowatt-hours reduced (for electricity) or tons of CO_2 reduced (for fossil fuels) *per EM dollar expended*. (Notice how focusing on public dollars, as opposed to the sum of public and private dollars, provides an incentive for cost sharing on the part of companies—putting more of their own money and less public money into the project raises the ratio of the savings per EM dollar and, hence, increases the likelihood of success of their proposed funding request.)

To be funded, all proposals must also pass a benefit-cost test to assure the resources are being used efficiently. EM's 2016 annual report notes that the FY2016 benefit-cost ratios for these large customers were 3.26 for the electric programs and 3.16 for the thermal programs. The comparable numbers for all EM programs were respectively 2.63 and 1.89.

The investments in energy efficiency incentivized by these funds have been very cost-effective. The data demonstrate that at the margin saving energy is cheaper than buying it. In other words investing in energy savings actually lowers energy costs. Lower energy costs have made participating Maine firms more cost competitive and have saved jobs and bolstered the local economy, while reducing emissions of one of the gases that contributes to climate change.

Sources: The Regional Greenhouse Gas Initiative auction results website: www.rggi.org/market/co2_auctions/results#state_proceeds (accessed June 19, 2017); Acadia Center. (2016). Regional greenhouse gas initiative status report: Part I—measuring success. Available at: http://acadiacenter.org/document/measuring-rggi-success/ (accessed June 19, 2017); Efficiency Maine (EM). (2016). *FY2016 Annual Report*. Available at: www.efficiencymaine.com/docs/FY2016-Annual-Report.pdf (accessed June 19, 2017).

Responses to Changes in the Regulatory Environment

One major additional difference between charges and allowances concerns the manner in which these two systems react to changes in external circumstances in the absence of further decisions by the control authority. This is an important consideration, because bureaucratic procedures are notoriously sluggish and changes in policies are usually rendered slowly.[8] We consider three such circumstances: growth in the number of sources, inflation, and technological progress.

If the number of sources were to increase in a cap-and-trade program, the demand for allowances would shift to the right. Given a fixed supply of allowances, the price would rise, as would the control costs, but the amount of emissions would remain the same. If charges were being used, in the absence of additional action by the control authority the charge level would remain the same. This implies that the amount the existing sources would control would be unchanged by the growth. Therefore, the arrival of new sources would cause a deterioration of air or water quality in the region due to the added emissions by the new sources. The costs of abatement would rise, since the costs of control paid by the new sources must be considered, but by a lesser amount than with cap-and-trade, because of the lower amount of pollution being controlled. If the economy is growing, the allowance system ensures that emissions will not rise.

Inflation in the cost of control would automatically result in higher allowance prices in a cap-and-trade program, but with a charge system it would result in lower control. Essentially, the real charge (the nominal charge adjusted for inflation) declines with inflation if the nominal charge remains the same.

We should not, however, conclude that over time, charges always result in less control than allowances. Suppose, for example, technological progress in designing pollution control equipment were to cause the marginal cost of abatement to fall. With cap-and-trade this would result in lower prices and lower abatement costs, but the same aggregate degree of control. With a charge system, the amount controlled would actually increase (see Figure 5.5) and, therefore, would result in more control than a cap-and-trade program that, prior to the fall in costs, controlled the same amount.

Instrument Choice under Uncertainty

Another major difference between allowances and charges involves the cost of being wrong. Suppose that we have very imprecise information on damages caused and avoidance costs incurred by various levels of pollution and yet we have to choose either a charge level or an allowance level and live with it. What can be said about the relative merits of allowances versus charges in the face of this uncertainty?

The answer depends on the circumstances. Allowances offer a greater amount of certainty about the quantity of emissions, while charges confer more certainty about the marginal cost of control. Allowance markets allow an aggregate emissions standard to be met with certainty, but they offer less certainty about marginal costs. When the objective is to minimize total costs (the sum of damage cost and control costs), allowances would be preferred when the costs of being wrong are more sensitive to changes in the quantity of emissions than to changes in the marginal cost of control. Charges would be preferred when control costs were more important. What circumstances give rise to a preference for one or the other?

When the marginal damage curve is steeply sloped and the marginal cost curve is rather flat, certainty about emissions is more important than certainty over control costs. Smaller deviations of actual emissions from expected emissions can cause a rather large deviation in damage costs, whereas control costs would be relatively insensitive to the degree of control.

Allowances would prevent large fluctuations in these damage costs and therefore would yield a lower cost of being wrong than charges.

Suppose, however, that the marginal control cost curve was steeply sloped, but the marginal damage curve was flat. Small changes in the degree of control would have a large effect on abatement costs but would not affect damages very much. In this case it makes sense to rely on charges to give more precise control over control costs, accepting the less dire consequences from possible fluctuations in damage costs.

Theory is not strong enough to dictate a choice. Empirical studies are necessary to establish a preference for particular situations.

One interesting current application of these insights involves the control of the gases that intensify climate change. As we will see in the next chapters, the shape of the marginal cost curve matters for the choice of policy instrument. For our most complex issue, greenhouse gases, growing scientific evidence suggests that climatic responses to temperature increases may well be highly nonlinear, characterized by thresholds or abrupt changes. This understanding of the science leads to a greater sensitivity of damages to the level of emissions reduction, shifting the preference toward cap-and-trade (Keohane, 2009). These cases suggest that a preference either for allowances or for charges in the face of uncertainty is not universal; it depends on the circumstances.

Summary

In this chapter we developed the conceptual framework needed to evaluate current approaches to pollution control policy. We have explored many different types of pollutants, and found that context matters. Different policy approaches are appropriate for different circumstances.

Stock pollutants pose the most serious intertemporal problems. The efficient production of a commodity that generates a stock pollutant could be expected to decline over time. Theoretically, a point would be reached when all of the pollutant would be recycled. After this point, the amount of the pollutant in the environment would not increase. The amount already accumulated, however, would continue to cause damage perpetually unless some natural process could reduce the amount of the pollutant over time.

The efficient amount of a fund pollutant was defined as the amount that minimizes the sum of damage and control costs. Using this definition, we were able to derive two propositions of interest: (1) the efficient level of pollution would vary from region to region; and (2) the efficient level of pollution would not generally be zero, although in some particular circumstances it might.

Since pollution is a classic externality, markets will generally produce more than the efficient amount of both fund pollutants and stock pollutants. For both types of pollutants, this will imply higher-than-efficient damages and lower-than-efficient control costs. For stock pollutants, an excessive amount of pollution would accumulate in the environment, imposing a detrimental externality on future generations as well as on current generations.

The market would not provide any automatic ameliorating response to the accumulation of pollution as it would in the case of natural resource scarcity. Firms attempting to unilaterally control their pollution could be placed at a competitive disadvantage. Hence, the case for some sort of government intervention is particularly strong for pollution control.

While policy instruments could, in principle, be defined to achieve an efficient level of pollution for every emitter, it is very difficult in practice because the amount of information required by the control authorities is unrealistically high.

Cost-effectiveness analysis provides a way out of this dilemma. In the case of uniformly mixed fund pollutants, uniform emissions charges or an allowance system focused purely on emissions could be used to attain the cost-effective allocation, even when the control authority has no information whatsoever on either control costs or damage costs. Uniform emissions standards would not, except by coincidence, be cost-effective. In addition, either emissions trading or charges would provide more incentives for technological progress in pollution control than would emissions standards.

The fact that auctioned allowances or taxes can raise revenue is also an important characteristic. If the revenue from pollution charges or auctioned allowances can be used to reduce revenue from other, more distortionary taxes (such as labor or income taxes), greater welfare gains can be achieved from revenue-raising instruments than instruments that raise no revenue. On the other hand, historically at least, transferring some or all of that revenue back to the sources either by gifting the allowances or including some sort of tax rebate has been an important aspect of securing the political support for implementing the system. Revenue use for this purpose, of course, cannot be used to reduce distortionary taxes or lower the regressive nature of the program.

The allowance approach and the charge approach respond differently to growth in the number of sources, to inflation, to technological change, and to uncertainty. As we shall see in the next few chapters, some countries have chosen to rely on emissions charges, while others have chosen to rely on cap-and-trade.

Discussion Question

1. In his book *What Price Incentives?*, Steven Kelman suggests that from an ethical point of view, the use of economic incentives (such as emissions charges or emissions trading) in environmental policy is undesirable. He argues that transforming our mental image of the environment from a sanctified preserve to a marketable commodity has detrimental effects not only on our use of the environment, but also on our attitude toward it. His point is that applying economic incentives to environmental policy weakens and cheapens our traditional values toward the environment.

    a. Consider the effects of economic incentive systems on prices paid by the poor, on employment, and on the speed of compliance with pollution-control laws—as well as the Kelman arguments. Are economic incentive systems more or less ethically justifiable than the traditional regulatory approach?

    b. Kelman seems to feel that because emissions allowances automatically prevent environmental degradation, they are more ethically desirable than emissions charges. Do you agree? Why or why not?

Self-Test Exercises

1. Two firms can control emissions at the following marginal costs: $MC_1 = \$200q_1$, $MC_2 = \$100q_2$, where q_1 and q_2 are, respectively, the amount of emissions reduced by the first and second firms. Assume that with no control at all, each firm would be emitting 20 units of emissions or a total of 40 units for both firms.

    Compute the cost-effective allocation of control responsibility if a total reduction of 21 units of emissions is necessary.

2. Assume that the control authority wanted to reach its objective in 1 by using an emissions charge system.

    a. What per-unit charge should be imposed?
    b. How much revenue would the control authority collect?

3. In a region that must reduce emissions, three polluters currently emit 30 units of emissions. The three firms have the following marginal abatement cost functions that describe how marginal costs vary with the amount of emissions each firm reduces.

Firm Emissions Reduction	Firm 1 Marginal Cost	Firm 2 Marginal Cost	Firm 3 Marginal Cost
1	$1.00	$1.00	$2.00
2	$1.50	$2.00	$3.00
3	$2.00	$3.00	$4.00
4	$2.50	$4.00	$5.00
5	$3.00	$5.00	$6.00
6	$3.50	$6.00	$7.00
7	$4.00	$7.00	$8.00
8	$4.50	$8.00	$9.00
9	$5.00	$9.00	$10.00
10	$5.50	$10.00	$11.00

Suppose this region needs to reduce emissions by 14 units and plans to do it using a form of cap-and-trade that auctions allowances off to the highest bidder.

    a. How many allowances will the control authority auction off? Why?
    b. Assuming no market power, how many of the allowances would each firm be expected to buy? Why?
    c. Assuming that demand equals supply, what price would be paid for those allowances? Why?
    d. If the control authority decided to use an emissions tax rather than cap-and-trade, what tax rate would achieve the 14-unit reduction cost-effectively? Why?

Notes

1 At this point, we can see why this formulation is equivalent to the net benefit formulation. Since the benefit is damage reduction, another way of stating this proposition is that marginal benefit must equal marginal cost. That is, of course, the familiar proposition derived by maximizing net benefits.

2 Note that pollution damage is not inevitably an externality. For any automobile rigged to send all exhaust gases into its interior, those exhaust gases would not be an externality to the occupants.

3 Actually the source certainly considers some of the costs, if only to avoid adverse public relations. The point, however, is that this consideration is likely to be incomplete; the source is unlikely to internalize all of the damage cost.

4 Affected parties do have an incentive to negotiate among themselves, a topic covered in Chapter 2. As pointed out there, however, that approach works well only in cases where the number of affected parties is small.

5 Another policy choice is to remove the people from the polluted area. The government has used this strategy for heavily contaminated toxic-waste sites, such as Times Beach, Missouri, and Love Canal, New York, as we shall see in Chapter 10.

6 This statement is true when marginal cost increases with the amount of emissions reduced as in Figure 5.3. Suppose that for some pollutants the marginal cost were to decrease with the amount of emissions reduced. What would be the cost-effective allocation in that admittedly unusual situation?

7 The literature contains a third reason. It suggests that, unless emitters cover all external costs via a revenue-raising instrument, the cost of production will be artificially low, production will be artificially high, and the industry will contain too many firms.

8 This is probably particularly true when the modification involves a change in the rate at which firms are charged for their emissions.

Further Reading

Baumol, W. J., & Oates. W. E. (1988). *The Theory of Environmental Policy*, 2nd ed. Cambridge: Cambridge University Press. A classic on the economic analysis of externalities. Accessible only to those with a thorough familiarity with multivariate calculus.

Freeman, Jody and Kolstad, Charles D. (Eds.). (2007). *Moving to Markets: Lessons from Twenty Years of Experience*. New York: Oxford University Press. A collection of 16 essays from leading scholars exploring what lessons can be extracted from actual experience with moving to market-based environmental regulation.

Harrington, W., Morgenstern, R. D., & Sterner, T. (2002). *Choosing Environmental Policy: Comparing Instruments and Outcomes in the United States and Europe*. Washington, DC: Resources for the Future. Uses paired case studies from the United States and Europe to contrast the costs and outcomes of direct regulation on one side of the Atlantic with an incentive-based policy on the other.

OECD. (1994). *Environment and Taxation: The Cases of the Netherlands, Sweden, and the United States*. Paris: OECD. Background case studies for a larger research project seeking to discover the extent to which fiscal and environmental policies could be made not only compatible but also mutually reinforcing.

Sterner, T., & Muller, Adrian (Eds.). (2016). *Environmental Taxation in Practice*, International Library of Environmental Economics and Policy. New York: Routledge. Focusing on environmental taxation in practice this book collects key contributions on a wide range of topics, including comparisons in different countries and key aspects of implementation.

Tietenberg, T. (2006). *Emissions Trading: Principles and Practice*, 2nd ed. Washington, DC: Resources for the Future. This book considers how the use of emissions trading to control pollution has evolved, looks at how these programs have been implemented in the US and internationally, and offers an objective evaluation of the resulting successes, failures, and lessons learned over the last 25 years.

Additional references and historically significant references are available on this book's Companion Website: www.routledge.com/cw/Tietenberg

Appendix

The Simple Mathematics of Cost-Effective Pollution Control

Suppose that each of N polluters would emit u_n units of emission in the absence of any control. Furthermore, suppose that the pollutant concentration K_R at some receptor R in the absence of control is

$$K_R = \sum_{n=1}^{N} a_n u_n + B \tag{1}$$

where B is the background concentration and a_n is the transfer coefficient. This KR is assumed to be greater than Φ, the legal concentration level. The regulatory problem, therefore, is to choose the cost-effective level of control q_n for each of the n sources. Symbolically, this can be expressed as minimizing the following Lagrangian with respect to the Nq_n control variables:

$$\min \sum_{n=1}^{N} C_n(q_n) + \lambda \left[\sum_{n=1}^{N} a_n(u_n - q_n) - \Phi \right] \tag{2}$$

where $C_n(q_n)$ is the cost of achieving the q_n level of control at the nth source and A is the Lagrangian multiplier.

The solution is found by partially differentiating (2) with respect to λ and the N q_n's. This yields

$$\frac{\partial C_n(q_n)}{\partial q} - \lambda * a_n \geq 0, n = 1, \ldots, N, \tag{3}$$

$$\sum_{n=1}^{N} a_n(u_n - q_n) + B - \Phi = 0. \tag{4}$$

Solving these equations produces the N-dimensional vector q^0 and the scalar λ.

Note that this same formulation can be used to reflect both the uniformly mixed and nonuniformly mixed single-receptor case. In the uniformly mixed case, every $a_n = 1$. This immediately implies that the marginal cost of control should be equal for all emitters who are required to engage in some control. (The first N equations would hold as equalities except for any source where the marginal cost of controlling the first unit exceeded the marginal cost necessary to meet the target.) For the nonuniformly mixed single-receptor case, in the cost-effective allocation the control responsibility would be allocated so as to ensure that the ratio of the marginal control costs for two emitters would be equal to the ratio of their transfer coefficients. For J receptors both $\lambda*$ and $\lambda*$ would become J-dimensional vectors.

Policy Instruments

A special meaning can be attached to λ. If emissions trading were being used, it would be the market-clearing price of an allowance. In the uniformly mixed case, A would be the price of an allowance to emit one unit of emission. In the nonuniformly mixed case, λ would be the price of being allowed to raise the concentration at the receptor location one unit. In the case of taxes, λ represents the value of the cost-effective tax.

Note how firms choose emissions control when the allowance price or tax is equal to λ. Each firm wants to minimize its costs. Assume that each firm is given allowances of Ω_n, where the regulatory authority ensures that

$$\sum_{n=1}^{N} a_n \Omega_n + B = \Phi \tag{5}$$

for the set of all emitters. Each firm would want to

$$\min c_n(q_n) + P^0 [a_n(u_n - q_n) - \Omega_n)]. \tag{6}$$

The minimum cost is achieved by choosing the value of $q_n(q_n{}^0)$ that satisfies

$$\frac{\partial C_n(q_n)}{\partial q_n} - P * a_n = 0. \tag{7}$$

This condition (marginal cost equals the price of a unit of concentration reduction) would hold for each of the N firms. Because P^* would equal λ^* and the number of allowances would be chosen to ensure the ambient standard would be met, this allocation would be cost-effective. Exactly the same result is achieved by substituting T^*, the cost-effective tax rate, for P^*.

Chapter 6

Stationary-Source Local and Regional Air Pollution

People are very open-minded about new things—as long as they're exactly like the old ones.
—Charles F. Kettering (American engineer, inventor of the electric starter, 1876–1958)

Introduction

Attaining and maintaining clean air is an exceedingly difficult policy task. In the United States, for example, an estimated 27,000 major stationary sources of air pollution are subject to control as well as hundreds of thousands of more minor sources. Many distinct production processes emit many different types of pollutants. The resulting damages range from minimal effects on plants and humans to the modification of the earth's climate.

The policy response to this problem has been continually evolving. The Clean Air Act Amendments of 1970 set a bold new direction that has been retained and refined by subsequent acts. By virtue of this legislation, the federal government assumed a much larger and much more vigorous direct role than previously had been the case. The US Environmental Protection Agency (EPA) was created in 1970 to implement and oversee this massive attempt to control the injection of pollutants into the nation's air. Individually tailored strategies were created to deal with mobile and stationary sources.

Conventional Pollutants

Conventional pollutants are relatively common substances, found in almost all parts of the country, and are thought, on the basis of research, to be dangerous only in high concentrations. In the United States, these pollutants are called *criteria pollutants* because the Act required the EPA to produce "criteria documents" to be used in setting acceptable standards for these pollutants. These documents summarize and evaluate all of the existing research on the various health and environmental effects associated with these pollutants. The central focus of air pollution control during the 1970s was on criteria pollutants.

The Command-and-Control Policy Framework

In Chapter 5 several possible approaches to controlling pollution were described and analyzed in theoretical terms. The historical approach to air pollution control, known popularly as "command-and-control" (CAC), depended primarily on emissions standards. In this section we outline the specific nature of this approach, analyze its shortcomings from an efficiency and cost-effectiveness perspective, and show how a series of reforms based on the logic advanced in the last chapter has worked to rectify some of these deficiencies.

For each of the conventional pollutants, the typical first step is to establish the National Ambient Air Quality Standards (NAAQS). These standards have to be met everywhere, although as a practical matter they are monitored at a large number of specific locations.

Ambient standards set legal ceilings on the allowable concentration of the pollutant in the outdoor air averaged over a specified time period. The allowable concentrations for many pollutants are defined in terms of both a long-term average (defined frequently as an annual average) and a short-term average (such as a 3-hour average). Compliance with short-term averages usually requires that the allowable concentrations be exceeded no more than once a year. Control costs can be quite sensitive to the level of these short-term averages.

In the United States, two ambient standards have been defined. The *primary standard* is designed to protect human health. It was the earliest standard to be determined, and had the earliest deadlines for compliance. All pollutants have a primary standard. The primary ambient standards are required by statute to be set at a level sufficient to protect even the most sensitive members of the population without any consideration given to the costs of meeting them.

The *secondary standard* is designed to protect other aspects of human welfare from those pollutants having separate effects. Currently, only three separate secondary standards have been set—nitrogen dioxide, sulfur oxides, and small particulates. For some other pollutants, the concentration levels allowed by the primary and secondary standards are the same. The secondary standards are designed to protect aesthetics (particularly visibility), physical objects (houses, monuments, and so on), and vegetation. When a separate secondary standard exists, both it and the primary standard must be met.[1]

While the EPA is responsible for defining the ambient standards, the primary responsibility for enforcement falls on the state control agencies. They exercise this responsibility by developing and executing an acceptable state implementation plan (SIP), which must be approved by the EPA. This plan divides the state into separate air-quality-control regions. Special procedures were developed for handling regions that cross state borders, such as metropolitan New York.

The SIP spells out for each control region the procedures and timetables for meeting local ambient standards and for abatement of the effects of locally emitted pollutants on other states. The required degree of control depends on the severity of the pollution problem in each of the control regions. All areas not meeting the deadlines were designated as *nonattainment regions*.

Recognizing that it is typically much easier and much cheaper to control new sources rather than existing ones, the Clean Air Act established the New Source Review (NSR) Program. This program requires all new major stationary sources (as well as those undergoing major modifications) in both attainment and nonattainment areas to seek a permit for operation. This permit requires compliance with the specified standards (more stringent in nonattainment areas than in attainment areas). The theory was that as old, dirtier plants became obsolete, this program would ensure that their replacements would be significantly less polluting. As Debate 6.1 points out, the New Source Review Program has stimulated some controversy.

The Efficiency of the Command-and-Control Approach

Efficiency requires that the allowable concentration levels authorized by the ambient standards are set where the marginal benefit equals the marginal cost. To ascertain whether or not the current standards are efficient, it is necessary to inquire into five aspects of the standard-setting process: (1) the threshold concept, on which the standards are based, (2) the level of the standard, (3) the choice of uniform standards over standards more tailored to the regions

---

DEBATE 6.1

Does Sound Policy Require Targeting New Sources via the New Source Review?

One of the characteristics of the New Source Review program is that it requires large stationary sources that are undergoing major modifications (not just routine maintenance) to meet the same stringent standards as new sources. Routine maintenance does not trigger a need to install the more stringent control technology. Due to this routine maintenance exemption, a number of older plants have historically avoided the major modification threshold and therefore were never upgraded. As a result, over time these older plants have become responsible for an increasing share of the total emissions.

One approach to dealing with this problem was to take enforcement actions against individual companies, including numerous electric utilities that own and operate coal-fired power plants in the Southeast and Midwest. The lawsuits alleged that plants that should have been retired years earlier were being modified and retained past their normal life under the cover of "routine maintenance." Using this exemption to prop up the plants was seen as an evasion of the principle of improving air quality over time by replacing older plants with modern, less polluting plants.

Opponents of the New Source Review process argue that it has been counterproductive, resulting in worse air quality, not better, and it should be replaced, not merely enforced more rigorously. According to this view, not only has the New Source Review deterred investment in newer, cleaner technologies, but it has also discouraged companies from keeping power plants adequately maintained, lest they trigger the major modification designation. The solution, they argue, is to use cap-and-trade to create a level-playing field, where all electricity generators (old and new) would face the same emissions constraint. Under this new policy, plant owners would pursue the investment and/or retirement strategies that secured the required emissions reductions at minimum cost. Artificial delay in replacing plants would no longer make any economic sense with the new incentives created by cap-and-trade—private and social goals would be harmonized.

Source: Stavins, R. (2006). Vintage-differentiated environmental regulation. *Stanford Environmental Law, 25*(1), 29–63.

involved, (4) the timing of emissions flows, and (5) the failure to incorporate the degree of human exposure in the standard-setting process.

The Threshold Concept. Since the Clean Air Act prohibits the balancing of costs and benefits, some alternative criterion must be used to set the standard. For the primary (health-related) standard, this criterion is known as the *health threshold*. In principle, this threshold is defined with a margin of safety sufficiently high that no adverse health effects would be suffered by any member of the population as long as the air quality was at least as good as the standard. This approach presumes the existence of a threshold such that concentrations below that level produce no adverse health effects.

If the threshold concept presumption were valid, the marginal damage function would be zero for concentrations under the threshold and would be positive at higher concentrations. In practice, this shape is not consistent with the latest evidence. Adverse health effects can occur at pollution levels lower than the ambient standards. The standard that produces no adverse health effects among the general population (which, of course, includes especially susceptible groups) is probably zero or close to it. It is certainly lower than the established ambient standards. What the standards purport to accomplish and what they actually accomplish are rather different.

The Level of the Ambient Standard. The absence of a defensible health threshold complicates the analysis (see Debate 6.2). Some other basis must be used for determining the level at which the standard should be established. Efficiency would dictate setting the standard in order to maximize the net benefit, which includes a consideration of costs as well as benefits.

The current policy explicitly excludes costs from consideration in setting the ambient standards. It is difficult to imagine that the process of setting the ambient standard would yield an efficient outcome when it is prohibited from considering one of the key elements of that outcome!

Unfortunately, for reasons that were discussed in some detail in Chapter 4, our current benefit measurements are not sufficiently reliable as to permit the identification of the efficient level with any confidence. For example, an early EPA study of the Clean Air Act found that the total monetized benefits of the Clean Air Act realized during the period from 1970 to 1990 ranged from $5.6 to $49.4 trillion, with a central estimate of $22.2 trillion. That is a very large band of uncertainty.

The study further noted that the central estimate of $22.2 trillion dollars in benefits might be a significant underestimate due to the exclusion of large numbers of benefit categories from the monetized benefit estimate (e.g., all air toxics effects; ecosystem effects; numerous human health effects).

The EPA's estimates suggest that a high degree of confidence can be attached to the belief that government intervention to control air pollution in the United States was economically justified; but they provide no evidence whatsoever on whether current policy was, or is, efficient.

Uniformity. The same primary and secondary standards apply to all parts of the country. No account is taken of the number of people exposed, the sensitivity of the local ecology, or the costs of compliance in various areas. All of these aspects of the problem would have some effect on the efficient standard and efficiency would, therefore, dictate different standards for different regions. Uniform ambient standards are inconsistent with an efficient allocation of pollution control resources. Spatially differentiated standards that target the level of control so as to reflect the damage caused would produce more damage reduction per dollar of

DEBATE 6.2

The Particulate and Smog Ambient Standards Controversy

During one of its periodic reviews of the ambient air-quality standards, the US EPA concluded that 125 million Americans, including 35 million children, were not adequately protected by the existing standards for ozone and particulates. More stringent standards were estimated to prevent 1 million serious respiratory illnesses each year, and 15,000 premature deaths.

The proposed revisions were controversial because the cost of compliance would be very high. No health threshold existed at the chosen level (some health effects would be noticed at even more stringent levels than those proposed) and the EPA was, by law, prohibited from using a benefit-cost justification. In the face of legal challenge, the EPA found it very difficult to defend the superiority of the chosen standards from slightly more stringent or slightly less stringent standards.

In its ruling on the issues raised in this case, the US Court of Appeals for the District of Columbia Circuit overturned the proposed revisions. In a 2–1 ruling, the three-judge panel rejected the EPA's approach to setting the level of those standards:

> the construction of the Clean Air Act on which EPA relied in promulgating the NAAQS at issue here effects an unconstitutional delegation of legislative power. . . . Although the factors EPA uses in determining the degree of public health concern associated with different levels of ozone and PM are reasonable, EPA appears to have articulated no "intelligible principle" to channel its application of these factors. . . . EPA's formulation of its policy judgement leaves it free to pick any point between zero and a hair below the concentrations yielding London's Killer Fog.

Although the threat to the EPA's authority from this decision was ultimately overturned by the US Supreme Court, the dilemma posed by the absence of a compelling health threshold remains unresolved.

abatement cost, but populations in less densely populated areas would face worse air quality. Spatially differentiated standards are efficient, but would they be fair to the people in rural areas? That is the policy conundrum.

Timing of Emissions Flows. Because ambient concentrations are important for criteria pollutants, the timing of emissions is an important policy concern. Emissions concentrated in time are as troublesome as emissions concentrated in space. One circumstance that gives rise to this concern involves those relatively rare, but devastating, occasions when thermal inversions prevent the normal dispersion and dilution of the pollutants. The resulting concentration levels can be quite dangerous. How should these circumstances be handled?

From an economic efficiency point of view, the most obvious approach is to tailor the degree of control to the circumstances. The most stringent control would be exercised when (and only when) meteorological conditions were relatively stagnant; less control would be applied under normal circumstances. A reliance on a constant degree of control, rather than allowing intermittent controls, raises compliance costs substantially, particularly when the required degree of control is high. The strong stand against intermittent controls in the Clean Air Act, however, rules out this approach.

Concentration versus Exposure. Presently ambient standards are defined in terms of pollutant concentrations in the outdoor air. Yet health effects are closely related to human exposure to pollutants and exposure is determined not only by the concentrations of air pollutants in each of the places in which people spend time, but also by the number of people exposed and the amount of time spent in each place. Since in the United States only about 10 percent of the population's person-hours are spent outdoors, indoor air becomes very important in designing strategies to improve the health risk of pollutants. To date, very little attention has been focused on controlling indoor air pollution despite its apparent importance.[2]

Cost-Effectiveness of the Command-and-Control Approach

While empirically determining the magnitude of the inefficiency of the ambient standards is difficult at best, determining their cost-effectiveness is somewhat easier. Although it does not allow us to shed any light on whether a particular ambient standard is efficient or not, cost-effectiveness does allow us to see whether the ambient standards are being met in the least costly manner possible.

The theory covered in Chapter 5 makes it clear that the CAC strategy will normally not be cost-effective. What the theory does not make clear, however, is the degree to which this strategy diverges from the least-cost ideal. If the divergence is small, the proponents of reform would not likely be able to overcome the inertia of the status quo. If the divergence is large, the case for reform is stronger.

The cost-effectiveness of the CAC approach depends on local circumstances such as prevailing meteorology, the spatial configuration of sources, stack heights, and the degree to which costs vary with the amount controlled. Several simulation models capable of dealing with these complexities have now been constructed for a number of different pollutants in a variety of airsheds. The vast majority of these studies have found that the costs associated with the command-and-control approach were considerably higher than a cost-effective approach.[3]

As Example 6.1 points out, the command-and-control program to control SO_2 emissions in Germany did experience some cost-ineffectiveness, but not for the traditional reason.

EXAMPLE 6.1

Controlling SO₂ Emissions by Command-and-Control in Germany

Germany and the United States took quite different approaches to controlling SO_2 emissions. Whereas the United States used a version of cap-and-trade, Germany used traditional command-and-control regulation. Theory would lead us to believe that the US approach, due to its flexibility, would achieve its goals at a considerably lower cost. The evidence suggests that it did, but the reasons are a bit more complicated than one might suppose.

Due to the large amount of forest death (Waldsterben) in Germany, in which SO_2 emissions were implicated, the pressure was on to significantly reduce SO_2 emission from large combustion sources in a relatively short period of time. Both the degree of control and the mandated deadlines for compliance were quite stringent.

The stringency of the targets and deadlines meant that sources had very little control flexibility. Only one main technology could meet the requirements, so every covered combustion source had to install that technology. Even if firms had been allowed to engage in allowance trading once the equipment was installed, the pretrade marginal costs would have been very similar. Since the purpose of trading is to equalize marginal costs, the fact that they were very similar before trading left little room for cost savings from trade.

The main cost disadvantage to the German system, however, was not found to be due to unequal marginal costs but rather to the temporal inflexibility of the command-and-control regulations. As Wätzold (2004) notes:

> The nearly simultaneous installation of desulfurization equipment in LCPs [Large Combustion Plants] all over Germany led to a surge in demand for this equipment with a resulting increase in prices. Furthermore, because Germany had little experience with the necessary technology, no learning effects were achieved; . . . shortcomings that should have come to light before the systems were introduced in the entire fleet of power stations . . . had to be remedied in all power stations.
>
> (p. 35)

This was quite different from the US experience with its sulfur allowance program. In the US program (described later in this chapter), the ability to bank or save allowances for subsequent use provided an incentive for some firms to comply early, and the phased deadline allowed much more flexibility in the timing of the installation of abatement controls; not all firms had to comply at the same time.

Source: Wätzold, F. F. (2004). SO_2 emissions in Germany: Regulations to fight Waldsterben. In W. Harrington, R. D. Morgenstern, & T. Sterner (Eds.), *Choosing Environmental Policy: Comparing Instruments and Outcomes in the United States and Europe*. Washington, DC: Resources for the Future, 23–40.

Table 6.1 Percentage Change in US Emissions, 1980–2015

	1980 vs 2015	1990 vs 2015	2000 vs 2015
Carbon Monoxide	−71	−65	−50
Lead	−99	−80	−50
Nitrogen Oxides (NO$_x$)	−58	−54	−49
Volatile Organic Compounds (VOC)	−54	−41	−19
Direct PM$_{10}$	−57	−17	−14
Direct PM$_{2.5}$	—	−24	−32
Sulfur Dioxide	−86	−84	−77

Source: www.epa.gov/air-trends/air-quality-national-summary. Accessed June 9, 2017.

Air Quality

Each year, the US Environmental Protection Agency publishes emission trends using measurements from monitors located across the country. Table 6.1 shows the reduction in emissions for various pollutants from 1980 to 2015. Notice that every pollutant experienced improvement and in some cases the improvements were dramatic.

How typical has the US experience been? Is pollution declining on a worldwide basis? The Global Environmental Monitoring System (GEMS), operating under the auspices of the World Health Organization and the United Nations Environment Program, monitors air quality around the globe. Scrutiny of its reports reveals that the US experience is typical for the industrialized nations, which have generally reduced pollution (both in terms of emissions and ambient outdoor air quality).

However, the air quality in most developing nations has steadily deteriorated, and the number of people exposed to unhealthy levels of pollution in those countries is frequently very high.[4] Since these countries typically are struggling merely to provide adequate employment and income to their citizens, they cannot afford to waste large sums of money on inefficient environmental policies, especially if the inefficiencies tend to subsidize the rich at the expense of the poor. Some cost-effective, yet fair means of improving air quality that works in the developing country context must be found.

Market-Based Approaches

Fortunately more cost-effective approaches are not only available, but are being used. Since various versions of these approaches have now been implemented around the world, we can learn from the experience gained from their implementation.

Emissions Charges

Economists typically envision two types of effluent or emissions charges. The first, an efficiency charge, is designed to force the polluter to compensate completely for all damage caused. The second, a cost-effective charge, is designed to achieve a predefined ambient standard or aggregate emissions level at the lowest possible control cost.

In Japan, the charge is based upon damages to human health. As a result of four important legal cases where Japanese industries were forced to compensate victims for pollution damages caused, in 1973 Japan passed the Law for the Compensation of Pollution-Related Health Injury. According to this law, victims of designated diseases, upon certification by a council of medical, legal, and other experts, are eligible for medical expenses, lost earnings, and other expenses; they are not eligible for other losses, such as pain and suffering. Two classes of diseases were funded: designated diseases, where the specific source is relatively clear, and nonspecific respiratory diseases, where all polluters are presumed to have some responsibility.

Victim compensation is funded by an emissions charge on sulfur dioxides and by an automobile weight tax. The level of the charge/tax is determined by the revenue needs of the compensation fund.

In contrast to cap-and-trade where allowance prices respond automatically to changing market conditions, emissions charges have to be determined by an administrative process. When the function of the charge is to raise revenue for a particular purpose, charge rates will be determined by the costs of achieving that purpose; when the costs of achieving the purpose rise, the level of the charge must also rise to secure the additional revenue.[5]

Sometimes that process produces an unintended dynamic. In Japan, for example, the charge is calculated on the basis of the amount of compensation paid to victims of air pollution in the previous year. While the amount of compensation was increasing, the amount of emissions (the base to which the charge is applied) was decreasing. As a result, unexpectedly high charge rates were necessary in order to raise sufficient revenue for the compensation system and these had quite a large incentive effect on emissions reduction.

In 1986 the law was amended to, among other changes, use the funds for pollution abatement research, medical expenses associated with pollution-related illnesses, and educating the public about research findings.

Emissions Trading

In the early days of pollution control, local areas adopted the motto "Dilution is the solution." As implemented, this approach suggested that the way to control local pollutants was to require tall stacks for emissions. By the time the pollutants hit the ground, according to this theory, the concentrations would be diluted, making it easier to meet the ambient standards at nearby monitors.

By the end of the 1980s, it had become painfully clear in the United States that the Clean Air Act was ill-suited to solving regional pollution problems. Revamping the legislation to do a better job of dealing with regional pollutants, such as acid rain, became a high priority.

Politically, that was a tall order. By virtue of the fact that these pollutants are transported long distances due to the tall stacks, the set of geographic areas receiving the damage is typically not the same as the set of geographic areas responsible for most of the emission causing the damage. In many cases the recipients and the emitters are even in different countries! In this political milieu, it should not be surprising that those bearing the costs of damages should call for a large, rapid reduction in emissions, whereas those responsible for bearing the costs of that cleanup should want to proceed more slowly and with greater caution.

Economic analysis was helpful in finding a feasible path through this political thicket. In particular, in 1986 a Congressional Budget Office (CBO) study helped to set the parameters of the debate by quantifying the consequences of various courses of action. To analyze the economic and political consequences of various strategies designed to achieve reductions of SO_2 emissions from utilities anywhere from 8 to 12 million tons below the emissions levels from those plants in 1980, the CBO used a computer-based simulation model that related utility emissions, utility costs, and coal-market supply and demand levels to the strategies under consideration.

The first implication of the analysis was that the marginal cost of additional control would rise rapidly, particularly after 10 million tons had been reduced. The cost of reducing a ton of SO_2 was estimated to rise from $270 for an 8-million-ton reduction to $360 for a 10-million-ton reduction, and it would rise to a rather dramatic $779 per ton for a 12-million-ton reduction. Costs would rise much more steeply as the amount of required reduction was increased, because reliance on the more expensive *scrubbers* would become necessary. (Scrubbers involve a chemical process to extract, or "scrub," sulfur gases before they escape into the atmosphere.)

The second insight, one that should be no surprise to readers of this book, is that the emissions charge would be more cost-effective than the comparable CAC strategy. Whereas the CAC strategy could secure a 10-million-ton reduction at about $360 a ton, the emissions charge could do it for $327 a ton. The superiority of the emissions charge was due to the fact that this approach would result in equalized marginal costs, a required condition for cost-effectiveness.

Although the emissions-charge approach may be the most cost-effective policy, it was not the most popular, particularly in states with a lot of old, heavily polluting power plants. With an emissions-charge approach, utilities not only have to pay the higher equipment and operating costs associated with the reductions, but also have to pay the emissions charge on all remaining uncontrolled emissions. The additional financial burden on utilities associated with controlling acid rain by this means would have been significant. Instead of paying the $3.2 billion for reducing 10 million tons under a CAC approach, utilities would be saddled with a $7.7 billion financial burden with an emissions charge. The savings from lower equipment and operating costs achieved because the emissions-charge approach is more cost-effective would have been more than outweighed by the additional expense of paying the emissions charges. The political dilemma posed by this additional financial burden was resolved by adopting an emissions trading system known as the *sulfur allowance trading program*. Adopted as part of the Clean Air Act Amendments of 1990, this approach was designed to complement, not replace, the traditional approach.

Under this program allowances to emit sulfur oxides were allocated to older sulfur-emitting, electricity-generating plants. The number of allowances was restricted in order to assure a reduction of 10 million tons in emissions from 1980 levels by the year 2010.

These allowances, which each provide a limited authorization to emit 1 ton of sulfur dioxide (SO_2), were defined for a specific calendar year, but unused allowances could be carried forward into the next year. They were transferable among the affected sources. Any plants reducing emissions more than required by the allowances could transfer the unused allowances to other plants. Emissions in any plant could not legally exceed the levels permitted by the allowances (allocated plus acquired) held by the managers of that plant. An annual year-end audit balanced emissions with allowances. Utilities that emitted more than authorized by their holdings of allowances were required to pay an "excess emissions" penalty and were required to forfeit an equivalent number of tons of emissions in the following year (equal to the amount of the excess emissions). The financial penalty was adjusted annually for inflation.

An important innovation in this program was the establishment of an auction market for the allowances. Each year the EPA withheld an allowance auction reserve of 2.8 percent of the allocated allowances; these went into the sealed bid auction. These withheld allowances were allocated to the highest bidders, with successful buyers paying their bid price (not the market clearing price). The proceeds were refunded to the utilities from whom the allowances were withheld, on a proportional basis. One main advantage of this auction is that it made allowance prices publicly transparent. By providing more information to investors, business investment strategies were facilitated.

Private allowance holders were also allowed to offer allowances for sale at these auctions. Potential sellers specify minimum acceptable prices. Once the withheld allowances have been disbursed, the EPA then matches the highest remaining bids with the lowest minimum acceptable prices on the private offerings and matches buyers and sellers until the sum of all remaining bids is less than that of the remaining minimum acceptable prices.

How did the program fare? Rather well in many respects, but not always for the expected reasons (see Example 6.2).

EXAMPLE 6.2

The Sulfur Allowance Program after 20 Years

An *ex post* analysis published in 2013 provides a thorough retrospective evaluation of the Sulfur Allowance Program. It found the following:

- The program was environmentally effective, with SO_2 emissions from electric power plants decreasing by 36 percent between 1990 and 2004, even though electricity generation from coal-fired power plants *increased* 25 percent over the same period.
- The program's long-term annual emissions goal was achieved early. However, it turns out that the ecological benefits of the program, the original focus, were relatively small. Reversing the acidification of ecosystems took longer than expected. In retrospect more than 95 percent of the benefits from this program were associated not with ecological impacts, but rather with human health improvements resulting from reduced levels of small airborne sulfate particles derived from SO_2 emissions.
- Due to effective penalties and continuous monitoring of emissions, compliance was nearly 100 percent.
- Some evidence suggests that the intertemporal allocation of abatement cost (via allowance banking) was at least approximately efficient.
- Although the law was clearly more cost-effective than a traditional command-and-control approach would have been, and it produced savings much larger than anticipated before the act was enacted, much of this reduced cost was due to an unanticipated consequence—the deregulation of railroad rates in the late 1970s and early 1980s. This event, which clearly preceded the 1990 enactment of this program, allowed more low-sulfur coal to flow eastward at a cheaper price than previously possible.
- In July 2011, the Cross-State Air Pollution Rule (CSAPR), a different regulation resulting from a court decision, restricted trading to *within* states, thereby eliminating the scope for cost-effective interstate trades. The SO_2 market collapsed, with allowance prices falling to record low levels.

The authors note a couple of ironies in this history:

- Although this market-based, cost-effective policy innovation (cap-and-trade) was championed and implemented by Republican administrations from President Ronald Reagan to President George W. Bush, in recent years this approach has come to be demonized by current conservative Republican politicians.
- Finally, court decisions and subsequent responses by the Obama administration led to the virtual collapse of the SO_2 market, demonstrating that what the government gives, the government can take away.

Source: Schmalensee, R., & Stavins, R. N. (2013). The SO_2 allowance trading system: The ironic history of a grand policy experiment. *Journal of Economic Perspectives*, 27(1), 103–122.

Since the sulfur allowance program, a number of other cap-and-trade programs have been implemented in other nations as well. How have these programs fared? Schmalensee and Stavins (2017), two economists who have been involved in this evolution, review this experience. They conclude their review with a cautious, but positive assessment:

> Overall, we have found that cap-and-trade systems, if well designed and appropriately implemented, can achieve their core objective of meeting targeted emissions reductions cost-effectively. But the devil is in the details, and design as well as the economic environment in which systems are implemented are very important.

The main cautionary caveats include:

- Some of the success can be attributed to factors other than the program. The timely arrival of railroad deregulation in the sulfur allowance program, noted in Example 6.2, was one instance, but another was the emergence of fracking. It expanded the availability of low-cost natural gas, which made the carbon reductions achieved by the Regional Greenhouse Gas Initiative, discussed in Chapter 8, deeper and less expensive than would have otherwise been possible.
- Provisions for allowance banking have proven to be very important for achieving maximum gains from trade, and the absence of banking provisions can lead to price spikes and collapses.
- The level of the cap is generally based upon expected emissions. Changing economic conditions can either reduce emissions sufficiently below this expectation that the cap becomes nonbinding, or increase emissions above expectations and drive allowance prices to politically unacceptable levels. As can be seen in more detail in Chapter 8, economists have come up with a means of meeting this challenge by incorporating something called a *price collar* into the design. Price collars reduce price volatility by combining an auction price floor with a price ceiling.

Summary

While air quality has improved in the industrial nations, it has deteriorated in the developing nations. Historically air pollution control has been based upon a traditional command-and-control approach. Although this has reduced emissions, it has been neither efficient nor cost-effective.

The command-and-control policy has not been efficient in part because it has been based on a legal fiction, a threshold below which no health damages are inflicted on any member of the population. In fact, damages occur at levels lower than the ambient standards. Sensitive members of the population, such as those with respiratory problems, are especially vulnerable. The attempt to formulate standards without considering control costs has been thwarted by the absence of a scientifically defensible health-based threshold.

In addition, the traditional policy failed to adequately consider the timing of emissions flows. By failing to target the greatest amount of control on those periods when the greatest damage is inflicted, the current policy encourages too little control in high-damage periods and excessive control during low-damage periods. Current policy has also failed to pay sufficient attention to indoor air pollution, which may well pose larger health risks than outdoor pollution, at least in developed countries. Unfortunately, because the existing benefit estimates have large confidence intervals, the size of the inefficiency associated with these aspects of the policy has not been measured with any precision.

Traditional regulatory policy has not been cost-effective either. The allocation of responsibility among emitters for reducing pollution has resulted in control costs that are typically several times higher than necessary to achieve the air-quality objective. This has been shown to be true for a variety of pollutants in a variety of geographic settings.

The recent move toward market-based policies is based on the cost-effective economic incentives they provide. Providing more flexibility in meeting the air-quality goals has reduced both the cost and the conflict between economic growth and the preservation of air quality.

What about the impact of environmental regulation on the diffusion of more environmentally benign technologies? Does the evidence suggest that new technologies with reduced environmental impact are being developed and adopted? As Example 6.3 points out, for chlorine manufacturing, the answer is a definite yes, but, as we have seen with earlier examples, the story of exactly how that happened is a bit more complex than simply observing all firms embracing the new technology.

EXAMPLE 6.3

Technology Diffusion in the Chlorine-Manufacturing Sector

Most of the world's chlorine is produced using one of three types of cells: the mercury cell, the diaphragm cell, and the membrane cell. Generally, the mercury-cell technology poses the highest environmental risk, with the diaphragm-cell technology posing the next highest risk.

Over the last 25 years, the mercury-cell share of the total production has fallen from 22 to 10 percent; the diaphragm-cell share has fallen from 73 to 67 percent, and the membrane-cell share has risen from less than 1 percent of the total to 20 percent.

What role did regulation play? One might normally expect that, prodded by regulation, chlorine manufacturers would have increasingly adopted the more environmentally benign production technique. But that is not what happened. Instead, other regulations made it beneficial for users of chlorine to switch to nonchlorine bleaches, thereby reducing the demand for chlorine. In response to this reduction in demand, a number of producers shut down, and a disproportionate share of the plants that remained open were the ones using the cleaner, membrane-cell production.

Source: Snyder, L. D., Miller, N. H., & Stavins, R. N. (2003).
The effects of environmental regulation on technology diffusion:
The case of chlorine manufacturing. *American Economic
Review, 93*(2), 431–435.

As the zone of influence of pollutants extends beyond local boundaries, the political difficulties of implementing comprehensive, cost-effective control measures increase. Pollutants crossing political boundaries impose external costs; neither the emitters nor the nations within which they emit have the proper incentives to institute efficient control measures.

Acid rain is a case in point. In the United States, the Clean Air Act had had a distinctly local focus until 1990. To control local pollution problems, state governments encouraged the installation of tall stacks to dilute the pollution before it hit ground level. In the process, a high proportion of the emissions were exported to other areas, reaching the ground hundreds of miles from the point of injection. A focus on local control made the regional problem worse.

Finding solutions to the acid rain problem was very difficult because those bearing the costs of further control were not those who would benefit from the control. In the United States, for example, opposition from the Midwestern and Appalachian states delayed action on acid rain legislation—stumbling blocks included the higher electricity prices that would result from the control and the employment impacts on those states that would suffer losses of jobs in the high-sulfur, coal-mining industry.

These barriers were overcome by the 1990 Clean Air Act Amendments, which instituted the sulfur allowance program. This program placed a cap on total emissions from the utility sector for the first time and implemented a flexible, cost-effective way of reducing emissions to the level specified by the cap.

Discussion Questions

1. The efficient regulation of hazardous pollutants should take exposure into account— the more persons exposed to a given pollutant concentration, the larger is the damage caused by it and therefore the smaller is the efficient concentration level, all other things being equal. An alternative point of view holds that this policy does not treat all citizens fairly. Rather, according to this point of view, fairness requires that all citizens be protected by a safe concentration threshold. What are the advantages and disadvantages of each approach? Which do you think represents the best approach? Why?

2. If you were in charge of an agency responsible for designing a cost-effective pollution control policy, would you prefer an approach based upon an emissions charge or on emissions trading? Why?

Self-Test Exercises

1. Would imposing the same tax rate on every unit of emissions normally be expected to yield a cost-effective allocation of pollution control responsibility? Does your answer depend on whether the environmental target is an aggregate emissions reduction or meeting an ambient standard? Why or why not?

2. Suppose in an emissions trading system the permits are allocated free of charge to emitters on the basis of how much they have historically emitted. Can that allocation be consistent with cost-effectiveness? Does your answer depend at all on whether this allocation scheme was announced well in advance of its implementation?

Notes

1 The actual standards can be found at www.epa.gov/criteria-air-pollutants/naaqs-table (accessed June 9, 2017).

2 The most obvious major policy response to indoor air pollution has been the large number of states that have passed legislation requiring "smoke-free" areas in public places to protect nonsmokers.

3 For a description of these studies and the sources of the results see Tietenberg, T. H. (2006). *Emissions Trading: Principles and Practice*, 2nd ed. Washington, DC: Resources of the Future, pp. 55–60.

4 For sulfur oxides, for example, the GEMS study estimates that only 30–35 percent of the world's population lives in areas where the air is at least as clean as recommended by World Health Organization guidelines.

5 While it is theoretically possible (depending on the elasticity of demand for pollution abatement) for a rise in the tax to produce less revenue, this has typically not been the case.

Further Reading

Ando, A. W., & Harrington, D. R. (2006). Tradable discharge permits: A student-friendly game. *The Journal of Economic Education (JEE)*, 37(2), 187–201. A classroom exercise to improve understanding of how tradable permits work.

Blackman, A. (2010). Alternative pollution control policies in developing countries. *Review of Environmental Economics and Policy*, 4(2), 234–253. This article reviews the effectiveness of the increasing tendency for developing countries to experiment with alternative approaches to control pollution.

Harrington, W., Morgenstern, R. D., & Sterner, T. (Eds.). (2004). *Choosing Environmental Policy: Comparing Instruments and Outcomes in the United States and Europe*. Washington, DC: Resources for the Future. A study that compares the evidence on the relative effectiveness of command-and-control and economic incentive polices for controlling pollution in Europe and the United States.

Hendrick, W., & Perry, L. (2010). Policy monitor: Trends in clean air legislation in Europe: Particulate matter and low emission zones. *Review of Environmental Economics and Policy*, 4(2), 293–308. This article describes developments in Europe concerning clean air legislation, focusing in particular on particulate matter (PM).

Hubbel, B. J., Crume, R. V., Evarts, D. M., & Cohen, J. M. (2010). Policy monitor: Regulation and progress under the 1990 Clean Air Act Amendments. *Review of Environmental Economics and Policy*, 4(1), 122–138. This article describes the 1990 CAA Amendments, regulations issued by EPA following their passage, progress made in air-quality management in the nearly 20 years since their enactment, and the likely future direction of US air-quality management programs at the federal level.

OECD. (2016). *The Economic Consequences of Outdoor Air Pollution*. Paris: OECD Publishing. http://dx.doi.org/10.1787/9789264257474-en. Covering the period 2015–2060, this report projects the economic consequences of high concentrations of particulate matter ($PM_{2.5}$) and ground level ozone in the outdoor air that would result from policy inaction.

Schmalensee, R., & Stavins, R. N. (2013). The SO_2 allowance trading system: The ironic history of a grand policy experiment. *The Journal of Economic Perspectives*, 27(1), 103–121. Evaluating the Sulfur Allowance Program after 20 years.

Schmalensee, R., & Stavins, R. N. (2017). Lessons learned from three decades of experience with cap and trade. *Review of Environmental Economics and Policy*, 11(1): 59–79. This article examines the design and performance of seven of the most prominent emissions trading systems that have been implemented over the past 30 years.

Additional references and historically significant references are available on this book's Companion Website: www.routledge.com/cw/Tietenberg

Chapter 7

Mobile-Source Air Pollution

There are two things you shouldn't watch being made, sausage and law.

—Anonymous

Introduction

Like its stationary-source counterpart, the control of mobile-source pollution began with a focus on conventional pollutants that imposed a risk to human health. As knowledge about climate change increased, the regulation of mobile sources began to focus on that challenge as well. At first the approach to this new challenge was based simply on an extension and intensification of the policies aimed at health concerns, but later it was recognized that to effectively control greenhouse gases the policies needed to be more comprehensive and treat mobile and stationary sources under the same regulatory umbrella. In this chapter we deal mainly with regulations designed to protect human health and how those regulations evolved as concerns over climate change heightened. In the next chapter we shall consider the policies that focus specifically on climate change.

Although they emit many of the same pollutants as stationary sources, mobile sources require a different policy approach. These differences arise from the mobility of the source, the number of vehicles involved, and the role of the automobile in daily life.

Mobility has two major impacts on policy. On the one hand, pollution is partly caused by the temporary location of the source—a case of being in the wrong place at the wrong time. This occurs, for example, during rush hour in metropolitan areas. Since the cars have to be where the people are, relocating them—as might be done with electric power plants—is not a viable strategy. On the other hand, it is more difficult to tailor vehicle emissions rates to local pollution patterns, since any particular vehicle may end up in many different urban and rural areas during the course of its useful life.

Mobile sources are also more numerous than stationary sources. In the United States, for example, while there are approximately 27,000 major stationary sources, well over 250 million motor vehicles have been registered, a number that has been growing steadily since the 1960s, when there were 74 million. Highway vehicle miles traveled (VMT) reached

3.1 million in 2015 after growing steadily since data started being collected in 1960 (US Bureau of Transportation Statistics).[1] Enforcement is obviously more difficult as the number of sources being controlled increases. Additionally, in the United States alone, 33 percent of carbon emissions from anthropogenic sources come from the transportation sector, 60 percent of which comes from the combustion of gasoline by motor vehicles. When the sources of pollution are mobile, the problem of creating appropriate incentives is much more complex than for stationary sources.

Where stationary sources generally are large and run by professional managers, automobiles are small and run by amateurs. Their small size makes it more difficult to control emissions without affecting performance, while amateur ownership makes it more likely that emissions control will deteriorate over time due to a lack of dependable maintenance and care.

These complications might lead us to conclude that perhaps we should ignore mobile sources and concentrate our control efforts solely on stationary sources. Unfortunately, that is not possible. Although each individual vehicle represents a miniscule part of the problem, mobile sources collectively represent a significant proportion of three criteria pollutants—ozone, carbon monoxide, and nitrogen dioxide—as well as a significant source of greenhouse gases.

For two of these—ozone and nitrogen dioxide—the process of reaching attainment has been particularly slow. With the increased use of diesel engines, mobile sources are becoming responsible for a rising proportion of particulate emissions.

Since it is necessary to control mobile sources, what policy options exist? What points of control are possible and what are the advantages or disadvantages of each? In exercising control over these sources, the government must first specify the agent charged with the responsibility for the reduction. The obvious candidates are the manufacturer and the owner-driver. The balancing of this responsibility should depend on a comparative analysis of costs and benefits, with particular reference to such factors as (1) the number of agents to be regulated, (2) the rate of deterioration while in use, (3) the life expectancy of automobiles, and (4) the availability, effectiveness, and cost of programs to reduce emissions at the point of production and at the point of use.

While automobiles are numerous and ubiquitous, they are manufactured by a small number of firms. It is easier and less expensive to administer a system that controls relatively few sources, so regulation at the production point has considerable appeal.

Some problems are associated with limiting controls solely to the point of production, however. If the factory-controlled emissions rate deteriorates during normal usage, control at the point of production may buy only temporary emissions reduction. Although the deterioration of emissions control can be combated with warranty and recall provisions, the costs of these supporting programs have to be balanced against the costs of local control.

Automobiles are durable, so new vehicles make up only a relatively small percentage of the total fleet of vehicles. Therefore, control at the point of production, which affects only new equipment, takes longer to produce a given reduction in aggregate emissions because newer, controlled cars replace old vehicles very slowly. Control at the point of production produces emissions reductions more slowly than a program securing emissions reductions from used as well as new vehicles.

Some possible means of reducing mobile-source pollution cannot be accomplished by regulating emissions at the point of production because they involve choices made by the owner-driver. The point-of-production strategy is oriented toward reducing the amount of emissions per mile driven in a particular type of car, but only the owner can decide what kind of car to drive, as well as when and where to drive it.

These are not trivial concerns. Diesel and hybrid automobiles, buses, trucks, and motorcycles emit different amounts of pollutants than do standard gasoline-powered automobiles.

Changing the mix of vehicles on the road affects the amount and type of emissions even if passenger miles remain unchanged.

Clustered emissions cause higher concentration levels than dispersed emissions; therefore, driving in urban areas causes more environmental damage than driving in rural areas. Local control strategies could internalize these location costs; a uniform national strategy focusing solely on the point of production could not.

Timing of emissions is particularly important because conventional commuting patterns lead to a clustering of emissions during the morning and evening rush hours. Indeed, plots of pollutant concentrations in urban areas during an average day typically produce a graph with two peaks, corresponding to the two rush hours.[2] Since high concentrations are more dangerous than low concentrations, some spreading over the 24-hour period could also prove beneficial.

Subsidies and Externalities

Vehicles emit an inefficiently high level of pollution because their owner-drivers are not bearing the full cost of that pollution. This inefficiently low cost, in turn, has two sources: (1) implicit subsidies for road transport and (2) a failure by drivers to internalize external costs.

Implicit Subsidies

Several categories of the social costs associated with transporting goods and people over roads are related to mileage driven, but the private costs do not reflect that relationship. For example:

- Road construction and maintenance costs, which are largely determined by vehicle miles, are mostly funded out of tax dollars. On average, states raise only 38 percent of their road funds from fuel taxes. The marginal private cost of an extra mile driven on road construction and maintenance funded from general taxes is zero, but the social cost is not.
- Despite the fact that building and maintaining parking space is expensive, parking is frequently supplied by employers at no marginal cost to the employee. The ability to park a car for free creates a bias toward private auto travel since other modes receive no comparable subsidy.

Other *transport subsidies* create a bias toward gas-guzzling vehicles that produce inefficiently high levels of emissions. In the United States, one example not long ago was that business owners who purchased large, gas-guzzling sport utility vehicles (SUVs) received a substantial tax break worth tens of thousands of dollars, while purchasers of small energy-efficient cars received none (Ball & Lundegaard, 2002). (Only vehicles weighing over 6000 pounds qualified.)

This tax break was established 20 years earlier for "light trucks," primarily to benefit small farmers who depended upon the trucks for chores around the farms. More recently, most purchasers of SUVs, considered "light trucks" for tax purposes, have nothing to do with farming.

Externalities

Road users also fail to bear the full cost of their choices because many of the costs associated with those choices are actually borne by others. For example:

- The social costs associated with accidents are a function of vehicle miles. The number of accidents rises as the number of miles driven rises. Generally the costs associated with these accidents are paid for by insurance, but the premiums for these insurance policies rarely reflect the mileage–accident relationship. As a result, the additional private cost of insurance for additional miles driven is typically zero, although the social cost is certainly not zero.
- Road congestion creates externalities by increasing the amount of time required to travel a given distance. Increased travel times also increase the amount of fuel used.
- The social costs associated with greenhouse gas emissions are also a function of vehicle miles. These costs are rarely borne by the driver of the vehicle.
- Recent studies have indicated high levels of pollution inside vehicles, caused mainly by the exhaust of cars in front.

Because the social costs of driving are not fully borne by motorists, the number of miles driven is inefficiently high.[3]

To elaborate on the congestion point, consider Figure 7.1. As traffic volumes get closer to the design capacity of the roadway, traffic flow decreases; it takes more time to travel between two points. At this point, the marginal private and social costs begin to diverge. The driver entering a congested roadway will certainly consider the extra time it will take her to travel that route, but she will not consider the extra time that her presence imposes on everyone else; it is an externality.

The efficient ratio of traffic volume to road capacity (V_e) occurs where the marginal benefits (as revealed by the demand curve) equal the marginal social cost. Because individual drivers do not internalize the external costs of their presence on this roadway, too many drivers will use the roadway and traffic volume will be too high (V_p). The resulting efficiency losses would be measured by the triangle ACD (the shaded area). One recent study estimates that highway congestion in 2014 caused 6.9 billion hours of delay, 3.1 billion gallons of additional fuel to be used, resulting in a cost of $160 billion to highway users.[4]

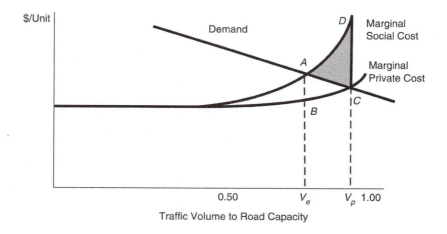

Figure 7.1 Congestion Inefficiency

Consequences

Understated road transport costs create a number of perverse incentives. Too many roads are crowded. Too many miles are driven. Too many trips are taken. Transport energy use is too high. Pollution from transportation is excessive. Competitive modes, including mass transit, bicycles, and walking, suffer from an inefficiently low demand.

Perhaps the most pernicious effect of understated transport cost, however, is its effect on land use. Low transport cost encourages dispersed settlement patterns. Residences can be located far from work and shopping because the costs of travel are so low. Unfortunately, this pattern of dispersal creates a path dependence that is hard to reverse. Once settlement patterns are dispersed, it is difficult to justify high-volume transportation alternatives (such as trains or buses). Both need high-density travel corridors in order to generate the ridership necessary to pay the high fixed cost associated with building and running these systems. With dispersed settlement patterns, sufficiently high travel densities are difficult, if not impossible, to generate.

Policy toward Mobile Sources

History of US Policy

Concern about mobile-source pollution originated in Southern California in the early 1950s, following a path-breaking study by Dr. A. J. Haagen-Smit of the California Institute of Technology. The study by Dr. Haagen-Smit identified motor vehicle emissions as a key culprit in forming the photochemical smog for which Southern California was becoming infamous.

In the United States, the Clean Air Act Amendments of 1965 set national standards for hydrocarbon and carbon monoxide emissions from automobiles to take effect during 1968. Interestingly, the impetus for this act came not only from the scientific data on the effects of automobile pollution, but also from the automobile industry itself. The industry saw uniform federal standards as a way to avoid a situation in which every state passed its own unique set of emissions standards, something the auto industry wanted to avoid. This pressure was successful in that the law prohibits all states, except California, from setting their own standards.

By 1970 the slow progress being made on air pollution control in general and automobile pollution in particular created the political will to act. In a "get tough" mood as it developed the Clean Air Act Amendments of 1970, Congress required new emissions standards that would reduce emissions by 90 percent below their uncontrolled levels. This reduction was to have been achieved by 1975 for hydrocarbon and carbon monoxide emissions and by 1976 for nitrogen dioxide. It was generally agreed at the time the Act was passed that the technology to meet the standards did not exist. By passing this tough Act, Congress hoped to force the development of an appropriate technology.

It did not work out that way. The following years ushered in a series of deadline extensions. In 1972 the automobile manufacturers requested a 1-year delay in the implementation of the standards. The administrator of the EPA denied the request and was taken to court. At the conclusion of the litigation in April 1973, the administrator granted a 1-year delay in the 1975 deadline for the hydrocarbon and carbon monoxide standards. Subsequently, in July 1973, a 1-year delay was granted for nitrogen oxides as well.[5] That was not the last deferred deadline.

The US and EU Policy Approaches

The overall design of US policies for addressing mobile-source air pollution has served as a model for mobile-source control in many other countries (particularly in Europe). The US approach represents a blend of controlling emissions at the point of manufacture with controlling emissions from vehicles in use. New car emissions standards are administered through a certification program and an associated enforcement program.

Certification and Enforcement Programs. The certification program tests prototypes of car models for conformity to federal standards. Only engine families with a certificate of conformity are allowed to be sold.

The certification program is complemented by an associated enforcement program that contains assembly-line testing, as well as recall and anti-tampering procedures and warranty provisions. If these tests reveal that more than 40 percent of the cars do not conform to federal standards, the certificate may be suspended or revoked.

In addition, the EPA conducts in-use (on-road) testing of vehicles, both at low mileage (at least 10,000 miles) and at high mileage (more than 50,000 miles).

The EPA has also been given the power to require manufacturers to recall and remedy manufacturing defects that cause emissions to exceed federal standards. If the EPA uncovers a defect, it usually requests the manufacturer to recall vehicles for corrective action. If the manufacturer refuses, the EPA can order a recall.

EU regulators pursue a similar testing approach, but EU tests tend to be less restrictive and do not include in-use testing. As Example 7.1 illustrates, these certification programs may not always provide the outcomes that they were designed to produce.

EXAMPLE 7.1

Monitoring and Enforcement: The Volkswagen Experience

On-road testing has some obvious advantages of pre-sale certification. It can, for example, take into consideration how durable the emissions control system is as the car ages. On the other hand, it is more expensive. So, from an economic point of view, whether the additional cost of on-road testing is worth it becomes of considerable interest. The US has chosen to incorporate on-road testing, while the EU has not.

Recently an experience where Volkswagen falsified their testing results has provided new information on the added value of on-road testing. In September of 2015, Volkswagen admitted to having programmed nearly 11 million vehicles to cheat on tailpipe emissions tests. According to the investigation the company created special software that could sense when the car was being tested and would activate equipment that reduced emissions. Once software sensed that the testing was concluded, it returned the car to a normal driving mode apparently to increase performance and drivability. Unfortunately this setting also resulted in emission levels far above legal limits.

The falsification was actually discovered in the United States via on-road testing. Some on-road testing in May 2014, conducted by researchers at West Virginia University, led the California Air Resources Board to investigate Volkswagen. Ultimately Volkswagen admitted the falsification.

In September 2015 the US Environmental Protection Agency ordered Volkswagen to recall its American car models with affected engines, amounting to nearly 600,000 vehicles. The vast majority of the cars—about 8.5 million—are in Europe, with much smaller numbers scattered around Asia, Africa, and South America.

This example suggests that certification may not always be as reliable as conventionally assumed and on-road testing may have an additional benefit—detecting fraud.

Sources: Gates, Gilbert, Ewing, Jack, Russell, Karl, & Watkins, Derek. (March 16, 2017). How Volkswagen's "defeat devices" worked. *The New York Times.* Available online at: www.nytimes.com/interactive/2015/business/international/vw-diesel-emissions-scandal-explained.html?_r=0 (accessed June 26, 2017); Klier, Thomas, & Linn, Joshua. (April 2016). Comparing US and EU approaches to regulating automotive emissions and fuel economy. Resources for the Future Policy Brief No. 16-03.

Lead Phaseout Program

Section 211 of the US Clean Air Act provides the EPA with the authority to regulate lead and any other fuel additives used in gasoline. Under this provision, gasoline suppliers were required to make unleaded gasoline available. By ensuring the availability of unleaded gasoline, this regulation sought to reduce the amount of airborne lead, as well as to protect the effectiveness of the catalytic converter, which was poisoned by lead.[6]

In the mid-1980s, prior to the issuance of new, more stringent regulations on lead in gasoline, the EPA announced the results of a benefit-cost analysis of their expected impact. The analysis concluded that the proposed 0.01 gram per leaded gallon (gplg) standard would result in $36 billion (1983 dollars) in benefits (from reduced adverse health effects) at an estimated cost to the refining industry of $2.6 billion. These actions followed a highly publicized series of medical research findings on the severe health and developmental consequences, particularly to small children, of even low levels of atmospheric lead. On March 7, 1985, the EPA issued regulations imposing strict new standards on the allowable lead content in refined gasoline. The primary phaseout of lead was completed by 1986.

Although the regulation was unquestionably justified on efficiency grounds, the EPA wanted to allow flexibility in how the deadlines were met without increasing the amount of lead used. While some refiners could meet early deadlines with ease, others could do so only with a significant increase in cost. Recognizing that meeting the goal did not require every refiner to meet every deadline, the EPA initiated an innovative program to provide additional flexibility in meeting the regulations (see Example 7.2). The program was successful in reducing both lead emissions and the concentration of lead in the ambient air. From 1981 to 2001, emissions of lead fell by 93 percent and concentrations of lead in the air fell by 94 percent.

By contrast, the European Union (EU) banned leaded gasoline in 2000 and implemented stricter emissions standards for light-duty vehicles in 2005. Russia, in principle, agreed to follow the example of Western Europe in introducing more stringent emissions controls, but the phaseout of lead has been much slower. By 1995, only eight of Russia's 25 oil refineries manufactured unleaded gasoline. This made up 40 percent of the gasoline produced in Russia. A 2001 World Bank study found that it would cost between $0.005 and $0.02 per liter of

EXAMPLE 7.2

Getting the Lead Out: The Lead Phaseout Program

Under the Lead Phaseout Program, a fixed number of lead rights (authorizing the use of a fixed amount of lead in gasoline produced during the period) were allocated to the 195 or so refineries. (Due to a loophole in the regulations, some new "alcohol blender" refineries were created to take advantage of the program, but their impact was very small.) The number of issued rights declined over time. Refiners who did not need their full share of authorized rights could sell their rights to other refiners.

Initially no banking of rights was allowed (rights had to be created and used in the same quarter), but the EPA subsequently allowed banking. Once banking was initiated, created rights could be used in that period or any subsequent period up to the end of the program in 1987. Prices of rights, which were initially about 0.75 cents per gram of lead, rose to 4 cents after banking was allowed.

Refiners had an incentive to eliminate the lead quickly because early reductions freed up rights for sale. Acquiring these credits made it possible for other refiners to comply with the deadlines, even in the face of equipment failures or acts of God; fighting the deadlines in court, the traditional response, was unnecessary. Designed purely as a means of facilitating the transition to this new regime, the lead banking program ended as scheduled on December 31, 1987.

Sources: Nussbaum, B. D. (1992). Phasing down lead in gasoline in the US: Mandates, incentives, trading and banking. In T. Jones & J. Corfee-Morlot (Eds.). *Climate Change: Designing a Tradeable Permit System*. Paris: Organisation for Economic Co-operation and Development Publication, 21–34; Hahn, R. W., & Hester, G. L. (1989). Marketable permits: Lessons from theory and practice. *Ecology Law Quarterly, 16*, 361–406.

gasoline to phase out lead at a less modern refinery in Russia. These costs could be cut in half, however, if the refinery's production were modified to meet market demand.[7]

Fuel Economy Standards—the US Approach

The Corporate Average Fuel Economy (CAFE) program, established in 1975, was designed to reduce American dependence on foreign oil by producing more fuel-efficient vehicles. Although it is not an emissions control program, fuel efficiency does affect emissions.

The program requires each automaker to meet government-set miles-per-gallon targets (CAFE standards) for all its car and light truck fleets sold in the United States each year. The unique feature is that the standard is a *fleet average*, not a standard applied to each vehicle. As a result, automakers can sell some low-mileage vehicles as long as they sell enough high-mileage vehicles to raise the average to the standard. The CAFE standards took effect in 1978, mandating a fleet average of 18 miles per gallon (mpg) for automobiles. The standard increased each year until 1985, when it reached 27.5 mpg. Most observers believe that the CAFE standards did, in fact, reduce oil imports. During the 1977–1986 period, oil imports fell from 47 to 27 percent of total oil consumption. The CAFE standard remained at 27.5 mpg until 2005 when a new set of rules was announced.

CAFE standards, however, have had their share of problems. When Congress instituted the CAFE standards, light trucks were allowed to meet a lower fuel-economy standard because they constituted only 20 percent of the vehicle market and were used primarily as work vehicles. Light truck standards were set at 17.2 mpg for the 1979 model year and went up to 20.7 mpg in 1996 (combined two-wheel and four-wheel drive). With the burgeoning popularity of SUVs, which are counted as light trucks, trucks now comprise nearly half of the market. In addition, intense lobbying by the auto industry resulted in an inability of Congress to raise the standards from 1985 until 2004. As a result of the lower standards for trucks and SUVs, the absence of any offsetting increase in the fuel tax, and the increasing importance of trucks and SUVs in the fleet of on-road vehicles, the average miles per gallon for all vehicles declined, rather than improved. In 2005 the standard for light trucks saw its first increase since 1996 to 21 miles per gallon.

In 2008 the EPA made an adjustment in how the fleet average is calculated, specifically taking the footprint of the vehicle into account. Vehicles with a larger footprint are subject to lower fuel economy requirements. Since the footprint and fuel economy are now interrelated, the recent decline in gasoline prices has reduced the overall level of fuel economy by an estimated 10 percent. This is due in part to a shift to larger vehicles (Leard et al., 2017).[8]

The standards have continued their upward trend. In 2010, new rules were announced for both fuel efficiency and greenhouse gas emissions. These rules cover the 2012–2016 model years and the CAFE standard was set to reach 34.1 miles per gallon by 2016. The US EPA and the National Highway Traffic Safety Administration (NHTSA) calculated benefits and costs of the proposed program for medium- and heavy-duty trucks. Using a social cost of carbon of $22/ton and a 3 percent discount rate, they find costs to the industry of $7.7 billion and societal benefits of $49 billion, for a total net benefit of approximately $41 billion.[9] Imagine if they made this calculation using the revised estimate of $37/ton for the social cost of carbon. In 2012, the standards rose yet again to a target of 54.5 mpg by 2025.

Since new fuel economy standards only affect new vehicles, overall fuel economy takes a long time to improve—up to 15 years or until all the older cars are off the roads. This, combined with the "rebound effect," which says that better fuel economy increases miles driven, raises the question of whether fuel taxation is a more efficient policy than a fuel economy standard (Anderson et al., 2011). Debate 7.1 and Example 7.3 look at the evidence.

DEBATE 7.1

CAFE Standards or Fuel Taxes?

Increasing the fuel efficiency of oil consumption could, in principle, be accomplished by increasing either fuel taxes or fuel-efficiency standards. By raising the cost of driving, the former would encourage auto purchasers to seek more fuel-efficient vehicles, while the latter would ensure that the average new vehicle sold was fuel efficient. Does it make a difference which strategy is followed?

It turns out that it does, and economics can help explain why. Think about what each strategy does to the marginal cost of driving an extra mile. Increased fuel taxes raise the marginal cost per mile driven, but fuel-economy standards lower it. In the first case, the marginal cost per mile rises because the tax raises the cost of the fuel. In the second case, the more fuel-efficient cars uses less fuel per mile so the cost has gone down.

Following economic logic leads immediately to the conclusion that even if both strategies resulted in the same fuel economy, the tax would reduce oil consumption by more because it would promote fewer miles driven. On these grounds, a tax is better than a fuel-economy standard.

Austin and Dinan (2005) test these ideas with a simulation model in which they compare an increase in the CAFE standards to a gasoline tax designed to save the same amount of gasoline. Using a 12 percent discount rate, they estimate that a per gallon tax designed to save the same amount of gasoline as a stipulated fuel economy standard would cost 71 percent less than the comparable change in fuel-economy standards!

Supporters of fuel-economy standards, however, counter with two arguments: (1) in the United States, sufficiently high gasoline taxes to produce that level of reduction could never have passed Congress, so the fuel-economy standards were better, indeed much better, than no policy at all, and (2) at least one careful empirical study has found that the increase in driving resulting from the fuel economy standards in practice is likely to be very small, and may even be non-existent. This latter finding implies that studies like the one discussed above are likely to considerably overstate the cost-effectiveness advantage of a gasoline tax. Can you see why?

Which argument do you find most compelling?

Sources: Austin, D., & Dinan, T. (2005). Clearing the air: The costs and consequences of higher CAFE standards and increased gasoline taxes. *Journal of Environmental Economics and Management, 50,* 562–582; West, Jeremy, Hoekstra, Mark, Meer, Jonathan, & Puller, Steven L. (May 2015). Vehicle miles (not) traveled: Why fuel economy requirements don't increase household driving. National Bureau of Economic Research Working Paper #21194.

EXAMPLE 7.3

Fuel Economy Standards When Fuel Prices Are Falling

Fuel economy standards are designed to reduce reliance on fossil fuels and to reduce emissions from vehicles. As we have seen in this chapter, fuel prices can counteract some of this effect if lower fuel prices cause increased vehicle miles traveled or if lower prices cause a shift toward the purchase of lower fuel economy cars. What about when fuel prices are rising?

Benjamin Leard, Joshua Linn, and Virginia McConnell, economists at think tank Resources for the Future, were curious about this question as well as the question of how standards based on vehicle attributes which also interact with market conditions might affect the overall effectiveness of the standards.

CAFE standards originally were based solely on a vehicle's class (car or light truck). Now, however, the standards also depend on the footprint of the vehicle. Consequently, automakers who sell larger vehicles are subject to lower fuel economy requirements (lowering overall fuel economy). For these more stringent standards, if gas prices fall, causing an increase in market share of low-fuel-economy cars, the manufacturer might have to respond by raising prices on those vehicles in order to meet the standard. Likewise, when fuel prices rise, market share of fuel-efficient cars will also rise.

Using data from 1996 to 2015, Leard et al. examine these questions statistically. Their data set includes periods of rising fuel prices, a period of relatively stable prices, a period from about 2008 to 2014 in which prices were quite volatile, and most recently when global crude oil prices dropped by about 25 percent. Interestingly, they find the effect of rising prices on market share of vehicles to be twice as large as falling prices. In other words, market shares respond more to price increases than price decreases and respond less after a period of prolonged high fuel prices.

Their results seem to suggest that because gas prices and overall fuel economy (market share) are interlinked, the best policy approach might be to combine the two approaches: standards and fuel taxes. What do you think?

Source: Leard, Benjamin, Linn, Joshua, & McConnell, Virginia. (2017). Fuel prices, new vehicle fuel economy, and implications for attribute based standards. *Journal of the Association of Environmental and Resource Economists*, 4(3); 659–700.

Gas Guzzler Tax

The Gas Guzzler Tax is levied on cars that do not meet fuel economy standards. Congress established this tax as part of the 1978 Energy Tax Act aimed at reducing the production and consumption of fuel inefficient vehicles. The tax is levied on the manufacturers and is over and above any CAFE fines the manufacturer might have to pay for not meeting its CAFE standard requirement. The tax is based on a formula that weights highway driving at 55 percent and city driving at 45 percent.[10]

Fuel Economy Standards in the European Union

The European Union has tackled the externalities from fuel consumption primarily through gas taxes and has some of the highest gas taxes in the world. Fuel economy standards are also higher than in the United States. The European Union standards are set to rise annually from the 2012 standard of 45 miles per gallon (5L/100 km). They also have a carbon dioxide target of 130 grams per kilometer. The European Union also combines standards with very high fuel taxes, which creates a larger demand for small cars (Anderson et al., 2011). EU countries also tax diesel at lower rates than gasoline and as such diesel's share of passenger cars has grown significantly. The Netherlands, Norway, Germany, and Sweden used differential tax rates to encourage consumers to purchase (and manufacturers to produce) low-emitting cars before subsequent regulations required all cars to be low emitting. Tax differentiation confers a tax advantage (and, hence, after-tax price advantage) on cleaner cars. The amount of the tax usually depends on (1) the emissions characteristics of the car (heavier taxes being levied on heavily polluting cars), (2) the size of the car (in Germany, heavier cars qualify for larger tax advantages to offset the relatively high control requirements placed upon them), and

(3) the year of purchase (the tax differential is declining since all cars will eventually have to meet the standards).

Apparently it worked. In Sweden, 87 percent of the new cars sold qualified for the tax advantage, while in Germany the comparable figure was more than 90 percent (Opschoor & Vos, 1989).

Europe not only has much higher gasoline prices, but also it has developed strategies to make better use of transportation capital. Its intercity rail system is better developed than the one in the United States, and public transit ridership is typically higher within cities. Europe was also a pioneer in the use of car-sharing arrangements, an idea that the United States has now begun to mimic (see Example 7.4).

EXAMPLE 7.4

Car-Sharing: Better Use of Automotive Capital?

One of the threats to sustainable development is the growing number of vehicles on the road. Though great progress has been made since the 1970s in limiting the pollution each vehicle emits per mile of travel, as the number of vehicles and the number of miles increase, the resulting increases in pollution offset much of the gains from the cleaner vehicles.

How to limit the number of vehicles? One strategy that started in Europe and has migrated to America is car-sharing. Car-sharing recognizes that the typical automobile sits idle most of the time, a classic case of excess capacity. (Studies in Germany suggest the average vehicle use per day is 1 hour.) Therefore the car-sharing strategy tries to spread ownership of a vehicle over several owners who share both the cost and the use.

Car sharing is now a major industry and there are car sharing programs in 30 countries on five continents.

The charges imposed by car-sharing clubs typically involve an upfront access fee plus fees based both on time of actual use and mileage. (Use during the peak periods usually costs more.) Some car-sharing clubs offer touch-tone automated booking, 24-hour dispatchers, and such amenities as child-safety seats, bike racks, and roof carriers.

Swiss and German clubs started in the late 1980s. As of 2013, 460,000 Germans belonged to car sharing clubs, up from 20,000 in 1997. An estimated 30 percent of customers sell their own cars after joining a car sharing program. The greatest concentrations of car-sharing vehicles in Europe are in the Netherlands, Austria, Germany, and Switzerland. The European idea of car-sharing was captured by some US entrepreneurs who started Zipcar, a company that now boasts 400,000 members and fleets of car-sharing vehicles in 50 cities in North America and the United Kingdom. Similar car-sharing companies can now be found in hundreds of cities.

The University of California, Berkeley's Transportation Sustainability Research Center (TSRC) and Susan Shaheen have been tracking car-sharing developments worldwide since 1997. They report that as of January 1, 2014, 24 US car-sharing programs claimed 1,228,573 members sharing 17,179 vehicles.

What could the contribution of car-sharing be to air pollution control in those areas where it catches on? It probably does lower the number of vehicles and the resulting congestion. Zipcar claims that each Zipcar takes 15–20 personally owned vehicles off the road. In addition, peak-hour pricing probably encourages use at the less polluted periods. On the other hand, it does not necessarily lower the number of miles driven, which is one of the keys to lowering pollution. The contribution of this particular innovation remains to be clarified by some solid empirical research.

Source: Oliviera Jr., Pedro (2013). Car sharing takes off in Germany. Available at: www.pri.org/stories/2013-10-04/car-sharing-takes-germany; What do you do when you are green, broke and connected? You share. (October 10, 2010). *The Economist.* Retrieved from: www.economist.com/node/17249322?story_id=17249322&fsrc=rss; www.zipcar.com; Shaheen, Susan, & Chan, Nelson. (March 2015). Mobility and the sharing economy: Impacts synopsis—spring 2015. Available at: http://innovativemobility.org/?project=mobility-and-the-sharing-economy-impacts-synopsis-2.

Fuel Economy Standards in Other Countries

Anderson et al. (2011) summarize fuel economy standards outside of the United States for countries including Japan, China, South Korea, Australia, and the United Kingdom. Japan has some of the most stringent standards with different standards for diesel and gasoline vehicles. China sets fuel consumption standards that are based on weight.

External Benefits of Fuel Economy Standards

Fuel economy standards create positive externalities in two ways. First, fuel efficiency lowers emissions. Lower carbon dioxide emissions as well as reduced dependence on foreign fuels are both positive externalities that flow from better fuel efficiency. These external benefits along with the political feasibility of fuel efficiency makes CAFE standards an appealing option.

Interestingly, in a thorough evaluation of the literature on consumer responses to fuel economy, Helfand and Wolverton (2011) find that automakers do not build in as much fuel economy as consumers are willing to purchase. Although the literature is so far inconclusive as to why this is the case, they posit that uncertainty, attribute bundling, and the vehicle design process all play a role. If manufacturers are risk adverse and returns to fuel economy are uncertain, they will provide a lower level of fuel economy. Automakers will also invest more in those attributes for which consumers have already exhibited a strong preference. These attributes include size and performance. Additionally, since attributes tend to be bundled, consumers can chose a bundle of attributes including color, features, and so on. Fuel economy is not a bundled attribute so it may not be a priorty for manufacturers to vary. Finally, new designs take time and as such manufacturers many not be as responsive to consumer's preferences in the short run (Helfand & Wolverton, 2011).

Alternative Fuels and Vehicles

Alternative Fuels. The Clean Air Act Amendments of 1990 required nonattainment areas to use cleaner-burning (oxygenated) automotive fuels during the winter months in some cases and year round (reformulated gasoline) in the worst cases. Ethanol and methyl tertiary butyl ether (MTBE) were the two additives most widely used to meet the oxygen content standard.

Largely due to cost, most non-Midwestern states opted for gasoline with the additive MTBE, rather than ethanol. MTBE was designed to make gasoline burn cleaner and more efficiently. Unfortunately, once it entered into widespread use, it was discovered to be a source of contaminated groundwater and drinking water. Once in soil or water, MTBE breaks down very slowly while accelerating the spread of other contaminants in gasoline, such as benzene, a known carcinogen. Once these properties became known, several states passed measures to ban or significantly limit the use of MTBE in gasoline.

The MTBE story provides an interesting case study of the problems that can occur with a strategy that relies on a "technical fix" to solve air pollution problems. Sometimes the effects of the "solution" can, in retrospect, turn out to be worse than the original problem.

Even before the MTBE water contamination issue surfaced, questions were also being raised about the cost-effectiveness of using oxygenated fuels. For example, when Rask (2004) compared the oxyfuel smog test results to emissions improvements resulting from emissions system repairs, he found increased maintenance and repairs to be a much more cost-effective strategy for lowering CO and hydrocarbon emissions than oxyfuels.

In 1989 the South Coast Air Quality Management District identified 120 options for reducing volatile hydrocarbons. The average cost-effectiveness of the 68 measures proposed was a stunning $12,250 per ton. While early estimates such as these should not determine the outcome, they certainly did suggest that some caution against proceeding too rapidly down this path would be appropriate.

Alternative Vehicles. In an attempt to foster the development of alternative vehicles and alternative fuels that would be less damaging to the environment, Congress and some states have passed legislation requiring their increased use.

California has pushed the envelope even further. In September 1990, the California Air Resources Board (CARB) passed its zero emission vehicle (ZEV) regulations.

Under the ZEV regulation, three distinct vehicle designs are considered "zero emission," though to varying degrees: (1) plug-in hybrid vehicles, which combine a conventional gasoline-powered engine with a battery, (2) battery electric vehicles, which run entirely on electricity, and (3) hydrogen fuel cell vehicles, which run on electricity produced from a fuel cell using hydrogen gas.

The program works by imposing increasingly stringent sales quotas on ZEV vehicles. The quotas are expressed as a percentage of new cars and light trucks sold in the state that must be zero emission vehicles.

The program is implemented using a credit system. The program assigns each automaker "ZEV credits," which represent the company's sales of electric cars and trucks. Automakers are then required to maintain ZEV credits equal to a set percentage of non-electric sales. The current percentage is 4.5 percent of sales in 2018, rising to 22 percent in 2025.[11]

Clearly, this is an attempt to force automotive technology using a rather innovative method—mandated sales quotas for clean vehicles. Notice that selling this number of clean vehicles depends not only on how many are manufactured, but also on whether demand for those vehicles is sufficient. If the demand is not sufficient, manufacturers will have to rely on factory rebates or other strategies to promote sufficient demand. Inadequate demand is not a legal defense for failing to meet the deadlines.

How well has this strategy worked in forcing the development and market penetration of new automotive technologies? According to the CARB, California is one of the world's largest markets for light-duty ZEVs. According to their data as of Summer 2016, Californians drive 47 percent of all ZEVs on the road in the US, while the US comprises about one-third of the world ZEV market.[12] Of course discerning the specific contribution of this program would require a deeper analysis and not merely a point in time comparison, but these data are intriguing.

Transportation Pricing

The pricing of transportation falls into several categories: fuel taxes; congestion pricing; emissions pricing; pricing of accident externalities; pricing of roads; and pricing or subsidizing public transport. Some of examples of road pricing are highlighted below.[13]

Fuel Taxes. As controls on manufacturers have become more common and vehicles have become cleaner, attention is increasingly turning to the user. Drivers have little incentive to drive or maintain their cars in a manner that minimizes emissions because the full social costs of road transport have not been internalized by current policy. How far from a full internalization of cost are we? Parry et al. (2007) compile estimates from the literature and find the sum of mileage-related external marginal costs to be approximately $2.10 per gallon.

Mileage-related externalities include local pollution, congestion, and accidents. Fuel external costs, such as oil dependency and climate change, are another $0.18 per gallon. Figure 7.2 illustrates current fuel taxes by country. These data suggest current fuel taxes would have to be much higher in many countries in order to internalize the full social cost of road transport.

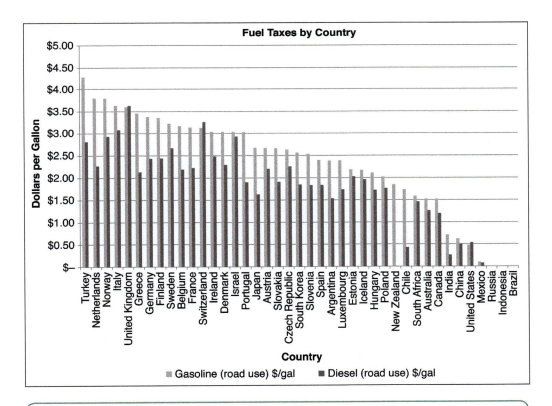

Figure 7.2 2016 Fuel Taxes in Selected Countries

Source: https://afdc.energy.gov/data/?q=fuel+taxes

Note: Tax rates are federal, with the exception of the United States and Canada, which include average state/provincial taxes.

But fuel taxes are not the only way to begin to internalize costs, and, by themselves, they would be a blunt instrument anyway because typically they would not take into account when and where the emissions occurred. One way to focus on these temporal and spatial concerns is through congestion pricing.

Congestion Pricing. Congestion is influenced not only by how many vehicle miles are traveled, but also where and when the driving occurs. Congestion pricing addresses the spatial and temporal externalities by charging for driving on congested roads or at congested times. Four different types of congestion pricing mechanisms are in current use: (1) cordon (area or zonal) pricing, (2) facilities pricing, (3) pricing lanes, and (4) high occupancy toll (HOT) lanes.[14] Congestion pricing of roads or zones has recently been gaining considerable attention as a targeted remedy for these time- and space-specific pollutant concentrations. Anas and Lindsey (2011) note that truly efficient congestion pricing is challenging to implement because the toll not only varies over time, but also varies with lane width, travel speed, and the types of vehicles on the road. The amount of information necessary to implement fully efficient tolls may be unrealistically high.

Toll rings have existed for some time in Oslo, Norway, and Milan, Italy. In the United States, electronic toll collection systems are currently in place in many states. Express lanes for cars with electronic meters reduce congestion at toll booths. Reserved express bus lanes during peak hour periods are also common in the United States for congested urban highways. (Reserved lanes for express buses lower the relative travel time for bus commuters, thereby providing an incentive for passengers to switch from cars to buses.) High occupancy vehicle (HOV) lanes have also been established for some highways. During certain hours, vehicles traveling in the HOV lanes must have more than one passenger. Honolulu, Hawaii, has a high occupancy "zipper lane." The zipper lane is in the middle of the highway; in the morning commute hours the traffic travels toward Honolulu and by mid-afternoon the lane is literally zipped up on one side and unzipped on the other, creating an additional lane for the outgoing evening commute.

Several cities have also undertaken some innovative approaches to congestion charges including London, Stockholm, and Singapore. Perhaps the most far-reaching can be found in Singapore (Example 7.5). Bangkok also bars vehicles from transporting goods from certain parts of the metropolitan area during various peak hours, leaving the roads available to buses, cars, and motorized tricycles.

Beijing is currently evaluating a draft proposal to charge a congestion fee for commuters who enter certain parts of the city. In Beijing there are 5.6 million vehicles, more than any other city in the world. Linn et al. (2015) find that the proposed fee will affect those who make discretionary trips rather than commuters. In part that is due to the nature of the affected commuters. The commuters most likely to be affected by the charge will be wealthier since they tend to live outside the congestion ring and typically drive to work, but they are likely to be less responsive than those with lower incomes would be.

Safirova et al. (2007) compare six different road-pricing instruments all aimed at internalizing the congestion externality. These include three types of cordon pricing schemes (area-based congestion taxes): a distance-based toll on highways, a distance-based toll on metro roads only, and a gas tax. Examining the effectiveness of these instruments for the Washington, DC, metropolitan area in 2000, they explicitly model how residential choice (and hence travel time) could be affected by the type of policy instrument employed. The question they ask is "But how do policies designed to address congestion alone fare, once the many other consequences associated with driving—traffic accidents, air pollution, oil

EXAMPLE 7.5

Zonal Mobile-Source Pollution-Control Strategies: Singapore

Singapore has one of the most comprehensive strategies to control vehicle pollution in the world. In addition to imposing very high vehicle-registration fees, this approach also includes the following:

- Central Business District parking fees that are higher during normal business hours than during the evenings and on weekends.
- An area-licensing scheme that requires the display of an area-specific purchased vehicle license in order to gain entry to restricted downtown zones during restricted hours. These licenses are expensive and penalties for not displaying them when required are very steep.
- Electronic peak-hour pricing on roadways. These charges, which are deducted automatically using a "smart card" technology, vary by roadway and by time of day. Conditions are reviewed and charges are adjusted every 3 months.
- An option for people to purchase an "off-peak" car. Identified by a distinctive red license plate that is welded to the vehicle, these vehicles can only be used during off-peak periods. Owners of these vehicles pay much lower registration fees and road taxes.
- Limiting the number of new vehicles that can be registered each year. In order to ensure that they can register a new car, potential buyers must first secure one of the fixed number of licenses by submitting a winning financial bid.
- An excellent mass-transit system that provides a viable alternative to automobile travel.

Has the program been effective? Apparently, it has been quite effective in two rather different ways. First, it has provided a significant amount of revenue for the government, which the government can use to reduce more burdensome taxes. (The revenues go into the general treasury; they are not earmarked for the transport sector.) Second, it has caused a large reduction in traffic-related pollution in the affected areas. The overall levels of carbon monoxide, lead, sulfur dioxide, and nitrogen dioxide are now all within the human-health guidelines established by both the World Health Organization and the US Environmental Protection Agency.

Source: Chia, N. C., & Phang, S.-Y. (2001). Motor vehicle taxes as an environmental management instrument: The case of Singapore. *Environmental Economics and Policy Studies*, 4(2), 67–93.

dependency, urban sprawl, and noise, to name a few—are taken into account?"[15] They find that using "social-cost pricing" (incorporating the social costs of driving) instead of simple congestion pricing affects the outcome of instrument choice. Specifically, when the policy goal is solely to reduce congestion, variable time-of-day pricing on the entire road network is the most effective and efficient policy. However, when additional social costs are factored in, the vehicle miles traveled (VMT) tax is almost as efficient.

Private Toll Roads. New policies are also being considered to ensure that road users pay all the costs of maintaining the highways, rather than transferring that burden to taxpayers. One strategy, which has been implemented in Mexico and in Orange County, California, is to allow construction of new private toll roads. The tolls are set high enough to recover all construction and maintenance costs and in some cases may include congestion pricing.

Parking Cash-Outs. Providing parking spaces for employees costs employers money, yet most of them provide this benefit free of charge. This employer-financed subsidy reduces one significant cost of driving to work. Since this subsidy only benefits those who drive to work, it lowers the relative cost of driving vis-à-vis all other transport choices, such as walking, biking, and public transport. Most of those choices create much less air pollution; therefore, the resulting bias toward driving creates an inefficiently high level of pollution.

One way to rectify this bias is for employers to compensate employees who do not use a parking space with an equivalent increase in income. This would transfer the employer's savings in not having to provide a parking spot to the employee and remove the bias toward driving to work.

Bike Sharing Programs. Expensive and hard to find city parking and congestion helps incentivize consumers to find alternative means of transportation. Urban bike sharing programs have emerged in cities and are growing in popularity. Large cities such as Denver, Montreal, Minneapolis, New Orleans, and others have adopted these systems. New York City's Citibike program logs over 60,000 riders on some days (www.citibikenyc.com/system-data).

Common pricing for these bike share programs involves a membership fee plus pricing based on the rental time used. Typically, 30 minutes or less is free and over 30 minutes is priced at an increasing block rate. Data suggests that many riders who are approaching the 30-minute mark will return that bike to a stand and take out another. That new bike now has 30 minutes for "free." This behavior of docking a bicycle to keep trip length under a time limit is called "daisy-chaining." Daisy-chaining adds time to a commute since riders might need to go a short distance out of their way to dock the bike and take out another, but the cost savings can be significant depending on the marginal price of the next 30 minutes.

Pricing Public Transport. The common notion is that public transit reduces vehicle miles and hence reduces both emissions and energy use. That outcome, however, is not inevitable and the fares charged on public transit should reflect the actual situation.

In the absence of congestion, public transportation fees should equal the marginal cost of the service minus a subsidy that reflects the external benefits of taking public transportation (Anas & Lindsey, 2011). If the public transport actually turns out to increase congestion, however, fares should also include a congestion charge.

The level of the external benefits subsidy should also reflect the local situation. Although the subsidy may attract new riders to public transit, the source of these riders is important in structuring the fares. Did they actually come from personal vehicles? Or were they riders that would not otherwise have taken a trip? Subsidies may also attract riders that use public transport (such as light rail) as a complement, rather than a substitute, for driving. Subsidies that were designed by assuming that all public transit trips represent shifts from private vehicles will be excessively high to the extent these other trip sources are prevalent (Anas & Lindsey, 2011).

Feebates. Some research has found that consumers may undervalue fuel economy. One study found that consumers only consider the first 3 years of fuel savings when choosing a more fuel-efficient vehicle. This understates the value of fuel savings by up to 60 percent (NRC, 2002). To remedy this undervaluation bias among consumers purchasing new vehicles, feebates combine taxes on purchases of new high-emitting (or high-fuel-consumption) vehicles with subsidies for purchases of new low-emitting/low-fuel-consumption vehicles. By raising the relative cost of high-emitting vehicles, it encourages consumers to take the environmental effects of those vehicles into account. Feebate system structures are based on a boundary that separates vehicles charged a tax from those entitled to rebates. The simplest feebate structure uses a constant dollar rate per gallon of fuel consumed. The revenue from the taxes can serve as the financing for the subsidies, but previous experience indicates that policies such as this are rarely revenue-neutral; the subsidy payouts typically exceed the revenue from the fee. Feebates are not yet widely used, but Ontario, Canada, and Austria have implemented feebates. Greene et al. (2005) find that feebates achieve fuel economy increases that are two times higher than those achieved by either rebates or gas guzzler taxes alone.

Tax Credits for Electric Vehicles. Tax credits subsidize the purchase of electric vehicles and can be as high as $7,500 per vehicle in the United States. Consumers who purchase electric vehicles not only receive a tax credit but also pay less in gasoline and emit fewer greenhouse gases, both of which have external benefits. However, tax credits also have a downside—they lower tax revenue. The loss of revenue due to tax credits has been estimated to be $7.5 billion through 2019. Yet, since they help manufacturers reduce their miles per gallon average for new cars, the sales of electric vehicles help them to meet the CAFE standards.[16]

The availability of credits for any particular manufacturer's cars expires after that automaker sells 200,000 qualified vehicles. The theory behind this number is that it should be enough sales to produce sufficient economies of scale to make their unsubsidized price competitive.

Pay-as-You-Drive (PAYD) Insurance. Another possibility for internalizing an environmental externality associated with automobile travel, thereby reducing both accidents and pollution, involves changing the way car insurance is financed. As Example 7.6 illustrates, small changes could potentially make a big difference.

Accelerated Retirement Strategies. A final reform possibility involves strategies to accelerate the retirement of older, polluting vehicles. This could be accomplished either by raising the cost of holding onto older vehicles (as with higher registration fees for vehicles that pollute more) or by providing a bounty of some sort to those retiring heavily polluting vehicles early.

Under one version of a bounty program, stationary sources were allowed to claim emissions reduction credits for heavily polluting vehicles that were removed from service. Heavily polluting vehicles were identified either by inspection and maintenance programs or remote sensing. Vehicle owners could bring their vehicle up to code, usually an expensive proposition, or they could sell it to the company running the retirement program. Purchased vehicles are usually disassembled for parts and the remainder is recycled. The number of emissions reduction credits earned by the company running the program depends on such factors as the remaining useful life of the car and the estimated number of miles it would be driven and is controlled so that the transaction results in a net increase in air quality.

EXAMPLE 7.6

Modifying Car Insurance as an Environmental Strategy

Although improvements in automobile technology (such as air bags and antilock brakes) have made driving much safer than in the past, the numbers of road deaths and injuries are still inefficiently high. Since people do not consider the full societal cost of accident risk when deciding how much and how often to drive, the number of vehicle miles traveled is excessive. Although drivers are very likely to take into account the risk of injury to themselves and family members, other risks are likely to be externalized. They include the risk of injury their driving poses for other drivers and pedestrians, the costs of vehicular damage that is covered through insurance claims, and the costs to other motorists held up in traffic congestion caused by accidents. Externalizing these costs artificially lowers the marginal cost of driving, thereby inefficiently increasing the pollution from the resulting high number of vehicle miles.

Implementing PAYD insurance could reduce those inefficiencies. With PAYD insurance, existing rating factors (such as age, gender, and previous driving experience) would be used by insurance companies to determine a driver's per-mile rate, and this rate would be multiplied by annual miles driven to calculate the annual insurance premium. This approach has the effect of drastically increasing the marginal cost of driving an extra mile without raising the amount people spend annually on insurance. Estimates by Harrington and Parry (2004) suggest that calculating these insurance costs on a per-mile basis would have the same effect as raising the federal gasoline tax from $0.184 to $1.50 per gallon for a vehicle that gets 20 miles per gallon. This is a substantial increase and could have a dramatic effect on people's transport choices (and, therefore, the pollution they emit) despite the fact that it imposes no additional financial burden on them.

Source: Harrington, W., & Parry, I. (2004). Pay-as-you-drive for car insurance. In R. Morgenstern & P. Portney (Eds.). *New Approaches on Energy and the Environment: Policy Advice for the President.* Washington, DC: Resources of the Future, 53–56.

Another accelerated retirement approach was undertaken in 2009 as a means to stimulate the economic recovery, while reducing emissions. Example 7.7 explores how well this Cash-for-Clunkers program worked.

We also have learned some things about what doesn't work very well. One increasingly common strategy involves limiting the days any particular vehicle can be used, as a means of limiting miles traveled. As Example 7.8 indicates, this strategy can backfire!

EXAMPLE 7.7

The Cash-for-Clunkers Program: Did It Work?

On July 27, 2009, the Obama administration launched the car allowance rebate system (CARS), known popularly as "Cash for Clunkers." This federal program had two goals: to provide stimulus to the economy by increasing auto sales, and to improve the environment by replacing old, fuel-inefficient vehicles with new, fuel-efficient ones.

Under the CARS program, consumers received a $3,500 or $4,500 discount from a car dealer when they traded in their old vehicle and purchased or leased a new, qualifying vehicle. In order to be eligible for the program, the trade-in passenger vehicle had (1) to be manufactured less than 25 years before the date it was traded in, (2) to have a combined city/highway fuel economy of 18 miles per gallon or less, (3) to be in drivable condition, and (4) to have been continuously insured and registered to the same owner for the full year before the trade-in. The end date was set at November 1, 2009, or whenever the money ran out. Since the latter condition prevailed, the program terminated on August 25, 2009.

During the program's nearly 1-month run, it generated 678,359 eligible transactions at a cost of $2.85 billion. Using Canada as the control group, one research group (Li et al., 2010) found that the program significantly shifted sales to July and August from other months.

In terms of environmental effects, this study found that the program resulted in a cost per ton ranging from $91 to $301, even including the benefits from reducing criteria pollutants. This is substantially higher than the per ton costs associated with other programs to reduce emissions, a finding that is consistent with other studies (Knittel, 2009; Gayer and Parker, 2013). In addition, the program was estimated to have created 3676 job-years in the auto assembly and parts industries from June to December of 2009. That effect decreased to 2050 by May 2010.

In summary, this study found mixed results. An increase in sales did occur, but much of it was simply shifting sales that would have occurred either earlier or later into July and August. And while it did produce positive environmental benefits, the approach was not a cost-effective way to achieve those benefits. This case study illustrates a more general principle, namely that trying to achieve two policy objectives with a single policy instrument rarely results in a cost-effective outcome.

Sources: United States Government Accountability Office. (2010). Report to Congressional Committees: Lessons Learned from Cash for Clunkers Program Report # GAO-10-486; Li, S., Linn, J., & Spiller, E. (2010). *Evaluating 'Cash-for-Clunkers': Program Effect on Auto Sales, Jobs and the Environment.* Washington, DC: Resources for the Future Discussion Paper 10–39; Knittel, C. R. (August 31, 2009). The implied cost of carbon dioxide under the cash for clunkers program. Retrieved from: http://ssrn.com/abstract=1630647; Gayer, T., & Parker, E. (2013). *Cash for Clunkers: An Evaluation of the Car Allowance Rebate System.* Washington, DC: Brookings Institution.

EXAMPLE 7.8

Counterproductive Policy Design

As one response to unacceptably high levels of traffic congestion and air pollution, the Mexico City administration imposed a regulation that banned each car from driving on a specific day of the week. The specific day when the car could not be driven was determined by the last digit of the license plate.

This approach appeared to offer the opportunity for considerable reductions in congestion and air pollution at a relatively low cost. In this case, however, the appearance was deceptive because of the way in which the population reacted to the ban.

An evaluation of the program by the World Bank found that in the short run the regulation was effective. Pollution and congestion were reduced. However, in the long run the regulation not only was ineffective; it was actually counterproductive (paradoxically it increased the level of congestion and pollution). This paradox occurred because a large number of residents reacted by buying an additional car (which would have a different banned day), and, once the additional cars became available, total driving actually increased. Policies that fail to anticipate and incorporate behavior reactions run the risk that actual and expected outcomes may diverge considerably.

Source: Eskeland, G. S., & Feyzioglu, T. (December 1995). Rationing can backfire: The "day without a car program" in Mexico City. World Bank Policy Research Working Paper 1554.

Summary

The current policy toward motor vehicle emissions blends point-of-production control with point-of-use control. It began with uniform emissions standards.

Grams-per-mile emissions standards, the core of the current approach in the United States and Europe, have had, in practice, many deficiencies. While they have achieved lower emissions per mile, they have been less effective in lowering aggregate emissions and in ensuring cost-effective reductions.

Aggregate mobile-source emissions have been reduced by less than expected because of the large offsetting increase in the number of miles traveled. Unlike sulfur emissions from power plants, aggregate mobile-source emissions are not capped, so, as miles increase, emissions increase.

The efficiency of the emissions standards has been diminished by their geographic uniformity. Too little control has been exercised in highly polluted areas, and too much control has been exercised in areas with air quality that exceeds the ambient standards.

Local approaches, such as targeted inspection and maintenance strategies and accelerated retirement strategies, have had mixed success in redressing this imbalance. Since a relatively small number of vehicles are typically responsible for a disproportionately large share of the emissions, a growing reliance on remote sensing to identify the most polluting vehicles is allowing the policy to target resources where they will produce the largest net benefit.

The historic low cost of auto travel has led to a dispersed pattern of development. Dispersed patterns of development make mass transit a less-viable alternative, which causes a downward spiral of population dispersal and low mass-transit ridership. In the long run, part of the strategy for meeting ambient standards will necessarily involve changing land-use patterns to create the kind of high-density travel corridors that are compatible with effective mass-transit use. Though these conditions already exist in much of Europe, it is likely to evolve in the United States over a long period of time. Ensuring that the true social costs of transportation are borne by those making residential and mode-of-travel choices will start the process moving in the right direction.

A couple of important insights about the conventional environmental policy wisdom can be derived from the history of mobile-source control. Contrary to the traditional belief that tougher laws produce more environmental results, the sanctions associated with meeting the grams-per-mile emissions standards were so severe that, when push came to shove, authorities were unwilling to impose them. Threatened sanctions will only promote the desired outcome if the threat is credible. The largest "club" does not necessarily produce the best incentive.

The second insight confronts the traditional belief that simply applying the right technical fix can solve environmental problems. The gasoline additive MTBE was advanced as a way to improve the nation's air. With the advantage of hindsight, we now know that its pollution effects on groundwater have dwarfed its positive effects on air quality. Though technical fixes can, and do, have a role to play in environmental policy, they also can have large, adverse, unintended consequences.

Looking toward the future of mobile-source air pollution control, two new emphases are emerging. The first involves encouraging the development and commercialization of new, cleaner automotive technologies ranging from gas–electric hybrids to fuel-cell vehicles powered by hydrogen. Policies such as fuel-economy standards, gasoline taxes, feebates, and sales quotas imposed on auto manufacturers for low-emitting vehicles are designed to accelerate their entry into the vehicle fleet.

The second new emphasis focuses on influencing driver choices. The range of available policies is impressive. One set of strategies focuses on bringing the private marginal cost of driving closer to the social marginal cost through such measures as congestion pricing and pay-as-you-drive auto insurance. Others, such as parking cash-outs, attempt to create a more level playing field for choices involving the mode of travel for the journey to work.

Complicating all of these strategies is the increased demand for cars in developing countries. In 2007, Tata Motors, the Indian automaker, introduced "the world's cheapest car," the Tata Nano. The Nano sells for about 100,000 rupees (US $2,500). Tata Motors expects to sell millions of these affordable, stripped-down vehicles. Fuel efficiency of these cars is quite good (over 50 miles per gallon), but the sheer number of vehicles implies sizable increases in the demand for fuel, congestion, and pollution emissions.

Appropriate regulation of emissions from mobile sources requires a great deal more than simply controlling the emissions from vehicles as they leave the factory. Vehicle purchases, driving behavior, fuel choice, and even residential and employment choices must eventually be affected by the need to reduce mobile-source emissions. Affecting the choices facing automobile owners can only transpire if the economic incentives associated with those choices are structured correctly.

Discussion Questions

1. When a threshold concentration is used as the basis for pollution control, as it is for air pollution, one possibility for meeting the threshold at minimum cost is to spread the emissions out over time. To achieve this, one might establish a peak-hour pricing system that charges more for emissions during peak periods.

    a. Would this represent a movement toward efficiency? Why or why not?
    b. What effects should this policy have on mass-transit usage, gasoline sales, downtown shopping, and travel patterns?

2. What are the advantages and disadvantages of using an increase in the gasoline tax to move road transport decisions toward both efficiency and sustainability?

Self-Test Exercises

1. "While gasoline taxes and fuel economy standards can both be effective in increasing the number of miles per gallon in new vehicles, gasoline taxes are superior means of reducing emissions from the vehicle fleet." Discuss.

2. Suppose the nation wished to reduce gasoline consumption not only to promote national security, but also to reduce the threats from climate change.

    a. How effective is a strategy relying on the labeling of the fuel efficiency of new cars likely to be? What are some of the advantages or disadvantages of this kind of approach?
    b. How effective would a strategy targeting the retirement of old, fuel-inefficient vehicles be? What are some of the advantages or disadvantages of this kind of approach?
    c. Would it make any economic sense to combine either of these polices with pay-as-you-drive insurance? Why or why not?

3. a. If a pay-as-you-drive insurance program is being implemented to cope with automobile-related externalities associated with driving, what factors should be considered in setting the premium?
    b. Would you expect a private insurance company to take all these factors into account? Why or why not?

Notes

1   www.bts.gov/product/national-transportation-statistics
2   The exception is ozone, formed by a chemical reaction involving hydrocarbons and nitrogen oxides in the presence of sunlight. Since, for the evening rush-hour emissions, too few hours of sunlight remain for the chemical reactions to be completed, graphs of daily ozone concentrations frequently exhibit a single peak.
3   Data on vehicle miles traveled for the United States can be found here: www.rita.dot.gov/bts/sites/rita.dot.gov.bts/files/publications/national_transportation_statistics/html/table_01_35.html
4   Annual Urban Mobility Report, Texas Transportation Institute. (2015). http://mobility.tamu.edu/ums/ and https://static.tti.tamu.edu/tti.tamu.edu/documents/mobility-scorecard-2015.pdf
5   The only legal basis for granting an extension was technological infeasibility. Only shortly before the extension was granted, the Japanese Honda CVCC engine was certified as meeting the original standards. It is interesting to speculate on what the outcome would have been if the company meeting the standards had been American, rather than Japanese.

6 Three tanks of leaded gas used in a car equipped with a catalytic converter would produce a 50 percent reduction in the effectiveness of the catalytic converter.
7 Lovei, Magolna. (2001). *Toward an Unleaded Environment: World Bank Support to Transition Economies*. Available at: www.worldbank.org/html/prddr/trans/m&j96/art5.htm
8 In 2017 the EPA updated the calculations that manufacturers use for fuel economy labels. These updates use data that better reflects new technology and the changing composition of manufacturers' fleets. See: www.epa.gov/fueleconomy/basic-information-fuel-economy-labeling
9 www.nhtsa.gov/staticfiles/rulemaking/pdf/cafe/CAFE_2014-18_Trucks_FactSheet-v1.pdf, October 2010.
10 Vehicles subject to the gas guzzler tax in 2016 can be found here: https://nepis.epa.gov/Exe/ZyPDF.cgi/P100OA3I.PDF?Dockey=P100OA3I.PDF
11 www.ucsusa.org/clean-vehicles/california-and-western-states/what-is-zev#.WVEqZsZlmV5 (accessed June 26, 2017).
12 CARB, The Zero Emission Vehicle Program: www.arb.ca.gov/msprog/zevprog/zevprog.htm (accessed June 29, 2017).
13 For a nice summary of road pricing, see Anas and Lindsey (2011).
14 Congressional Budget Office. (2009). *Using Pricing to Reduce Traffic Congestion*. Washington, DC: A CBO Study.
15 www.rff.org/rff/News/Releases/2008Releases/MarginalSocialCostTrafficCongestion.cfm
16 www.cbo.gov/publication/43633

Further Reading

Anas, A., & Lindsey, R. (2011). Reducing urban road transportation externalities: Road pricing in theory and in practice. *Review of Environmental Economics and Policy*, 5(1), 66–88. A survey of the literature on road pricing and policy.

Anderson, S. T., Parry, I. W. H., Sallee, J. M., & Fischer, C. (2011). Automobile fuel economy standards: Impacts, efficiency, and alternatives. *Review of Environmental Economics and Policy*, 5(1), 89–108. A comprehensive summary and assessment of fuel economy standards.

Harrington, W., & McConnell, V. (2003). Motor vehicles and the environment. In H. Folmer & T. Tietenberg (Eds.) *International Yearbook of Environmental and Resource Economics 2003/2004*. Cheltenham, UK: Edward Elgar, 190–268. A comprehensive survey of what we have learned from economic analysis about cost-effective ways to control pollution from motor vehicles.

Additional references and historically significant references are available on this book's Companion Website: www.routledge.com/cw/Tietenberg

Chapter 8

Climate Change

Everything should be made as simple as possible, but not simpler.

—Albert Einstein

Introduction

As pollutants flow beyond local boundaries, the political difficulties of implementing comprehensive, cost-effective control measures are compounded. Pollutants crossing national boundaries impose external costs; neither emitters nor the political jurisdictions within which they emit have the proper incentives for controlling the emissions.

Compounding the problem of improper incentives is the scientific uncertainty that limits our understanding of these complex problems. Our knowledge about various relationships that form the basis for our understanding of the magnitude of the problems and the effectiveness of various strategies to control them is far from complete. Unfortunately, the problems are so important and the potential consequences of inaction so drastic that procrastination is not usually an optimal strategy. To avoid having to act in the future under emergency conditions when the remaining choices have dwindled, strategies to preserve options with desirable properties must be formulated now on the basis of the available information, as limited as it may be.

The costs of inaction are not limited to the direct damages caused. International cooperation among such traditional allies as the United States, Mexico, and Canada and the countries of Europe has historically been undermined by disputes over the proper control of transboundary pollution. The potential for future international conflicts is heightened by impending climate-intensified scarcities (water, for example) and the expected border-crossing surge of refugees fleeing extreme weather-related disasters.

In this chapter we survey the evidence on the unique challenges and opportunities posed by climate change. Having laid the groundwork in the two previous chapters by focusing on national strategies targeted respectively on stationary and mobile sources, in this chapter we consider not only the additional important aspect of the international context associated with climate change, but also more comprehensive strategies and policies that treat mobile and stationary sources together in a way that enhances the cost-effectiveness of the policy approach.

The Science of Climate Change

One class of global pollutants, greenhouse gases, absorb the long-wavelength (infrared) radiation from the earth's surface and atmosphere, trapping heat that would otherwise radiate into space. The mix and distribution of these gases within the atmosphere is in no small part responsible for both the hospitable climate on the earth and the inhospitable climate on other planets; changing the mix of these gases, however, can modify the climate.

Although carbon dioxide is the most abundant and the most studied of these greenhouse gases, many others have similar thermal radiation properties. These include the chlorofluorocarbons, nitrous oxide, and methane.

The current concern over the effect of this class of pollutants on climate arises not only because emissions of these gases are increasing over time, changing their mix in the atmosphere, but also because many of them have very long residence times in the atmosphere. Once emissions enter the atmosphere they can affect climate for a very long time.

By burning fossil fuels, leveling tropical forests, and injecting more of the other greenhouse gases into the atmosphere, humans are creating a thermal blanket capable of trapping enough heat to raise the temperature of the earth's surface.

The Intergovernmental Panel on Climate Change (IPCC), the body charged with compiling and assessing the scientific information on climate change, reported its findings in 2013 on the sources of climate change. It noted the following:

- Warming of the climate system is unequivocal, and since the 1950s many of the observed changes are unprecedented over decades to millennia.
- Most aspects of climate change will persist for many centuries even if emissions of CO_2 are stopped.
- It is extremely likely that human influence has been the dominant cause of the observed warming since the mid-twentieth century. . . . This is evident from the increasing greenhouse gas concentrations in the atmosphere, positive radiative forcing, observed warming, and understanding of the climate system.

Scientists have also uncovered evidence to suggest that climate change may occur rather more abruptly than previously thought. Since the rate of temperature increase is a significant determinant of how well ecosystems can adapt to temperature change, abrupt climate change has become a matter of intensified concern. An example that raises this concern is the large quantities of methane trapped in the frozen tundra of the north. As temperatures warm, the tundra can thaw, releasing the trapped methane. Since methane is a powerful greenhouse gas, this release accelerates the rate of warming.

These climate changes are expected to result in adverse human health impacts including heat waves and the migration of disease vectors to new areas, in rising sea levels that when coupled with storm surges could inundate coastal areas, in precipitating more intense storms, in triggering an increase in both droughts and floods, and in intensifying ocean acidification, among other impacts.

While most scientists accept this view of the state of the science, not all observers do. And some are even willing to put their money where their mouth is (Example 8.1).

EXAMPLE 8.1

Betting on Climate Science

In 2011 Economist Chris Hope was at a conference at Cambridge, UK. As he describes the situation in an article in *The Guardian*:

> most of the participants were skeptical about the influence of humans on the climate. I took the microphone and asked if any of them would care to make a £1,000 bet with me about whether 2015 would be hotter than 2008. Two brave souls, Ian Plimer and Sir Alan Rudge, agreed.

Cole then found a climate scientist, James Annan, who was willing make a side bet that would give Cole 5 to 1 odds against 2015 being cooler than 2008. (Specifically, if 2015 were warmer Cole would pay Annan £666 and if 2015 were colder Annan would pay Cole £3,333.) Although the numbers look a bit odd, in fact this side bet provided a perfect hedge for Cole. He would win £1,333 if 2015 were cooler than 2008, and £1,334 if it were warmer. This side bet had shifted the downside risk (the risk of losing) to Annan, who was willing to accept it due to his confidence that this risk was very small.

We now know that 2015 was hotter than 2008 and Plimer and Rudge each lost £1,000, which was split between Cole (£1,334) and Annan (£666) based upon their side bet.

Did the specific starting and ending dates matter in this bet? While global temperatures have in general been rising, it turns out this was a particularly bad set of dates for betting against climate change. To start with, 2008 was a relatively cool year. According to the NASA Goddard Institute for Space Studies, a strong cyclical effect known as La Niña caused much of the Pacific Ocean to be cooler than the long-term average for that year.

In contrast, the ending year, 2015, was the hottest year on record up to that time. Notice that every bet against a warmer temperature involving an ending date of 2015 would have lost.

Would a different set of 7-year intervals involving earlier starting and ending dates have produced a different result? Gather the data, do the calculations and find out for yourself. Start with 1998 and examine every 7-year period, ending with the 2008 period used in this bet. In general, what do these data show about the wisdom of betting against climate change?

Sources: Hope, Chris. (July 28, 2016). Making a safe bet on climate change. In his Keeping an Eye on Climate Change blog. Available at: www.chrishopepolicy. com/2016/07/making-a-safe-bet-on-dangerous-climate-change/; NASA Goddard Institute for Space Studies (GISS). (February 23, 2009). 2008 was earth's coolest year since 2000. Available at: www.nasa. gov/topics/earth/features/2008_temps.html

Negotiations over Climate Change Policy

Characterizing the Broad Strategies

What can be done? Three strategies have been identified: (1) climate engineering, (2) adaptation, and (3) mitigation.

Climate engineering or, alternatively, *geoengineering*, approaches can be divided into two very different categories: carbon dioxide removal and solar-radiation management. While approaches in the former category, such as direct air capture or ocean fertilization, seek to reduce the concentrations of greenhouse gases, approaches in the second category, such as injecting stratospheric aerosols, aim to cool the planet by reflecting a fraction of the incoming sunlight away from earth. Some propose that one or more of these strategies could provide a cost-effective alternative to mitigation, but recent other reviews have emphasized that such approaches are fraught with uncertainties and have potential adverse effects. Thus they cannot currently be considered a reasonable substitute for comprehensive mitigation until such time as it is too late for conventional policies. Research continues, while the ultimate role for geoengineering remains to be determined.

Adaptation strategies involve efforts to modify natural or human systems in order to minimize harm from climate change impacts. Examples include modifying development planning to increase the resilience of damage-prone areas, such as relocating transportation systems and waste treatment facilities away from areas vulnerable to sea-level rise, and preparing public health facilities to handle the larger burdens resulting from the changing disease impacts of a warmer climate.

Mitigation attempts to moderate the temperature rise by using strategies designed to reduce emissions or to increase the planet's natural capacity to absorb greenhouse gases.

In this chapter we shall focus mainly on mitigation and adaptation. The most significant mitigation strategy deals with our use of fossil-fuel energy. Combustion of fossil fuels results in the creation of carbon dioxide. Carbon dioxide emissions can be reduced either by using less energy or by using alternative energy sources (such as wind, photovoltaics, or hydro) that produce less or no carbon dioxide. Any serious reduction in carbon dioxide emissions would involve significant changes in our energy-consumption patterns and those changes could come with an economic cost. Thus, the debate over how vigorously this strategy is to be followed is a controversial public-policy issue.

Another possible strategy involves encouraging activities that increase the amount of carbon that is absorbed by trees or soils. As Debate 8.1 points out, however, the desirability of this approach is also heavily debated in current climate change negotiations.

Finding a global solution to climate change is certainly one of the most challenging and pressing problems of our time, but it is not the first global pollutant to be the subject of international negotiations. As we shall examine more closely subsequently in this chapter the negotiations aimed at reducing ozone-depleting gases broke the ice.

Game Theory as a Window on Global Climate Negotiations

One area of economics that has been used to study the incentives in situations such as this (where participant outcomes are jointly determined) is *game theory*. Outcomes are jointly determined in the sense that the payoff to any nation from its participation in an international agreement or not depends not only on its decisions, but also on the decisions of other nations.

One particularly interesting strain of game theory investigates the conditions that support self-enforcing agreements (Barrett, 1994)—namely those where the incentives are sufficient

DEBATE 8.1

Should Carbon Sequestration in the Terrestrial Biosphere Be Credited?

Both forests and soils sequester (store) a significant amount of carbon. Research suggests that with appropriate changes in practices they could store much more. Increased *carbon sequestration* in turn would mean less carbon in the atmosphere. Recognition of this potential has created a strong push in the climate change negotiations to give credit in carbon markets or toward carbon taxes for actions that result in more carbon uptake by soils and forests. Whether this should be allowed, and, if so, how it would be done are currently heavily debated.

Proponents argue that this form of carbon sequestration is typically quite cost-effective. Cost-effectiveness not only implies that the given goal can be achieved at lower cost, but also it may increase the willingness to accept more stringent goals with closer deadlines. Allowing credit for carbon absorption may also add economic value to sustainable practices (such as limiting deforestation or preventing soil erosion), thereby providing additional incentives for those practices. Proponents further point out that many of the prime beneficiaries of this increase in value would be the poorest people in the poorest countries.

Opponents say that our knowledge of the science of carbon sequestration in the terrestrial biosphere is in its infancy, so the amount of credit that should be granted is not at all clear. Obtaining estimates of the amount of carbon sequestered could be both expensive (if done right) and subject to considerable uncertainty. Because carbon absorption could be easily reversed at any time (from wildfires, by cutting down trees, or by changing agricultural practices), continual monitoring and enforcement would be required, adding even more cost. Even in carefully enforced systems, the sequestration is likely to be temporary (even the carbon in completely preserved forests, for example, may ultimately be released into the atmosphere by decay). And finally, the practices that may be encouraged by crediting sequestration will not necessarily be desirable, as when slow-growing old-growth forests are cut down and replaced with fast-growing plantation forests in order to increase the amount of carbon uptake.

to encourage both joining the agreement and, once a member, continuing to abide by the rules. Since no country can be forced to sign an international agreement, and signatories can always withdraw after signing, self-enforcing agreements are those where the incentives are most likely to create successful, stable coalitions.

A main difficulty in constructing self-enforcing agreements is the *free-rider* effect. Climate change involves a global pollutant and the effects of emissions reductions are a public good. All nations receive the benefits of emissions reductions whether those nations contributed to those reductions or not. Individual nations therefore bear all of the costs of their reductions, but gain only a portion of the resulting benefits. This means the private marginal benefit for any nation's reduction effort is lower than the social marginal benefit, which is the sum of the marginal benefits received by all nations. Therefore when an individual nation reduces emissions until its private marginal cost of reduction is equal to its private marginal benefit, this private optimum results in too little reduction.

The Barrett model assumes that signatories choose their strategies in order to maximize their collective net benefits. In the structure of this game when a country joins the international agreement the other signatories respond by increasing their abatement levels, and hence reward the country for participating in the agreement; when a country withdraws, the remaining signatories reduce their abatement levels, and hence punish the country for withdrawing from the agreement. These punishments and rewards are credible, because the signatories always choose their levels in order to maximize their collective net benefits. The questions of interest are under what conditions is a stable, successful coalition achieved? and how well do these conditions fit the current climate negotiations?

The Barrett analysis finds that a stable successful agreement can only be achieved when the difference between the cooperative (where all nations actually cooperate so that collective net benefits are maximized) and noncooperative outcomes (where each nation simply acts independently in pursuit of its own self-interest) is small. Why? Unless the free-rider effect is small in this agreement it seriously undermines cooperation. Unfortunately, this analysis demonstrates that in precisely those cases where the gains from cooperation are greatest, the incentives for individual nations to become free-riders are also greatest, thereby inhibiting the formation of a stable successful agreement.

More recent work (Barrett, 2013) has focused on whether the existence of a catastrophe threshold (known as a "tipping point") ups the ante sufficiently so that cooperation is more likely. This analysis finds that when the specifics of a climate catastrophe threshold are known with certainty and the benefits of avoiding catastrophe are high relative to the costs, self-enforcing treaties can coordinate countries' behavior so as to avoid the catastrophe. Where the net benefits of avoiding catastrophe are lower relative to the costs, however, agreements typically fail to avoid catastrophe; only modest cuts in emissions are sustained. This analysis also finds that uncertainty about the magnitude of the temperature rise that would trigger the catastrophic threshold normally causes coordination to collapse as well. Since our understanding of the precise temperatures that trigger various tipping points is limited, this is a concerning result.

Another game theory study (Jacquet, 2013), which relies on a lab experiment, reveals even more barriers to cooperation—the nature and timing of the payoffs to cooperation. At the start of this experiment, which is played with real money for ten rounds, each of six participants is allotted a fixed amount of money (40 euros) to invest in a climate account. Each round these players choose how much of their allotted money they want to put into the account.

At the end of ten rounds, if the climate account grows to 120 euros from the contributions made by the six players over the ten rounds, the participants in that game are deemed to have won their game (averted "dangerous climate change"). Each participant in a game that successfully averts dangerous climate change receives a bonus in addition to the money they each have leftover after their contributions to the climate account. However, if after ten rounds the climate account ends up smaller than 120 euros, the participants in that game are deemed to have lost the game and they receive no bonus.

The game was played with three different sets of rules. The first treatment involved ten groups, while the second and third involved 11. In the first scenario, where the earned bonus (45 euros) would be received the next day, seven out of the ten groups averted dangerous climate change. In the second scenario, where the earned bonus (still 45 euros) would be received seven weeks later, only four of the 11 groups succeeded. In the final scenario, where the bonus was used to plant oak trees in order to sequester carbon, and thus provide the greatest benefit to future generations, none of the 11 groups reached the target. Apparently the fact that payoffs from action on climate change occur with a lag is yet another factor that makes successful agreements harder to achieve.

In general these results are very discouraging because they suggest that under precisely the conditions currently prevailing in the climate policy arena, a close examination of the incentives facing nations seeking to form stable, effective agreements to mitigate greenhouse gases suggests that global cooperation is at best an elusive outcome.

Fortunately, the current climate arena also includes some aspects of international co-operation that are not included in these models, but that suggests somewhat greater possibilities for success. One such area involves co-benefits, the benefits that are derived from mitigating other nontargeted pollutants in the process of mitigating greenhouse gases. One important example is the reduction in adverse human health impacts from reduced particulate pollution when low- or no-carbon fuels are substituted for coal. Since all the health benefits from mitigating these local pollutants are received by the mitgating nation, the free-rider effect does not come into play. Co-benefits can add a powerful additional incentive for individual participants receiving those co-benefits to mitigate. Some argue that this can explain, for example, China's recent increased interest in reducing greenhouse gases.

Another strategy designed to improve the odds of a successful agreement involves "issue linkage" in which countries simultaneously negotiate a climate change agreement and a linked economic agreement. Typical candidates for linkage are agreements on trade liberalization, or cooperation on either research and development (R&D) or international debt. The intuition behind this approach is that some countries gain from resolving the first issue, while others gain from the second. Linking the two issues increases the chances that cooperation may result in mutual gain and, hence, increases the incentives to join and abide by the combined agreement.

To understand how this works, consider a research-and-development example from Cararro (2002). To counteract the incentive to free ride on the benefits from climate change, suppose only ratifiers of both agreements share in the insights gained from research and development in the ratifying countries. The fact that this benefit can only be obtained by ratifying both the climate change agreement and the R&D agreement provides an incentive to ratify both since these benefits do not create a free-rider effect. Nations choosing not to ratify can be excluded from the research-and-development benefits; they would have to join the agreement to gain this benefit.

Another strategy for encouraging participation involves transfers from the gainers to the losers. Some countries have more to gain from an effective agreement than others. If the gainers were willing to share some of those gains with reluctant nations who have more to lose, the reluctant nations could be encouraged to join. Some interesting early work (Chandler & Tulkens, 1997) has shown that it is possible to define a specific set of transfers such that each country is better off participating than not participating. That is a powerful, comforting result, but is it practical?

In terms of operationalizing the concept of using transfers as an inducement to join the agreement, the Bali Climate Change Conference in 2007 established a funding mechanism for adaptation. It was established to finance specific adaptation projects and programs in developing countries that are parties to the Kyoto Protocol (www.adaptation-fund.org). The fund, which falls under the auspices of the Global Environmental Facility, is financed primarily from a 2 percent levy on proceeds from Clean Development Mechanism projects. Note that while this fund is directed toward adaptation, rather than mitigation, the fact that it is available only to parties to the agreement provides an incentive for potential holdouts to participate.

As a complementary measure, the Conference of Parties (COP) to the United Nations Framework Convention on Climate Change (UNFCCC) decided in 2010 to also establish the Green Climate Fund, which would raise significantly more funding. This fund is intended to provide support to developing countries as they limit or reduce their greenhouse gas emissions and as they adapt to the impacts of climate change, focusing especially on those developing countries that are particularly vulnerable to the adverse effects of climate change.[1] As of July 2016 some 50 proposals had been approved, with the funds having been disbursed for ten of them.

And, finally, choosing cost-effective policies can positively affect the level of participation. Since cost-effective policies reduce the cost, but not the benefits, of participation, those policies should make participation more likely by increasing the net benefits from joining the agreement.

How have all of these factors interacted in the process of seeking agreements? Historically, climate change agreements have been based upon a top-down approach where the goals and responsibilities were defined collectively by the agreement itself. That was not producing the intended results because many of the world's countries, especially the developing countries, remained on the sidelines.

The Paris Accord, which was passed in December 2015 and went into force in October 2016, shifted to a more bottom-up approach. Each individual country was asked to define their own contribution, called a "nationally determined contribution" (NDC), to achieve the worldwide goal. The NDCs are not binding (enforceable) as a matter of international law.

After the Paris Accord was concluded, experts did the calculations to find out if the sum of all NDCs would be large enough to meet the temperature increase goals embodied in the agreement, assuming that all counties lived up to their commitments in their NDC.

The experts found that the sum of the NDCs would be insufficient to keep global emissions within levels necessary to stay within the temperature-increase targets. Additionally, soon after he won the 2016 US presidential election, Donald Trump announced his intention to withdraw the United States from the Paris Accord. Apparently so far it seems that the public good effects outweigh the effects of co-benefits, linkages, and financial transfers.

The Precedent: Reducing Ozone-Depleting Gases

Fortunately not all international agreements designed to manage global pollutant challenges have had such a dismal experience. Are there lessons to be learned from those earlier agreements? Consider the experience of the Montreal Protocol, which was designed to control ozone-depleting gases.

In the stratosphere, the portion of the atmosphere lying just above the troposphere, rather small amounts of ozone present have a crucial positive role to play in determining the quality of life on the planet. In particular, by absorbing the ultraviolet wavelengths, stratospheric ozone shields people, plants, and animals from harmful radiation, and by absorbing infrared radiation, it is a factor in determining the earth's climate.

Chlorofluorocarbons (CFCs), which are greenhouse gases, also deplete the stratospheric ozone shield as a result of a complicated series of chemical reactions. These chemical compounds were used as aerosol propellants and in cushioning foams, packaging, and insulating foams, industrial cleaning of metals and electronics components, food freezing, medical instrument sterilization, refrigeration for homes and food stores, and air-conditioning of automobiles and commercial buildings.

The major known health effect of the increased ultraviolet radiation resulting from *tropospheric ozone depletion* is an increase in nonmelanoma skin cancer. Other potential effects, such as an increase in the more serious melanoma form of skin cancer, suppression of the human immunological systems, damage to plants, eye cancer in cattle, and an acceleration of degradation in certain polymer materials, were suspected, but not as well established.

Responding to the ozone-depletion threat, an initial group of 24 nations signed the *Montreal Protocol* in September 1988. A subsequent series of new agreements generally broadened the number of covered substances and established specific schedules for phasing out their production and use. Currently, some 96 chemicals are controlled by these agreements to some degree.

In terms of reducing its target emissions the protocol is generally considered to have been a noteworthy success. As of 2008, more than 95 percent of listed ozone-depleting substances have been phased out and the ozone layer was expected to return to its pre-1980 levels no later than 2075.

How did this treaty avoid the free-rider pitfalls identified previously? One reason for the success of this approach was an early recognition of the need to solicit the active participation of developing countries. One component of the success in eliciting that participation resulted from offering later phaseout deadlines for developing countries. Another involved the creation of a *Multilateral Fund*.

In 1990 the parties agreed to establish the Multilateral Fund, which was designed to cover the incremental costs that developing countries incur as a result of taking action to eliminate the production and use of ozone-depleting chemicals. Contributions to the Multilateral Fund come from the industrialized countries. The fund has been replenished multiple times. As of April 2013, the contributions made to the Multilateral Fund by some 45 countries (including countries with economies in transition, or CEIT countries) totaled over US $3.09 billion.

The fund promotes technical change and facilitates the transfer of more environmentally safe products, materials, and equipment to developing countries. Developing countries that have ratified the agreement have access to technical expertise, information on new replacement technologies, training and demonstration projects, and financial assistance for projects to eliminate the use of ozone-depleting substances.

The existence of the Multilateral Fund, however, does not deserve the bulk of the credit for the success of the Montreal Protocol. The success of ozone protection was possible in no small measure because producers were able to develop and commercialize alternatives to ozone-depleting chemicals. In many cases the companies that would be forced to stop producing ozone-depleting chemicals were the same companies that would produce the substitutes. Countries and producers ended the use of CFCs faster and cheaper than was originally anticipated due both to the availability of these substitutes and the fact that profit from their sale would offset any losses from stopping production of the ozone-depleting chemicals.

In retrospect we now know that one class of the substitutes, HFCs, had a detrimental side effect—it turned out to be a potent greenhouse gas. Although HFCs have a shorter residence time in the atmosphere than carbon dioxide, they turn out to be a much more powerful greenhouse gas on a pound for pound basis.

Responding to this challenge a deal to phaseout HFCs was reached in Kigali, Rwanda, in October 2016 that could on its own prevent a 0.5°C (0.9°F) rise in temperature by 2100 and, hence, be a healthy complement to the Paris Accord.

Economics and the Mitigation Policy Choice

Early in climate change negotiations it became clear that using cost-effective mitigation strategies was a priority. For reasons explained in Chapter 6 and the fact that they simultaneously control both mobile and stationary sources, the policy choices quickly narrowed down to a carbon tax and the cap-and-trade version of emissions trading.

In general, historically Europe tended to favor carbon taxes, while the United States preferred cap-and-trade. In practice, as shown in Table 8.1, we now have experience with both approaches.

Providing Context: A Brief Look at Two Illustrative Carbon Pricing Programs

Emissions trading and a carbon tax are both forms of carbon pricing, but they operate rather differently. In emissions trading the government sets the magnitude of allowed emissions and allows the market to determine the price, while the carbon tax sets the price on emissions and allows the market to determine the amount of emissions. To provide some feel for how these two types of programs work in practice consider two examples: (1) the British Columbia carbon tax, and (2) the European Union's Emissions Trading Scheme.

British Columbia Carbon Tax Program. Since 2008, British Columbia has imposed a carbon tax on each metric ton of carbon dioxide equivalent (CO_2–e) emissions from the combustion of fuel. The tax rose from 10 Canadian dollars per ton of carbon dioxide in 2008 to 30 dollars by 2012. This program affects an estimated 77 percent of British Columbia's total greenhouse gas (GHG) emissions.

Under this program, CO_2–e is defined as the amount of CO_2, methane, and nitrous oxide (N_2O) released into the atmosphere, with the methane and N_2O emission levels adjusted to a CO_2–e basis that accounts for their impact on global warming relative to CO_2. Certain fuels, such as fuel for commercial aviation and ships, are exempted. To facilitate implementation, the carbon tax is applied and collected at the wholesale level, using the traditional administrative

Table 8.1 Selected Carbon Markets and Carbon Taxes

Carbon Markets	Carbon Taxes
The Kyoto Protocol's Clean Development and Joint Implementation Mechanisms (2005)	Finland (1990)
	Sweden (1991)
The European Union Emissions Trading Scheme (2005)	Norway (1991)
Regional Greenhouse Gas Initiative US (2009)	United Kingdom (2001)
New Zealand (2010)	Denmark (2005)
California, USA (2013)	Alberta, Canada (2007)
Quebec, Canada (2013)	Switzerland (2007)
	British Columbia, Canada (2008)
Peoples Republic of China Pilot Programs (2013) and National Program (2019)	India (2010)
	Japan (2012)
South Korea (2015)	

channels for collecting motor fuel taxes. The cost of the tax is ultimately passed forward to consumers via higher prices.

This carbon tax program is revenue neutral (i.e., all revenue generated is returned to British Columbians through rebates or cuts in other taxes). To help protect low-income households, the Low Income Climate Action Tax Credit program provides adult residents with lump sum tax credits that are reduced by 2 percent of net family income above specified income thresholds.

After 4 years in effect, BC's per capita consumption of fuels subject to the tax was found to have declined by 19 percent compared to the rest of Canada while its economy kept pace with the rest of Canada. When a new government took over in 2012, it retained the program, but it stopped the annual rise in the tax rate. Carbon emissions in BC started rising again after the province froze the tax. In part the new government did not want to get too far ahead of other nations, lest they start losing their competitive edge.

Since then, Canadian Prime Minister Justin Trudeau has established his national climate plan, which requires all provinces and territories to put in place either a carbon tax or a cap-and-trade plan by 2022.

European Union Emissions Trading Scheme (EU ETS). Launched in 2005, the EU ETS operates in 31 countries and is the largest emissions trading system in the world. The program establishes a cap on the total amount of certain GHGs that can be emitted from installations covered by the system. Under this cap, companies receive emission allowances, which they can sell to, or buy from, one another as needed. At the end of the year each company must surrender enough allowances to cover all its emissions or pay penalties on any excess. Companies can bank any spare allowances for future sale or for covering their future needs. The cap (and, hence, the number of allowances) is reduced over time so that total emissions will fall.

The EU ETS operates in all 28 EU countries plus Iceland, Liechtenstein, and Norway. It limits emissions from more than 11,000 heavy energy-using installations (power stations and industrial plants) as well as airlines operating between these countries, and it covers around 45 percent of the EU's greenhouse gas emissions.

Emissions in the EU were reduced by 22 percent between 1990 and 2015 while the economy grew by 50 percent over the same period. According to the European Environment Agency (EEA) the decrease was mostly driven by emissions reductions in power generation. Emission reductions slowed down in the later period as an excess of allowances for sale developed.

Carbon Markets and Taxes: How Have These Approaches Worked in Practice?

Cost Savings. Two types of studies have conventionally been used to assess cost savings: *ex ante* analyses, based on computer simulations, and *ex post* analyses, which examine actual implementation experience. A substantial majority, though not all, of the large number of *ex ante* analyses have found that a change from more traditional regulatory measures based upon source-specific limits to more cost-effective market-based measures such as emissions trading or pollution taxes could potentially achieve either similar reductions at a much lower cost or much larger reductions at a similar cost. The evidence also finds, as the theory would lead us to expect, that these two instruments typically produce more emissions reduction per unit expenditure than other types of polices such as renewable resource subsidies or mandates.

Although the number of existing detailed *ex post* studies is small, they typically also find, however, that the cost savings from shifting to these market-based measures are positive, but less than would have been achieved if the final outcome had been fully cost-effective. In other words, while both taxes and emissions trading are fully cost-effective in principle, they fall somewhat short of that in practice.

Emissions Reductions. In one study that attempts to control for other factors that could affect emissions outcomes, Lin and Li (2011) compared the change in per capita CO_2 emissions over time between countries that do and do not use a carbon tax. They found that in general carbon taxes have reduced emissions, but the role of carbon taxes was statistically significant only for Finland. The authors attributed this lack of statistical significance for the other countries to the relatively common practice of granting tax exemptions to certain energy intensive industries.

Among emissions trading markets, as noted above, emissions in the EU were reduced by 22 percent between 1990 and 2015. In the Northeastern US, the Regional Greenhouse Gas Initiative (RGGI) emissions from all covered sources were reduced 37 percent during the 2008–2015 period despite a rather weak cap. While the recession played some role, the main sources of the RGGI reductions were (1) substituting to renewable resources and lower carbon fossil fuels such as natural gas, aided considerably by lower natural gas prices, and (2) energy efficiency investments, that reduced the amount of energy used per unit of output.

Not all countries or regions regulate their greenhouse gases, of course, and that raises the specter of leakage. When leakage occurs it means that the actual emissions reductions are smaller than those recorded at the regulated site, because some emissions have been merely transferred to another location, not reduced. Leakage can occur when pressure on the regulated source to reduce emissions results in a diversion of emissions to unregulated, or lesser regulated, locations. Common channels for this diversion involves firms moving their polluting factories to countries with lower environmental standards or consumers increasing their reliance on imported products from countries with unregulated sources. Generally, to date, however, the evidence suggests that actual carbon leakage effects have been rather small despite initial concerns that they might be quite large.

Three Carbon Pricing Program Design Issues: Using the Revenue, Offsets, and Price Volatility

Using the Revenue. Either form of carbon pricing can raise revenue while reducing emissions. What difference do the various choices about revenue use make?

Revenues could be used to reduce the financial burden of the policy on low-income populations, to boost the economy, to increase the magnitude of the emissions reductions, to aid workers displaced by the policy, and even to increase the likelihood that a carbon-pricing policy might be enacted in the first place. While in some cases particular revenue choices can simultaneously achieve multiple objectives, others require political trade-offs.

Various strategies have been designed to achieve one or more of these objectives. They include: (1) giving the revenue back to households in the form of a lump-sum rebate on a per capita basis, (2) lowering various taxes such as the corporate tax, the income tax, the capital gains tax, the payroll tax, and so on, (3) subsidizing further emissions reductions, or (4) helping workers who are displaced by the shift to a lower-carbon energy supply.

Some of these revenue strategies can be designed to be "revenue-neutral." By definition, no revenue from a revenue neutral policy can be used to fund new or expanded programs.

Revenue neutrality can be achieved either by rebating all the carbon-pricing revenues to households, or by lowering other tax rates such that the lost revenue to the government from the lower rates is equal to the revenue derived from carbon pricing. Revenue neutrality is also seen as helpful in building support for the policy among those who do not want to see an increase in the size of government.

Issuing lump-sum rebates to households (for example a fixed monthly check for each member of every eligible household up to four) is an effective strategy for reducing the burden from carbon pricing on lower-income populations. Indeed economic studies find that of the various strategies lump-sum rebates are the most effective choice in pursuing this particular objective, and they boost the economy, but they are not the most effective choice for boosting the economy.

Economists have found that using the revenue to lower tax rates on such taxes as the capital gains tax or the corporate income tax would produce the largest boost to the economy but because the beneficiaries from these approaches are primarily upper-income groups, they would have the least effect on reducing the burden on the low-income populations.

Some programs that are not revenue neutral use the revenue to incentivize greater emissions reductions. Common strategies include using the revenue to pick up part of the cost for those households or businesses who invest in energy efficiency or in renewable energy such as wind or solar. Some energy efficiency programs have been shown to boost the economy in high energy cost regions not only by lowering the energy costs, but also by keeping the revenue in the local area rather than exporting it to import fuels. Studies find, however, that they are not as effective in boosting the economy as lowering the capital gains or corporate tax rates. Although energy efficiency programs frequently target some of the subsidies at the poor and the resulting investments do lower participants' energy cost, they are not particularly effective at lowering the burden on low-income populations in general since only those that choose to participate actually benefit.

Finally, carbon-pricing policies induce a shift away from high-carbon fuels and toward low- or zero-carbon fuels. While employment in the low- or zero-carbon fuel industries would rise, employment in the high-carbon fuel industries would fall. Studies indicate that the coal industry would be the hardest hit. Some of the revenue could be targeted specially at helping these displaced coal workers make the transition. This strategy could be useful in reducing the burden on this specific population and potentially in reducing the opposition to carbon-pricing in coal-mining regions.

Fortunately, economic studies have also found that it is not necessary to make an either–or decision among these revenue using choices. Because substantial revenue is commonly involved in carbon pricing programs, some strategies can be used simultaneously, thereby covering several bases at once.

Offsets. While both emissions trading and a carbon tax cover emissions from sources specifically subject to those programs, offsets allow emissions reductions from sources that are not subject to either the tax or the cap to be certified as offsets. Offsets, like allowances, can be used to cover emissions in a cap-and-trade program, sold, or used to reduce the tax base in carbon taxation. Offsets or offset tax credits perform several roles in pricing GHGs:

- First, increasing the number of reduction opportunities lowers the cost of compliance.
- Second, lowering the cost in this manner could increase the likelihood of enacting a carbon-pricing program by making compliance easier.
- Third, offsets extend the reach of a program by providing economic incentives for reducing sources that are not covered by the tax or cap.

- Finally, because offset credits separate the source of financing from the source providing the reduction, it secures some reductions (in developing countries, for example) that for affordability reasons might not be secured otherwise.

The challenge for establishing an effective offset program is assuring that the primary requirements (namely, that the reductions be quantifiable, enforceable, and additional) are all met. One obstacle is the tradeoff between the administrative costs associated with verifying the validity of offsets and the degree of offset validity. Assuring valid offsets is not cheap.

In response to concerns over the validity of offsets, most programs now try to limit their use. One historical approach has been to restrict the use of offsets (domestic, foreign, or both) to some stipulated percentage of the total required allowances. In the Regional Greenhouse Gas Initiative (RGGI) in the Northeastern US states, for example, CO_2 offset allowances may be used to satisfy only 3.3 percent of a source's total compliance obligation during a control period, although this may be expanded to 5 percent and 10 percent if certain CO_2 allowance price thresholds are reached. In contrast, in 2011, Germany announced that it would not allow *any* offsets to be used to pursue its reduction goals.

The Role of Price Volatility. A tax system fixes prices, and unless some administrative intervention changes those fixed prices, price volatility is not an issue. This is not the case with emissions trading in either principle or practice.

Experience not only validates the concern that emissions trading can be plagued by volatile prices, but also demonstrates that price volatility is not a rare event. In the EU ETS case, two early price declines were attributable to inadequate public knowledge of actual emissions relative to the cap and a failure to permit allowances in the first phase to be banked for use in the second phase. A subsequent dramatic price decline in 2012 stemmed from an over-allocation of permits, recession, and long-term uncertainty about the stability of climate policy.

This experience demonstrates that the design of an emissions trading system is vulnerable to unstable prices in two rather fundamental ways:

- First, because the cap establishes a fixed supply of allowances, demand shifts (due, for example, to other regulatory actions, recessions, or shifts in prices of lower carbon fuels) can trigger large changes in allowance prices (since supply cannot respond).
- Second, the demand for allowances is derived from satisfying compliance obligations. Changing circumstances (due either to external factors or simply greater than anticipated success in lowering carbon emissions) can create a surplus of allowances. This surplus may cause the price to drop precipitously since lower prices do not stimulate any increase in the quantity demanded. Both the RGGI and the EU ETS markets have experienced precisely this kind of price-dropping surplus.

One approach, called a price collar, is included in California's cap-and-trade program, as a means of dealing with price volatility. It couples a safety valve price ceiling backed by an allowance reserve with a price floor. Establishing a safety valve ceiling allows sources to purchase additional allowances from a reserve at a predetermined price, one that is set sufficiently high to make it unlikely to have any effect unless unexpected spikes in allowance prices occur. In 2013 the three fixed-price tiers in California were $40, $45, and $50, but they would rise over time with inflation. To prevent these purchases from causing the emissions cap to be exceeded, the reserve is established by allocating a specified percentage of allowances (originally 4 percent) from each annual budget between 2013 and 2020. As of 2016 the reserve had not been used and market prices were below the reserve tier prices, but the mere fact it exists serves to reduce price uncertainty.

Controversy: The Morality of Emissions Trading

Emissions trading has not avoided controversy. One element of that controversy raises the rather important question of whether the greenhouse gas trading concept violates conventional norms of international ethics (see Debate 8.2).

DEBATE 8.2

Is Global Greenhouse Gas Trading Immoral?

In a December 1997 editorial in the *New York Times*, Michael Sandel, a Harvard government professor, suggested that greenhouse gas trading is immoral. He argued that treating pollution as a commodity to be bought and sold not only removes the moral stigma that is appropriately associated with polluting, but also trading reductions undermines an important sense of shared responsibilities that global cooperation requires. He illustrated the point by suggesting that legitimizing further emission by offsetting it with a credit acquired from a project in a poorer nation would be very different from penalizing the firm for emitting, even if the cost of the credit were equal to the penalty. Not only would the now-authorized emission become inappropriately "socially acceptable" but also the wealthier nation would have met its moral obligation by paying a poorer nation to fulfill a responsibility that should have been fulfilled by a domestic emissions reduction.

Published responses to this editorial countered with several points. First, it was pointed out that since it is voluntary, international emissions trading typically benefits both nations; one nation is not imposing its will on another. Second, the historical use of these programs has resulted in much cleaner air at a much lower cost than would otherwise have been possible, so the ends would seem to justify the means. Third, with few exceptions, virtually all pollution-control regulations allow some emission that is not penalized; this is simply a recognition that zero pollution is rarely either efficient or politically feasible.

Source: Sandel, M. J. (December 17, 1997). It's immoral to buy the right to pollute. With replies by Steven Shavell, Robert Stavins, Sanford Gaines, and Eric Maskin. *New York Times*; excerpts reprinted in Stavins, R. N. (Ed.) (2000). *Economics of the Environment: Selected Readings*, 4th ed. New York: W.W. Norton & Company, 449–452.

Mitigation Policy: Timing

Most studies find that taking action to mitigate emissions enhances, rather than reduces, future economic well-being. Not only do we know how to design cost-effective carbon pricing strategies that hold the cost of action down, but the savings from avoided damages are potentially huge. A recent OECD study found, for example, that a climate-friendly policy package could increase long-run output by up to 2.8 percent on average across the G20 nations by 2050. If avoided climate damage is also taken into account, this rises to nearly 5 percent.[2]

How does the timing of the action matter? The US withdrawal from the Paris Accord seems likely to at least delay the timing of global emissions reductions. What can economics say about the optimal level of current investments in greenhouse gas reduction and how the costs are affected by delay in implementing those investments?

The earliest benefit-cost studies of options for controlling climate change suggested a "go slow" or "wait-and-see" policy. The reasons for these results are instructive. First, the benefits from current control are experienced well into the future, while the costs occur now. The present-value criterion in benefit-cost analysis discounts future values more than current values. Second, both energy-using and energy-producing capital are long-lived. Replacing them all at an accelerated pace now would be more expensive than replacing them in sequence closer to the end of their useful lives. Finally, the models anticipate that the number of new emissions-reducing technologies would be larger in the future and, due to this larger menu of options, the costs of reduction would be lower if actions are delayed until those technologies emerge.

Two concerns about that earlier conclusion, however, strengthen the case for beginning the process now. The use of benefit-cost analysis in climate change discussion is controversial due to the role of the present-value criterion. Although, as we demonstrated earlier, this approach is not inherently biased against future generations, their interests will only be adequately protected if they are adequately compensated for the damage inflicted on them. The uncertainty associated with this particular solution place the interests of future generations in maintaining a stable climate in jeopardy, raising an important ethical concern (Portney & Weyant, 1999).

Second, while the reasons for caution have economic merit, they do not necessarily imply a "wait-and-see" policy. Spreading the capital investment decisions over time implies that some investments take place now as current capital is replaced. Furthermore, the expectation that future technical change can reduce costs will only be fulfilled if the incentives for producing the technical change are in place now. In both cases, waiting simply postpones the process of change.

As time has passed the case for wait-and-see has diminished even further. The rise in atmospheric emissions can mean that the costs of mitigation rise as well. A recent study by the MIT Joint Program on the Science and Policy of Global Change found that delaying the abatement policy would substantially increase the mitigation cost. To be specific, they found that delaying the start of policy to 2030, as opposed to starting it in 2010, would raise the mitigation costs in 2050 and 2100 by 52.0 percent and 26.4 percent, respectively.[3]

Another powerful consideration in the debate over the timing of control investments involves uncertainty about both the costs and the benefits of climate change. Governments must act without complete knowledge. How can they respond reasonably to this uncertainty?

As economic analysis points out, the risks of being wrong are clearly asymmetric. If it turns out in retrospect that policy controlled more emissions than necessary, current generations could bear a larger-than-necessary cost. On the other hand, if the problem turns out to be as serious as the worst predictions indicate, catastrophic and largely irreversible damage to the planet could be inflicted on future generations. The second error clearly imposes higher costs than the former.

Yohe, Andronova, and Schlesinger (2004) investigate both consequences of being wrong using a standard, well-respected global climate model. Their model assumes that decision makers would choose global mitigation policies that would be in effect for 30 years, but after 30 years the policymakers would be able to modify the policies to take into account the better understanding of climate change consequences that would have been afforded by the intervening years. The specific source of uncertainty in their model results from our imperfect knowledge about the relationship between the atmospheric greenhouse gas concentrations and the resulting change in climate impacts. The specific question they examine is "What is the best strategy now?"

They found at that time that a hedging strategy that involved modest reductions dominated a "wait-and-see" strategy. Not only did current action initiate the capital turnover process and provide incentives for technical change, but also it allowed the avoidance of very costly and potentially irreversible mistakes later. If at the end of 30 years, for example, scientists discover that greenhouse gas concentrations must be stabilized at a more stringent level than previously thought to avoid exceeding important thresholds (such as the methane example discussed previously), that may not only be much more difficult and much more expensive to do later, but it may actually be impossible (due to the residence time in the atmosphere of past emissions). Now that we have higher concentrations in the atmosphere, most studies are indicating that the longer we wait to take action, the more costs will rise.

The Role of Adaptation Policy

Whereas mitigation strategies try to limit damage by limiting the emissions that cause the impacts, adaptation tends to limit damage by reducing the damage caused by the impacts that do occur. The two strategies are complements in the sense that the optimal policy response contains both adaptation and mitigation. Since the marginal cost function for each strategy is upward-sloping, this normally means that an optimal strategy would employ both mitigation and adaptation. Deviating from this optimum necessarily means that costs would be higher than necessary.

In another, equally meaningful sense the two strategies are also substitutes: more of one typically means less is needed of the other. To understand how they can be substitutes remember that the optimal level of either strategy would be to invest up to the point where the marginal cost of an additional unit of that strategy is equal to the marginal damages reduced by that unit. So for either strategy higher marginal damages imply a higher demand for investing more in that strategy.

If the strategies are substitutes, a reduction in the marginal cost of mitigation, for example, should lower the demand for adaptation. Why? Let's think this through. In an optimal policy a lower marginal cost of mitigation with an unchanged marginal damage would imply a higher optimal level of mitigation. This increased level of mitigation would lower the resulting marginal damage not only for additional units of mitigation, but for additional units of adaptation as well. The lower resulting marginal damages for adaptation would lower the demand for it. In this sense mitigation and adaptation are substitutes: increase the amount of one and you decrease the efficient amount of the other.

If you peruse the web you will discover that some pundits think about mitigation and adaptation as an either/or choice. They further suggest that policymakers should choose the one that is cheaper. Economic analysis points out that this is a false choice.

- First of all, as noted above, upward-sloping marginal cost functions for each strategy normally mean that an optimal approach would employ both strategies. Deviating from this optimum means that costs would be higher than necessary.
- Second, to the extent that adaptation and mitigation are substitutes, they are not perfect substitutes. Adaptation strategies are necessarily targeted at specific problems in specific geographic areas, whereas mitigation strategies have broader damage-reduction effects around the globe.
- Third, to some extent their timing may differ. Mitigation is necessarily done early to prevent emissions from building up in the atmosphere. Some adaptation can be done early as well, but some can also be delayed until a better understanding of the intensity and location of damages emerges.

As one World Bank study put it:

> There is a need for an integrated portfolio of actions ranging from avoiding emissions (mitigation) to coping with impacts (adaptation) and to consciously accepting residual damages. . . . However, some irreversible losses cannot be compensated for. Thus, mitigation might be in many cases the cheapest long-term solution to climate change problems and the most important to avoid thresholds that may trigger truly catastrophic consequences.[4]

What forms can adaptation strategies take? They range from large-scale infrastructure changes—such as building sea walls to protect against sea-level rise—to behavioral shifts as when individuals waste less water, farmers plant different crops, and households relocate their dwellings to higher land for flood protection. They can also involve a mix of public and private strategies, with private strategies ranging from improved early warning systems to building codes that prohibit new structures that are inefficiently vulnerable and would only be purchased by an uninformed buyer.

One way to think about the optimal respective roles for the public and private sectors is to look closely at the role private decision makers—households and businesses—can be expected to play (and indeed have already played in response to climate threats that have already occurred). Will private agents adapt to a modified climate? Are those reactions likely to be both effective and sufficient or is there a role for the public sector to fill in gaps?

A review of economic research in this this area by Fankhauser (2016) makes it clear that the answer to the first question is a resounding "yes!" Private agents do adapt. One of the most studied sectors, agriculture, reveals clear differences in agricultural practices, such as crop choices, under different climate conditions. In the longer term, farmers also respond to weather fluctuations by adjusting the size of their farm or moving into non-farm activities.

Although few studies examine business investments in adaptation, the fact that households adjust their energy consumption to climatic factors is well documented. Both energy demand and the demand for associated products like air conditioning units are found (as expected) to vary both seasonally and across climate zones. Further these private responses have been found to produce substantial social benefits in terms of reduced mortality and enhanced well-being.

So while the literature does provide compelling evidence that private agents do adapt, it does not provide compelling evidence that these responses are either completely effective or sufficient. To start with, the number of adaptation investment situations that have been studied is very limited. Further, few of those that have been studied focus on adaptation to the kinds of major damages that are expected from a changing climate. More importantly, however, the literature documents a number of barriers that inhibit private actions, thereby reducing the effectiveness of a purely private adaptation strategy.

- Property rights matter. Because they would incur the losses caused by property damages, renters also have lower incentives than owners to invest in adaptation. In general, ambiguous or compromised property rights can be a barrier to effective private action.
- Effective private action depends on good information on both the nature of risks and options for adapting to them. Much of this information about future risks is a public good, which means that it will be undersupplied unless the government supplies it or participates in its supply.
- Adaptation choices can also be limited by affordability, including how a low income diminishes the ability to borrow.
- Finally, much of the adaptation would involve public capital like roads or public transportation systems, and the desirability of many private adaptation responses would be affected by those public adaptation responses.

Even this brief list suggests a multi-faceted role for governments.

- It should identify circumstances that lead to adaptation market failures and adopt policies that correct or remove the distortions in incentives that lead to the failures.
- It should provide public information on the risks being posed by a changing climate.
- It should provide financial mechanisms for assisting populations facing affordability problems with adaptation.
- It should develop adaptation plans for publicly owned capital such as the transportation infrastructure.

Summary

The first global pollutant problem confronted by the international community arose when ozone-depleting gases were implicated in the destruction of the stratospheric ozone shield that protects the earth's surface from harmful ultraviolet radiation. Because these are accumulating pollutants, an efficient response to this problem involves reducing their emissions over time.

To restrict their accumulation in the atmosphere, the international agreements on ozone-depleting substances created a system of limits on production and consumption. Internationally, this system is considered a success in part because the Multilateral Fund and other incentives, such as delayed compliance deadlines, facilitated the participation of developing countries and in part because the losses imposed on producers of ozone-depleting chemicals when those chemicals were phased out were offset by the profits gained by many of the same producers as they produced and sold the substitutes.

Climate change is appropriately considered an even more difficult problem. Not only must policy cope with the free-rider problem and the fact that the current generation bears the costs while the benefits accrue in the future, but climate change presents some additional challenges. At the top of the list is the fact that in this case controlling greenhouse gases means controlling energy use from fossil fuels, the lynchpin of modern society.

Fortunately, economic analysis of the climate change problem not only defines the need for action, but also sheds light on effective forms that action might take. The empirical studies suggest that it makes sense to take action not only to mitigate emissions, but to develop and implement adaptation strategies.

Economics also sheds light on the barriers to effective participation in climate change agreements and some potential solutions as well. Game theory studies reveal that the free-rider effect is a significant barrier to participation as is the long horizon over which the effects of current polices are felt. Game theory studies with a broader scope, however, point out specific strategies (such as international transfers and issue linkage) that can be used to build stronger incentives for participation. Some international cost sharing is also likely to be as necessary an ingredient in a successful attack on the climate problem as it was in the ozone-depletion case.

Since carbon pricing is the main form of cost-effective policy on climate change, the fact that the number of existing regional and national carbon pricing programs is growing and the list of participating countries includes some important players is good news indeed.

The evidence demonstrates that these programs are achieving emissions reductions in a relatively cost-effective manner, but some issues, such as volatile prices and the appropriate role for offsets, are still in the process of being resolved.

During the next few decades, options must not only be preserved, they must be enhanced. Responding in a timely and effective fashion to global and regional pollution problems will not be easy. Our political institutions are not configured in such a way as to make decision making on a global scale simple. International organizations exist at the pleasure of the nations they serve. Only time will tell if the mechanisms of international agreements described in this chapter will prove equal to the task.

Discussion Questions

1. Concerned individuals can now seek to reduce their carbon footprint by buying offsets. Air travelers, for example, are now asked if they wish to purchase offsets when they buy their ticket. Is this a complement or substitute for a national climate change policy? Why?
2. What is your national, regional, or state government doing about climate change? Has it adopted a form of carbon pricing? If so, how is it working out? Is anyone working on an adaptation plan in your area? Do the basics of those approaches seem consistent with some of the characteristics of an efficient strategy discussed in this chapter? Why or why not?

Self-Test Exercises

1. Explain why a climate policy using emissions-charge revenue to provide capital and operating subsidies for carbon capture technologies is less cost-effective than an emissions-charge policy alone.
2. The revenues from an emissions-charge approach to controlling climate change would be unusually large in comparison to other pollutants. What circumstances would lead to high revenues?
3. Label the following as true, false, or uncertain, and explain your choice. (Uncertain means that it can be either true or false depending upon the circumstances.)

    a. The imposition of a tax on currently uncontrolled greenhouse gas emissions would represent a move toward efficiency.

    b.   Relying on a series of regional systems (like the EU ETS), rather than a true global system, for controlling greenhouse gases increases the importance of the leakage problem.

4.   Suppose two countries with domestic cap-and-trade polices are considering linking their two systems. Country A has a cap of 20 tons of emissions, a domestic marginal cost of abatement of \$10 and an uncontrolled emissions level of 60 tons, while Country B has a cap of 40 tons, a domestic marginal cost of abatement of \$1q, where q = the tons of emission abatement, and an uncontrolled emissions level of 80 tons.

    a.   Before linkage what would be the prices in the two separate markets and how much abatement would each country choose?

    b.   If these two markets were linked by allowing each country to buy from and sell allowances to the other, what would be the prices in the two markets? How much would each country abate? Describe the transfer of allowances, if any, that would take place between the two countries.

5.   In negotiations over a public good such as a greenhouse gas emissions reduction, a cooperative agreement always produces higher aggregate benefits than a noncooperative agreement so cooperation will dominate noncooperation. Discuss.

Notes

1   How difficult these negotiations are can be illustrated by the fact that the magnitude of US pledges to the Green Climate Fund was one example President Trump gave of the US's unfair burden under the Paris Accord. Although the Green Climate Fund actually precedes the Paris Accords by about 5 years, it wasn't until 2013 that the GCF started its first round of fundraising.

2   OECD. (2017). *Investing in Climate, Investing in Growth*. Paris: OECD Publishing.

3   Chen, Y.-H. H., Babiker, M., Paltsev, S., & Reilly, H. (2016). Costs of climate mitigation policies. MIT Joint Program on the Science and Policy of climate Change Report 292. Available at: https://globalchange.mit.edu/publication/15766 (accessed June 14, 2017).

4   Shalizi, Z. and Lecocq, F. (August 2010). To mitigate or to adapt: Is that the question? Observations on an appropriate response to the climate change challenge to development strategies. *The World Bank Research Observer*, 25(2), 295–321, p. 295.

Further Reading

Calvo, E., & Santiago J. R. (2012). Dynamic models of international environmental agreements: A differential game approach. *International Review of Environmental and Resource Economics*, 6, 289–339. A survey of dynamic models of international environmental agreements.

Fankhauser, Sam. (2016). Adaptation to climate change. Grantham Research Institute on Climate Change and the Environment Working Paper No. 255. Available at: www.lse.ac.uk/GranthamInstitute/publication/adaptation-to-climate-change/. Last accessed April 1, 2017. A survey of the economics of adaptation.

Fell, Harrison, Burtraw, Dallas, Morgenstern, Richard D., & Palmer, Karen L. (2012). Soft and hard price collars in a cap-and-trade system: A comparative analysis. *Journal of Environmental Economics and Management*, 64(2): 183–198. Compares price collars (price ceilings and floors) in a cap-and-trade system involving uncertainty with respect to the level of baseline emissions and costs.

Mendelsohn, R., Dinar, A., et al. (2006). The distributional impacts of climate change on rich and poor countries. *Environment and Development Economics*, *11*, 159–178. This economic analysis concludes that poor countries will suffer the bulk of the damages from climate change, due primarily to their location.

Metcalf, G. E. (2009). Designing a carbon tax to reduce US greenhouse gas emissions. *Review of Environmental Economics and Policy*, *3*(1), 63–83. Describes considerations for designing a carbon tax to control greenhouse gas emissions in the United States.

Stavins, R. N. (2008). Addressing climate change with a comprehensive US cap-and-trade system. *Oxford Review of Economic Policy*, *24*(2), 298–321. Describes considerations for designing a cap-and-trade policy to control greenhouse gas emissions in the United States.

Stern, N. (2008). The economics of climate change. *American Economic Review*, *98*(2), 1–37. As assessment by the former chief economist of the World Bank.

Tietenberg, T. H. (Summer 2013). Reflections—Carbon pricing in practice. *Review of Environmental Economics and Policy*, *7*, 313–329. A review of the existing carbon pricing programs that considers their effectiveness and the emerging design lessons.

US Environmental Protection Agency. 2016. Climate change indicators in the United States, 2016, 4th ed. EPA 430-R-16-004. www.epa.gov/climate-indicators. This report presents 37 indicators to help readers understand changes observed from long-term records related to the causes and effects of climate change, the signicance of these changes, and their possible consequences for people, the environment, and society.

Williams III, Roberton C. (June, 2016). Environmental taxation. Resources for the Future Discussion Paper 16-24. Available at: www.rff.org/files/document/file/RFF-DP-16-24.pdf. This paper evaluates the economic and environmental effects of potential environmental tax reforms, based on a review of recent economic research.

Additional references and historically significant references are available on this book's Companion Website: www.routledge.com/cw/Tietenberg

Chapter 9

Water Pollution

It was the best of times, it was the worst of times, it was the age of wisdom, it was the age of foolishness, it was the epoch of belief, it was the epoch of incredulity.
—Charles Dickens, *A Tale of Two Cities* (1859)

Introduction

While various types of pollution share common attributes, important differences are apparent as well. These differences form the basis for the elements of policy unique to each pollutant. We have seen, for example, that although the types of pollutants emitted by mobile and stationary sources are often identical, the policy approaches differ considerably.

Water pollution control has its own unique characteristics as well. The following stand out as having particular relevance for policy:

1. Recreation benefits are much more important for water pollution control than for air pollution control.
2. Large economies of scale in treating sewage and other wastes create the possibility for large, centralized treatment plants as one control strategy, while for air pollution on-site control is the standard approach.
3. Many causes of water pollution are more difficult to trace to a particular source. Runoff from streets and agriculture as well as atmospheric deposition of pollutants are major diffuse sources of water pollution. Control of these sources adds additional complexities for water pollution control.

These characteristics create a need for yet another policy approach. In this chapter we explore the problems and prospects for controlling this unique and important form of pollution.

Nature of Water Pollution Problems

Types of Waste-Receiving Water

Three primary types of water are susceptible to contamination. The first, *surface water*, consists of the rivers, lakes, and oceans covering most of the earth's surface. Historically, policymakers have focused almost exclusively on preventing and cleaning up lake and river water pollution.

Groundwater, once considered a pristine resource, has been shown to be subject to considerable contamination from toxic chemicals. *Groundwater* is water beneath the earth's surface in soils or rocks, or in geological formations that are fully saturated.

The third, *oceans*, has only recently begun receiving attention.

While surface water serves as a significant source of drinking water, it has many other uses as well. Recreational benefits, such as swimming, fishing, and boating, are important determinants of surface water policy in areas where the water is not used for drinking. Groundwater is used primarily for irrigation and as a source of drinking water.

Sources of Contamination

For pollution policy purposes, it is useful to distinguish between two sources of contamination—point and nonpoint—even though the distinction is not always crystal clear. *Point sources* generally discharge into surface waters at a specific location through a pipe, outfall, or ditch, while *nonpoint sources* usually affect the water in a more indirect and diffuse way. Examples of nonpoint source pollution include the runoff of fertilizers and pesticides from lawns and

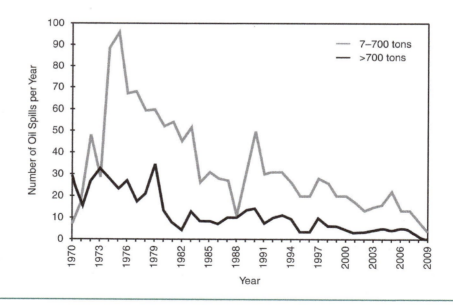

Figure 9.1 The Decreasing Frequency of Oil Spills from Tankers and Barges

Source: International Tanker Owners Pollution Federation Limited website: www.itopf.com/informationservices/data-and-statistics/statistics/index.html

farms after rainstorms. From the policy point of view, nonpoint sources are more difficult to control because both the source and timing are hard to predict and, as such, they have received little legislative attention until recently. As a result of the gains made in controlling point sources, nonpoint sources now compose over half of the waste load borne by the nation's waters.

Contamination of groundwater occurs when polluting substances leach into a water-saturated region. Many potential contaminants are removed by filtration and adsorption as the water moves slowly through the layers of rock and soil. Toxic organic chemicals are one major example of a pollutant that may not be filtered out during migration. Once these substances enter groundwater, very little, if any, further cleansing takes place. Moreover, since the rate of replenishment for many groundwater sources, relative to the stock, is small, very little mixing and dilution of the contaminants occur.

Three primary sources of ocean pollution are oil spills, ocean dumping, and trash (primarily plastics) that ends up in the ocean. Oil spills from tankers have become less frequent and have decreased in magnitude since 1970 (see Figure 9.1). Spills, however, are still not uncommon, as shown in Table 9.1, and off-shore drilling has increased those risks, as the recent "BP spill" in the Gulf of Mexico illustrated. Various unwanted by-products of modern life have also been dumped into ocean waters based upon the mistaken belief that the vastness of the

Table 9.1 Notable Oil Spills from Tankers

Rank	Spill Size (tons)	Ship Name	Year	Location
1	287,000	*Atlantic Empress*	1979	Off Tobago, West Indies
2	260,000	*ABT Summer*	1991	700 nautical miles off Angola
3	252,000	*Castillo de Bellver*	1983	Off Saldanha Bay, South Africa
4	223,000	*Amoco Cadiz*	1978	Off Brittany, France
5	144,000	*Haven*	1991	Genoa, Italy
6	132,000	*Odyssey*	1988	700 nautical miles off Nova Scotia, Canada
7	119,000	*Torrey Canyon*	1967	Scilly Isles, the United Kingdom
8	115,000	*Sea Star*	1972	Gulf of Oman
9	100,000	*Irenes Serenade*	1980	Navarino Bay, Greece
10	100,000	*Urquiola*	1976	La Coruna, Spain
11	95,000	*Hawaiian Patriot*	1977	300 nautical miles off Honolulu
12	94,000	*Independenta*	1979	Bosphorus, Turkey
13	88,000	*Jakob Maersk*	1975	Oporto, Portugal
14	85,000	*Braer*	1993	Shetland Islands, the United Kingdom
15	74,000	*Aegean Sea*	1992	La Coruna, Spain
16	72,000	*Sea Empress*	1996	Milford Haven, the United Kingdom
17	70,000	*Khark 5*	1989	120 nautical miles off Atlantic coast of Morocco
18	70,000	*Nova*	1985	Off Kharg Island, Gulf of Iran
19	67,000	*Katina P*	1992	Off Maputo, Mozambique
20	63,000	*Prestige*	2002	Off Galicia, Spain
35	37,000	*Exxon Valdez*	1989	Prince William Sound, Alaska, USA
131	11,000	*Hebei Spirit*	2007	South Korea

Source: International Tanker Owners Pollution Federation Limited website, updated June 2017: www.itopf.com/knowledge-resources/data-statistics/statistics/#major. Reprinted with permission from ITOPF.

oceans allows them to absorb large quantities of waste without suffering noticeable damage. Dumped materials have included sewage and sewage sludge, unwanted chemicals, trace metals, and even radioactive materials. More recently, vast amounts of plastics have been found in the ocean. Much of this plastic gets ingested by sea life and kills thousands of marine birds and mammals each year.

Types of Pollutants

For our purposes, the large number of water pollutants can be usefully classified by means of the taxonomy developed in Chapter 5.

Fund Pollutants. Fund pollutants are those for which the environment has some assimilative capacity. If the absorptive capacity is high enough relative to the rate of discharge, they may not accumulate at all. One type of fund water pollutant is called *degradable* because it degrades, or breaks into its component parts, within the water. Degradable wastes are normally organic residuals that are attacked and broken down by bacteria in the stream.

The process by which organic wastes are broken down into component parts consumes oxygen. The amount of oxygen consumed depends upon the magnitude of the waste load. All of the higher life-forms in watercourses are *aerobic*; they require oxygen for survival. As a stream's oxygen levels fall, fish mortality increases, with the less tolerant fish becoming the first to succumb. The oxygen level can become low enough that even the aerobic bacteria die. When this happens, the stream becomes *anaerobic* and the ecology changes drastically. This is an extremely unpleasant circumstance because the stream takes on a dark hue, and the stream water stinks![1]

To control these waste loads, two different types of monitoring are needed: (1) monitoring the ambient conditions in the watercourse; and (2) monitoring the magnitude of emissions, or effluent as it is commonly labeled for water pollutants. One measure commonly used to keep track of ambient conditions for these conventional fund pollutants is *dissolved oxygen* (DO). The amount of dissolved oxygen in a body of water is a function of ambient conditions, such as temperature, stream flow, and the waste load. The measure of the oxygen demand placed on a stream by any particular volume of effluent is called the *biochemical oxygen demand* (BOD).

Using modeling techniques, effluent (measured as BOD) at a certain point can be translated into DO measures at various receptor locations along a stream. This step is necessary in order to implement an ambient permit system or an ambient emissions charge.

If we were to develop a profile of dissolved oxygen readings on a stream where organic effluent is being discharged, that profile would typically exhibit one or more minimum points called *oxygen sags*. These oxygen sags represent locations along the stream where the dissolved oxygen content is lower than at other points. An ambient permit or ambient charge system would be designed to reach a desired DO level at those sag points, while a cap-and-trade or effluent charge system would simply try to hit a particular BOD reduction target. The former would take the location of the emitter into account, while the latter would not. Later in this chapter we examine studies that model these systems on particular watercourses.

A second type of fund pollutant, thermal pollution, is caused by the injection of heat into a watercourse. Typically, *thermal pollution* is caused when an industrial plant or electric utility uses surface water as a coolant, returning the heated water to the watercourse. This heat is dissipated in the receiving waters by evaporation. By raising the temperature of the water near the outfall, thermal pollution lowers the dissolved oxygen content and can result in dramatic ecological changes in that area.

Yet another example is provided by a class of pollutants, such as nitrogen and phosphorus, that are plant nutrients. These pollutants stimulate the growth of aquatic plant life, such as algae and water weeds. In excess, these plants can produce odor, taste, and aesthetic problems. A lake with an excessive supply of nutrients is called *eutrophic*.

The various types of fund pollutants could be ordered on a spectrum. On one end of the spectrum would be pollutants for which the environment has a very large absorptive capacity and on the other end pollutants for which the absorptive capacity is virtually nil. The limiting case, with no absorptive capacity, is stock pollutants.

Near the end of that spectrum is a class of inorganic synthetic chemicals called *persistent* pollutants. These substances are called persistent because their complex molecular structures are not effectively broken down in the stream. Some degradation takes place, but so slowly that these pollutants can travel long distances in water in a virtually unchanged form.

These persistent pollutants accumulate, not only in the watercourses, but also in the food chain. The concentration levels in the tissues of living organisms rise with the order of the species. Concentrations in lower life-forms such as plankton may be relatively small, but because small fish eat a lot of plankton and do not excrete the chemical, the concentrations in small fish would be higher. The magnification continues as large fish consume small fish; concentration levels in the larger fish would be even higher.

Because they accumulate in the food chains, persistent pollutants present an interesting monitoring challenge. The traditional approach would involve measurements of pollutant concentration in the water, but that is not the only variable of interest. The damage is related not only to its concentration in the water, but its concentration in the food chain as well. Although monitoring the environmental effects of these pollutants may be more compelling than for other pollutants, it is also more difficult.

Infectious organisms such as bacteria and viruses can be carried into surface water and groundwater by human and animal wastes and by wastes from such industries as tanning and meatpacking. These live organisms may either thrive and multiply in water or their population may decline over time, depending upon how hospitable or hostile the watercourse is for continued growth.

Most recently, medicinal waste has been found in watercourses and in fish tissue. In 2002, the USGS tested 139 rivers in 30 states and found that 80 percent of the streams sampled resulted in evidence of residuals from drugs such as birth-control pills and antidepressants. Residuals from soaps, perfumes, and caffeine were also found. While the magnitude of the damage that will ultimately be caused by these substances is not yet clear, it is certainly a challenge for water pollution control policy.

Stock Pollutants. The most troublesome cases of pollution result from stock pollutants, which merely accumulate in the environment. No natural process removes or transforms stock pollutants; the watercourse cannot cleanse itself of them.

Inorganic chemicals and minerals comprise the main examples of stock pollutants. Perhaps the most notorious members of this group are the heavy metals, such as lead, cadmium, and mercury. Extreme examples of poisoning by these metals have occurred in Japan. One ocean-dumping case was responsible for *Minamata disease*, named for the location where it occurred. Some 52 people died and 150 others suffered serious brain and nerve damage. Scientists puzzled for years over the source of the ailments until tracing it to an organic form of mercury that had accumulated in the tissues of fish eaten three times a day by local residents.

In the United States, mercury contamination of fish has led to consumption advisories for many freshwater and migratory fish. Women of childbearing age and children especially are cautioned against eating large amounts of certain species. Debate 9.1 examines the effects of fish consumption advisories on consumer behavior.

In another case in Japan, known as the *itai itai* (literally, *ouch-ouch*) *disease*, scientists traced the source of a previously undiagnosed, extremely painful bone disease to the ingestion of cadmium. Nearby mines were the source of the cadmium, which apparently was ingested by eating contaminated rice and soybeans.

DEBATE 9.1

Toxics in Fish Tissue: Do Fish Consumption Advisories Change Behavior?

Since mercury persists and bioaccumulates, the concentrations of mercury rise as you move up the food chain. Ingested mercury has been linked to neurological disorders in infants and children. In January 2001, the Food and Drug Administration (FDA) released an advisory on methyl mercury in fish. An updated advisory was issued in 2004 and again in 2006. Part of that advisory reads as follows:

> However, nearly all fish and shellfish contain traces of mercury. For most people, the risk from mercury by eating fish and shellfish is not a health concern. Yet, some fish and shellfish contain higher levels of mercury that may harm an unborn baby or young child's developing nervous system. The risks from mercury in fish and shellfish depend on the amount of fish and shellfish eaten and the levels of mercury in the fish and shellfish. Therefore, the Food and Drug Administration (FDA) and the Environmental Protection Agency (EPA) are advising women who may become pregnant, pregnant women, nursing mothers, and young children to avoid some types of fish and eat fish and shellfish that are lower in mercury

The FDA targeted women planning on becoming pregnant within 6 months, pregnant women, and nursing women to receive information about the new advisory on methyl mercury.

Using the Bureau of Labor Statistics' Consumer Expenditure Survey, Shimshack, Ward, and Beatty (2007) examined the effectiveness of advisories in affecting consumer choices. In particular, they looked at the effects of the advisory on the consumption of canned fish during 1999–2002, a time period that includes 2 years before and 2 years after the advisory. They examined whether the groups targeted reduced their consumption of canned fish and what determined the responses.

Comparing target households (those with young children) to nontarget households, they found that targeted consumers significantly reduced their canned fish consumption as a result of the warning. College-educated consumers responded quite strongly. Additionally, they found that newspaper and magazine readership were significant in influencing the postadvisory reduction in fish consumption, but health consciousness was not. Interestingly, they also found evidence of spillover effects; nontargeted consumers also reduced their consumption of canned fish.

Access to information is clearly important to the success of a health advisory. At-risk consumers who were less educated and nonreaders did not significantly reduce consumption. The authors suggest that this particular group is also less likely to be able to withstand negative health shocks.

What is the best way to get information to different population groups? Unequal access to information creates unevenly distributed health risks and might be labeled an environmental justice issue.

Sources: Shimshack, J. P., Ward, M. B., and Beatty, T. K. M. (2007). Mercury advisories: Information, education and fish consumption. *Journal of Environmental Economics and Management, 53*(2), 158–179; www.fda.gov; www.cfsan.fda.gov/~dms/admehg3.html.

As is typical with persistent pollutants, some of the stock pollutants are difficult to monitor. Those accumulated in the food chains give rise to the same problem as is presented by persistent pollutants. Ambient sampling must be supplemented by sampling tissues from members of the food chain. To further complicate matters, the heavy metals may sink rapidly to the bottom, remaining in the sediment. While these could be detected in sediment samples, merely drawing samples from the water itself would allow these pollutants to escape detection.

Traditional Water Pollution Control Policy

Water pollution control policies vary around the world. In this section we begin with a detailed discussion of US policy, which provides a rich example of a typical legal approach to regulation. Later in the chapter we will look at the European approach, which has depended more heavily on economic incentives.

US policy for water pollution control predates federal air pollution control. We might suppose that the policy for water pollution control would, therefore, be superior, since authorities have had more time to profit from early mistakes. Unfortunately, that is not the case.

The US Experience

Early Legislation

The first federal legislation dealing with discharge into the nation's waterways occurred when Congress passed the 1899 Refuse Act. Designed primarily to protect navigation, this act focused on preventing any discharge that would interfere with using rivers as transport links. All discharges into a river were prohibited unless approved by a permit from the Chief of the US Engineers. Most permits were issued to contractors dredging the rivers, and they dealt mainly with the disposal of the removed material. This act was virtually unenforced for other pollutants until 1970, when this permit program was rediscovered and used briefly (with little success) as the basis for federal enforcement actions.

The Water Pollution Control Act of 1948 represented the first attempt by the federal government to exercise some direct influence over what previously had been a state and local function. A hesitant move, since it reaffirmed that the primary responsibility for water pollution control rested with the states, it did initiate the authority of the federal government to conduct investigations, research, and surveys.

Early hints of the current approach are found in the amendments to the Water Pollution Control Act, which were passed in 1956. Two provisions of this Act were especially important: (1) federal financial support for the construction of waste treatment plants, and (2) direct federal regulation of waste discharges via a mechanism known as the *enforcement conference*.

The first of these provisions envisioned a control strategy based on subsidizing the construction of a particular control activity—waste water treatment plants. Municipalities could receive federal grants to cover up to 55 percent of the construction of municipal sewage treatment plants. This approach not only lowered the cost to the local governments of constructing these facilities, but also it lowered the cost to users. Since the federal government contribution was a grant, rather than a loan, the fees users were charged did not reflect the federally subsidized construction portion of the cost. The user fees were set at a lower rate that was high enough to cover merely the unsubsidized portion of construction cost, as well as operating and maintenance costs.

The 1956 amendments envisioned a relatively narrow federal role in the regulation of discharges. Initially, only polluters contributing to interstate pollution were included, but subsequent laws have broadened the coverage. By 1961, discharges into all navigable water were covered.

The mechanism created by the amendments of 1956 to enforce the regulation of discharges was the enforcement conference. Under this approach, the designated federal control authority could call for a conference to deal with any interstate water pollution problem, or it could be requested to do so by the governor of an affected state. The fact that this authority was discretionary and not mandatory and that the control authority had very few means of enforcing any decisions reached meant that the conferences simply did not achieve the intended results.

The Water Quality Act of 1965 attempted to improve the process by establishing ambient water quality standards for interstate watercourses and by requiring states to file implementation plans. This sounds like the approach currently being used in air pollution control, but there are important differences. The plans forthcoming from states in response to the 1965 Act were vague and did not attempt to link specific effluent standards on discharges to the ambient standards. They generally took the easy way out and called for secondary treatment, which removes 80–90 percent of BOD and 85 percent of suspended solids. The fact that these standards bore no particular relationship to ambient quality made them difficult to enforce in the courts, since the legal authority for them was based on this relationship.

Subsequent Legislation

Point Sources. An air of frustration regarding pollution control pervaded Washington in the 1970s. As with air pollution legislation, this frustration led to the enactment of a very tough water pollution control law. The tone of the 1972 Ammendments to the Water Pollution Control Act, now commonly called the Clean Water Act (CWA), is established immediately in the preamble, which calls for the achievement of two goals: (1) "that the discharge of pollutants into the navigable waters be eliminated by 1985"; and (2) "that wherever attainable, an interim goal of water quality which provides for the protection and propagation of fish, shellfish, and wildlife and provides for recreation in and on the water be achieved by June 1, 1983." The stringency of these goals represented a major departure from previous policy.

This Act also introduced new procedures for implementing the law. Permits were required of all dischargers (replacing the 1899 Refuse Act, which, because of its navigation focus, was difficult to enforce). The permits would be granted only when the dischargers met certain technology-based effluent standards. The ambient standards were completely bypassed as these effluent standards were uniformly imposed and, hence, could not depend on local water conditions.[2]

According to the CWA, the effluent standards were to be implemented in two stages. By 1977, industrial dischargers, as a condition of their permit, were required to meet effluent limitations based on the "best practicable control technology currently available" (BPT). In setting these national standards, the EPA was required to consider the total costs of these technologies and their relation to the benefits received, but not to consider the conditions of the individual source or the particular waters into which it was discharged. In addition, all publicly owned treatment plants were to have achieved secondary treatment by 1977. By 1983, industrial discharges were required to meet effluent limitations based on the presumably more stringent "best available technology economically achievable" (BAT), while publicly owned treatment plants were required to meet effluent limitations that depended on the "best practicable waste treatment technology."

The program of subsidizing municipal water treatment plants, begun in 1956, was continued in a slightly modified form by the CWA. Whereas the 1965 Act allowed the federal government to subsidize up to 55 percent of the cost of construction of waste treatment plants, the 1972 Act raised the ceiling to 75 percent. The 1972 Act also increased the funds available for this program. In 1981, the federal share was returned to 55 percent.

The 1977 amendments to the CWA continued this regulatory approach, but with some major modifications. This legislation drew a more careful distinction between conventional and toxic pollutants, with more stringent requirements placed on the latter, and it extended virtually all of the deadlines in the 1972 Act.

For conventional pollutants, a new treatment standard was created to replace the BAT standards. The effluent limitations for these pollutants were to be based on the "best conventional technology," and the deadline for these standards was set at July 1, 1984. In setting these standards, the EPA was required to consider whether the costs of adding the pollution control equipment were reasonable when compared with the improvement in water quality. For unconventional pollutants and toxics (any pollutant not specifically included on the list of conventional pollutants), the BAT requirement was retained but the deadline was shifted to 1984.

The final modification made by the 1977 amendments involved the introduction of pretreatment standards for waste being sent to a publicly owned treatment system. These standards were designed to prevent discharges that could inhibit the treatment process and to prevent the introduction of toxic pollutants that would not be treated by the waste treatment facility.

Nonpoint Sources. In contrast to the control of point sources, the EPA was given no specific authority to regulate nonpoint sources. This type of pollution was seen by Congress as a state responsibility.

Section 208 of the CWA authorized federal grants for state-initiated planning that would provide implementable plans for area-wide waste-treatment management. Section 208 further specified that this area-wide plan must identify significant non-point sources of pollution, as well as procedures and methods for controlling them. The reauthorization of the Clean Water Act, passed over President Reagan's veto during February 1987, authorized an additional $400 million for a new program to help states control runoff, but it still left the chief responsibility for controlling nonpoint sources to the states.

The main federal role for controlling nonpoint sources has been the Conservation Reserve Program run by the US Department of Agriculture rather than the EPA. Designed to remove some 40–45 million acres of highly erodible land from cultivation, this act provides subsidies to farmers for planting grass or trees. These subsidies are designed to result in reduced erosion and to reduce loadings of nitrogen, phosphorus, and total suspended solids.

Since the late 1980s, efforts focused on nonpoint sources have increased dramatically. Voluntary programs and cost-sharing programs with landowners have been the most common tools. Section 319 of the Clean Water Act specifies guidelines for state implementation of nonpoint source-management plans. In 2003, the EPA devoted a large portion of its Section 319 funds ($100 million) to address areas where nonpoint source pollution has significantly impaired water quality.[3] Another recent role for municipalities has been the separation of storm water and sewer drains so that sewage treatment plants do not overflow during rainstorms. Federal subsidies have also assisted with these projects.

The TMDL Program

In 1999, recognizing the problems with both the technology-based national effluent standards and the growing importance of nonpoint pollution control, the US EPA proposed new rules designed to breathe fresh life into the previously unenforced *Total Maximum Daily Load (TMDL) program* of the Clean Water Act. A TMDL is a calculation of the maximum amount of a pollutant that a water body can receive and still meet water quality standards as well as an allocation of that amount to the pollutant's sources. The calculation must include a margin of safety to ensure that the water body can be used for its designated purpose. The calculation must also account for seasonable variation in water quality.

The TMDL program moves water pollution control toward the ambient standard approach long used to control air pollution. Under this program, water quality standards are promulgated by states, territories, and/or tribes. The promulgated standards are tailored to the designated uses for each water body (such as drinking water supply or recreational uses such as swimming and/or fishing). The states must then undertake strategies for achieving the standards, including significantly bringing nonpoint source pollutants under control.

The Safe Drinking Water Act

The 1972 Act focused on achieving water quality sufficiently high for fishing and swimming. Because that quality is not high enough for drinking water, the Safe Drinking Water Act of 1974 issued more stringent standards for community water systems. The primary drinking water regulations set maximum allowable concentration levels for bacteria, turbidity (muddiness), and chemical-radiological contaminants. National secondary drinking water regulations were also established to protect "public welfare" from odor and aesthetic problems that may cause a substantial number of people to stop using the affected water system. The secondary standards are advisory for the states; they cannot be enforced by the EPA.

The 1986 Amendments to the Safe Drinking Water Act required the EPA to (1) issue primary standards within three years for 83 contaminants and by 1991 for at least 25 more, (2) set standards based on the BAT, and (3) monitor public water systems for both regulated and unregulated chemical contaminants. Approximately 60,000 public water systems are subject to these regulations. Civil and criminal penalties for any violations of the standards were also increased by the amendments.

More recent drinking water rules and standards cover MTBE, arsenic, radon, lead, microbials, and disinfection by-products. In 2007, the EPA issued a final ruling on lead and copper in drinking water, two contaminants that enter through plumbing materials. Many older homes have faucets or fittings of brass, which contain some lead, lead pipes, or copper pipes with solder.

The Clean Water Rule

The Clean Water Rule, enacted by the Obama administration in 2017, was designed to take the existing federal protections on large water bodies and expand them to include the wetlands and small tributaries that flow into these larger waters. This rule closed loopholes that had left streams wetlands at risk for pollution.

In 2015, the EPA and the US Department of the Army issued a report examining the costs and benefits of expanding the definition of the "waters of the United States." Their estimate concluded that the water protections would indeed come at an economic cost—between $236 million and $465 million annually, *but* the report also concluded that the economic benefits of preventing water pollution would be much greater: between $555 million and $572 million. As we have seen throughout this book, estimating both the costs and the benefits informs decision making on environmental policy.

Ocean Pollution

Oil Spills. The Clean Water Act prohibits discharges of "harmful quantities" of oil into navigable waters. Since the EPA regulations define "harmful" to include all discharges that "violate applicable water quality standards or cause a film or sheen upon the surface of the water," virtually all discharges are prohibited.

Industry responsibilities include complying with Coast Guard regulations (which deal with contingency planning in case of a spill and various accident avoidance requirements) and assuming the financial liability for any accident. If a spill does occur, it must be immediately reported to the Coast Guard or the EPA. Failure to report a spill can result in a fine up to $10,000 and/or imprisonment for up to 1 year.

In addition to giving notice, the discharger must either contain the spill or pay the cost of cleanup by a responsible government agency. The discharger's liability for the government's actual removal cost is limited to $50 million unless willful negligence or willful misconduct can be proved. Successful proof of willful negligence or willful misconduct eliminates the liability limit. In addition to cleanup costs, removal costs also include compensation for damages to natural resources. (Natural resource damages are defined as "any costs or expenses incurred by the federal government or any state government in the restoration or replacement of natural resources damaged or destroyed as a result of a discharge of oil.") Example 9.4, later in this chapter, presents damage estimates for the Deepwater Horizon oil spill.

Ocean Dumping. Except for oil spills, which are covered by the Clean Water Act and the Oil Pollution Act of 1990, discharges to the ocean are covered by the Marine Protection Research and Sanctuaries Act of 1972. This act governs all discharges of wastes to ocean waters within US territorial limits and discharges of wastes in ocean waters by US vessels or persons regardless of where the dumping occurs. With only a few exceptions, no ocean dumping of industrial wastes or sewer sludge is now permitted. Radiological, chemical, and biological warfare agents and high-level radioactive wastes are specifically prohibited by the statute. Under the amended statute, the only ocean-dumping activities permitted are the disposal of dredged soil, fish wastes, human remains, and submerged vessels. This dumping is subject to specific regulations and is approved on a case-by-case basis.

Ocean Trash. Similar to nonpoint source pollution, floating trash found in the ocean comes from a variety of sources and is almost impossible to attribute to a particular location. Marine debris, in particular plastics, are harmful to marine life that frequently mistakes plastics for food. Ingesting the plastic objects, many of which contain toxics, kills thousands of sea birds and other sea life each year. Sea turtles and albatross have both been known to mistake the plastics for food and feed pieces to their young.

The "Great Pacific Garbage Patch" also known as the Pacific Trash Vortex is a giant floating mass of marine garbage located in the North Pacific Ocean. Scientists are not sure of its exact size, but all of the estimates are enormous.

Few laws govern ocean trash except for explicit dumping. Some states and countries have bans or fees for the use of plastic bags in grocery stores. Hawaii has a statewide ban on plastic bags, though it is difficult to enforce.[4]

Efficiency and Cost-Effectiveness

The companion book on natural resource economics presents the theory that shows that the efficient allocation of uncontaminated water requires marginal net benefits to be equalized across all uses. However, if return flows are contaminated, this can alter the efficient allocation.[5]

Figure 9.2 demonstrates the effect of return flow contamination on the efficient allocation in the case of two users: an upper basin (*UB*) user and a downstream lower basin (*LB*) user. Efficiency dictates that water should be allocated at the point of equal marginal net benefits across the two users. If the two users have identical marginal net benefits for uncontaminated water, the two users should receive equal amounts of water. However, subtracting the effect of contaminated return flows from the upper basin marginal net benefit function (MB_{UB}) (internalizing this externality) changes the efficient allocation to one with unequal sharing. In particular, more water would be allocated to the lower basin user (Q_{LB}) and less to the upper basin user (Q_{UB}). (See Bennett, 2000 for a more detailed discussion.) Accounting for water quality can be an important and often-overlooked factor in allocation decisions.

Ambient Standards and the Zero-Discharge Goal

The 1956 amendments to the Water Pollution Control Act defined ambient standards as a means of quantifying the objectives being sought. A system of ambient standards allows the control authority to tailor the quality of a particular body of water to its use. Water used for drinking would be subject to the highest standards, swimming the next highest, and so on. Once the ambient standards are defined, the control responsibility could be allocated among sources. Greater efforts to control pollution would be expended where the gap between desired and actual water quality was the largest.

Unfortunately, the early experience with ambient standards for water was not reassuring. Rather than strengthening the legal basis for the effluent standards, while retaining their connection to the ambient standards, Congress chose to downgrade the importance of ambient standards by specifying a zero-discharge goal. Additionally, the effluent standards were given

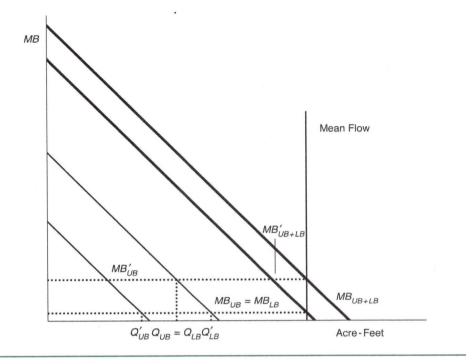

Figure 9.2 Economic Efficiency When Return Flows Are Contaminated

Source: Adapted from Bennett, L. L. (2000). The integration of water quality into transboundary allocation agreements: Lessons from the southwestern United States. *Agricultural Economics, 24,* 113–125.

their own legal status apart from any connection with ambient standards. The wrong inference was drawn from the early lack of legislative success.

In his own inimitable style, Mark Twain (1893) put the essential point rather well:

> We should be careful to get out of an experience only the wisdom that is in it—and stop there; lest we be like the cat that sits down on a hot stove lid. She will never sit down on a hot stove lid again—and that is well; but also she will never sit down on a cold one anymore.
>
> (p. 125)

The most fundamental problem with the current approach is that it rests on the faulty assumption that the tougher the law, the more that is accomplished. The zero-discharge goal provides one example of a case in which passing a tough standard, in the hopes of actually achieving a weaker one, can backfire. Kneese and Schultze (1975) point out that in the late 1960s the French experimented with a law that required zero discharge and imposed severe penalties for violations. The result was that the law was never enforced because it was universally viewed as unreasonable. Less control was accomplished under this stringent, but unenforceable law than would have been accomplished with a less stringent but enforceable one.

Is the US case comparable? It appears to be. In 1972, the EPA published an estimate of the costs of meeting a zero-discharge goal, assuming that it was feasible. They concluded that over the decade from 1971 to 1981, removing 85–90 percent of the pollutants from all industrial and municipal effluents would cost $62 billion. Removing all of the pollutants was estimated to cost $317 billion, more than five times as much, and this figure probably understates the true cost (Kneese & Schultze, 1975).

Is this cost justified? Probably not for all pollutants, though for some it may be. Unfortunately, the zero-discharge goal makes no distinction among pollutant types. For some fund pollutants it seems extreme. Perhaps the legislators realized this because when the legislation was drafted, no specific timetables or procedures were established to ensure that the zero-discharge goal would be met by 1985 or, for that matter, anytime.

National Effluent Standards

The first prong in the two-pronged congressional attack on water pollution was the national effluent standards. Deciding on the appropriate levels for these standards for each of the estimated 60,000 sources is not a trivial task. Not surprisingly, difficulties arose. Challenges with enforcement and allocating control responsibility were so prevalent that it took many years for the types of economic incentives we have seen for air pollution to emerge for water pollution.

In allocating the control responsibility among various sources, the EPA was constrained by the inherent difficulty of making unique determinations for each source and by limitations in the Act itself, such as the need to apply relatively uniform standards. We know from Chapter 5 that uniform effluent standards are not cost-effective, but it remains an open question whether or not the resulting increases in cost are sufficiently large to recommend an alternative approach, such as effluent charges or allowances. The fact that the cost increases are large in the control of stationary-source air pollution does not automatically imply that they are large for water pollution control as well.

Municipal Wastewater Treatment Subsidies

The second phase of the two-pronged water pollution control program involves subsidies for wastewater treatment plants. This program has run into problems as well, ranging from deficiencies in the allocation of the subsidies to the incentives created by the program.

The Allocation of Funds. Since the available funds were initially allocated on a first-come, first-served basis, it is not surprising that the funds were not spent in areas having the greatest impact. It was not uncommon, for example, for completed treatment plants to dump effluent that was significantly cleaner than the receiving water. Also, federal funds have traditionally been concentrated on smaller, largely suburban communities, rather than on the larger cities with the most serious pollution problems.

The 1977 CWA amendments attempted to deal with this problem by requiring states to set priorities for funding treatment works, while giving the EPA the right, after holding public hearings, to not only veto a state's priority list but also to request a revised list. This tendency to ensure that the funds are allocated to the highest-priority projects was reinforced with the passage of the Municipal Wastewater Treatment Construction Grant Amendments of 1981. Under this Act, states were required to establish project priorities for targeting funds to projects with the most significant water quality and public health consequences.

Operation and Maintenance. This approach subsidized the *construction* of treatment facilities but provided no incentive to *operate* them effectively. The existence of a municipal wastewater treatment plant does not by itself guarantee cleaner water. The EPA's annual inspection surveys of operating plants in 1976 and 1977 found only about half of the plants performing satisfactorily. Later surveys found that the general level of wastewater treatment performance had remained substantially unchanged from previous years.

When sewage treatment plants chronically or critically malfunction, the EPA may take a city to court to force compliance with either a direct order or a fine. Because of various constitutional legal barriers, it is very difficult to force a city to pay a fine to the federal treasury. Without an effective and credible sanction, the EPA is in a difficult position to deal with municipalities. Therefore, the end of the treatment-plant malfunction problem cannot yet be pronounced with any assurance.

Capital Costs. Due to the federal subsidies, local areas ended up paying only a fraction of the true cost of constructing these facilities. Since much of the money came from federal taxpayers, local communities had less incentive to hold construction costs down. The Congressional Budget Office (1985) estimated that substantially increasing the local share could reduce capital costs by as much as 30 percent. Local areas would be expected to be more careful with their own money.

Pretreatment Standards

To deal with untreatable hazardous wastes entering municipal wastewater treatment plants, the EPA has defined pretreatment standards regulating the quality of the wastewater flowing into the plants. These standards suffer the same deficiencies as other effluent standards; they are not cost-effective. The control over wastewater flows into treatment plants provides one more aspect of environmental policy where economic incentive approaches offer yet another unclaimed opportunity to achieve equivalent results at a lower cost.

Nonpoint Source Pollution

Nonpoint source pollution has become, in many areas, a significant part of the total problem. In some ways, the government has tried to compensate for this uneven coverage by placing more intensive controls on point sources. Is this emphasis efficient?

It could conceivably be justified on two grounds. If the marginal damages caused by nonpoint sources are significantly smaller than those of point sources, then a lower level of control could well be justified. Since in many cases, nonpoint source pollutants are not the same as point source pollutants, this is a logical possibility.

Or, if the costs of controlling nonpoint sources even to a small degree are very high, this could justify benign neglect as well. Are either of these conditions met in practice?

Costs. The research on economic incentives for nonpoint source pollution control is relatively thin as cost information is relatively scarce. Some of the case-specific studies available, however, can give us a sense of the economic analysis. Most of the available studies focus on nonpoint source pollution from agriculture.

McCann and Easter (1999) measured the size of transaction costs associated with various agricultural nonpoint source pollution control policies. Transaction costs (the administrative costs associated with implementing a policy) are an important consideration for nonpoint source pollution control because monitoring costs tend to be much higher than for point sources. The net gain from implementing a policy is the abatement cost savings minus the transaction costs; if the transaction costs are too high, they can offset all or a major part of the abatement cost gains from implementing the policy.

McCann and Easter looked specifically at the Minnesota River, where severe water quality problems made the river "unswimmable, unfishable and uncanoeable" near the Twin Cities. Four policies aimed at reducing agricultural sources of phosphorus were considered: education about best management practices, a conservation tillage requirement, expansion of a program that obtained permanent development rights, and a tax on phosphorus fertilizers. They found that a tax on phosphorus fertilizers had the lowest transaction costs ($0.94 million). Educational programs had the second-lowest transaction costs at $3.11 million. Conservation tillage and expansion of the conservation easement program had the highest transaction costs at $7.85 million and $9.37 million, respectively. In terms of transaction costs, their results suggest a comparative advantage for input taxes relative to the other approaches. However, since the price elasticity of demand for phosphorus fertilizers is low (it has been estimated at between -0.25 and -0.29), a considerable tax increase would be needed to guarantee the desired level of water-quality improvements.

Schwabe (2001) examines various policy options for nonpoint source pollution control for the Neuse River in North Carolina. He compares cost-effectiveness of both the initial and final proposed rules considered by the State of North Carolina. In 1998, nutrient loads in the Neuse River basin were so high that the basin received a *nutrient sensitive waters* classification.[6] In the 2 years prior to his study, two large swine waste spills caused major algal blooms and killed 11 million fish. The state of North Carolina initially proposed a rule requiring all farms with land adjacent to a stream to install vegetative filter strips. This was compared to a uniform rollback that measured loadings by county with the objective of a 30 percent reduction in total nitrogen loadings. Using a least-cost mathematical programming model, Schwabe finds that the uniform rollback is the more cost-effective strategy, especially since the 30 percent reduction target would be unlikely to be met using the vegetative strips. However, the author notes that the dominance of the uniform strategy is specific to this particular setting and should not be taken as a general proposition.

Despite this evidence, the regulatory reform movement that played such an important role for air pollution control has been much slower to emerge for water pollution control. An early attempt at trading was implemented for the Fox River in Wisconsin, but only one trade was completed in the first 10 years after implementation.

Watershed-Based Trading

More recently, watershed-based trading programs have been gaining attention. In 1996, the EPA began exploring trading programs for the Tar-Pamlico River in North Carolina, Long Island Sound, Chesapeake Bay, and the Snake and Lower Boise rivers in Idaho. Dozens more followed. Worldwide, 57 trading programs are now in various stages of operation; 26 active, 21 under development, and 10 inactive. All but six of these are in the United States (Selman et al., 2009). Trading for water pollution control typically involves point source polluters meeting water quality standards by purchasing reductions from other sources (point or nonpoint sources) that have lower marginal costs of abatement.

Most of the markets currently in place focus on either nitrogen or phosphorus trading and most are too new to evaluate, but at least 23 US water trading programs have carried out at least one trade (for some examples see Table 9.2). The six trading programs outside of the United States include four in Australia (three of which are active and one under development), one in Canada, and one in New Zealand (Selman et al., 2009).

Table 9.2 Summary of NPDES Trading Programs that Have Traded at Least Once as of June 2007

Point–Point Trades	Pollutant(s) Traded	Point–Nonpoint Trades	Pollutant(s) Traded
Long Island Sound, CT	Total Nitrogen	Wayland Center, MA	Total Phosphorus
Bear Creek, CO	Total Phosphorus	Croton Watershed, NY	Total Phosphorus
Neuse River, NC	Total Nitrogen	Pinnacle, DE	Total Nitrogen, Total Phosphorus
Charlotte-Mecklenburg, NC	Total Phosphorus	Rahr Malting, MN	Offset Biological Oxygen Demand with Total Phosphorus
Cobb County, GA	Total Phosphorus	Southern MN Beetsugar Cooperative, MN	Total Phosphorus
City of Newman, GA	Total Phosphorus	Red Cedar River, WI	Total Phosphorus
MN General Permit	Total Phosphorus	Great Miami River, OH	Total Nitrogen, Total Phosphorus
Las Vegas Wash, NV	Total Ammonia, Total Phosphorus	Taos Ski Valley, NM	Total Nitrogen
		Carlota Copper, AZ	Copper
		Clean Water Services, OR	Temperature
		Cherry Creek, CO	Total Phosphorus
		Chatfield Res, CO	Total Phosphorus
		Lake Dillon, CO	Total Phosphorus

Source: Table from Summary of NPDES Trading Programs that have Traded at Least Once as of June 2007. Retrieved from www.ecosystemmarketplace.com/pages/dynamic/article.page.php?page_id=5335&section=home&eod=1. Reprinted with permission of Ecosystem Marketplace.

EXAMPLE 9.1

Effluent Trading for Nitrogen in Long Island Sound

Long Island Sound experiences severe hypoxia (low levels of dissolved oxygen) during the summer months. This *eutrophication* is caused primarily by excess nitrogen discharges from municipal sewage-treatment plants. As discussed earlier in this chapter, most past policies for water pollution control focused on technology standards to control discharges. Economic theory suggests that lower costs can be achieved by providing flexibility to the plants via a permit-trading program. In the late 1990s, Connecticut, New York, and the US EPA began exploring this possibility for sewage-treatment plants with discharges reaching Long Island Sound. The plan targeted trading to certain management zones. The overall goal of this management plan was a 58.5 percent reduction in nitrogen over 15 years, beginning in 1999.

Bennett et al. (2000) estimate the costs associated with the proposed scheme, whereby trading is restricted to the 11 management zones designated by the *Long Island Sound Study*. They then estimate the cost savings of alternative programs that expand the zone of trading to (1) trading among sources and across zones, but within state boundaries, and (2) trading across all sources. For each trading scenario, polluting sources are grouped into trading "bubbles" that are based on geographic location. Trading is allowed to take place within each bubble, but not among bubbles.

Bennett et al. find what economic theory would predict—that cost savings rise (and rise substantially) as the scope of trading expands (meaning, fewer bubbles). Expanding trading across the two state bubbles could save up to 20 percent or $156 million, based on their estimates. The following table is reproduced from their results.

Number of Trading Bubbles	Present Value of Total Costs ($ million)	Cost Savings Relative to 11 Bubbles ($ million)	Percentage Savings
11	781.44	—	—
2	740.55	40.89	5.23
1	625.14	156.30	20.00

Not all discharges have the same impact. In fact, discharges from zones in the eastern portion of Long Island Sound and the northern parts of Connecticut do not have as detrimental effects as those closer to New York City. Despite differences in abatement cost, the proposed management plan recommends that each management zone be responsible for an equal percentage of nitrogen reduction.

While marginal abatement costs vary widely across management zones (suggesting that trades could reduce costs), the marginal contributions to damages also vary widely, thus ruling out a simple system of ton-for-ton effluent trades. (As Chapter 6 pointed out, more complicated ambient trades would be required to achieve cost-effectiveness for this nonuniformly mixed pollutant.) Currently, in recognition of this complexity, trading is not being considered across the boundaries of the 11 management zones despite the apparent potential cost savings.

Between 2002 and 2004, Connecticut's Long Island Sound program reduced more total nitrogen via trading than was needed to meet the TMDL requirement. Between 2002 and 2009, 15.5 million nitrogen credits were exchanged at a total value of $45.9 million. Cost savings through trading are estimated at $300 to $400 million. The credit price in 2002 was $1.65 and rose to $4.54 in 2009. As it turns out, however, the price is set by the state and trades go through the nitrogen credit exchange, so potential gains from trade resulting from allowance price fluctuations are not captured.

Source: Bennett, L. L., Thorpe, S. G., & Guse, A. J. (December 2000). Cost-effective control of nitrogen loadings in Long Island Sound. *Water Resources Research, 36*(12), 3711–3720; Kibler, V., & Kasturi, K. (2007). Status of water quality trading programs today. Katoomba Group's Ecosystem Marketplace. Retrieved from www.ecosystemmarketplace.com; Connecticut Department of Environmental Protection. (2010). Retrieved from www.ct.gov/deep/cwp/view. asp?a=2719&q=325572&deepNav_GID=1635%20

Ex ante studies, however, suggest that the economic benefits can be large. Example 9.1 illustrates the potential for tradable effluent cost savings for treating hypoxic (low levels of dissolved oxygen) conditions in Long Island Sound. Allowing firms the flexibility to exploit economies of scale in pollution-control technology can provide for large savings. This point–point trading program has resulted in cheaper *and* faster cleanup.

The EPA supports market-based programs for certain pollutants if they can help meet Clean Water Act goals. In 2008, the EPA issued a Water Quality Trading Evaluation and found significant cost savings and nutrient (nitrogen and phosphorus) reductions for the trading programs they evaluated. Comparing across programs is somewhat challenging, however, since they do not all rely on the same trading mechanism. Some trades are case-by-case, while others are open-market trades. Some rely on a broker, while others operate through direct negotiations. And some are not based on market mechanisms at all.[7] Watershed-based trading is complicated by the difficulties of accounting for spatial distribution of pollutants, thus requiring complicated trading ratios (Olmstead, 2010). A trading ratio ensures that the reduction in pollution after a trade is equal to the required reduction. Important features of the trading ratio are the location of the sources, the distance between buyers and sellers, uncertainty if nonpoint source pollutants are involved and whether or not the pollutant is equivalent after discharge. Complicated trading ratios may be one barrier to trade. Using the Upper Ohio River Basin as a case study, Farrow et al. (2005) demonstrate that social costs can be minimized if trading ratios are based on relative damages between sources. Of course, calculating the damages remains a challenge.

Water quality trading is frequently complicated by measurement and enforcement challenges (especially for nonpoint sources), abatement cost differentials, sufficient trading volumes, and trading flexibility (Fisher-Vanden & Olmstead, 2013). Where markets are thin (few traders) or when cost differentials are slight, there will be very few feasible trades. Large differences in marginal abatement costs can result in the largest gains from trade; the most significant gains are likely to come from point–nonpoint source trades. Lack of flexibility in trading over time and space has also inhibited water quality trading (Fisher-Vanden & Olmstead, 2013).

The fact that point and nonpoint sources have received such different treatment from the EPA, however, suggests the possibility that costs could be lowered by a more careful balancing of these control options. Point sources have received the most attention and have cleaned up considerably. Nonpoint sources have received very little attention. This suggests that perhaps the marginal cost of additional abatement for point sources is now sufficiently high that it justifies moving control toward nonpoint sources. Figure 9.3 portrays the current situation. The marginal cost of abatement of point sources (MC_{PS}) is everywhere lower than the marginal cost of abatement of nonpoint sources (MC_{NPS}). However, with policy focus on the point source, the point source has cleaned up, meaning that source is on a higher portion of its marginal cost curve. Without policy addressing the nonpoint source, the nonpoint source is still at zero cleanup. Now, comparing the two at their different cleanup levels, the nonpoint source has a *lower* marginal cost of abatement! Consider a scenario in which point sources have already cleaned up 50 percent of their discharges (point d in Figure 9.3) and the nonpoint source has cleaned up none. Suppose the regulatory agency is seeking additional cleanup of 10 percent. Can you see how the total cost of this additional abatement would be less for the nonpoint source than the point source? The point source could clean up 10 percent at a total cost of area defg. Or the nonpoint source could clean up the same amount for the smaller cost of area 0abc. In other words, the total cost for the point source of additional cleanup (or area defg) is more than the total cost for the same amount of cleanup from the nonpoint source (0abc). These two sources can reduce total cost by trading until marginal cost is equalized at the dotted line. After that point, all gains from trade would be eliminated.

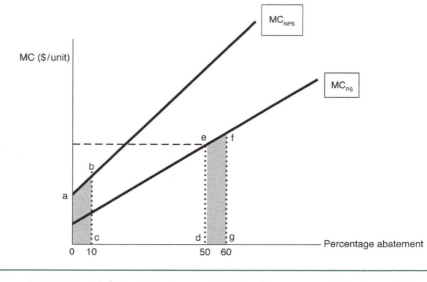

Figure 9.3 Potential Cost Savings with Trading across Point and Nonpoint Sources

Such a scenario also offers an incentive for point source–nonpoint source trading. One situation like this happened in Colorado. An Industrial Economics, Inc. (1984) study of phosphorus control in the Dillon reservoir in Colorado provides empirical support that such point–nonpoint trading could be more cost-effective.

In this reservoir, four municipalities constitute the only point sources of phosphorus, while numerous uncontrolled nonpoint sources are in the area. The combined phosphorus load on the reservoir from point and nonpoint sources was projected to exceed its assimilative capacity.

The traditional way to rescue the projected phosphorus load would be to impose even more stringent controls on the point sources. The study found, however, that by following a balanced program controlling both point and nonpoint sources, the desired phosphorus target could be achieved at a cost of approximately $1 million a year less than would be spent if only point sources were controlled more stringently. The more general point to be carried away from this study is that as point sources are controlled to higher and higher degrees, rising marginal control costs will begin to make controlling nonpoint sources increasingly attractive. As the list of 13 point–nonpoint trades in Table 9.2 demonstrates, we have apparently already reached that point.

Trades can sometimes achieve greater effluent reductions in addition to cost savings. Kibler and Kasturi (2007) describe one case for which reductions have actually been much greater than anticipated. When the Southern Minnesota Sugar Beet Industry needed to offset 6500 pounds of total phosphorus per year, they actually achieved 15,767 pounds per year reductions by trading. Does your state have a water pollutant trading program?

Water Quality, Watershed-Based Trading, and GIS. Land use change significantly affects watershed health.[8] Agricultural and urban runoff into rivers, streams, and estuaries is the largest contributor to water pollution. Hascic and Wu (2006) use digital land use maps to examine the relationship between land use and water quality. They find that the levels of nutrient and conventional water pollutants are significantly affected by the amount of land in agriculture and urban development, while the level of toxic pollution is dependent on land in transportation or mining. Their results suggest that water quality trading programs should take into account land uses within the watershed as well as the overall watershed health. GIS technology is a powerful tool for understanding these relationships.

Atmospheric Deposition of Pollution

An additional complexity comes in the form of the nonpoint source pollution from the atmosphere that ends up in water bodies. Airborne pollutants, such as sulfur dioxide, mercury, and nitrogen, eventually find their way to rivers and lakes via atmospheric deposition. *Wet deposition* refers to pollutants that travel to the ground with rainfall. *Dry deposition* occurs when pollutants become too heavy and fall to the ground even in the absence of precipitation.

Debate 9.1 highlighted some of the issues surrounding one approach to dealing with airborne deposition—fish consumption advisories due to mercury levels found in many fish. A quite different complication for water pollution control stems from a lack of coordination with air quality regulations. Simply put, they may or may not take into consideration the impacts of the air quality regulation on the soil (or in the water). The external benefits from air quality improvements are likely to be quite large. What does this suggest about the optimal level of air quality and the fact that air and water quality are controlled by separate offices within EPA?

The European Experience

European water legislation originated in the 1970s with standards for drinking water and set targets for fish and shellfish, bathing and groundwater. In 1988, a second phase of water legislation began with the adoption of the Urban Waste Water Treatment Directive, a Nitrates Directive, and a revised Drinking Water Objective. In 1996, a Directive for Integrated Pollution and Prevention Control (IPPC) was adopted to address pollution from large industrial installations.[9]

Economic incentives have been important in water pollution control in Europe, where effluent charges play a prominent role in a number of countries. These charge systems have taken a number of forms. One common approach, illustrated by the former Republic of Czechoslovakia, used charges to achieve predetermined ambient standards. Others, such as the former West Germany, used charges mainly to encourage firms to control more than their legal requirements. A third group, illustrated by Hungary and the former East Germany, combined charge systems with effluent standards.

The former Republic of Czechoslovakia used effluent charges to maintain water quality at predetermined levels for several decades. A basic charge was placed on BOD and suspended solids and complemented by a surcharge ranging from 10 to 100 percent, depending upon the contribution of the individual discharge to ambient pollutant concentrations. The basic rates could be adjusted to reflect the quality of the receiving water. This system is conceptually very close to the ambient emissions charge system known to be cost-effective.

The charge system in the former West Germany was announced in 1976 and implemented in 1981. The level of charge was related to the degree of compliance with the standards. Firms failing to meet their required standards paid a charge on all actual emissions. If, according to the issued permit, federal emissions standards (which are separately defined for each industrial sector) were met, the charge was lowered to 50 percent of the base rate and was applied to the level of discharge implied by the minimum standard. If the discharge was lower than 75 percent of minimum standards, one-half of the base rate was applied to the (lower) actual discharge level. The charge was waived for 3 years prior to the installation of new pollution control equipment promising further reductions of at least 20 percent. Revenues from the charges could be used by the administering authorities for administrative costs and financial assistance to public and private pollution abatement activities.

The approach used in Hungary and the former East Germany combined effluent charges with effluent standards. The charges are levied on discharges in excess of fixed effluent limits. In the Hungarian system, the level of the charge is based on the condition of the receiving waters, among other factors. Initially the Hungarian charges had little effect, but when the charge levels were raised, a flurry of wastewater treatment activity resulted. France charges an effluent tax that is proportional to the quantity of the pollution. The revenues are then used for subsidizing wastewater treatment.

Though these European approaches differ from one another and are not all cost-effective, their existence suggests that a variety of effluent charge systems are possible and practical. The German Council of Experts on Environmental Questions estimated the German effluent charge policy to be about one-third cheaper for the polluters as a group than an otherwise comparable uniform treatment policy. Furthermore, it encouraged firms to go beyond the uniform standards when it was cost-justified.

In a very different approach, Bystrom (1998) examines reducing nonpoint source nitrogen pollution by constructing wetlands in Sweden, where reducing nitrogen loads to the Baltic Sea is an important policy goal. Although it is well known that wetlands can help reduce nitrogen concentrations through the uptake of biomass, how cost-effective is this approach when it is compared to alternative, more traditional methods of control?

To answer this question, Bystrom estimates nonpoint source abatement costs for constructed wetlands and compares them to the costs of reducing nitrogen by means of land-use changes, such as the planting of fuel woods. This study finds that marginal abatement costs for wetlands are lower than transitioning to different crops, but still higher than the marginal costs of simply reducing the use of nitrogen fertilizer.

The European Water Framework Directive (WFD) was adopted in October of 2000 with a goal of achieving "'good status' for all ground and surface waters (rivers, lakes, transitional waters, and coastal waters) in the EU by 2015."

Ek and Persson (2016) evaluate the implementation of the WFD in Sweden and find that cost-effectiveness is challenged by the complexities of water management. While the directive emphasizes the role of economic tools, the goals are not based on economic efficiency. The absolute targets make designing an effective economic instrument challenging at best. The existing system in Sweden is also based primarily on command and control. In the Netherlands and in France, charges have been used for heavy metals and other discharges with revenues going toward water infrastructure (Olmstead, 2010).

Effluent is not the only water pollution problem. Plastics are a growing source of pollution, much of which ends up in the ocean. Ireland was the first country to tax the use of plastic bags. Example 9.2 examines the effect of the Irish bag levy.

Developing Country Experience

The move from command-and-control regulations to economic incentives for water pollution control has not seen as rapid a transition in developing countries. Several attempts to use discharge fees and marketable permits have failed. This may be due to lack of regulatory capacity—for example, lack of technical, political, and financial means to set up and monitor a fee or permit program effectively. Noncompliance and lack of infrastructure have hampered many programs. Example 9.3 explores Colombia's experience with a discharge fee program—one case deemed successful.

EXAMPLE 9.2

The Irish Bag Levy

Rapid economic growth in Ireland in the 1990s was marked by a significant increase in the amount of solid waste per capita. The lack of adequate landfill sites resulted in escalating costs of waste disposal, which in turn led to more illegal dumping and littering. It was feared that tourism, one of Ireland's largest industries, would be negatively affected as a consequence of the degradation of the environment. The food industry, which based a significant amount of its marketing strategies on a healthy, wholesome reputation, also suffered as a result of the public perception of its role in the increased litter.

The most visible element of litter was plastic bags, so in 2002 the government introduced the Plastic Bag Environmental Levy on all plastic shopping bags (the "PlasTax"), with a few exceptions that were sanctioned for health and safety reasons. Retailers were charged a fee of 15 cents per plastic bag, which they were obliged, by the government, to pass on to the consumer. This levy was designed to alter consumer behavior by creating financial incentives for consumers to choose more environmentally friendly alternatives to plastic, such as "bags-for-life." (Bags-for-life are heavy-duty, reusable cloth or woven bags, which were made available in all supermarkets, at an average cost of €1.27.)

Expectations that this levy would bring about a 50 percent reduction in the number of plastic bags used were exceeded when the estimated actual reduction turned out to be 95 percent! In a single year, Irish consumers reduced their consumption of plastic bags from 1.26 billion to 120,000, while concurrently raising approximately €10 million in revenue for the government. Placed in the Environmental Fund, this revenue finances environmental initiatives such as recycling, waste management, and, most importantly, anti-litter campaigns.

This levy has been viewed as a major success by the government and environmental groups alike. It has also been enthusiastically embraced by Irish consumers, thanks to an intensive environmental-awareness campaign that was launched in conjunction with the levy. Irish retailers, although skeptical in the beginning, have also recognized the huge benefits of this levy. Estimates suggest that their costs were offset by the savings from no longer providing disposable bags to customers free of charge, as well as the profit margin earned on the sale of "bags-for-life," whose sales have increased by 600–700 percent since the introduction of the levy. The amount of plastic being sent to Irish landfills has been dramatically reduced, bringing about a clear visual improvement. The success of this case has promoted the diffusion of this idea. For example, in 2008 China banned super-thin plastic bags and imposed a fee on other plastic bags.

Source: Dungan, L. What were the effects of the plastic bag environmental levy on the litter problem in Ireland? Retrieved from http://personal.colby.edu/personal/t/thtieten/litter.htm

For developing countries, water pollution control is further complicated by poverty, lack of enforcement, and lack of technology. Deaths from waterborne diseases are much more frequent in developing countries. Of the 1.6 million deaths in 2003 attributed to water and sanitation, 90 percent were children under 5 and most were from developing countries. In 2004, 2331

EXAMPLE 9.3

Economic Incentives for Water Pollution Control: The Case of Colombia

In 1997, Colombia experimented with a new nationwide program of pollution discharge fees. Polluters would be charged per unit of pollution emitted. Colombia has 33 regional environmental authorities (CARs), some of which had discharge fees in place for 30 years. This was the first nationwide program.

This new program mandated that CARs would first collect and map out data on all discharging facilities that generated biological oxygen demand (BOD) and total suspended solids (TSS). They were then to set 5-year reduction goals for aggregate discharge in each basin and charge a fee per unit of BOD and TSS. The ministry set a minimum fee, but CARs could adjust this fee upward every 6 months if reduction targets were not being met.

The program ran into several problems, including uneven levels of implementation across CARs, incomplete coverage of dischargers, and widespread noncompliance by municipal sewage authorities. Between the start of the program in 1997 and 2003, municipal sewage authorities were assessed over 30 percent of all discharge fees, but only paid 40 percent of what they were charged. Given that some CARs were raising fees based on meeting reduction targets, noncompliance by one group of dischargers was responsible for large rate hikes for others.

Was the Colombia program thus unsuccessful? Surprisingly, evidence actually suggests it was successful! In a number of basins, discharges dropped significantly between 1997 and 2003. BOD discharge from point sources in the program dropped by 27 percent and TSS discharges fell by 45 percent.

One suggested reason for the apparent success of the program is that previously lacking enforcement had to be improved simply to set up a discharge program. Collecting information on discharge amounts and locations is also a necessary component for successful implementation. Increased transparency over command-and-control programs contributed to the program's success.

The author of this study suggests that one of the most important components of a successful program is adequate infrastructure.

Source: Blackman, A. (Spring 2006). Economic incentives to control water pollution in developing countries: How well has Colombia's wastewater discharge fee program worked and why? *Resources*, 20–23.

---

deaths from cholera occurred in Africa. No deaths from cholera were recorded in the Americas. According to the World Health Organization, improved water supply reduces diarrhea morbidity by 6–25 percent, and improved sanitation reduces diarrhea morbidity by 32 percent.

A study on the costs and benefits of meeting the United Nations Millennium Development Goal of halving the proportion of people without sustainable access to improved water supply and sanitation determined it would:

definitely bring economic benefits, ranging from US$3 to US$34 per US dollar invested, depending on the region. Additional improvement of drinking water quality, such as point-of-use disinfection, in addition to access to improved water and sanitation would lead to benefits ranging from US$5 to US$60 per US dollar invested.

(Hutton & Haller, 2004)

China has implemented a different approach to enforcement than the type of sanction commonly used in the United States and Canada. China imposes a graduated pollution levy where the per-unit fine rises with the level of noncompliance (Wang & Wheeler, 2005). China also relies on self-reporting. Wang and Wheeler examine data from 3000 Chinese factories and estimate a model that incorporates the joint determination of levy and emissions. They show that progressive penalties, combined with self-reporting, are a significant deterrent. Regional variation in local enforcement, however, is a factor and inhibits universal compliance.

Oil Spills—Tankers and Off-Shore Drilling

One of the chief characteristics of the current approach to oil spills is that it depends heavily on the ability of the legal system to internalize the costs of a spill through liability law. In principle, the approach is straightforward. Consider how liability for spills might affect the incentives for a tanker fleet. Forcing the owner of a vessel to pay for the costs of cleaning up the spill, including compensation for natural resource damages, creates a powerful incentive to exercise care. But is the outcome likely to be efficient in practice?

One problem with legal remedies is their high administrative cost; assigning the appropriate penalties is no trivial matter. Even if the court were able to act expeditiously, the doctrines it imposes are not necessarily efficient since the financial liability for cleaning up spills is limited by statute. This point is demonstrated in Figure 9.4, which depicts the incentives of a vessel owner to take precautions. The owner will minimize costs by choosing the level of precaution that equates the marginal cost of additional precaution, with the resulting reduction in the marginal expected penalty. The marginal reduction in expected penalty is a function of two factors: the likelihood of a spill and the magnitude of financial obligation it would trigger. This function slopes downward because larger amounts of precaution are presumed to yield smaller marginal reductions in both the likelihood and magnitude of resulting accidents.

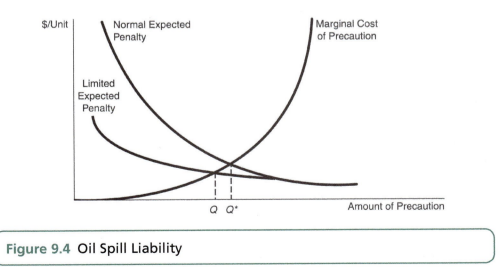

Figure 9.4 Oil Spill Liability

The vessel owner's cost-minimizing choice with unlimited liability is shown as Q^*. As long as the imposed penalty equaled the actual damage and the probability of having to pay the damage once an accident occurred was 1.0, this outcome would normally be efficient. The external costs would be internalized. The owner's private costs would be minimized by taking all possible cost-justified precaution measures to reduce both the likelihood and the seriousness of any resulting spill; taking precautions would simply be cheaper than paying for the cleanup.

Limited liability, however, produces a different outcome. With limited liability, the expected penalty function rotates inward for levels of precaution lower than that level that would produce an accident resulting in damages exactly equal to the limit.[10] Lower levels of precaution imply damages that exceed the limit, but the vessel owner would not have to pay anything above the limit. (The only benefit to the vessel owner faced with limited liability of increasing precaution at lower levels of precaution is the reduction in the likelihood of a spill; in this range, increasing precaution does not reduce the magnitude of the financial payment should a spill occur.) The deviation in the magnitude of the limited expected penalty function from the normal expected penalty function is greatest at lower levels of precaution; it declines to zero at that precaution level where the expected magnitude of an accident is equal to the liability limit.

What is the effect of limited liability on the vessel owner's choice of precaution levels? As long as the liability limit is binding (which appears to routinely be the case with recent spills), the owner will choose too little precaution. (The owner's choice is shown as Q in Figure 9.4.) Both the number and magnitude of resulting spills would be inefficiently large.[11]

Garza-Gil et al. (2006) estimate the economic losses from the *Prestige* oil spill off the Spanish city of Galicia. Ultimately 63,000 tons were spilled (Table 9.1) and the tanker sank. This spill was considered one of the worst tanker spills due not only to the size of the spill but also to the "black tides" caused by the spill in valuable tourist regions of Northern Spain and Southern France. Garza-Gil et al. consider short-term (immediately following the spill) damages to the fishing industry and the tourism sector and find losses of almost 200 million euros. Including cleanup and restoration costs brings the total to 762 million euros. They were not able to include lost recreation opportunities or passive use-value losses. The current international liability framework does not allow for the inclusion of these values. (Recall the importance of these for the *Exxon Valdez* damage estimates discussed in Chapter 4.) What effect would omitting these values be expected to have on the incentives for risk-aversion by tanker owners?

While the frequency of spills from tankers has diminished significantly, off-shore drilling has been increasing the risk of spills. In 2010, the Deepwater Horizon, a rig operated by British Petroleum (BP), exploded in the Gulf of Mexico, spewing 134 million gallons of oil, the largest spill on record in the United States. Example 9.4 examines the economic damages from this spill. Increasing interest in off-shore drilling, especially in the Arctic waters, raises the risk of more spills like this one.

An Overall Assessment

Although the benefit estimates from water pollution control are subject to much uncertainty, they do exist.

One early study concluded that the net benefits from water pollution control policy were positive but were likely to become negative as costs escalate in the future. Relying on benefits estimates derived from contingent valuation, Carson and Mitchell (1993) estimated that aggregate benefits from water pollution control in 1990 exceeded aggregate costs by $6.4 billion. They also found, however, that projected aggregate costs would exceed projected

EXAMPLE 9.4

Deepwater Horizon BP Oil Spill—Estimating the Damages

In the spring of 2010, the Deepwater Horizon, a rig operated by British Petroleum (BP) in the Gulf of Mexico, exploded and began spewing oil. By the time the leaking well was capped in August 2010, an estimated 134 million gallons had been spread through the Gulf of Mexico, almost 20 times greater than the *Exxon Valdez* spill, and the largest maritime spill in US history.

In 2016, after a six-year study of the impacts, economists estimated the damages to the natural resources from the spill at $17.2 billion. This number represents the "benefits to the public to protect against damages that could result from a future oil spill in the Gulf of a similar magnitude."[12]

Using the first nationally represented, stated preference survey (recall from Chapter 4), Bishop et al. (2017) estimated the monetary value of natural resource damages from the spill. They interviewed a random sample of American adults. Respondents were told about the state of the Gulf prior to the spill, and about the accident—causes and injuries.

They were then told about a proposed program for preventing a similar accident. Respondents were asked how much their household would be willing to pay for a one-time tax based on their income to prevent future spills. The money would be used to pay for a second pipe safety feature intended to prevent a spill like this. There were two versions of the survey. Version A described the harm to three items: birds (brown pelicans, northern gannets, and royal terns), marshes, and recreation. Version B described harm to more animals and plants including snails, sea turtles, and bottlenose dolphins.[13]

Using state-of-the-art survey design techniques, they used a combined approach of both mail surveys and face-to-face interviews. They specifically tried to reduce bias including social desirability bias. Social desirability bias occurs when respondents try to present themselves in a favorable light, the common example being voters claiming to have voted when they did not. Survey administrators were concerned that respondents might over exaggerate their willingness to pay given the scenario. The alternative was that they might underestimate (or protest) their willingness to pay given that taxation for Americans is frequently seen as socially *undesirable*. They did not receive a large number of protest votes even though the payment vehicle was increased taxes.

The Oil Pollution Act of 1990 specifies that both use and nonuse values be included in natural resource damage assessments and these assessments can inform settlements. It also allows for damages to be assessed for the losses experienced by the entire US population.

The calculation of total economic loss is conducted by multiplying the estimated population lower bound marginal willingness to pay (MWTP) by the appropriate number of households. For Version A the point estimate of economic losses is $15,332,412,434 (112,647,215 households multiplied by $136.11). For Version B, the point estimate of economic losses is $17,236,150,367 (112,647,215 households multiplied by $153.01).

The case was settled in 2016 for $20.8 billion, of which $8.8 billion was for natural resource damages. This amount is in addition to the approximately $30 billion already spent on cleanup.

Sources: www.fws.gov/doiddata/dwh-ar-documents/980/DWH-AR0290376a.pdf; www.fws.gov/doiddata/dwh-ar-documents/980/DWH-AR0290122a.pdf; www.fws.gov/doiddata/dwh-ar-documents/980/DWH-AR0302133.pdf; Bishop, R. C. et al. (2017). Putting a value on injuries to natural assets: The BP oil spill. *Science, 356*(6335), 253–254.

aggregate benefits because of the high marginal costs and the low marginal benefits associated with bringing the remaining bodies of water up to swimmable quality.

Griffiths and Wheeler (2005) summarize the costs and benefits of the most economically significant[14] water quality rules that are subject to benefit-cost analysis. For the five rules that relate to surface water, they find that two of them do not pass a benefit-cost analysis and for the other three the range of benefits estimates bounds the costs. They point out that policies do not necessarily have to pass a benefit-cost test to be adopted; benefit-cost calculations are simply one source of information for the decision-making process.

Using cost-effective policies rather than the current approach, it would be possible to reduce costs substantially, without affecting the benefits. Cost-effectiveness would require the development of better strategies for point source control and for achieving a better balance between point and nonpoint source control. The resulting reduction in costs probably would allow net benefits to remain positive even with the more stringent control levels envisioned for the future. Even positive net benefits would not necessarily make the policy efficient, however, because the level of control might still be too high or too low (meaning the present value of net benefits would not have been maximized). Unfortunately, the evidence is not rich enough to prove whether the overall level of control maximizes the net benefit.

In addition to promoting current cost-effectiveness, economic incentive approaches would stimulate and facilitate change better than a system of rigid, technology-based standards. Russell (1981) assessed the importance of the facilitating role by simulating the effects on the allocation of pollution-control responsibility in response to regional economic growth, changing technology, and changing product mix. Focusing on the steel, paper, and petroleum-refining industries in the 11-county Delaware Estuary Region, his study estimated the change in permit use for three water pollutants (BOD, total suspended solids, and ammonia) that would have resulted if a marketable permit system had been in place over the 1940–1978 period. The calculations assume that the plants existing in 1940 would have been allocated permits to legitimize their emissions at that time, that new sources would have had to purchase permits, and that plant shutdowns or contractions would free up permits for others to purchase.

This study found that for almost every decade and pollutant a substantial number of permits would have been made available by plant closing, capacity contractions, product-mix changes, and/or by the availability of new technologies. In the absence of a marketable permit program, a control authority would not only have to keep abreast of all technological developments so emissions standards could be adjusted accordingly, but it would also have to ensure an overall balance between effluent increases and decreases so as to preserve water quality. This tough assignment is handled completely by the market in a tradable permit system, thereby facilitating the evolution of the economy by responding flexibly and predictably to change.

Tradable effluent permits encourage, as well as facilitate, this evolution. Since permits have value, in order to minimize costs firms must continually be looking for new opportunities to control emissions at lower cost. This search eventually results in the adoption of new technologies and in the initiation of changes in the product mix that result in lower amounts of emissions. The pressure on sources to continually search for better ways to control pollution is a distinct advantage that economic incentive systems have over bureaucratically defined standards.

Summary

Historically, policies for controlling water pollution have been concerned with conventional pollutants discharged into surface waters. More recently, concerns have shifted toward toxic pollutants, which apparently are more prevalent than previously believed; toward groundwater, which traditionally was thought to be an invulnerable pristine resource; and toward the oceans, which were mistakenly considered immune from most pollution problems because of their vast size.

Early attempts at controlling water pollution followed a path similar to that of air pollution control. Legislation prior to the 1970s had little impact on the problem. Frustration then led to the enactment of a tough federal law that was so ambitious and unrealistic that little progress resulted.

There the similarity ends. Whereas in air pollution a wave of recent reforms have improved the process by making it more cost-effective, little parallel exists for control of water pollution. Policy toward cleaning up rivers and lakes was based upon the subsidization of municipal waste-treatment facilities and national effluent standards imposed on industrial sources.

The former approach was hampered by delays, by problems in allocating funds, and by the fact that about half of the constructed plants were not performing satisfactorily. The latter approach gave rise to delays and to the need to define the standards in a series of court suits. In addition, effluent standards have assigned the control responsibility among point sources in a way that excessively raises cost. Nonpoint pollution sources have, until recently, been virtually ignored. Technological progress is inhibited, rather than stimulated, by the current approach.

This lack of progress could have been avoided. It did not result from a lack of toughness. Rather, it has resulted from a reliance on direct regulation, rather than on emissions charges or tradable effluent permits, which are more flexible and cost-effective in both the dynamic and static sense. Recognizing this deficiency, watershed-based new trading programs are now gaining attention. The European Water Framework Directive, by contrast, has focused on economic tools, but not necessarily economic efficiency.

It is largely the court system that controls oil spills, in that it ensures that those responsible for the spills assume the financial liability for cleaning up the site and compensating for any resulting damages to natural resources. While in principle this approach can be efficient, in practice it has been hampered by liability limitations and the huge administrative burden an oil spill trial entails.

Discussion Questions

1. "The only permanent solution to water pollution control will occur when all production by-products are routinely recycled. The zero-discharge goal recognizes this reality and forces all dischargers to work steadily toward this solution. Less stringent policies are at best temporary palliatives." Discuss.
2. "In exercising its responsibility to protect the nation's drinking water, the government needs to intervene only in the case of public-water supplies. Private-water supplies will be adequately protected without any government intervention." Discuss.
3. The Deepwater Horizon "BP" oil spill in the Gulf of Mexico was the largest spill in US history. How do natural resource damage assessments such as the one presented in Example 9.4 help decision makers who may be grappling with increased well-permitting requests? Do the benefits outweigh the risks?

Self-Test Exercises

1. Consider the situation posed in Problem 1(a) in Chapter 5.

   a. Compute the allocation that would result if ten tradable effluent permits were given to the second source and nine were given to the first source. What would be the market permit price? How many permits would each source end up with after trading? What would the net permit expenditure be for each source after trading?

   b. Suppose a new source entered the area with a constant marginal cost of control equal to $1,600 per unit of emission reduced. Assume further that it would add ten units in the absence of any control. What would be the resulting allocation of control responsibility if the cap of only 19 total units of effluent allowed were retained? How much would each firm clean up? What would happen to the permit price? What trades would take place?

2. Suppose you have three production facilities that are polluting a river. Each emits ten units of pollution. Their marginal cost functions for reducing emissions are, respectively, $MC_1 = \$3$, $MC_2 = \$4$, and $MC_3 = \$5$.

   a. If the objective is to cut emissions in half (to 15) cost-effectively, how much reduction should be assigned to each firm?

   b. What would be the total variable cost of controlling these emissions?

   c. What would be the total variable cost that would result from forcing each facility to control one-half of its emissions? Is this different from the cost associated with the cost-effective allocation? Why or why not?

Notes

1 The danger of anaerobic conditions is highest in the late summer and early fall, when temperatures are high and the stream flow is low.

2 Actually, the ambient standards were not completely bypassed. If the uniform controls were not sufficient to meet the desired standard, the effluent limitation would have to be tightened accordingly.

3 *US Federal Register* Vol. 68, No. 205 (October 2003).

4 For a full list of legislation on plastic bags, see www.ncsl.org/issues-research/env-res/plastic-bag-legislation.aspx

5 Return flow is a measure of the unused portion of water. For example, in agriculture, water withdrawal is the amount of water taken from a source and applied to a field. Consumptive use is the amount actually used by the plant. Return flow is the unconsumed portion that will eventually return to the watercourse and is frequently claimed by a downstream user. Return flows will bring with them leached contaminants, pesticides, fertilizers, and salts from the soil.

6 Nutrient sensitive waters are defined as waters subject to excessive plant growth and requiring limitations on nutrient inputs.

7 US EPA Water Quality Trading page: www.epa.gov/npdes/water-quality-trading

8 The US EPA maintains digital data by watershed with indicators of conventional ambient water quality, toxic ambient water quality, and other water-quality indicators. See www.epa.gov/surf

9 http://ec.europa.eu/environment/water/water-framework/info/intro_en.htm

10 To avoid confusion, note that the marginal expected penalty for additional precaution when the damage would exceed the liability limit is not zero. While further precaution does not lower the ultimate penalty in this range, it does lower the likelihood of an accident and, hence, the expected penalty.

11 Suppose, at the efficient level of precaution, the magnitude of a resulting spill was less than the liability limit. How would this be depicted graphically? Would you expect the vessel owner's choice to be efficient?

12 www.sciencedaily.com/releases/2017/04/170420141825.htm

13 www.fws.gov/doiddata/dwh-ar-documents/980/DWH-AR0290122a.pdf

14 Defined as rules with an economic impact of more than $100 million.

Further Reading

Brouwer, R., & Pearce, E. (Eds.). (2005). *Cost Benefit Analysis and Water Resources Management*. Cheltenham, UK: Edward Elgar. A collection of benefit/cost analysis case studies for water pollution control projects, flood control, and water allocation. Most of the cases occurred in Europe.

Fisher-Vanden, K., & Olmstead, S. (Winter 2013). Moving pollution trading from air to water: Potential problems and prognosis. *Journal of Economic Perspectives*, 27(1),147–172. An analysis of water quality trading programs to date and the challenges that remain to implementing water quality trading.

Olmstead, S. M. (Winter 2010). The economics of water quality trading. *Review of Environmental Economics and Policy*, 4(1), 44–62. A thorough review of the literature on the economics of water quality.

Selman, M., Greenhalgh, S., Branosky, E., Jones, C., & Guiling, J. (March 2009). Water quality trading programs: An international overview. *WRI Issue Brief*, 1. WRI (World Resources Institute). An overview and analysis of 57 water quality trading programs worldwide.

Additional references and historically significant references are available on this book's Companion Website: www.routledge.com/cw/Tietenberg

Chapter 10

Toxic Substances and Environmental Justice

The fact that a problem will certainly take a long time to solve, and that it will demand the attention of many minds for several generations, is no justification for postponing the study. . . . Our difficulties of the moment must always be dealt with somehow, but our permanent difficulties are difficulties of every moment.

—T. S. Eliot, *Christianity and Culture* (1949)

Introduction

In one of the ironies of history, the place that focused public attention in the United States on toxic substances is called the Love Canal. *Love* is not a word any impartial observer would choose to describe the relationships among the parties to that incident.

The Love Canal typifies in many ways the dilemma posed by toxic substances. Until 1953, Hooker Electrochemical (subsequently Hooker Chemical, a subsidiary of Occidental Petroleum Corporation) dumped waste chemicals into an old abandoned waterway known as the Love Canal, near Niagara Falls, New York. (Hooker was acquired by Occidental in 1968.) At the time it seemed a reasonable solution, since the chemicals were buried in what was then considered to be impermeable clay.

In 1953, Hooker deeded the Love Canal property for $1 to the Niagara Falls Board of Education, which then built an elementary school on the site. The deed specifically excused Hooker from any damages that might be caused by the chemicals. Residential development of the area around the school soon followed.

The site became the center of controversy when, in 1978, residents complained of chemicals leaking to the surface. News reports emanating from the area included stories of spontaneous fires and vapors in basements. Medical reports suggested that the residents had experienced abnormally high rates of miscarriage, birth defects, and liver disease.

Similar contamination experiences befell Europe and Asia. In 1976, an accident at an F. Hoffmann-La Roche & Co. plant in Sevesco spewed dioxin over the Italian countryside. Subsequently, explosions in a Union Carbide plant in Bhopal, India, spread deadly gases over nearby residential neighborhoods with significant loss of life, and water used to quell a warehouse fire at a Sandoz warehouse near Basel, Switzerland, carried an estimated 30 tons of toxic chemicals into the Rhine River, a source of drinking water for several towns in Germany. In 2010, an explosion and fire at the BP/Deepwater Horizon drilling rig off Louisiana's coast in the Gulf of Mexico killed 11 people and ruptured an underwater pipe that caused a massive oil spill.

In previous chapters, we touched on a few of the policy instruments used to combat toxic substance problems. Emissions standards govern the types and amounts of substances that can be injected into the air. Effluent standards regulate what can be discharged directly into water sources, and pretreatment standards control the flow of toxics into wastewater treatment plants. Maximum concentration levels have been established for many substances in drinking water.

This impressive array of policies is not sufficient to resolve the Love Canal problem or others having similar characteristics. As Flint, Michigan's water contamination disaster demonstrated in 2015, for example, by the time violations of the standards for drinking water are detected, the water is already contaminated. Specifying maximum contaminant levels helps to identify when a problem exists, but it does nothing to prevent or contain the problem. The various standards for air and water emissions that do protect against *point* sources do little to prevent contamination by *nonpoint* sources. Furthermore, most waterborne toxic pollutants are stock pollutants, not fund pollutants; they cannot be absorbed by the receiving waters. Therefore, temporally constant controls on emissions (a traditional method used for fund pollutants) are inappropriate for these toxic substances since they would allow a steady rise in the concentration over time. Finally controlling accidental discharges may require a rather different set of policies. Some additional form of control is necessary.

In this chapter, we describe and evaluate the main policies that deal specifically with the creation, use, transportation, and disposal of toxic substances and how those policies affect environmental justice. Many dimensions will be considered: what are appropriate ways to dispose of toxic substances? How can the government ensure that all waste is appropriately disposed of in a way that does not disproportionately disadvantage some socioeconomic groups? How do we prevent surreptitious dumping? Who should clean up old sites and how should the cleanup be financed? Should victims be compensated for damages caused by toxic substances under the control of someone else? If so, by whom? What are the appropriate roles for the legislature and the judiciary in creating the proper set of incentives?

Nature of Toxic Substance Pollution

A main objective of the current legal system for controlling toxic substances is to protect human health, although protecting other forms of life is a secondary objective. The potential health danger depends upon the toxicity of a substance to humans and their exposure to the substance. *Toxicity* occurs when a living organism experiences detrimental effects following exposure to a substance. In normal concentrations, most chemicals are not toxic. Others, such as pesticides, are toxic by design. Yet, in excess concentrations, even a benign substance such as table salt can be toxic.

While a degree of risk is involved when using any chemical substance, there are benefits as well. The task for public policy is to define an acceptable risk by balancing the costs and benefits of controlling the use of chemical substances.

Health Effects

Two main health concerns associated with toxic substances are risk of cancer and effects on reproduction.

Cancer. While many suspect the mortality rate for cancer may be related to increased exposure to carcinogens, proving or disproving this link is very difficult due to the latency of the disease. *Latency* refers to the state of being concealed during the period between exposure to the carcinogen and the detection of cancer. Latency periods for cancer run from 15 to 40 years, and have been known to run as long as 75 years.

In the United States, part of the increase in cancer has been convincingly linked to smoking, particularly among women. As the proportion of women who smoke has increased, the incidence of lung cancer has increased as well. Smoking does not account for all of the increase in cancer, however.

Although it is not entirely clear what other agents may be responsible, one suggested cause is the rise in the manufacture and use of synthetic chemicals since World War II. A number of these chemicals have been shown in the laboratory to be carcinogenic. That evidence is not necessarily sufficient to implicate them in the rise of cancer, however, because it does not take exposure into account. The laboratory can reveal, through animal tests, the relationship between dosage and resulting effects. To track down the significance of any chemical in causing cancer in the general population would require an estimate of how many people were exposed to specific doses. Currently, our data are not extensive enough to allow these kinds of calculations to be done with any confidence.

Reproductive Effects. Tracing the influence of environmental effects on human reproduction is still a new science. A growing body of scientific evidence, however, suggests that exposure to smoking, alcohol, and chemicals known as endocrine disruptors may contribute to infertility, may affect the viability of the fetus and the health of the infant after birth, and may cause genetic defects that can be passed on for generations.

Problems exist for both men and women. In men, exposure to toxic substances has resulted in lower sperm counts, malformed sperm, and genetic damage. In women, exposure can also result in sterility or birth defects in their children.

These are not the only health concerns, however, since exposure to toxic substances can have much more pervasive effects. Muir and Zegarac (2001) found, for example, that at least 10 percent, and up to 50 percent of the cumulative costs in Canada and the United States associated with four specific health problems—diabetes, Parkinson's disease (PD), neurodevelopmental effects and hypothyroidism, and deficits in intelligence quotient (IQ)— are environmentally induced.[1]

Policy Issues

Many aspects of the toxic substance problem make it difficult to resolve. Three important aspects that add to this difficulty are the number of substances involved, latency, and uncertainty.

Number of Substances. Of the tens of millions of known chemical compounds, approximately 100,000 are actively used in commerce. Many exhibit little or no toxicity, and even a very toxic substance represents little risk as long as it is isolated. The trick is to identify problem substances and to design appropriate policies as responses. The massive number of substances involved makes that a difficult assignment.

Latency. The period of latency exhibited by many of these relationships compounds the problem. Two kinds of toxicity are exhibited: acute and chronic. *Acute toxicity* is present when a short-term exposure to the substance produces a detrimental effect on the exposed organisms. *Chronic toxicity* is present when the detrimental effect arises from exposure of a continued or prolonged nature. One size does *not* fit all.

The process of screening chemicals as potentially serious causes of chronic illness is even more complicated than that of screening for acute illness. The traditional technique for determining acute toxicity is the lethal-dose determination, a relatively quick test performed on animals that calculates the dose that results in the death of 50 percent of the animal population. This test is less well suited for screening substances that exhibit chronic toxicity.

The appropriate tests for discovering chronic toxicity typically have involved subjecting animal populations to sustained low-level doses of the substance over an extended period of time. These tests are very expensive and time consuming. If the EPA were to perform these tests, given its limited resources, it could only test a few of the estimated 700 new chemicals introduced each year. If the industries were to do the tests, the expense could preclude the introduction of many potentially valuable new chemicals that have limited, specialized markets.

Uncertainty. Another dilemma inhibiting policymakers is the uncertainty surrounding the scientific evidence on which regulation is based. Effects uncovered by laboratory studies on animals are not perfectly correlated with effects on humans. Large doses administered over a 3-year period may not produce the same effects as an equivalent amount spread over a 20-year period. Some of the effects are *synergistic*—that is, their effects are intensified or diminished by the presence of other variable factors. (Asbestos workers who smoke are 30 times more likely than their nonsmoking fellow workers to get lung cancer, for example.) Once cancer is detected, in most cases it does not bear the imprint of a particular source. Policymakers have to act in the face of limited information (see Example 10.1).

From an economic point of view, how the policy process reacts to this dilemma should depend on how well the market handles toxic substance problems. To the extent that the

---

EXAMPLE 10.1

The Arduous Path to Managing Toxic Risk: Bisphenol A

One example of a potentially toxic substance that is working its way through the government regulatory bureaucracy is Bisphenol A (BPA). The food industry was using more than 6 billion pounds of BPA every year to make the resins that line food cans and the polycarbonate plastics used to make baby bottles and many other products. The Centers for Disease Control and Prevention (CDC) says that 95 percent of us carry measurable amounts of BPA in our blood.

In April 2008, the National Toxicology Program (NTP) at the National Institutes of Health (NIH) expressed some concern that exposure to BPA during pregnancy and childhood could impact the developing breast and prostate, hasten puberty, and affect behavior in American children. Not long after those concerns were expressed, the Canadian government moved to ban polycarbonate infant bottles containing BPA, the most popular type of bottle on the market.

Despite the absence of any such ruling from the US government, after the Canadian move the US market reacted. Major BPA manufacturers, including Playtex (which makes bottles and cups) and Nalgene, which makes portable water bottles, announced a shift to BPA-free products. Major retailers, including Walmart and Toys "R" Us, announced they would quickly phase out BPA-containing baby bottles. Furthermore since 2009 13 states and the District of Columbia enacted further restrictions.

In January 2010, the US Food and Drug Administration (FDA), which had previously found BPA to be safe, announced:

> On the basis of results from recent studies using novel approaches to test for subtle effects, both the National Toxicology Program at the National Institutes of Health and FDA have some concern about the potential effects of BPA on the brain, behavior, and prostate gland in fetuses, infants, and young children.

In July 2012, the agency announced that it would no longer allow BPA in baby bottles and children's drinking cups. The agency did not restrict its use in other consumer products.

How this risk was handled in the United States is especially noteworthy in that both the market and the states reacted before federal regulation was in place, but the federal government did ultimately follow their lead.

Sources: The National Institutes of Health website: www.niehs.nih.gov/health/topics/agents/sya-bpa/ (accessed December 5, 2016); Food and Drug Administration website: www.fda.gov/NewsEvents/PublicHealthFocus/ucm064437.htm (accessed May 23, 2013); Environmental Working Group website: www.ewg.org/bpa/ (accessed December 5, 2016)

market generates the correct information and provides the appropriate incentives, policy may not be needed. On the other hand, when the government can best generate information or create the appropriate incentive, intervention may be called for. As the following sections demonstrate, the nature and the form of the most appropriate policy response may depend crucially on how the toxic source and the affected party or parties are related.

Market Allocations and Toxic Substances

Toxic substance contamination can arise in a variety of settings. In order to define the efficient policy response, we must examine what responses would be forthcoming in the normal operation of the market. Let's look at three possible relationships between the source of the contamination and the victim: employer–employee, producer–consumer, and producer–third party. The first two involve normal contractual relations among the parties, while the latter involves noncontracting parties, whose connection is defined solely by the contamination.

Occupational Hazards

Many occupations involve risk, including, for some people, exposure to toxic substances. Do employers and employees have sufficient incentives to act in concert toward achieving safety in the workplace?

The caricature of the market used by the most ardent proponents of regulation suggests not. In this view, the employer's desire to maximize profits precludes spending enough money on safety. Sick workers can simply be replaced. Therefore, the workers are powerless to do anything about it; if they complain, they are fired and replaced with others who are less vocal.

The most ardent opponents of regulation respond that this caricature overlooks or purposefully ignores significant market pressures, such as employee incentives and the feedback effects of those incentives on employers. When the full story that includes these pressures is considered, regulation may be unnecessary or even counterproductive.

According to this market incentives worldview, employees will only accept work in a potentially hazardous environment if appropriately compensated for taking that risk. Riskier occupations should call forth higher wages. The increase in wages should be sufficient to compensate them for the increased risk, otherwise they will work elsewhere. These higher wages represent a real cost of the hazardous situation to the employer. They also produce an incentive to create a safer work environment, since greater safety would result in a lower risk premium and, hence, lower wages. One cost could be balanced against the other. What was spent on safety could be recovered in lower wages (see Figure 10.1).

The first type of cost, the marginal increase in wages, is drawn to reflect the fact that the lower the level of precaution, the higher the wage bill. Two such curves are drawn to reflect high-exposure and low-exposure situations. The high-exposure case assumes larger numbers of workers are exposed than in the low-exposure case. The low-exposure cost curve rises more slowly because the situation is less dangerous at the margin.

The second type of curve, the marginal cost of providing precaution, reflects an increasing marginal cost. The two different curves depict different production situations. A firm with a few expensive precautionary options will face a steeply sloped marginal cost curve, while a

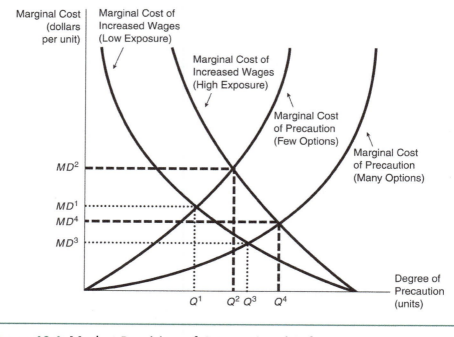

Figure 10.1 Market Provision of Occupational Safety

firm with many cheaper options will face a lower marginal cost at every comparable degree of precaution chosen.

The graph depicts four possible outcomes—one for each possible combination of these four marginal cost curves. Note that very different choices will be made, depending on the circumstances. Also note that the level of risk chosen (as indicated by the marginal damage, labeled MD) and the degree of precaution are not perfectly correlated. The highest marginal risk is MD^2, but the associated level of precaution (Q^2) is not the largest. The reason, of course, is that the cost of taking precautions matters, and sometimes it is cheaper to accept the risk and compensate for it than it is to prevent it.

Because the marginal increased wages curve accurately reflects marginal damages (since the higher wages are demanded by workers to compensate them for damages), these market equilibria are also efficient. Thus, the efficient resolution of the occupational hazards problem varies not only from substance to substance, but also from plant to plant. As long as this stylized view of the world is correct, the market will tailor the appropriate degree of precaution to the situation.

Proponents of this view point out that this allocation would also allow more choices for workers than would, for example, a system requiring all workplaces to be equally safe. With varying occupational risk, those occupations with more risk (such as working to clean up toxic spills) would attract people who were less averse to risk. These workers would receive higher-than-average wages (to compensate them for the increased risk), but paying these higher wages would be cheaper to the firm (and, hence, consumers) than requiring every workplace to meet the same risk standard. The risk-averse workers would be free to choose less risky occupations.

Do wages actually reflect risk? Existing empirical studies make clear that wages in risky occupations in countries like the United States do contain a risk premium (Viscusi & Aldy, 2003). Two conclusions about these risk premiums seem clear from these studies: (1) the willingness to pay for apparently similar risk reductions varies significantly across individuals, and (2) the revealed willingness to pay for risk reduction is substantial.

In those cases where wages accurately reflect risk is there any appropriate role for the government in controlling contamination in the workplace? Perhaps. The efficient solution may not always be considered the most ethical solution, a point that has been addressed in the courts. For example, if the employee is a pregnant woman and the occupational hazard involves potential damage to the fetus, does the expectant mother have the right to risk the unborn child, or is some added protection for the fetus needed? Furthermore, if the lowest-cost solution is to ban pregnant, or even fertile, women from a workplace that poses a risk to a fetus, is that an acceptable solution, or is it unfair discrimination against women? As Example 10.2 suggests, these are not idle concerns.

Ethical concerns are not the only challenges for market solutions. Wages may not reflect the actual risk. The ability of the worker to respond to a hazardous situation depends on his or her knowledge of the seriousness of the danger. With toxic substances, that knowledge is likely to be incomplete in general, but completely inadequate in settings such as developing countries. Consequently, the marginal increased wages function may be artificially rotated toward the origin. In this case, the employer would choose too little precaution and the market will not provide sufficient pressure to rectify this worker hazard. By having access to the health records of all employees, the employer could potentially be in the best position to assess the degree of risk posed, but the employer also has an incentive to suppress that information since publicizing the risk would mean demands for higher compensatory wages and possible lawsuits.

Information on the dangers posed by exposure to a particular toxic substance is a public good to employees; each employee has an incentive to be a free rider on the discoveries of others. Individual employees do not have an incentive to bear the cost of doing the necessary

> ## EXAMPLE 10.2
>
> # Susceptible Populations in the Hazardous Workplace: An Historical Example
>
> Some employees are especially susceptible to occupational hazards. Pregnant women and women in the childbearing years are particularly vulnerable. When an employer attempts to manage a work situation that poses a hazardous threat, either the susceptible population can be separated from the hazard or the hazard can be controlled to a sufficient level that its risk is acceptable to even the most susceptible employees.
>
> The economic aspects of this choice are easily deduced from Figure 10.1. Suppose that the firm has few control options and is on the uppermost of the two marginal cost of precaution curves. By removing the susceptible population, it could face the low-exposure curve. Removal of the susceptible population results in lower marginal risk to the workers, lower costs to the firm, and less precaution taken. But is it fair to those who are removed from their jobs?
>
> This issue came to a head in 1978 when American Cyanamid decided to respond to an occupational risk by banning all fertile women from jobs in the section manufacturing lead chromate pigment at Willow Island, West Virginia. After reviewing the decision, the Occupational Safety and Health Administration (OSHA) cited the company under the general duty clause of the Occupational Safety and Health Act, which requires an employer to provide a workplace free of hazards, and fined it $10,000. That was not the end of the story. In early 1980, the Oil, Chemical, and Atomic Workers Union sued the company under the 1964 Civil Rights Act on the grounds that the company had discriminated unfairly against women. In March 1991, the Supreme Court ruled that banning fertile women from any workplace posing a risk to a fetus was not an acceptable way to control risk. The workplace must be made safe for all.
>
> *Source: International Union v. Johnson Controls, 499 US 187 (1991).*

research to uncover the degree of risk. Thus, it seems neither employers nor employees can be expected to produce the efficient amount of information on the magnitude of risk.[2]

As a result, the government may play a substantial role in setting the boundaries on ethical responses, in stimulating research on the nature of hazards, and in providing for the dissemination of information to affected parties. It does not necessarily follow, however, that the government should be responsible for determining the level of safety in the workplace once this information is available and the ethical boundaries are determined. For situations that are sufficiently dangerous that no rational worker would voluntarily choose to work there, the role of the government would be to set and enforce a safety threshold.

This analysis suggesting that the market is not likely to provide an efficient level of information on occupational risk is consistent with the enactment of "right-to-know" laws in several states. These laws require businesses to disclose to their employees and to the public any potential health hazards associated with toxic substances used on the job. Generally employers are required to (1) label toxic substance containers, (2) inventory all toxic substances used in the workplace, and (3) provide adequate training on the handling of these substances to all affected employees. Significantly, proponents of these laws suggest that the targets are not the large chemical companies, which generally have excellent disclosure programs, but the smaller, largely nonunion plants.

Product Safety

Exposure to a hazardous or potentially hazardous substance can also occur as a result of using a product, as when eating food containing chemical additives. Does the market efficiently supply safe products?

One view holds that the market pressures on both parties (consumers and producers) are sufficient to yield an efficient level of safety. Safer products are generally more expensive to produce and carry a higher price tag. If consumers feel that the additional safety justifies the cost, they will purchase the safer product. Otherwise they won't. Producers supplying excessively risky products will find their market drying up, because consumers will switch to competing brands that are safer, despite their higher price. Similarly, producers selling excessively safe products (meaning they eliminate, at great cost, risks consumers are perfectly willing to take in return for a lower purchase price) find their markets drying up as well. Consumers will choose the cheaper, riskier product.

This theory also suggests that the market will not (and should not) yield a uniform level of safety for all products. Different consumers will have different degrees of risk aversion. While some consumers might purchase riskier, but cheaper, products, others might prefer safer, but more expensive, products.[3]

Under this worldview it would be common to find products with various safety levels supplied simultaneously, reflecting and satisfying different consumer preferences for risk. Forcing all similar products to conform to a single level of risk would not be efficient. Uniform product safety is no more efficient than uniform occupational safety.

If this view of the market were completely accurate, government intervention to protect consumers would not be necessary to ensure the efficient level of risk. By the force of their collective buying habits, consumers would protect themselves.

The problem with the market's ability to provide such self-regulation is, once again, the availability of information on product safety. The consumer generally acquires his or her information about a product either from personal experience or from labels and warnings. With toxic substances the latency period may be so long as to preclude any effective market reaction arising from personal experience. Even when some damage results several years later, it is difficult for the consumer to associate it with a particular source. While an examination of the relationships between purchasing patterns of a large number of consumers and their subsequent health might well reveal some suggestive correlations, it would be difficult for any individual consumer to deduce this correlation. Furthermore, it may be that the risk is so large that no knowledgeable consumer would accept that risk so that banning the product is the appropriate remedy. (Note that banning was the choice of several states in managing the risk from BPA, as described in Example 10.1.)

In situations where adequate information is available on the risks, consumers should have a substantial role in choosing the acceptable level of risk through their purchases, but varying levels of access to information can make this problematic. (Recall Debate 9.1 on fish consumption advisories.)

Third Parties

The final case involves *third parties*, victims who have no contractual relationship to the source. Oil spills are one example. Another occurs when groundwater is contaminated by a neighboring wastewater treatment facility, by surreptitious dumping of toxic wastes, or by a neighbor's improper application of a pesticide. In all of these examples the victims are third parties. Since in third-party situations the affected party cannot bring any direct market pressure to bear on the source, the case for additional government intervention is stronger.

This does not necessarily imply, however, that executive or legislative remedies are appropriate. The most appropriate response may come from simply requiring better information on the risk or from using the judicial system to impose liability.

Liability law provides one judicial avenue for internalizing the external costs in third-party situations. If the court finds (1) that damage occurred, (2) that it was caused by a toxic substance, and (3) that a particular source was responsible for the presence of the substance, the source can be forced to compensate the victim for the damages caused. Unlike regulations that are uniformly (and, hence, inefficiently) applied, a court decision can be tailored to the exact circumstances involved in the suit. Furthermore, the impact of any particular liability assignment can go well beyond the parties to that case. A decision for one plaintiff can remind other sources that they should take the efficient level of precaution now to avoid paying damages later.

In principle, liability law can force potential sources of toxic discharges, including nonpoint sources, to choose efficient levels of precaution. Unlike regulation, liability law can provide compensation to the victims. Bringing suit to recover damages, however, is a costly process so these administrative costs must be balanced against the potential gains in efficiency when choosing the appropriate remedy for any particular situation.

Using liability law to resolve toxic situations can also take a long time. In the famous case of Flint, Michigan, decisions made as early as 2007 resulted in lead contamination of the city's water supply. A flurry of lawsuits followed, but it wasn't until March 2017 that a federal judge approved a $97 million settlement.

The Incidence of Hazardous Waste Siting Decisions

Flint, Michigan's population is 56.6 percent African American and 41 percent of the population live below the poverty line. Did the fact that this was largely a poor, minority community play any role in what happened and how long it took to resolve the problem?

For some historical context for thinking about the possible linkages between race and exposure to toxic substances, it may be instructive to review what we know about the role of race in the siting of toxic waste facilitates.

History

In 1979, Robert Bullard, then a sociologist at Texas Southern University, completed a report describing a futile attempt by an affluent African American neighborhood in Houston, Texas, to block the location of a hazardous waste site within their community. His analysis suggested that race, not just income status, was a probable factor in this local land use decision.

Environmental justice, as revealed though the siting of hazardous waste plants, became a national issue in 1982 when some 500 demonstrators protested against the location of a proposed PCB landfill in a predominantly low-income community in North Carolina. On returning from the protests, Walter Fauntroy, the District of Columbia congressional delegate, asked the General Accounting Office (GAO) to study the characteristics of hazardous waste sites in the EPA's Region 4 (Georgia, Florida, Mississippi, Alabama, Kentucky, Tennessee, North Carolina, and South Carolina). The 1983 study found that three out of four commercial hazardous waste facilities were in predominantly African American communities, and the fourth was in a low-income community.

In 1987, the United Church of Christ Commission for Racial Justice examined the issue of hazardous waste siting for the nation as a whole. According to their statistical analysis of communities with commercial hazardous waste facilities, they determined that:

> Race proved to be the most significant among the variables tested in association with the location of commercial hazardous waste facilities. This represented a consistent national pattern.

In 1994, the Center for Policy Alternatives issued "Toxic Wastes and Race Revisited: An Update of the 1987 Report." That study found that commercial toxic waste facilities were even more likely to be located in minority communities at that time than in 1980, despite growing national attention to the issue.

Not all studies have reached this conclusion, but in a detailed review of the literature, Hamilton (2003) found that, for most US studies, low-income and minority residents do indeed face higher risks from hazardous waste facilities. Less detailed information exists on the exposure of these populations to hazardous waste risks in other industrialized countries.

Environmental Justice Research and the Emerging Role of GIS

The application of geographic information systems (GIS) technology has allowed studies of the distributional inequities with respect to either pollution or hazardous waste site location to become more sophisticated. GIS technology also allows analyses to be conducted at the facility level, the city level, or another geographical area. Most regional offices of the EPA, for example, now use demographic data from the US Census Bureau, combined with GIS mapping. This technique allows for the overlay of census data onto concentric rings around a hazardous waste facility or a Superfund site, for example, in order to discover who lives in close proximity to the site. The distribution of risks can also be estimated by combining assumptions about the radius of the externalities around a facility with data from epidemiological studies (Hamilton, 2006).

What have these studies found? The results from these studies are quite varied, but they demonstrate that using only one measure of equity, such as low income, could prove misleading. Hamilton and Viscusi (1999), for example, consider multiple measures of equity, including racial distribution, mean household income, and potential cancer risks, and their work demonstrates how sensitive the results are to the specific measure that is used.

Other studies have utilized the EPA's Toxic Release Inventory (TRI) data. This data set contains self-reported information on toxic releases from all plants that are required to report. Studies using these data have found that demographic groups most likely to face the threat of exposure to toxic air emissions include minorities, renters, people with incomes below the poverty line, and individuals with fewer years of schooling. Studies have also found significant negative effects of pollution on house values and incomes in New England states (Example 10.3).

What explains these findings? What do these findings imply for policy?

The Economics of Site Location

One point of departure is to understand the dynamics of hazardous waste treatment site location and how both income and race might play a role. Our analysis begins by recognizing

EXAMPLE 10.3

Do New Polluting Facilities Affect Housing Values and Incomes? Evidence from New England

Combining census data for New England for 1980 and 1990 with Toxics Release Inventory (TRI) data for manufacturing firms that began operations during that period, Hanna (2007) explores the effect of polluting facilities on the surrounding neighborhoods. The study looks specifically at how prices, wages, pollution, and incomes vary among census tracts in the New England states.

Hanna uses data on new plants with an index of pollution exposure calculated as a weighted sum of the distance between the census tract and the pollution source times the TRI-reported releases for that pollution source. Some 167 New England sites were in the TRI data. Ten percent of the new plant emissions were of dichloromethane, an airborne contaminant classified as a probable human carcinogen. Significant negative effects of pollution on house values and incomes were found. Their estimates suggest that a house located 1 mile closer to a polluting manufacturing plant has its value reduced by 1.9 percent.

Source: Hanna, B. G. (2007). House values, incomes, and industrial pollution. *Journal of Environmental Economics and Management, 54,* 100–112.

that hazardous waste facilities are generally unpopular neighbors. Even if the treatment of hazardous waste makes sense for society as a whole, all potential recipient communities must face the NIMBY (Not in My Backyard) opposition.

Understanding the economics of site location requires consideration of the incentives facing both the owners of the proposed facility and the incentives of the host community. Since the owners want to maximize profits, they will look for a site that can process the wastes at a low cost. Being located near the sources of the waste would be attractive as a means of holding down transport costs. Lower land costs would also be attractive since these facilities are frequently land-intensive. Finally, the site should pose as few liability risks as possible in order to limit future payouts.

The host community has its own agenda in order to ensure that it reaps benefits that outweigh costs. They would want to ensure, insofar as possible, that the site was safe for both employees and the inhabitants of the surrounding community. They would also want adequate compensation for assuming the risk of being near these sites. This compensation could take many forms (for example, employment, enhanced tax revenues, or new public services).

What does efficiency suggest about the characteristics of host communities? Low-income communities become attractive as disposal sites not only because land prices are relatively low in those communities, but also because those communities will typically require less compensation in order to accept the risk. Targeting low-income communities would be the expected, not the exceptional, outcome. Furthermore, once hazardous waste facilities are located in a community, the composition of that community is likely to become even poorer due to migration and the negative effects on surrounding property values. Assuming that the willingness to pay for risk-avoidance is higher for higher-income families, more lower-income families may be attracted by the unusually low land prices (or rents), while higher-income families may depart for less risky neighborhoods. Even if the community were not low income at the time of the siting, it is likely to become more so over time.

While even an efficient siting process might target a disproportionate share of these facilities in low-income communities, it is much more difficult to develop a clear economic rationale for why race is a more important predictor than income. Explaining that finding requires greater attention to market failures.

Efficient location requires both full information and adequate enforcement of agreements. In the absence of full information, host communities can fail to fully understand the risk and therefore are likely to undervalue it. One hypothesis explains the importance of race by noting that minority communities have less access to full information than comparably situated white communities. This would imply they are more likely to be unwittingly subject to flawed agreements that are biased against them. Another hypothesis is that they lack the power to enforce community will, perhaps because of underrepresentation on governing boards. This hypothesis implies that even potentially efficient agreements may be inefficiently implemented

---

EXAMPLE 10.4

Which Came First—The Toxic Facility or the Minority Neighborhood?

Pastor et al. (2001) explore "which came first" in Los Angeles County. Using data from 1970 to 1990, they explore whether toxic storage and disposal facilities (TSDFs) moved into a minority neighborhood or whether the TSDF was there first. Using geo-coded site locations and GIS, they were able to identify affected census tracts. By mapping the facility location and creating circular buffers of one-quarter mile and 1 mile, they were able to determine the potentially affected residents. Their data set contains 83 TSDFs, 39 of which are high capacity and handle most of the waste. Some 55 census tracts were within one-quarter mile of these facilities and 245 tracts were within 1 mile.

They find that areas receiving TSDFs during this time period were indeed low-income, minority areas with a disproportionate number of renters. After the TDSFs were in place, however, increases in minority residents occurred, but were not disproportionate to the rest of the "move-ins." In other words, prior to any siting decision, neighborhoods with below-average incomes and above-average percentages of Latinos and African Americans were more likely to receive a TSDF. After the siting decision, little evidence suggests disproportionate in-migration along racial or ethnic lines.

The authors acknowledge two limitations of this study. One is that any analysis at the neighborhood level does not capture individual exposure rates, which may vary within the neighborhood. A second limitation arises from the fact that the perceived risks of living near a site are not certain. Some evidence suggests that people are more worried about hazards to which they have been exposed involuntarily.

Source: Pastor, Jr., M., Sadd, J., & Hipp, J. (2001). Which came first? Toxic facilities, minority move-in and environmental justice. *Journal of Urban Affairs, 23*, 1–21.

(Bullard, 1990). Taken as a whole, this evidence on the prominence of race as an independent predictor variable (over and above income) suggests not only that the current siting process may be discriminatory, but also that it is not efficient. Until such time as recipient communities can be guaranteed both full information and the capability to enforce the community's will, the hazardous waste siting process will remain seriously flawed.

One lingering issue of debate has to do with the direction of causality. Consider two quite different possibilities. In the first case these population groups could face higher exposures because a hazardous facility was attracted by low land prices. In the other case, attracted by lower land and/or housing prices, people could have moved in <u>after</u> the hazardous waste site located in that community. This chicken-and-egg question has been explored in a few studies.[4] Example 10.4 illustrates one such study in Los Angeles.

The Policy Response

Environmental Justice and Hazardous Waste Sites. In recognition of the problems associated with locating hazardous waste sites, the Office of Environmental Equity was officially established within the US Environmental Protection Agency on November 6, 1992. Its mandate is to deal with environmental impacts affecting people of color and low-income communities. Although the issue that precipitated the creation of this office was largely focused on the siting of hazardous waste facilities, the concerns of this office go well beyond that. Initial efforts are focused on gathering more information about the problem and strengthening enforcement inspections and compliance monitoring in impacted communities.

In 1994, President Clinton issued Executive Order 12898, "Federal Action to Address Environmental Justice in Minority Populations and Low-Income Populations." The goal of this order was to make sure that minority groups and low-income populations are not subjected to an unequal or disproportionately high level of environmental risks.

How effective has the order been? In 2004, the EPA issued an evaluation report of this Executive Order and did not award a good grade. In fact, the report suggests that Executive Order 12898 has not been fully implemented and that the EPA has "not consistently integrated environmental justice into its day-to-day operations." The report also states that the "EPA has not . . . identified populations addressed in the Executive Order, and has neither defined nor developed criteria for determining the disproportionately impacted."[5]

In 2014, Dr. Robert Bullard summed up his sense of what had been the result of Executive Order 12898 on the twentieth anniversary of its enactment:

> After decades of hard work, struggle, and some victories along the way, the quest for environmental justice for all communities has yet to be achieved. Even in 2014, the most potent predictor of health is zip code. Race and poverty are also powerful predictors of students who attend schools near polluting facilities, the location of polluted neighborhoods that pose the greatest threat to human health, hazardous waste facilities, urban heat islands, and access to healthy foods, parks, and tree cover.[6]

Simultaneous exposures to various types of risk make discerning the causal relationships even more complex. Those with lower incomes may live close to a plant with high emissions, but lower incomes are also associated with a poorer diet and less access to health care, both of which can also be associated with increased levels of illness (Hamilton, 2006).

Environmental Justice in Canada and Europe. The number of empirical studies outside the United States is rather limited, but some case studies have been conducted, particularly in Canada and Europe. These case studies are useful in helping to discern what kinds of strategies can be effective in the quest to achieve environmental justice in the siting of hazardous waste facilities.

Public participation has been cited as an important factor in the successful siting of hazardous waste facilities in the Canadian provinces of Alberta and Manitoba. ("Successful" in this case means not only that the facility was able to find a home, but also that no environmental justice concerns have arisen after the fact in the host communities.) The siting process in these provinces is not only voluntary, but it also provides multiple stages at which the community can exercise veto power over the project.

Interestingly, the resulting locations are not always in low-income neighborhoods. In fact, one such location, the town of Swan Hills, has an average household income significantly higher than the average in the province and one of the lowest levels of unemployment.

Why would any community accept such a facility? Potential jobs at the facilities are apparently one large factor, as is the property tax revenue that might accrue.

One corollary of the jobs hypothesis might be that we would expect the presence of local high unemployment to increase the likelihood a community would accept a hazardous waste facility. That seems to be the case. In a survey of successful sitings in France, Hungary, Italy, the Netherlands, and Spain, for example, Dente et al. (1998) found that areas with higher unemployment are, as expected, more likely to accept facilities. They also found, however, that communities are more likely to accept waste if it is seen as "local" since, in that case, the residents of the host community will also be reaping the benefits from employment in the plants generating the waste.

The Role of Risk Perception. The NIMBY attitude has been explored in both the economics and cognitive psychology literatures. Delving into the psychology of risk perception, Messer et al. (2006) summarize the results of a study that evaluated the benefits of hazardous waste cleanup under the Comprehensive Environmental Response, Compensation, and Liability Act (CERCLA), more commonly known as Superfund. Although this legislation was passed in 1980, legal complexities in the Act have delayed the cleanup of many Superfund sites. These authors wanted to know if the length of delay affected the ultimate recovery of property values after the cleanup.

The authors examined four Superfund sites: Operating Industries, a landfill in Los Angeles; Montclair, West Orange, and Glen Ridge Townships in New Jersey, formerly the site of US Radium Corporation; Industri-plex and Water Wells G&H in Woburn, Massachusetts; and Eagle Mine in Colorado. Cleanup was significantly delayed and/or hampered at all of these sites.

They found that the designation of the site as a Superfund site, the cleanup itself, and the associated news items all negatively affected the property values. Media announcements were found to affect public perceptions of risk so profoundly that a "shunning" of the property may result. Current owners may not be willing to stay in their homes if their perceived costs of remaining are greater than the value of their homes and potential buyers are likely to be few and far between. In this study, property values continued to fall over time as cleanup was delayed. If cleanup were delayed for 20 years, for example, they found that the benefits of cleanup (measured by the recovery of property values) would be negligible in present value economic terms, since it would take another 5 to 10 years for property values to recover.

Compensation as a Policy Instrument. One policy device for attempting to achieve environmental justice is paying compensation or host fees to communities accepting hazardous waste facilities. In principle, this would serve to make sure that benefits, not merely costs, accrue to the local community. Additionally, paying the compensation would internalize the cost of the environmental risk as that cost was passed on to those whose waste was being treated.

While compensation frequently is an effective device for finding common ground, as Debate 10.1 suggests, that is not always the case!

The Toxic Release Inventory

The Toxic Release Inventory (TRI) was enacted by the US Congress in January 1986 as a part of the Environmental Protection and Community Right to Know Act (EPCRA). EPCRA was enacted partially in response to two incidents. In 1984, methyl isocyanate killed thousands of people in Bhopal, India. A chemical release at a sister plant in West Virginia happened soon after. The public's (workers' and community members') demand for information about toxic chemicals was the impetus for EPCRA. Together with the Pollution Prevention Act (PPA) of 1990, it mandates the collection of data on toxic chemicals that are treated on-site, recycled, and combusted for energy recovery. The TRI is a publicly available database designed to provide information to the public on releases of toxic substances into the environment. Most of the substances involved are not themselves subject to release standards.

TRI states that firms that *use* 10,000 or more pounds of a listed chemical in a given calendar year or firms that *import, process, or manufacture* 25,000 or more pounds of a listed chemical must file a report on each of the chemicals in existence within the plant if they also have ten or more full-time employees. Approximately 650 chemicals are covered in the TRI. Most recently the TRI has been expanded to include lower reporting thresholds for certain persistent bioaccumulative toxic (PBT) chemicals. PBT chemicals are stock pollutants and can accumulate in body tissue. PBT chemicals include mercury, pesticides, and dioxins.

Reporting of emissions or use of listed chemicals is accomplished annually. (For the data, see www.epa.gov/tri/tridata/index.htm.) The reports include such information as the name of the company, the name of the parent company if it exists, the toxic released and frequency of release, and the medium in which the chemical is released. Data by state are also available and all data are available to the public. Firms must also separately report emissions to their state and local authorities as well as to fire and emergency officials.

Several other countries now use similar reporting mechanisms, known as Pollutant Release and Transfer Registers (PRTR). All have slight variations on the TRI. In Japan, the PRTR includes data on diffuse sources (e.g., automobiles). The Canadian PRTR, called the National Pollutant Release Inventory (NPRI), also collects data on the number of employees at each facility. The Mexican PRTR is voluntary and so data are limited. Australia, the Czech Republic, Norway, and the United Kingdom also all have PRTRs with on-site release data.

Has the existence of the TRI reduced toxic emissions into the environment? EPA's annual reports reveal that substantial reductions have occurred. Although careful examination of the filings (e.g., Natan & Miller, 1998) found that some of these reductions merely reflect a change in definition, other reductions have been found to be genuine. Apparently, the reported magnitude of the reductions is overstated, but real reductions have occurred. Among the chemicals that are reported to TRI, about 180 are known or suspected carcinogens. In 2011, the EPA reported that the air releases of these carcinogens decreased by 50 percent between 2003 and 2011.

DEBATE 10.1

Does Offering Compensation for Accepting an Environmental Risk Always Increase the Willingness to Accept the Risk?

One week before a referendum in Switzerland on the siting of a nuclear-waste repository, a survey was conducted in the community where the repository was to be located. Researchers found that an offer of compensation to accept the facility *reduced* willingness to accept it! Specifically, Frey and Oberholzer-Gee (1997) and Frey et al. (1996) found that when asked whether they would accept a nuclear-waste repository without compensation, 50.8 percent of the respondents said "yes." This rate dropped to 24.6 percent when compensation was offered! The researchers suggest that acceptance rates drop with compensation because offering the compensation crowds out a feeling of civic duty. If respondents feel that accepting a facility is part of his or her civic duty, he or she will be less likely to feel this sense of responsibility once a payment is introduced. In this context, the authors believe that the compensation was viewed as a morally unacceptable bribe and, hence, should be rejected.

An alternative explanation might suggest that compensation could play a signaling role. Perhaps the risks are perceived as being small until such time as compensation is offered. At that moment, introducing compensation into the mix might be taken by the community as a signal that the risks are much higher than previously thought—indeed, so high that compensation must be paid!

How common is this outcome? In a very different setting (Japan), Lesbirel (1998) examined the siting of energy plants. In this context, the author found that compensation did, as expected, actually facilitate the siting of these plants. He interprets his findings as consistent with the belief that in Japan, institutional structures facilitate participatory negotiations on risk-management strategies that result in productive bargaining between the plants and host communities. This process effectively removes the moral stigma and eliminates the signaling role of compensation. Whether this characterization of the Japanese process continues to be valid following the Fukushima nuclear accident remains to be seen.

What is the moral of the story? This evidence suggests that compensation does not automatically increase the likelihood of a community accepting a hazardous facility, but it might. The context matters.

Sources: Frey, B. S., & Oberholzer-Gee, F. (1997). The cost of price incentives: An empirical analysis of motivation crowding out. *American Economic Review, 87*(4), 746–755; Frey, B. S, Oberholzer-Gee, F., & Eichenberger, R. (1996). The old lady visits your backyard: A tale of morals and markets. *Journal of Political Economy, 104*(6). Lesbirel, S. Hayden (1998) "NIMBY Politics in Japan: Energy Siting and the Management of Environmental Conflict" (Ithaca: Cornell University Press).

Proposition 65

Proposition 65, the *Safe Drinking Water and Toxic Enforcement Act of 1986*, was established in the state of California by popular vote in November 1986, following the inception of the Toxic Release Inventory by the EPA. Proposition 65 is intended to protect California citizens and the state's drinking water sources from toxic chemicals. Proposition 65 requires companies producing, using, or transporting one or more of the listed chemicals to notify those who are potentially impacted. Chemicals are listed as carcinogenic or as causing reproductive harm. When their use or potential exposure levels exceed "safe harbor numbers" established by a group of approved scientists, the impacted people must be notified. The "safe harbor" threshold is uniquely determined for each chemical and depends upon its intrinsic potency or the potency of a released mixture. Proposition 65 also requires the governor of California to publish, at least annually, a list of chemicals known to the state to cause cancer or reproductive toxicity.

The program involves three forms of notification: (1) warning labels must be placed on all products that will cause adverse health effects when used for a prolonged period of time; (2) a company whose toxic emissions to air, ground, or water exceed levels deemed safe for prolonged exposure must provide public notification; and (3) workers must be warned of the potential danger if toxic chemicals defined by Proposition 65 are used in manufacturing a product or are created as a by-product of manufacturing.

Only companies with ten or more full-time workers are required to notify people of exposure. Nonprofit organizations like hospitals, recycling plants, and government organizations, which account for over 65 percent of California's pollution, are not required to comply with Proposition 65.

Under the proposition, private citizens, other industry members, and environmental groups can sue companies that fail to notify people of exposure appropriately. Plaintiffs who make a successful legal claim can keep a substantial portion of the settlement; this encourages private enforcement of the law and reduces the need for government monitoring. Industry members also have a strong incentive to monitor each other, so that one company does not cheat and look greener than its rivals.

Did this program change behavior? At least in controlling exposure to lead, it clearly did (see Example 10.5).

International Agreements

One of the issues erupting during the 1990s concerned the efficiency and morality of exporting hazardous waste to areas that are willing to accept it in return for suitably large compensation. A number of areas, particularly poor countries, appear ready to accept hazardous waste under the "right conditions." The right conditions usually involve alleviating safety concerns and providing adequate compensation (in employment opportunities, money, and public services) so as to make acceptance of the wastes desirable from the receiving community's point of view. Generally, the compensation required is less than the costs of dealing in other ways with the hazardous waste, so the exporting nations find these agreements attractive as well.

A strong backlash against these arrangements arose when opponents argued that communities receiving hazardous waste were poorly informed about the risks they faced and were not equipped to handle the volumes of material that could be expected to cross international boundaries safely. In extreme cases, the communities were completely uninformed as sites were secretly located by individuals, with no public participation in the process at all.

EXAMPLE 10.5

Regulating through Mandatory Disclosure: The Case of Lead

Rechtschaffen (1999) describes a particularly interesting case study involving how Proposition 65 produced a major reduction in the amount of lead exposure by promoting new technologies, production-process changes, and pollution-prevention measures. He even goes so far as to suggest that Proposition 65 seemed even more effective than federal law in addressing certain lead hazards from drinking water, consumer products, and other sources.

Rechtschaffen identifies several characteristics about Proposition 65 that explain its relative success. We mention two here.

First, despite periodic calls for such an integrated strategy, no coordinated federal approach to controlling lead hazards had emerged. Rather, lead exposures were regulated by an array of agencies acting under a multitude of regulatory authorities. In contrast, the Proposition 65 warning requirement applies without limitation to *any* exposure to a listed chemical unless the exposure falls under the safe harbor standard, regardless of its source. Thus, the coverage of circumstances leading to lead exposure is very high and the standards requiring disclosure are universally applied.

Second, unlike federal law, Proposition 65 is self-executing. Once a chemical is listed by the state as causing cancer or reproductive harm, Proposition 65 applies. This contrasts with federal statutes, where private activity causing lead exposures is permitted until and unless the government sets a restrictive standard. Whereas under the federal approach fighting the establishment of a restrictive standard made economic sense (by delaying the date when the provisions would apply), under Proposition 65 exactly the opposite incentives prevail. In the latter case, since the provisions took effect soon after enactment, the only refuge from the statute rested on the existence of a safe harbor standard that could insulate small exposures from the statute's warning requirements. For Proposition 65, at least some subset of firms had an incentive to make sure the safe harbor standard was in place; delay in implementing the standard was costly, not beneficial.

Source: Rechtschaffen, C. (1999). How to reduce lead exposure with one simple statute: The experience with Proposition 65. *Environmental Law Reporter, 29,* 10581–10591.

The Basel Convention on the Control of Transboundary Movements of Hazardous Wastes and Their Disposal was developed in 1989 to provide a satisfactory response to these concerns. Under this convention, the 24 nations that belong to the Organisation for Economic Co-operation and Development (OECD) were required to obtain written permission from the government of any developing country before exporting toxic waste there for disposal or recycling. This was followed, in 1994, by an additional agreement on the part of most, but not all, industrialized nations to completely prohibit the export of toxic wastes from any OECD country to any non-OECD country.

With the huge growth in sales of electronic devices and the valuable materials in the postconsumer e-waste resulting from these sales, enforcement of laws on exporting toxic materials in e-waste is getting more difficult.

Some used electronic goods exported to developing countries become electronic waste (e-waste) that is usually disassembled in those developing countries. The concern is that the recovery process can be dangerous to the health of the disassemblers, particularly if it is done without the proper safeguards. E-waste often contains toxic substances such as lead, mercury, cadmium, and flame retardants.

Kinnaman and Yokoo (2011) report on studies that have found the following:

- Ambient dioxin and furan concentrations in the air around an e-waste dismantling site in China are the highest in the world. As a result, blood lead levels in children within proximity to this Chinese dismantling site significantly exceed the Chinese mean.
- Concentrations of lead, dioxins, and furans in e-waste dismantling sites in India also exceed World Health Organization guidelines.

A bill titled the Responsible Electronics Recycling Act, which would have banned US exports of electronic waste, was introduced in Congress in 2011, but not enacted.

Summary

The potential for contamination of the environmental asset by toxic substances is one of the most complex environmental problems. The number of substances that are potentially toxic is in the millions. Some 100,000 of these are in active use.

Although it is not always sufficient to provide an efficient outcome, the market provides a considerable amount of pressure toward resolving toxic substance problems as they affect employees and consumers. With reliable information at their disposal, all parties have an incentive to reduce hazards to acceptable levels. This pressure is absent, however, in cases involving third parties. Here, the problem frequently takes the form of an external cost imposed on innocent bystanders.

The efficient role of government can range from ensuring the provision of sufficient information (so that participants in the market can make informed choices) to setting exposure limits on hazardous substances. Unfortunately, the scientific basis for decision making is weak. Only limited information on the effects of these substances is available, and the cost of acquiring complete information is prohibitive. Therefore, priorities must be established and tests developed to screen substances so that efforts can be concentrated on those substances that seem most dangerous.

In contrast to air and water pollution, the toxic substance problem is one in which the courts may play a particularly important role. Liability law not only creates a market pressure for more and better information on potential damages associated with chemical substances, but also it provides some incentives to manufacturers of substances, the generators of waste, the transporters of waste, and those who dispose of it to exercise precaution. Judicial remedies also allow the level of precaution to vary with the occupational circumstances and provide a means of compensating victims.

Judicial remedies, however, are insufficient. They are expensive and ill-suited for dealing with problems affecting large numbers of people. The burden of proof under the current American system is difficult to surmount, although in Japan some radical new approaches have been developed to deal with this problem. Furthermore, court cases may take a considerable amount of time to resolve.

Is the burden posed by environmental risks and the policies used to reduce them distributed fairly? Apparently not. The siting of hazardous waste facilities seems to have resulted in a distribution of risks that disproportionately burdens low-income populations, and minority communities. This outcome suggests that current siting policies are neither efficient nor fair. The responsibility for this policy failure seems to lie mainly with the failure to ensure informed consent of residents in recipient communities and very uneven enforcement of existing legal protections.

The theologian Reinhold Niebuhr once said, "Democracy is finding proximate solutions to insoluble problems." That seems an apt description of the institutional response to the toxic substance problem. Our political institutions have created a staggering array of legislative and judicial responses to this problem that are neither efficient nor complete. They do, however, represent a positive first step in what must be an evolutionary process.

Discussion Questions

1. Did the courts resolve the dilemma posed in Example 10.2 correctly in your opinion? Why or why not?
2. Over the last several decades in product liability law, there has been a movement in the court system from *caveat emptor* ("buyer beware") to *caveat venditor* ("seller beware"). The liability for using and consuming risky products has been shifted from buyers to sellers. Does this shift represent a movement toward or away from an efficient allocation of risk? Why?
3. Would the export of hazardous waste to developing countries be efficient? Sometimes? Always? Never? Would it be moral? Sometimes? Always? Never? Make clear the specific reasons for your judgments.
4. How should the public sector handle a toxic gas, such as radon, that occurs naturally and seeps into some houses through the basement or the water supply? Is this a case of an externality? Does the homeowner have the appropriate incentives to take an efficient level of precaution?

Self-Test Exercises

1. Firms whose economic activity might pose an environmental risk are sometimes required to post performance bonds before the activity is allowed to commence. The amount of the required bond would be equal to the present value of anticipated damages. Any restoration of the site resulting from a hazardous waste leak could be funded directly and immediately from the accumulated funds. Any unused proceeds would be redeemable at specified dates if the environmental costs turned out to be lower than anticipated.

   What is the difference in practice between an approach relying on performance bonds and one imposing strict liability for cleanup costs on any firm for a toxic substance spill?
2. Is informing the consumer about any toxic substances used in the manufacture of a product sufficient to produce an efficient level of toxic substance use for that product? Why or why not?

Notes

1 Muir, T., & Zegarac, M. (2001). Societal costs of exposure to toxic substances: Economic and health costs of four case studies that are candidates for environmental causation. *Environmental Health Perspectives, 109*(Suppl 6), 885–903.
2 Unions would be expected to produce more efficient information flows since they represent many workers and can take advantage of economies of scale in the collection, interpretation, and dissemination of risk information. Available evidence suggests that the preponderance of wage premiums for risk has been derived from data involving unionized workers.
3 A classic example is provided by the manner in which Americans choose their automobiles. It is quite clear that some larger cars are safer and more expensive than smaller, cheaper ones, at least to their owners. Some consumers are willing to pay for this additional level of safety, and others are not.
4 Boyce (2007) reviews some of the debate on the *direction* of environmental protection.
5 Report of the Office of the Inspector General, March 1, 2004.
6 Bullard, Robert. (2014). New report tracks environmental justice movement over five decades. Available at: www.nrdc.org/experts/albert-huang/20th-anniversary-president-clintons-executive-order-12898-environmental-justice. Accessed December 7, 2016.

Further Reading

Jenkins, R. R., Klemicky, H., Kopitsz, E., & Marten, A. (2012). Policy monitor–US Emergency response and removal: Superfund's overlooked cleanup program. *Review of Environmental Economics and Policy, 6*(2), 278–297. Describes and evaluates a key component of the nation's response capability regulations to respond to actual and threatened hazardous releases, including deliberate releases by terrorists: the Superfund Emergency Response and Removal (ERR) Program.

Mendelsohn, R., & Olmstead, S. (2009). The economic valuation of environmental amenities and disamenities: Methods and applications. *Annual Review of Environment and Resources, 34*, 325–347. Reviews the evolution of our ability to estimate the economic value of environmental amenities and disamenities over the last four decades.

Sigman, H., & Stafford, S. (2011). Management of hazardous waste and contaminated land. *Annual Review of Resource Economics, 3*. A review of the hazardous-waste management from an economic perspective.

Additional references and historically significant references are available on this book's Companion Website: www.routledge.com/cw/Tietenberg

The Quest for Sustainable Development

The challenge of finding sustainable development paths ought to provide the impetus—indeed the imperative—for a renewed search for multilateral solutions and a restructured international economic system of co-operation. These challenges cut across the divides of national sovereignty, of limited strategies for economic gain, and of separated disciplines of science.

—Gro Harlem Brundtland, Prime Minister of Norway, *Our Common Future* (1987)

Introduction

Delegations from 178 countries met in Rio de Janeiro during the first 2 weeks of June 1992 to begin the process of charting a sustainable development course for the future global economy. Billed by its organizers as the largest summit ever held, the United Nations Conference on Environment and Development (known popularly as the Earth Summit) sought to lay the groundwork for solving global environmental problems. The central focus for this meeting was sustainable development.

What is sustainable development? According to the Brundtland Report, which is widely credited with raising the concept to its current level of importance, "Sustainable development is development that meets the needs of the present without compromising the ability of future generations to meet their own needs" (World Commission on Environment and Development, 1987). But that is far from the only possible definition. Part of the widespread appeal of the concept, according to critics, is due to its vagueness. Being all things to all people can build a large following, but it also has a substantial disadvantage; close inspection may reveal the concept to be vacuous. As the emperor discovered about his new clothes, things are not always what they seem.

In this chapter, we take a hard look at the concept of sustainable development and whether or not it is useful as a guide to the future. What are the basic principles of sustainable development? What does sustainable development imply about changes in the way our system operates? How could the transition to sustainable development be managed? Will the global economic system automatically produce sustainable development or will policy changes be needed? What policy changes?

Sustainability of Development

Suppose we were to map out possible future trends in the long-term welfare of the average citizen. Using a timescale measured in centuries on the horizontal axis (see Figure 11.1), four basic societal trends emerge, labeled A, B, C, and D, with t^0 representing the present. D portrays continued exponential growth in which the future becomes a simple repetition of the past. Although this scenario is generally considered to be infeasible, it is worth thinking about its implications if it were feasible. In this scenario not only would current welfare levels be sustainable, but also growth in welfare would be sustainable. Our concern for intergenerational justice would lead us to favor current generations, since they would be the poorest. Worrying about future generations would be unnecessary if unlimited growth were possible.

The second scenario (C) envisions slowly diminished growth culminating in a steady state where growth diminishes to zero. Each future generation is at least as well-off as all previous generations. Current welfare levels are sustainable, although current levels of welfare growth would not be. Since the level of welfare of each generation is sustainable, artificial constraints on the process would be unnecessary. To constrain growth would injure all subsequent generations.

The third scenario (B) is similar in that it envisions initial growth followed by a steady state, but with an important difference—those generations between t^1 and t^2 are worse off than the generation preceding them. Neither growth nor welfare levels are sustainable at current levels, and the sustainability criterion would call for policy to transform the economy so that earlier generations do not benefit themselves at the expense of future generations.

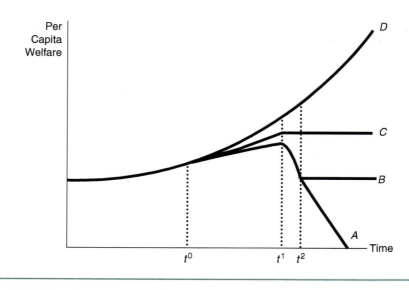

Figure 11.1 Possible Alternative Futures

The final scenario (*A*) denies the existence of sustainable per capita welfare levels, suggesting that the only possible sustainable level is zero. All consumption by the current generation serves simply to hasten the end of civilization.

These scenarios suggest three important dimensions of the sustainability issue: (1) the existence of a positive sustainable level of welfare; (2) the magnitude of the ultimate sustainable level of welfare vis-à-vis current welfare levels; and (3) the sensitivity of the future level of welfare to actions by previous generations. The first dimension is important because if positive sustainable levels of welfare are possible, scenario *A*, which in some ways is the most philosophically difficult, is ruled out. The second is important because if the ultimately sustainable welfare level is higher than the current level, radical surgery to cut current living standards is not necessary. The final dimension raises the issue of whether the ultimate sustainable level of welfare can be increased or reduced by the actions of current generations. If so, the sustainability criterion would suggest taking these impacts into account, lest future generations be unnecessarily impoverished by involuntary wealth transfers to previous generations.

The first dimension is relatively easy to dispense with. The existence of positive sustainable welfare levels is guaranteed by the existence of renewable resources, particularly solar energy, as well as by nature's ability to assimilate a certain amount of waste.[1] Therefore, we can rule out scenario *A*.

Scenarios *B* and *C* require actions to assure the maintenance of a sustainable level of welfare. They differ in terms of how radical the actions must be. Although no one knows exactly what level of economic activity can ultimately be sustained, the ecological footprint measurements discussed later in this chapter suggest that current welfare levels are not sustainable. If that controversial assessment is valid, more stringent measures are called for. If scenario *C* is more likely, then the actions could be less drastic, but still necessary.

Current generations can affect the sustainable welfare levels of future generations both positively and negatively. We could use our resources to accumulate a capital stock, providing future generations with shelter, productivity, and transportation, but machines and buildings do not last forever. Even capital that physically stands the test of time may become economically obsolete by being ill suited to the needs of subsequent generations.

One lasting contribution to future generations would come from what economists call human capital—investments in people. Though the people who receive education and training are mortal, the ideas they bring forth are not: knowledge endures.[2]

Current actions could also reduce future welfare levels, however. Fossil fuel combustion could modify the climate to the detriment of future generations. Current chlorofluorocarbon emissions can, by depleting the atmosphere's ozone, raise the incidence of skin cancer. The storage of radioactive wastes could increase the likelihood of genetic damage in the future. The reduction of genetic diversity in the stock of plants and animals could well reduce future medical discoveries.

Suppose that higher levels of sustainable welfare are feasible. Would our market system automatically choose a growth path that produces sustainable welfare levels, or could it choose one that enriches current generations at the expense of future generations?

Market Allocations

Market imperfections, including intertemporal externalities, open-access resources, and market power, create incentives that can interfere in important ways with the quest for sustainable development.

Allowing open access to resources can, and commonly does, promote unsustainable allocations. When resources are allocated by open access, even the existence of renewable resources cannot assure sustainability. Diminished stocks are left for the future. In the extreme, it is even possible that some harvested species would become extinct.

Intertemporal externalities also undermine the ability of the market to produce sustainable outcomes. Emissions of greenhouse gases impose a cost on future generations that is external to current generations. Current actions to reduce the gases will impose costs on this generation, but the bulk of the benefits would not be felt until significantly later. Economic theory clearly forecasts that too many greenhouse gas emissions would be forthcoming for the sustainability criterion to be satisfied.

While market imperfections normally do exacerbate the problem of unsustainability, the more general conclusion that they always promote unsustainability, however, is not correct. Markets can sometimes provide a safety valve to ensure sustainability even when the supply of a renewable resource is threatened. Fish farming is one example where declining supplies of a renewable resource trigger the availability of an alternative renewable substitute. Even when the government intervenes detrimentally in a way that benefits current generations at the expense of future generations, the market can in the right circumstances limit the damage by making substitutes available.

The flexibility and responsiveness of markets to scarcity can be an important component of the transition to sustainability, but the notion that markets would, if left to their own devices, automatically provide for a sustainable future is naïve, despite their apparent success in providing for generations in the past.

Efficiency and Sustainability

Suppose future governments were able to eliminate all market imperfections, restoring efficiency to the global economic system. In this idealized world, intertemporal and contemporaneous externalities would be reduced to efficient levels. Access to common resources would be restricted to efficient levels and excess harvesting capacity would be eliminated. Competition would be restored to previously cartelized natural resource markets. Would this package of policies be sufficient to achieve sustainability, or is something more required?

One way to examine this question is to examine a number of different models that capture the essence of intertemporal resource allocation. For each model the question becomes, "Will efficient markets automatically produce sustainable development?" The conclusion to be drawn from these models is very clear: restoring efficiency is *not* always sufficient to produce sustainability.

Take the allocation of depletable resources over time. Imagine a simple economy where the only activity is the extraction and consumption of a single depletable resource. Even when the population is constant and demand curves are temporally stable, the efficient quantity profiles show declining consumption over time. In this hypothetical world, later generations would be unambiguously worse off unless current generations transferred some of the net benefits into the future. Even an efficient market allocation would not be sustainable in the absence of transfers.

The existence of an abundant renewable backstop resource would not solve the problem. Even in this more congenial set of circumstances, the quantity profile of the depletable resource would still involve declining consumption until the backstop was reached. In the absence of compensating transfers, even efficient markets would use depletable resources to support a higher current standard of living than could ultimately be permanently supported.

In an historically important article, Dasgupta and Heal (1979) found a similar result for a slightly more realistic model. They assume an economy in which a single consumption good is produced by combining capital with a depletable resource. The finite supply of the depletable resource can either be used to produce capital or it can be used in combination with capital to produce the consumption good. The more capital produced, the higher is the marginal product of the remaining depletable resource in making the consumption good.

They prove that a sustainable constant consumption level exists in this model. The rising capital stock (implying a rising marginal product for the depletable resource) would compensate for the declining availability of the depletable resource. They also prove, however, that the use of any positive discount rate would necessarily result in declining consumption levels, a violation of the sustainability criterion. Discounting, of course, is an inherent component of dynamically efficient allocations.

In this model, sustainable development is possible, but it is not the choice made by markets, even efficient markets. Why not? What would it take to ensure sustainable allocations? Hartwick (1977) shows that the achievement of a constant per capita consumption path (which would satisfy our definition of sustainability) results when all scarcity rent is invested in capital. None of it should be consumed by current generations.

Would this be the normal outcome? No, it would not. Positive discount rates imply that some of the scarcity rent is consumed, thereby violating the Hartwick rule. The point is profound. Restoring efficiency will typically represent a move toward sustainability, but it may not, by itself, *always* be sufficient. Additional policies must be implemented to guarantee sustainable outcomes.

Not all economic models reach this discouraging conclusion. Specifically, a class of models with endogenous technical progress allows the possibility that efficient markets will produce sustainable outcomes. Endogenous technical progress means that the economic incentives inherent in the growth process produce a rate of technological progress that benefits future generations (remember that technological process shifts out the production possibilities). If the resulting rate is large enough to offset the declines to future generations caused by previous generations, efficient markets can produce sustainable outcomes.

Can we count on the fact that the endogenous rate of technological progress will be sufficiently high to generate a sustainable outcome? It is not guaranteed.

According to early work by Asheim (1994) and elaborated on by Pezzey (1994), we cannot. Rising net wealth can coincide with unsustainability when the capital stock is being valued at the wrong (i.e., unsustainable) prices. When nonrenewable resources are being used up too rapidly, prices are driven down by the excess current supply. Using these (artificially depressed) prices can create the false impression that the value of the depletion is less than the value of the additional investment and, therefore, that the value of the capital stock is rising. In fact, at the correct prices, the value of the capital stock may be falling.

Another study, by Howarth and Norgaard (1990), reaches a similar conclusion from a different perspective. They derive competitive resource allocations across generations, assuming that each generation is assigned a specific share of the available depletable resources. This share is then varied and a new allocation calculated for each to reveal the effect of this intertemporal assignment of property rights to resources among generations. For our purposes, two of their conclusions are relevant: (1) the resulting allocations are sensitive to the initial allocation of the resource rights across generations; and (2) assigning all of the rights to the first generation would not produce a sustainable outcome. This study provides yet another perspective underlying the conclusion that efficient allocations of depletable resources do not necessarily produce sustainable outcomes.

How about with renewable resources? At least renewable resource flows could, in principle, endure forever. Are efficient market allocations of renewable resources compatible with sustainable development? John Pezzey (1992) has examined the sustainability of an allocation of a single renewable resource (such as corn) over time. Sustained growth of welfare can occur in this model, but only if two conditions hold: (1) the resource growth rate exceeds the sum of the discount rate and the population growth rate; and (2) the initial food supply is sufficient for the existing population. The first condition is sometimes difficult to meet, particularly with rapid population growth and slow-growing biological resources. A main moral of this finding is that sustainable development of renewable resources is much harder in the presence of rapid population growth rates because the pressure to exceed sustainable harvest rates becomes harder to resist.

The second condition raises a more general and a more difficult concern. It implies the distinct possibility that if the starting conditions are sufficiently far from a sustainable path, sustainable outcomes may not be achievable without outside intervention. The simplest way to see this point is to note that a poor country that is reduced to eating all the seed corn to survive sacrifices its future in order to survive in the present. The double message that can be derived from these results is that (1) it is important to ensure, by acting quickly, that conditions do not deteriorate to the extent that survival strategies preclude investment; and (2) foreign aid is likely to be an essential part of sustainability policies for the poorest nations.

We must be careful to distinguish between what has been said and what has not been said. Restoring efficiency may well result in an improvement in sustainability, but efficiency may be neither necessary nor sufficient for sustainability. Three different cases can emerge. In the first case, the private inefficient outcome is sustainable and the efficient outcome is also sustainable. In this case, restoring efficiency will raise well-being, but it is not necessary for sustainability. This case might prevail when resources are extraordinarily abundant relative to their use. In the second case, the private inefficient equilibrium is unsustainable, but the efficient outcome is sustainable. In this case, restoring efficiency not only increases current well-being, but it is also sufficient to ensure sustainability. In the final case, neither the private inefficient outcome nor the efficient outcome is sustainable. In this case, restoring efficiency will not be enough to produce a sustainable outcome. Some sacrifice by current generations would be necessary to ensure adequate protection for the well-being of future generations.

While efficient markets cannot always achieve sustainable development paths, this does not mean that unsustainability would be the norm. Indeed, the historical record suggests that the incompatibility of the efficiency criterion and the sustainability criterion has been the exception, not the rule. Capital accumulation and technological progress have expanded the ways in which resources could be used and have increased subsequent welfare levels in spite of a declining resource base. Nonetheless, the two criteria are certainly not inevitably compatible. As resource bases diminish and global externalities increase, the conflict between these criteria will become intensified.

Trade and the Environment

One of the traditional paths to development involves opening up the economy to trade. Freer international markets provide lower prices for consumer goods (due to the availability of and competition from imported products) and the opportunity for domestic producers to serve foreign markets. The law of comparative advantage suggests that trade can benefit both parties. One might suspect (correctly) that as one moves from theory to practice the story would become a bit more complicated.

The Role of Property Rights. From our previous studies in this book, it should be clear that trade can certainly inflict detrimental (and inefficient) effects on the environment. One case is when some nations (presumably those in the less developed South) have poorly defined property rights or have not internalized their externalities (such as pollution). In this kind of situation, the tragedy of the commons can become greatly intensified by freer trade. Poorly defined property rights in the exporting nations encourage the importing nations (by artificially lowering prices) to greatly expand their consumption of the underpriced resources. In this scenario, trade intensifies environmental problems by increasing the pressure on open-access resources and hastening their degradation.

One example is the effect of trade on endangered wildlife such as elephants. The current approach to meeting this challenge involves a ban on ivory trading. Could a limited relaxation of that ban actually increase protection against elephant poaching? See Debate 11.1.

DEBATE 11.1

Would the Protection of Elephant Populations Be Enhanced or Diminished By Allowing Limited International Trade in Ivory?

Since elephant populations were being endangered by poaching and other illegal activities, in 1990 a cross-border ivory ban was imposed by CITES (the Convention on International Trade in Endangered Species). That ban has not been sufficient to solve the problem, since Central Africa lost 64 percent of its elephants in a decade.

One proposed change suggests allowing trade in ivory from stockpiled sources. Since no elephants are harmed in its collection, CITES considers this stockpiled ivory legal to hold, along with the ivory from elephants shot for justifiable management reasons (such as controlling problem animals).

The proposed trade would be based on regular auctions of legal ivory from African countries that have stable elephant populations and are motivated enough to organize credible recovery and stockpiling systems. The proceeds would be used to bolster currently unfunded elephant conservation programs. Buying countries would be limited to those that have transparent enforcement and are equally motivated to prevent illicit trafficking. CITES could revoke a country's selling or buying status at any time.

Opponents maintain that the assumption that the ivory collected from Africa's elephant populations through natural mortality and sustainable management practices can supply enough to satisfy demand is naïve. Currently, they note, the majority of African countries with elephant populations oppose the trade in ivory. If legal supply is based merely on supply from a handful of countries that support trade, other populations in countries that oppose trade will continue to be targeted and the illegal market will continue to thrive.

They further suggest that distinguishing between legal and illegal ivory trade is too difficult to manage as demonstrated by the fact that existing permitting and regulation systems clearly do not work.

Opponents also argue that what's needed is not reopening a limited ivory market, but better regulation and enforcement of the existing ban.

If you were on the CITES governing board, how would you vote? Why?

Sources: Scriber, Brad. (August 18, 2014). 100,000 elephants killed by poachers in just three years, landmark analysis finds. *National Geographic*. Available at: http://news. nationalgeographic.com/news/2014/08/140818-elephants-africa-poaching-cites-census/; Rice, Mary. (October 13, 2014). The case against a legal ivory trade: It will lead to more killing of elephants. *Environment 360*. Available at: http://e360.yale.edu/feature/counterpoint_the_case_against_a_legal_ivory_trade_it_will_lead_to_more_killing_of_elephants/2815/; Walker, John Frederick. (October 13, 2014). The case for a legal ivory trade: It could help stop the slaughter. *Environment 360*. Available at: http://e360.yale.edu/feature/point_the_case_for_a_legal_ivory_trade_it_could_help_stop_the_slaughter/2814/

Pollution Havens and the Race to the Bottom. The failure to control externalities such as pollution provides another possible route, known as the "pollution havens" hypothesis, for trade to induce or to intensify environmental degradation. According to this hypothesis, producers affected by stricter environmental regulations in one country will either move their dirtiest production facilities to countries (pollution havens) with less stringent environmental regulations (presumed to be lower-income countries) or face a loss of market share due to the cheaper goods produced in the pollution havens.

Pollution levels in the pollution havens can change for three different reasons: (1) the composition effect, (2) the technique effect, or (3) the scale effect. According to the *composition effect*, emissions change as the mix of dirty and clean industries changes; as the ratio of dirty to clean industries increases, emissions increase, even if total output remains the same. (Note that this is the expected outcome from the pollution havens hypothesis.) The *technique effect* involves the ratio of emissions per unit output in each industry. Emissions could increase in pollution havens via this effect if each firm in the pollution haven became dirtier as a result of openness to trade. And finally, the *scale effect* looks at the role of output level on emissions; even if the composition and technique effects were zero, emissions could increase in pollution havens simply because output levels increased.

In addition to suggesting a channel for degradation, the pollution havens hypothesis, if correct, could provide a justification for developing countries to accept lower environmental standards. In this view, lower environmental standards protect against job loss. In other words, it suggests a "race to the bottom" feedback mechanism where competitive incentives among nations force developing countries to keep environmental standards weak in order to attract jobs, and jobs move to those locations in search of the lower costs resulting from lower standards.

What is the evidence on the empirical validity of the pollution havens hypothesis and its race to the bottom implication? Early surveys of the empirical work, such as Dean (1992), found absolutely no support for the effect of environmental regulation on either trade or capital flows. Jaffe et al. (1995) reach the same conclusion in their survey of the effect of environmental regulations on US competitiveness. More recent studies reviewed by Copeland and Taylor (2004), however, have begun to find that environmental regulation can influence trade flows and plant location, all other things being equal, though the effects were still small.

Has there been a discernible exodus of dirty industries to developing countries? Apparently not. Studies that attempt to isolate composition, technique, and scale effects generally find that the composition effect (the most important effect for confirming the pollution havens hypothesis) is small relative to scale effects. Furthermore, in practice, technique effects normally result in less, not more, pollution (Hettige, Mani, & Wheeler, 2000). Though trade can increase pollution through the scale effect, these findings are quite different from what we would expect from a race to the bottom.

Actually, these results should not be surprising. Because pollution control costs comprise a relatively small part of the costs of production, it would be surprising if lowering environmental standards could become a major determinant of either firm location decisions or the direction of trade unless the costs of meeting those standards became a significant component of production cost.

The Porter "Induced Innovation" Hypothesis. The story does not end there. Michael Porter (1991), a Harvard Business School professor, has argued that more environmental protection can, under the right circumstances, promote jobs, not destroy them. Now known as the "Porter 'induced innovation' hypothesis," this view suggests that firms in nations with the most stringent regulations experience a competitive advantage rather than a competitive disadvantage. Under this nontraditional view, strict environmental regulations force firms to innovate, and innovative firms ultimately tend to be more competitive. This advantage is particularly pronounced for firms producing pollution control equipment (which can then be exported to firms in countries subsequently raising their environmental standards), but it might also be present for firms that find, in retrospect, that meeting environmental regulations actually lowered their production costs. Some specific instances of regulation-induced lower production costs have been recorded in the historic literature (Barbera & McConnell, 1990), but few studies have found the Porter hypothesis to be universally true.

While it seems clear that innovation induced by environmental regulation could simultaneously increase productivity (lower costs) and lower emissions, it is less clear why this would necessarily always or even normally be the case. And if it were universally true, it is not clear why all firms would fail to adopt these techniques even in the absence of regulations.

The Porter hypothesis is valuable because it reminds us that a particularly ingrained piece of conventional wisdom ("environmental regulation reduces firm competitiveness") can be wrong. It would be a mistake, however, to use the Porter hypothesis as confirmation of the much stronger proposition that environmental regulation is universally good for competitiveness.

The Environmental Kuznets Curve (EKC). Although its proponents have come to recognize the potential problems for the environment posed by free trade, particularly in the face of externalities or poor property right regimes in the exporting countries, they tend to suggest that these problems will be self-correcting. Specifically, they argue that as freer trade increases incomes, the higher incomes will promote more environmental protection.

The specific functional relationship underlying this view comes from some earlier work by Simon Kuznets, a now deceased Harvard professor, and so has become known as the Environmental Kuznets Curve. According to this relationship, environmental degradation increases with higher per capita incomes up to some income level (the turning point). After the turning point, however, higher incomes result in reductions in environmental degradation. Some apparent confirmation of this view came from early studies that plotted variables such as SO_2 concentrations against per capita incomes using countries as the units of observation (data points).

The notion that increasing income from trade involves a self-correcting mechanism would have quite a different meaning if part of that correction involved exporting the pollution-intensive industries to other countries. This would change the meaning of the Kuznets curve considerably since it would involve a transfer of pollution, not a reduction of pollution. This conjecture is especially important in a finite world because it implies that developing countries would never experience the Kuznets turning point. Since they would have nowhere to go, the pollution-intensive industries could not be transferred again.

How is the EKC relationship affected by trade? Cole (2004) examines this question and finds that explicit consideration of trade effects in estimating the EKC relationship does not eliminate the turning point for most pollutants, but it does affect the timing. In particular, controlling for the transfer of pollution-intensive industries makes the actual turning point occur later than without considering these effects.

How about the general proposition that pollution problems are self-correcting with development? In general, that proposition has little empirical support (Neumayer, 2001; Pasten & Figueroa, 2012). The early studies used different nations as data points, but the interpretation suggested that an individual country would eventually increase environmental protection as its income increased. Studies that looked specifically at how environmental protection varied over time as income increased within an individual country frequently did not find the expected relationship (Deacon & Norman, 2006; Vincent, 1997). Other studies found that it seemed to apply to some pollutants (such as SO_2) but not to others (such as CO_2) (List & Gallet, 1999; World Bank, 1992). And finally, as Example 11.1 illustrates, some case studies in countries that have experienced considerably freer trade regimes have generally experienced intensified, not reduced, environmental degradation.

What are we to make of this evidence? Apparently, environmental regulations are not yet a major determinant of either firm location decisions or the direction of trade. This implies that reasonable environmental regulations should not be held hostage to threats that polluters will leave the area and take their jobs with them; with few exceptions, firms that are going to move will move anyway, while firms that are not going to move will tend to stay whatever the regulatory environment.

When deterioration is caused by inadequate local property right regimes or inadequate internalization of externalities, it may not be necessary or desirable to prevent trade, but rather to correct these sources of market failure. These inefficiencies associated with trade could be solved with adequate property regimes and appropriate pollution control mechanisms. On the other hand, if establishing appropriate property regimes or pollution control mechanisms is not politically feasible, other means of protecting the resources must be found, including possibly restricting detrimental trade. However, caution must be used in imposing these trade restrictions, since they are a second-best policy instrument in this case and can even be counterproductive.[3]

While the foregoing argument suggests that the starkest claims against the environmental effects of free trade do not bear up under close scrutiny, it would be equally wrong to suggest that opening borders to freer trade inevitably results in a gain in efficiency and/or sustainability. The truth, it seems, depends on the circumstances, so pure ideology does not get us very far. The context matters.

Since new trade institutions are now emerging, new issues with enormous implications for the environment are emerging with them. Of particular interest are the environmental

EXAMPLE 11.1

Has NAFTA Improved the Environment in Mexico?

The North American Free Trade Agreement (NAFTA) took effect in 1994. By lowering tariff barriers and promoting the freer flow of goods and capital, NAFTA integrated the United States, Canada, and Mexico into a single, giant market. The agreement has apparently been successful in promoting trade and investment. Has it also been successful in promoting environmental protection in Mexico?

According to a study by Kevin Gallagher (2004), it has not, although not necessarily due to the forces identified by the pollution havens hypothesis. Some effects clearly resulted in less pollution and others more, although on balance, air quality has deteriorated.

The pollution havens hypothesis might lead us to expect a relocation of heavily polluting firms from the United States to Mexico, but that apparently did not happen. None of the numerous statistical tests performed by the author supported that hypothesis.

In terms of positive effects on air quality from trade, Gallagher found significant shifts in Mexican industry away from pollution-intensive sectors; the post-trade Mexican industrial mix was less polluting than the pretrade industrial mix (the opposite of what would be expected from the pollution havens hypothesis). He even found that some Mexican industries (specifically steel and cement) were cleaner than their counterparts in the United States, a fact he attributes to their success in securing new investment for more modern plants with cleaner technologies.

The largest trade-related source of air quality degradation was the scale effect. Although the post-trade industrial mix generally shifted away from the most polluting sectors (meaning fewer average emissions per unit output), the promotion of exports increased output levels considerably. Increased output meant more emissions (in this case, almost a doubling).

One expectation emanating from the Environmental Kuznets Curve is that the increased incomes from trade would result in more environmental regulation, which, in turn, would curb emissions. That expectation was not met either. Gallagher found that both real government spending on environmental policy and the number of Mexican plant-level environmental compliance inspections fell by 45 percent after NAFTA, despite the fact that income levels reached the turning point expected by the pretrade studies.

Source: Gallagher, K. P. (2004). *Free Trade and the Environment: Mexico, NAFTA and Beyond.* Palo Alto, CA: Stanford University Press.

consequences of international trade rules under the General Agreement on Tariffs and Trade (GATT) and the World Trade Organization (WTO).

Trade Rules under GATT and the WTO

The General Agreement on Tariffs and Trade (GATT), the international agreement that laid the groundwork for the World Trade Organization (WTO), was first signed in 1947.

That agreement provided an international forum for encouraging free trade between member states by regulating and reducing tariffs on traded goods and by providing a common mechanism for resolving trade disputes. Having now replaced the GATT forum, the WTO is the sole global international organization dealing with the rules of trade between nations.

As an organization devoted to freer trade, the WTO adjudicates disputes among trading nations through the lens of its effect on trade. Domestic restrictions on trade of any kind (including environmental restrictions) are suspect unless they pass muster. To decide whether they pass muster or not, the WTO has evolved a set of rules to define the border between acceptable actions and unacceptable actions.

These rules examine, for example, such things as "differential treatment." A disputed environmental action that discriminates against goods from another country (rather than holding imports and domestically produced goods to the same standard) is deemed differential treatment and is unacceptable. Disputed actions that are not the lowest-cost (and least injurious to trade) action that could have been taken to address the particular environmental problem are also unacceptable.

One of the most controversial rules involves a distinction between "product" concerns and "process" concerns (see Debate 11.2). At the risk of oversimplification, regulations that address product concerns (such as mandating the highest acceptable residual pesticide levels in foods) are acceptable, but regulations addressing the process by which the product was made or harvested (such as banning steel from a particular country because it is manufactured in coal-burning plants) are not acceptable. In the latter case, the steel from coal-burning plants is considered by the WTO to be indistinguishable from steel made by other processes, so the product is considered to be homogeneous and treating it as different is unacceptable.

The inability of any country to address process concerns in its imports clearly limits its ability to internalize externalities. In light of this interpretation, one way to internalize externalities in other countries would be to use means other than trade (international agreements to limit carbon emissions, for example). Another, as Debate 11.2 points out, is to use ecolabeling as a means of putting at least some market pressure on the disputed practices. How far that labeling can go without triggering a negative WTO ruling remains to be seen.

DEBATE 11.2

Should an Importing Country Be Able to Use Trade Restrictions to Influence Harmful Fishing Practices in an Exporting Nation?

Yellowfin tuna in the Eastern Tropical Pacific often travel in the company of dolphins. Recognizing that this connection could be exploited to more readily locate tuna, tuna fishermen used it to increase their catch with deadly effects for dolphins. Having located dolphins, tuna vessels would use giant purse seines to encircle and trap the tuna, capturing (and frequently killing) dolphins at the same time.

In response to public outrage at this technique, the United States enacted the Marine Mammal Protection Act (MMPA). This act prohibited the importation of fish caught with commercial fishing technology that results in the incidental kill or serious injury of ocean mammals in excess of US standards.

In 1991, a GATT panel ruled on an action brought by Mexico asserting that US law violated GATT rules because it treated physically identical goods (tuna) differently. According to this ruling, countries could regulate products that were harmful (as long as they treated domestic and imported products the same), but not the processes by which the products were harvested or produced in foreign countries. Using domestic regulations to selectively ban products as a means of securing change in the production or harvesting decisions of other countries was ruled a violation of the international trade rules.

The United States responded by mandating an ecolabeling program. Under this law, tuna caught in ways that killed dolphins could be imported, but those imports were not allowed to use the "dolphin-safe" label. Tuna caught with purse seines could only use the "dolphin-safe" label if special on-board observers witnessed no dolphin deaths. Disputes over some of the technical aspects of how this program is implemented are continuing.

Source: The official history of the case can be found at www.wto.org/english/tratop_e/dispu_e/cases_e/ds381_e.htm#top (accessed December 21, 2016).

Natural Disasters

One threat to sustainability comes from natural disasters such as hurricanes, floods, and wildfires. In its 2012 report The National Research Council notes:

> In 2011 the United States was struck by multiple disasters—including 14 related to weather and climate—that caused more than $55 billion in economic damages, breaking all records since these data were first reported in 1980. Nearly 600 Americans died, and many thousands more were displaced.

The report goes on to suggest that building a culture of resilience could reduce the nation's vulnerability to disasters as well as the costs they impose.

What exactly is resilience? According to the report, "Resilience is the ability to prepare and plan for, absorb, recover from, and more successfully adapt to adverse events."

How much difference could an increase in resilience make? A study conducted by the Multihazard Mitigation Council found that for every dollar spent on pre-disaster investments in resilience to prepare for earthquakes, wind, and flooding, about $4 were saved in post-disaster damages.

Readers of this book will recognize some of the strategies that could promote resilience. One involves providing better information to homeowners, businesses, and governments to apprise them of both the risks being faced and cost-effective ways of mitigating those risks. Another would be to implement policies that provide incentives for private risk reduction investments.

One instrument that can be used to promote resilience in the face of flood risk is flood insurance. A flood is one of the most prevalent and most costly types of natural disaster. In principle a well-designed flood insurance program could both reduce the economic damages caused and provide funds to lower the recovery time following a flood. With climate change intensifying flood risks, enhanced resilience could be very cost-effective.

As Example 11.2 points out, however, the policy has to be both well-designed and implemented appropriately if it is to be effective; otherwise it can end up increasing the damages. The devil really is in the details.

EXAMPLE 11.2

Enhancing Resilience Against Natural Disasters with Flood Insurance

Among other characteristics an efficient flood insurance design requires (1) premium levels high enough to cover the claims and (2) a structure of premiums that reflects the actual severity of the risk faced by the individual premium payers.

In the United States the National Flood Insurance Program (NFIP) was set up in 1968. NFIP flood insurance isn't mandatory, but homes and businesses in designated flood-prone areas must carry flood insurance to qualify for federally backed mortgages. Maps are used not only to designate areas that are flood-prone, but also to characterize their degree of risk.

Does this program meet the two efficiency tests? In a nutshell . . . it does not.

Premium levels have historically been too low to cover the claims. In 2016 the NFIP debt, resulting from claims exceeding premium revenue, was $23 billion. Furthermore attempts by Congress to raise premiums produced a backlash, resulting in a political inability to raise premiums to the efficient level.

An added factor involves the maps that are used to characterize the risk. Since climate change is intensifying flood risk, older maps necessarily underestimate the risk. Unfortunately the process of updating the maps has not kept pace, so underestimates are common.

Some problems with the structure of premiums have emerged as well. In efficient policy designs policy-holders who undertake measures that lower the risk to their structures should face lower premiums to reflect the lower risk. These premium discounts would provide the motivation for homeowners and businesses to reduce risks. As Kousky and Shabman (2016) report, the NFIP has been offering substantial premium reductions for elevating the structures, but not for other effective flood mitigation measures. As a result those other measures are underutilized and damages are higher than necessary. As a practical matter the program mainly enables people to rebuild in the same areas without doing enough to mitigate future risks.

One would expect that these incentives would lead to higher future claims.

A study by the Natural Resources Defense Council found that some 2109 NIFP-covered properties across the United States have flooded more than ten times, and the NFIP paid to rebuild them after each flood. One covered home has flooded 40 times and received a total of $428,379 in flood insurance payments.

The mere existence of a flood insurance program is not, by itself, evidence of efficient resilience.

Sources: National Research Council. (2012). *Disaster Resilience: A National Imperative.* Washington, DC: The National Academies Press; Kousky, Carolyn, & Shabman, Leonard A. (July 29, 2016). The role of insurance in promoting resilience. This blog is available at: www.rff.org/blog/2016/role-insurance-promoting-resilience; Moore, Rob. (August 11, 2016). Flood, rebuild, repeat: The need for flood insurance reforms. This blog is available at: www.nrdc.org.

The Natural Resource Curse

One especially intriguing possible barrier to development might plague resource-abundant nations. Common sense suggests that those countries blessed with abundant resource endowments would be more likely to prosper. In fact, the evidence suggests the opposite—resource-abundant countries are less likely to experience rapid development (see Example 11.3).

EXAMPLE 11.3

The "Natural Resource Curse" Hypothesis

Perhaps surprisingly, robust evidence suggests that countries endowed with an abundance of natural resources are likely to develop less rapidly than countries with a more modest natural resource base. And it is not merely because resource-rich countries are subject to volatile commodity prices.

Why might a large resource endowment exert a drag on growth? Several possibilities have been suggested. Most share the characteristic that resource-rich sectors are thought to "crowd out" investment in other sectors that might be more likely to support development:

- One popular explanation, known as the "Dutch Disease," is usually triggered by a significant increase in revenues from raw material exports. The resulting boom draws both labor and capital out of traditional manufacturing and causes it to decline.
- Another explanation focuses on how the increase in domestic prices that typically accompanies the resource boom impedes the international competitiveness of manufactured exports and therefore export-led development.
- A third explanation suggests that the large rents to be gained from the resource sectors in resource-abundant countries would cause entrepreneurial talent and innovation to be siphoned away from other sectors. Thus, resource-rich countries could be expected to have lower rates of innovation, which, in turn, results in lower rates of development.
- Finally, countries endowed with natural resources can give rise to domestic institutions in which autocratic or corrupt political elites finance themselves through physical control of the natural resources.

While countries with large resource endowments may not experience the development success that might have been expected, it is encouraging to note that lots of countries without large resource endowments have not been precluded from achieving significant levels of development.

Sources: Sachs, J. D., & Warner, A. M. (2001). The curse of natural resources. *European Economic Review, 45*(4–6), 827–838; Auty, R. M. *Sustaining Development in Mineral Economies: The Resource Curse Thesis*. London: Routledge; Kromenberg, T. (2004). The curse of natural resources in the transition economies. *Economics of Transition, 12*(3), 399–426; Frankel, J. A. (April 2012). The natural resource curse: A survey of diagnoses and some prescriptions. *Harvard Kennedy School Faculty Research Working Paper Series RWP12-014.*

The Growth–Development Relationship

Has economic growth historically served as a vehicle for development? Has growth really made the average person better off? Would the lowest-income members of the United States and the world fare better with economic growth or without it?

These turn out to be difficult questions to answer in a way that satisfies everyone, but we must start somewhere. One appropriate point of departure is clarifying what we mean by *development*. Some of the disenchantment with development can be traced to the way that development is measured. It is not so much that all growth is bad, but that increases in conventional indicators of development are not always good. Some of the enthusiasm for constrained economic growth stems from the fact that economic development, as currently measured, can be shown to have several undesirable characteristics.

Conventional Measures

A true measure of development would increase whenever we, as a nation or as a world, were better off and decrease whenever we were worse off. Such a measure is called a *welfare measure* and no conventional existing measure is designed to be a welfare measure.

In contrast the conventional measures of national accounting we currently use are *output measures*, which attempt to indicate how many goods and services have been produced, not how well off we are. Measuring output sounds fairly simple, but it is not. The measure of economic development with which most are familiar is based upon the GDP (gross domestic product). This number represents the sum of the outputs of goods and services produced by the economy in any year. Prices are used to weight the importance of these goods and services in GDP. Conceptually, this is accomplished by adding up the value added by each sector of the production process until the product is sold.

Why weight by prices? Some means of comparing the value of extremely dissimilar commodities is needed. Prices provide a readily available system of weights that takes into account the value of those commodities to consumers. From early chapters we know that prices should reflect both the marginal benefit to the consumer and the marginal cost to the producer.

GDP is not a measure of welfare and was never meant to be one. Therefore, increases in this indicator (growth) may not represent increases in development or well-being. One limitation of this indicator as a measure of welfare is that it includes the value of new machines that are replacing worn-out ones, rather than increasing the size of the capital stock. To compensate for the fact that some investment merely replaces old machines and does not add to the size of capital stock, a new concept known as net domestic product (NDP) was introduced. NDP is defined as the gross domestic product minus depreciation.

NDP and GDP share the deficiency that they are both influenced by inflation. If the flow of all goods and services were to remain the same while prices doubled, both NDP and GDP would also double. Since neither welfare nor output would have increased, an accurate indicator should reflect that fact.

To resolve this problem, national income accountants present data on *constant-dollar* GDP and *constant-dollar* NDP. These numbers are derived by "cleansing" the actual GDP and NDP data to take out the effects of price rises. Conceptually, this is accomplished by defining a market basket of goods that stays the same over time. Each year, this same basket is repriced. If the cost of the goods in the basket went up 10 percent, then because the quantities are held constant, we know that prices went up by 10 percent. This information is used to remove the effects of prices on the indicators; remaining increases should be due to an increased production of goods and services.

This correction does not solve all problems. For one thing, not all components of GDP contribute equally to welfare. Probably the closest, though still deficient, we could use in the existing system of accounts would be consumption, the amount of goods and services consumed by households. It leaves out government expenditures, investments, exports, and imports.

The final correction that could easily be made to the existing accounts would involve dividing real consumption by the population to get *real consumption per capita*. This correction allows us to differentiate between increases in output needed to maintain the same standard of living for a growing population and increases indicating more goods and services consumed by the average member of that population.

Real consumption per capita is about as close as we can get to a welfare-oriented output measure using conventional accounting data. Yet it is a far cry from being an ideal welfare indicator.

In particular, changes in real consumption per capita fail to distinguish between economic growth resulting from a true increase in income, and economic growth resulting from a depreciation in what economists have come to call "natural capital," the stock of environmentally provided assets, such as the soil, the atmosphere, the forests, wildlife, and water.

The traditional definition of income was articulated by Sir John Hicks (1939):

> The purpose of income calculations in practical affairs is to give people an indication of the amount they can consume without impoverishing themselves. Following out this idea, it would seem that we ought to define a man's income as the maximum value which he can consume during a week, and still expect to be as well off at the end of the week as he was at the beginning.
>
> (p. 172)

While human-created capital (such as buildings and bridges) is treated in a manner consistent with this definition, natural capital is not. As human-created physical capital wears out, the accounts set aside an amount called depreciation to compensate for the decline in value as the equipment wears out. No increase in economic activity is recorded as an increase in income until depreciation has been subtracted from gross returns. That portion of the gains that merely serves to replace worn-out capital is not appropriately considered income.

No such adjustment is made for natural capital in the standard national income accounting system. Depreciation of the stock of natural capital is by default therefore incorrectly counted as income. Development strategies that "cash in" on the endowment of natural resources are in these accounts indistinguishable from development strategies that do not depreciate the natural capital stock; the returns from both are treated as income.

Consider an analogy. Many high-quality private educational institutions in the United States have large financial endowments. When considering their budgets for the year, these institutions take the revenue from tuition and other fees and add in some proportion of the interest and capital gains earned from the endowment. Except in extraordinary circumstances, standard financial practice, however, does not allow the institution to attack the principal. Drawing down the endowment and treating this increase in cash flow as income is not allowed.

Yet that is precisely what the traditional national accounts allow us to do in terms of natural resources. We can deplete our soils, cut down our forests, and douse ocean coves with oil, and the resulting economic activity is treated as income, not as a decline in the endowment of natural capital.

Because the Hicksian definition is violated for natural capital, policymakers can be misled. By relying upon misleading information, policymakers are more likely to undertake unsustainable development strategies. Adjusting the national income accounts to apply the Hicksian definition uniformly to human-made and natural capital could, in resource-dependent countries, make quite a difference.

Motivated by a recognition of these serious flaws in the current system of accounts, a number of other industrial countries have now proposed (or in a few cases have already set up) systems of adjusted accounts, including Norway, France, Canada, Japan, the Netherlands, and Germany. Significant differences of opinion on such issues as whether the changes should be incorporated into a complementary system of accounts or into a complete revision of the standard accounts remain to be resolved.

Alternative Measures

Are we fulfilling the sustainability criterion or not? Although that turns out to be a difficult question to answer, a number of indicators have now been designed to allow us to make some headway. These indicators differ in both their construction and the insights that can be derived from them.

Ecological Footprint. One example of an indicator, the Ecological Footprint, differs considerably from the others in that it is based upon a physical measure rather than an economic measure. The Ecological Footprint indicator attempts to measure the amount of renewable and nonrenewable ecologically productive land area that is required either to support the resource demands or to absorb the wastes of a given population or specific activities.[4] The footprint is expressed in "global acres." Each unit corresponds to 1 acre of biologically productive space with "world average productivity." Every year has its own set of equivalence factors since land-use productivities change over time. By comparing this "footprint" to the amount of ecologically available land, deficits or surpluses can be uncovered.

This indicator calculates national consumption by adding imports to, and subtracting exports from, domestic production. This balance is computed for 72 categories, such as cereals, timber, fishmeal, coal, and cotton. The footprint (in terms of acres) for each category of resource uses is calculated by dividing the total amount consumed in each category by its ecological productivity (or yield per unit area). In the case of carbon dioxide (CO_2) emissions, the footprint is calculated by dividing the emissions by the average assimilative capacity of forests to find the number of acres necessary to absorb the pollutants.

According to this indicator, the industrialized nations have the most unsustainable consumption levels (meaning that their consumption requires more ecologically productive land than is domestically available). This analysis also suggests that current global consumption levels cannot be sustained indefinitely by the current amount of ecologically productive land—we are in a deficit situation.

The Genuine Progress Indicator. Another alternative indicator that has been developed is the Genuine Progress Indicator (GPI). While GDP is a measure of current production, the GPI is designed to measure the economic welfare generated by economic activity, essentially counting the depreciation of community capital as an economic cost. GPI starts with Personal Consumption Expenditures (a major component of GDP), but adjusts that data using 24 different components, including income distribution, environmental costs, and negative activities like crime and pollution, among others. GPI also adds positive components that are not included in the GDP, including the benefits of volunteering and household labor. Following an extensive analysis of the GPI both over time and across counties Kubiszewski et al. (2013) find a significant variation among these countries, but some major trends over the 1950–2003 period:

- "Global GPI/capita peaked in 1978, about the same time that global Ecological Footprint exceeded global biocapacity."
- "Life Satisfaction in almost all countries has also not improved significantly since 1975."
- "Globally, GPI/capita does not increase beyond a GDP/capita of around $7000/capita."

The Human Development Index. One reason for dissatisfaction with all of these measures of well-being is their focus on an average citizen. To the extent that the most serious problems of deprivation are not experienced by the average member of society, this focus may leave a highly misleading impression about well-being. To rectify this problem, in 1990, the United Nations Development Program (UNDP) constructed an alternative measure, the Human Development Index (HDI). This index has three major components: longevity, knowledge, and income.

Though highly controversial, because both the measures to be included in this index and the weights assigned to each component are rather arbitrary, the UNDP (2015) has drawn some interesting conclusions:

- Major progress has been made over the last 25 years, with 2 billion people lifted out of low human development levels. Between 1990 and 2014, the number of people living in countries with very high values of human development index more than doubled from 0.5 billion to 1.2 billion people, as 34 countries moved up to this category.
- Human development as measured by the Human Development Index (HDI) continues to improve, but at a slower pace. The HDI for developing countries grew by 1.2 percent annually between 2000 and 2010, but by only 0.7 percent annually for the period 2010–2014.
- Economic growth does not automatically translate into higher human development. For example, Equatorial Guinea and Chile have similar incomes but very different HDIs (0.592 and 0.847, respectively).
- The top five countries in rank order of HDI are: Norway [0.944], Australia [0.935], Switzerland [0.930], Denmark [0.923], and the Netherlands [0.922]. There are no changes from 2014 in these rankings. The bottom five countries in rank order of HDI are: Niger [0.348], Central African Republic [0.350], Eritrea [0.391], Chad [0.392], and Burundi [0.400].

Gross National Happiness. Bhutan is a small Asian country situated at the eastern end of the Himalayas. It shares borders with India and the People's Republic of China. In November 2008, the country adopted the Gross National Happiness index as an alternative to more conventional measures to guide its development strategy. This single number, Gross National Happiness index, which is based upon an extensive survey of the citizens of Bhutan, is based upon nine core *dimensions* that are regarded as components of happiness and well-being in Bhutan. The nine dimensions are as follows:

1. *Psychological well-being*
2. *Time use*
3. *Community vitality*

4. *Culture*
5. *Health*
6. *Education*
7. *Environmental diversity*
8. *Living standard*
9. *Governance*

Gross national happiness is deemed to have risen over time if sufficient achievements in these nine dimensions have been obtained. Since it is new, how well this index serves its intended purpose remains to be seen. Some results from 2015 indicate that overall fewer women are happy than men, people living in urban areas are happier than rural residents, single and married people are happier than the widowed, divorced, or separated, more-educated people are happier than their less-educated counterparts, and finally farmers are less happy than other occupational groups.

How important is money to happiness? It seems like a simple question, but that simplicity can be deceptive (see Example 11.4).

Summary

Sustainable development refers to a process for providing for the needs of the present generation (particularly those in poverty) without compromising the ability of future generations to meet their own needs.

Market imperfections frequently make sustainable development less likely. Intergenerational externalities such as climate modification impose excessive costs on future generations. Free access to biological common property resources can lead to excessive exploitation and even extinction of the species.

Even efficient markets do not necessarily guarantee development that can be sustained. Restoring efficiency is desirable and helpful but can be insufficient as a means for producing sustainable welfare levels. While in principle dynamically efficient allocations are compatible with the interests of future generations, in practice this is not necessarily the case. When trade is used as part of the development strategy, it must be used carefully. The effects of trade on the environment are neither universally benign nor universally detrimental. Context matters.

We have examined a series of indicators that attempt to shed light on the degree to which current national practices are sustainable. Though all of these indicators are both incomplete and flawed, they all convey some important insights.

The Ecological Footprint provides helpful reminders that scale does matter and that the earth on which we all depend is ultimately limited in its ability to fulfill our unlimited wants. Though the Ecological Footprint finding that we have already exceeded the earth's carrying capacity is controversial, it does usefully lay to rest the naïve view that our ability to consume is limitless and emphasize that we had better start thinking about how to stay within natural limits. The Ecological Footprint is also helpful in pointing out that affluence is fully as big a challenge to sustainability as poverty.

The Human Development Index reminds us that the relationship between income growth and the well-being of the poorest citizens of the world is far from a sure thing, in contrast to what some would have us believe. While national income growth can provide a means for empowerment for the poor, it can only do so when accompanied by appropriate policy measures, such as ensuring universal health care and education and limiting the perverse effects

EXAMPLE 11.4

Happiness Economics: Does Money Buy Happiness?

In recent years, economists and psychologists have become interested in what has become known as the economics of happiness. What is it that makes people happy and what role does income play?

A psychologist and an economist (Kahneman & Deaton, 2010) analyzed the responses of more than 450,000 US residents surveyed in 2008 and 2009 to several questions about their subjective well-being. Their results suggest a rather complex answer to this question, suggesting that it is sensitive to how well-being is measured.

The authors defined two rather different subjective measures of well-being.

- One measure, labeled "Emotional Well-Being," refers to the emotional quality of an individual's everyday experience—the frequency and intensity of experiences of joy, fascination, anxiety, sadness, anger, and affection that make one's life pleasant or unpleasant. In this study emotional well-being is captured by two variables. The first, which deals with aspects of positive well-being, sums three binary (1 or 0) variables measuring self-reported happiness, enjoyment, and frequent smiling and laughter. The second, capturing a "blue effect," takes the average of two binary variables, measuring stress and worry. All questions asked the respondent to respond relative to his or her experience the previous day.

- The second measure, which the authors label "Life Evaluation," has the respondent rate his or her current life on a ladder scale in which 0 is "the worst possible life for you" and 10 is "the best possible life for you." Unlike the previous measure, which focuses on a snapshot of feelings at a specific point in time, this question is a more overarching measure of well-being.

Before getting to the statistical results of how income affects these measures of well-being, consider some comparative observations revealed by these data. The authors found that most people were quite happy and satisfied with their lives. These results indicate that the US population ranks high on the Life Evaluation Index (ninth after the Scandinavian countries, Canada, the Netherlands, Switzerland, and New Zealand), and also does well in terms of happiness (5th), but much less well on worry (89th from least worried), sadness (69th from least sad), and anger (75th). Americans report very high levels of stress (5th among 151 countries).

In terms of income, the present study finds that "a lack of money brings both emotional misery and low life evaluation. . . . Beyond $75,000 (in 2008–2009) in the contemporary United States, however, higher income is neither the road to experienced happiness nor the road to the relief of unhappiness or stress, although higher income continues to improve individuals' life evaluations" (p. 16491).

Sources: Bruni, L., & Porta, P. L. (2005). *Economics and Happiness: Framing the Analysis.* Oxford: Oxford University Press; Kahneman, D., & Deaton, A. (2010). High income improves evaluation of life but not emotional well-being. *Proceedings of the National Academy of Sciences, 107*(38), 16489–16493.

of corruption. The Human Development Index identifies a number of low-income countries that have made great strides in ensuring that the fruits of development do reach the poor.

New sustainable forms of development are possible, but they will not inevitably be adopted. Economic incentive policies can facilitate the transition from unsustainable to sustainable activities. The search for solutions must recognize that market forces are extremely powerful. Attempts that ignore those forces are probably doomed to failure. Nonetheless, it is possible to harness those forces and channel them in directions that enhance the possibilities of sustainable outcomes. To take these steps will require thinking and acting in somewhat unconventional ways. Whether the world community is equal to the task remains to be seen.

Discussion Questions

1. Consider a possible mechanism for controlling population. According to an idea first put forth by Kenneth Boulding in 1964, each individual would be given the right to produce one (and only one!) child. Because this scheme over a generation allows each member of the current population to replace himself or herself, births would necessarily equal deaths and population stability would be achieved.

   This scheme would award each person a certificate, entitling the holder to have one child. Couples could pool their certificates to have two. Every time a child was born, a certificate would be surrendered. Failure to produce a certificate would cause the child to be put up for adoption. Certificates would be fully transferable.

   Is this a good idea? What are its advantages and disadvantages? Would it be appropriate to implement this policy now in the United States? For those who believe that it would, what are the crucial reasons? For those who believe it is not appropriate, are there any circumstances in any countries where it might be appropriate? Why or why not?

2. "Every molecule of a nonrenewable energy resource used today precludes its use by future generations. Therefore, the only morally defensible policy for any generation is to use only renewable resources." Discuss.

3. "Future generations can cast neither votes in current elections nor dollars in current market decisions. Therefore, it should not come as a surprise to anyone that the interests of future generations are ignored in a market economy." Discuss.

4. "Trade simply represents economic imperialism where one country exploits another. The environment is the inevitable victim." Discuss.

5. Suppose someone developed a high-quality synthetic ivory that could be used in products currently made from natural ivory. What effect might a legal trade in synthetic ivory have on the price of natural ivory? Would you support trade in synthetic ivory? Why or why not?

Self-Test Exercises

1. Because export taxes are frequently seen as falling on foreign consumers, they tend to be favored as revenue sources by many countries. What assumptions are necessary for export taxes to be borne entirely by foreign consumers? How likely is it that this set of assumptions characterizes the current world market for food commodities such as coffee or oranges?

2. If a natural disaster, such as the 2010 drought in Russia, hits food production, use supply and demand analysis to figure out how this affects consumers and producers. Does everyone lose or are some groups better off? Why?

3. Suppose the United States imposed a tariff on imported sugar. What are the consequences of this on consumers, domestic and foreign producers, and land use?

Notes

1   One study estimates that humans are currently using approximately 19–25 percent of the renewable energy available from photosynthesis. On land the estimate is more likely 40 percent (Vitousek et al., 1986).
2   While it is true that ideas can last forever, the value of those ideas may decline with time as they are supplanted by new ideas. The person who conceived of horseshoes made an enormous contribution to society at the time, but the value of that insight to society has diminished along with our reliance on horses for transportation.
3   Barbier and Schulz (1997) note a case in which a trade restriction designed to protect against deforestation from excessive export logging produced the opposite effect. Apparently the policy sufficiently lowered the value of the forest that the land was deforested to facilitate its conversion to agriculture.
4   The details about this indicator can also be found on the Global Footprint Network website at www.footprintnetwork.org/en/index.php/gfn/page/footprint_basics_overview/ (accessed December 21, 2016). Anyone can have his or her own ecological footprint calculated by answering a few questions at www.footprintnetwork.org/en/index.php/GFN/page/calculators/ (accessed December 21, 2016).

Further Reading

Copeland, B. R., & Taylor, M. S. (March 2004). Trade, growth, and the environment. *Journal of Economic Literature*, 42, 7–71. An excellent survey of the lessons to be derived from the theory and empirical work focusing on the relationship between trade and the environment.

Deacon, R. T., & Norman, C. S. (2006). Does the environmental Kuznets curve describe how individual countries behave? *Land Economics*, 82(2), 291–315. Examining time series data within countries, the authors find weak evidence of the existence of a Kuznets curve for SO_2 in wealthier countries, but no evidence for a Kuznets curve for other pollutants and for poorer countries.

De Soysa, I., & Neumayer, E. (2005). False prophet or genuine savior? Assessing the effects of economic openness on sustainable development, 1980–1999. *International Organization*, 59(3), 731–772. Estimates the effects of a dependence on trade and foreign direct investment on sustainability as measured by the genuine saving rate. They find openness enhances sustainability.

Fischer, C. (2010). Does trade help or hinder the conservation of natural resources? *Review of Environmental Economics and Policy*, 4(1), 103–121. This article reviews and takes stock of the lessons from the recent economics literature on the links between trade and the conservation of natural resources.

Frankel, J. A. (April 2012). The natural resource curse: A survey of diagnoses and some prescriptions. *Harvard Kennedy School Faculty Research Working Paper Series RWP12-014*. This paper reviews the literature on the Natural Resource Curse, focusing on six channels of causation that have been proposed.

Kubiszewski, I., Costanza, R., Franco, C., Lawn, P., Talberth, J., Jackson, T., & Aylmer, C. (2013). Beyond GDP: Measuring and achieving global genuine progress. *Ecological Economics*, 93, 57–68. A synthesis of estimates of GPI over the 1950–2003 time period for 17 countries for which GPI has been estimated and analysis of the results.

Layard, R. (2005). *Happiness: Lessons from a New Science*. New York: Penguin Press. Using integrated insights from psychology, economics, neuroscience, and sociology, a distinguished British economist explores the sources of human happiness.

Pasten, R., & Figueroa, E. B. (2012). The environmental Kuznets curve: A survey of the theoretical literature. *International Review of Environmental and Resource Economics*, 6(3), 195–224. This paper reviews and summarizes most of the literature on the Environmental Kuznets Curve.

Speth, James Gustave. (2016). Getting to the Next System: Guideposts on the way to a new political economy. The Next System Project Report #2. Available at: http://thenextsystem. org/gettowhatsnext/. A vision of how we might move toward a more "just, sustainable, and democratic future."

Additional references and historically significant references are available on this book's Companion Website: www.routledge.com/cw/Tietenberg

Chapter 12

Visions of the Future Revisited

Distinguishing the signal from the noise requires both scientific knowledge and self-knowledge: the serenity to accept the things we cannot predict, the courage to predict the things we can, and the wisdom to know the difference.

—Nate Silver, *The Signal and the Noise:*
Why So Many Predictions Fail—But Some Don't (2012)

Introduction

We have now come full circle. Having begun our study with two lofty, but conflicting visions of the future, we proceeded to dissect the details of the various components of these visions —the management of depletable and renewable resources, pollution, and the development process itself. During these investigations we gained a number of useful insights about individual environmental and natural resource problems. Now it is time to step back and coalesce those insights into a systematic assessment of the two visions.

Addressing the Issues

In Chapter 1, we posed a number of questions to serve as our focus for the overarching issue of growth in a finite environment. Those questions addressed three major issues: (1) How is the problem correctly conceptualized? (2) Can our economic and political institutions respond in a timely and democratic fashion to the challenges presented? (3) Can the needs of the present generation be met without compromising the ability of future generations to meet their own needs? Can short-term and long-term goals be harmonized? The next three segments of this section summarize and interpret the evidence.

Conceptualizing the Problem

At the beginning of this book, we suggested that if the problem is characterized as an exponential growth in demand coupled with a finite supply of resources, the resources must eventually be exhausted. If those resources are essential, society will collapse when the resources are exhausted.

These are big "ifs." We have seen that this is an excessively harsh and somewhat misleading characterization of the situation we face. The growth in the demand for resources is not insensitive to their scarcity. Prices matter.

Price is not the only factor that retards demand growth. Declines in population growth also play a significant role. Since the developed nations appropriate a disproportionate share of the world's resources, the dramatic declines in population growth in those countries has had a disproportionate effect on slowing the demand for resources. On the other hand, the rapidly rising consumption levels in high-growth, densely populated countries like China and India are having the opposite effect.

Characterizing the resource base as finite—the second aspect of the model—is also excessively harsh: (1) this characterization ignores the existence of a substantial renewable resource base and (2) it focuses attention on the wrong issue.

In a very real sense, a significant portion of the resource base is not finite. Plentiful supplies of renewable resources including, significantly, energy are available. The normal market reaction to increasing scarcity of individual depletable resources, such as oil, is to switch to renewable resources. That is clearly happening. The most dramatic examples can be found in the transition to wind, hydro, solar, and hydrogen fuel cells.

In addition, labeling the resource base as finite is also misleading because it implies that our concern should be with "running out." In fact, for most resources we shall never run out. Millions of years of finite resources are left at current consumption rates. For most of these resources the rising cost (including environmental cost) of extracting and using those resources is the chief threat to future standards of living, not the potential for their exhaustion. The limits on our uses of these resources are not determined by their scarcity in the crust of the earth, but rather by the costs of extracting them, including the environmental costs that accompany their use. The implications of climate change, including rising sea level, heat extremes, droughts, and storm surges, are potentially so severe as to force a major reevaluation of our carbon-based energy choices. Similarly, the loss of biodiversity, which would be intensified by climate change, could irreversibly alter our ecosystems and reduce their resilience to future shocks.

Resource scarcity can be countered without violating sustainability by finding new sources of conventional materials, as well as discovering new uses for unconventional materials, including what was previously considered waste. We can also stretch the useful life of existing reserves by reducing the amount of materials needed to produce the products or the services they provide. Striking examples include the diminishing size of a typical computer system needed to process a given amount of information and the substantially diminished amount of energy needed to heat a well-designed home.

For energy sources the issue is whether the transition to low-carbon fuels can proceed with sufficient speed and effectiveness so as to maintain economic well-being while preventing serious climate change damages. That question has been raised most starkly in the United States with the election of President Trump, who is dismantling the existing carbon-reduction policies and exiting the global agreement to hold this risk in check.

Paradoxically, some of the most obvious cases of intensifying scarcity involve renewable resources, rather than depletable resources. Demand pressure, whether driven by population growth or rising incomes, is a key contributor to this phenomenon. Expanding demand forces the cultivation of marginal lands and the deforestation of large, biologically rich tracts. The erosion of overworked soils diminishes their fertility and, ultimately, their productivity. Demand pressure can also contribute to the overexploitation of biological resources such as fisheries, even to the point of extinction. Trade can intensify these processes, especially when property regimes do not adequately protect the resources. For many resources the problem is not their finiteness, but the way in which they have been managed. It is important to recognize that "renewable" and "sustainable" are not synonyms.

Correct conceptualization of the resource scarcity problem suggests that both extremely pessimistic and extremely optimistic views are wrong. Impenetrable proximate physical limits on resource availability are typically less of a problem than the adverse atmospheric and biological consequences of their use. Transitions to renewable resources, recycled resources, carbon-free fuels, and more efficient use of resources have already begun. Whether the pace of the transition is sufficient remains to be seen.

Institutional Responses

One of the keys to understanding how society will cope with increasing resource scarcity and environmental damage lies in understanding how social institutions will react. Are market systems, with their emphasis on decentralized, profit-driven decision making, and democratic political systems, with their commitment to public participation and majority rule, equal to the challenge?

Our examination of the record seems to suggest that while our economic and political systems are far from infallible and have some rather glaring deficiencies, some serious flaws have been revealed by our historical experience, but no fatal ones . . . (yet?)

On the positive side, markets have responded swiftly and automatically to deal with those resources experiencing higher prices. Demand has been reduced and both substitution and reducing wasteful use have been encouraged. Markets for recycling are growing and consumer habits are changing. Green buildings with more efficient lighting and heating systems are proliferating. Renewable energy sources are being developed. Although government incentives may increase the pace, the government is typically not the principal driver. As long as property rights are well defined, the market system provides incentives for consumers and producers to respond to scarcity in a variety of useful ways (see Example 12.1).

As compelling as the evidence is for this point of view, it does not support the stronger conclusion that, left to itself, the market would automatically choose a dynamically efficient or a sustainable path for the future. Market imperfections frequently make sustainable development less likely. Treating resources such as the fish we eat, the air we breathe, and the water we drink as free-access resources can undermine their sustainable use. Left to its own devices a market will overexploit free-access resources, substantially lowering the net benefits received by future generations. In the absence of sufficient compensating increases in net benefits elsewhere in the economy, such exploitation could result in a violation of the sustainability criterion.

Externalities are also a barrier in the transition to sustainability. When many of the costs of using unsustainable resources are borne by someone other than those making the resource choices, private and social costs will not align and the market process will be biased. Only when the externalities are internalized can sustainable resources compete on a level playing field. The pressing need for an effective climate change policy is an obvious case in point.

Even efficient markets do not necessarily produce sustainable development. Restoring efficiency is frequently a desirable, but often insufficient means for producing sustainable welfare levels. While in principle dynamically efficient allocations can produce extraction profiles for depletable resources that are compatible with the interests of future generations, as we have seen in practice this is not automatically or even normally the case. The market

EXAMPLE 12.1

Private Incentives for Sustainable Development: Can Adopting Sustainable Practices Be Profitable?

Motivated by what it perceived to be great inefficiencies associated with its industry, the Interface Corporation, a carpet manufacturer founded by Ray Anderson, totally transformed the nature of its business. How it managed this transformation is instructive.

First, the company recognized that unworn carpet, usually under furniture, did not need to be replaced. In response, the company switched from selling traditional wall-to-wall carpet to selling a carpet tile system. Whereas, in traditional practice, wear in any part of the carpet meant that the entire carpet had to be replaced; with carpet tiles only those specific tiles showing wear are replaced. As an added benefit, the reduction in carpet replacement simultaneously reduces the amount of potentially harmful glue fumes being released into the indoor air.

Next, Interface totally changed its relationship with its customers. Rather than selling carpet, Interface leased it. In effect, it became a seller of carpet services rather than a seller of carpets. Carpet tiles can be easily replaced overnight by Interface employees, eliminating the loss of productivity that could occur from halting company activities during the day. The cost to consumers is substantially lower not only because less carpet is replaced but also because leasing allows tax advantages. Leased carpet is treated by the tax code as an expense, not an asset, and, hence, lowers taxes.

The environment also benefited. In traditional industry practice, most used carpet was transported to landfill. Much of the rest was remanufactured into much-lower-valued uses. Seeing that as a waste of resources, Interface created an entirely new product that, when recycled at the end of its useful life, could be remanufactured back into carpet. Not only was this production process less wasteful in terms of its drain on energy and raw materials, the product was also reportedly highly stain-resistant, four times as durable as regular carpet material, and easily cleaned with water.

These moves toward more sustainable manufacturing did not result from government mandates. Rather, an innovative company found that it could benefit itself and the environment at the same time.

The Interface story is a compelling one. Fifteen years after Anderson's initiative, Interface has:

- Cut greenhouse gas emissions by 94 percent
- Cut fossil fuel consumption by 60 percent
- Cut waste by 80 percent
- Cut water use by 80 percent
- Invented and patented new machines, materials, and manufacturing processes
- Increased sales by 66 percent, doubled earnings, and raised profit margins.

Source: Hawken, P., Lovins, A., & Lovins, L. H. (1999). *Natural Capitalism: Creating the Next Industrial Revolution*. Boston, MA: Little, Brown and Company; Anderson, Ray, with Robin White. (2011). *Business Lessons from a Radical Industrialist*. New York: St. Martin's Griffin.

does have some capacity for self-correction. The decline of overexploited fish populations, for example, led to the rise of private aquaculture. In this case the artificial scarcity created by imperfectly defined property rights gave rise to incentives for the development of a private property substitute.

This capacity of the market for self-healing, while comforting, is not always adequate. In some cases, government action to prevent the deterioration of the original natural resource base is both cheaper and more effective. Preventive medicine is frequently superior to corrective surgery. In other cases, such as when our air is polluted, no adequate private substitutes are available. To provide an adequate response, it is sometimes necessary to complement market decisions with regulatory actions.

The case for government intervention is especially compelling in controlling pollution. Uncontrolled markets not only produce too much pollution, but also they tend to underprice commodities (such as coal) that contribute to pollution either when produced or consumed. Firms that unilaterally attempt to control their pollution in the absence of regulations run the risk of pricing themselves out of the market. Government intervention is needed to ensure that firms that neglect environmental damage in their operating decisions do not thereby gain a competitive edge.

Significant progress has been made in reducing the amount of pollution, particularly conventional air pollution. Regulatory innovations, such as the sulfur allowance program and the California Global Warming Solutions Act represent major steps toward the development of a flexible but powerful framework for controlling air pollutants. By making it less costly to achieve environmental goals, these reforms can limit the potential for a backlash against the policy. They have brought perceived costs more in line with perceived benefits.

It would be a great mistake, however, to assume that government intervention has been uniformly benign. The acid-rain problem, for example, was almost certainly made worse by an initial policy structure that focused on local rather than regional pollution problems, and using MTBE as a gasoline additive to reduce air pollution ended up contaminating water supplies. While the former encouraged the export of pollution via tall stacks, the latter simply shifted the problem from air to water.

One aspect of the policy process that does not seem to have been handled well is the speed with which improvement has been sought. Public opinion polls have unambiguously shown that the general public supports efficient environmental protection even when it raises costs and lowers employment. Historically, as shown by the early regulation of automobile pollution, policymakers reacted to this resolve by writing very tough legislation designed to force rapid technological development.

Common sense suggests that tough legislation with early deadlines can achieve environmental goals more rapidly than weaker legislation with less tight deadlines. In the automobile pollution case common sense was frequently wrong. Writing excessively tough legislation with unreasonably early deadlines had the opposite effect. Those regulations were virtually impossible to enforce. Recognizing this situation, polluters repeatedly exploited this weakness by seeking (and receiving) delays in compliance. In this particular regulatory regime it was frequently better, from the polluter's point of view, to spend resources to change the regulations than to comply with them. This would not have been the case with less stringent regulations, since the firms would have had no legally supportable grounds for delay.

As in most things, however, the need is for balance. The message is *not* slow is always better. Sometimes timely responses are a crucial part of the efficient solution. The classic example is climate change policy, where analysis has made clear that delays in taking action will raise the cost.

Another flagrant example of counterproductive government intervention is to be found in treatment of both energy and water. By imposing price ceilings on natural gas and oil, the government removed much of the normal resiliency of the economic system. With price controls, the incentives for expanding the supply are reduced and the time profile of consumption is tilted toward the present. A similar story can be told about water. By holding water prices below the marginal cost of supply, water authorities have subsidized excess use.

In summary, the record compiled by our economic and political institutions has been mixed. It seems clear that simple ideological prescriptions such as "leave it to the market" or "let the government handle it" simply do not bear up under a close scrutiny of the record. The relationship between the economic and political sectors has to be one of selective engagement, complemented in some areas by selective disengagement. Each problem has to be treated on a case-by-case basis. As we have seen in our examination of a variety of environmental and natural resource problems, the efficiency and sustainability criteria allow such distinctions to be drawn, and those distinctions can serve as a basis for policy reform.

Sustainable Development

Historically, increases in inputs and technological progress have been important sources of economic growth in the industrialized nations. In the future, some factors of production, such as labor, will not increase as rapidly as they have in the past, at least in the developed world. The effect of this decline on growth depends on the interplay among the law of diminishing marginal productivity, substitution possibilities, and technological progress. The law of diminishing marginal productivity suggests slower growth rates, while technological progress and the availability of substitutes counteract this drag.

One view suggests that the development of new technologies such as self-driving cars and manufacturing robots will act as labor substitutes and, hence, will reduce the drag caused by diminishing labor supplies. Another view foresees limits to technological progress imposed by the second law of thermodynamics, implying that the growth process must culminate in a steady or stationary state where growth ultimately, but inevitably, diminishes to zero.

The economy is currently being transformed. It is not business as usual. The increasing corporate focus on sustainability is playing a role. Additionally, as citizens become better informed about the consequences of their choices, they are beginning to use their power as consumers, employees, shareholders, and voters to let companies know that they support business behavior that is compatible with sustainable outcomes.

Recognizing that conventional measures of economic growth shed little light on the question, some crude attempts have been made to estimate whether or not growth in the industrialized countries has historically made the citizens of those countries better off. Results of some of these studies suggest that because growth has ultimately generated more leisure, longer life expectancy, and more goods and services, it has, on balance, been beneficial. Yet, other measures, such as the ecological footprint, convey a more cautionary story. They remind us that our inability to measure precisely the earth's carrying capacity for supporting human activity in no way diminishes the existence and importance of those potentially existential limits.

Our examination of the evidence suggests that the notion that all of the world's people are automatically benefited by economic growth is naïve. Economic growth has demonstrably benefited some citizens, but that outcome is certainly not inevitable for all people in all settings. Expanding pollution and diminishing access to crucial resources such as water or land can offset or even more than offset the gains for at least some subset of the population. New sustainable forms of development are possible and desirable, but they will not automatically be adopted in either the high-income or the low-income nations.

The economic incentives approach to environmental and natural resource regulation has become a significant component of environmental and natural resource policy. Instead of mandating prescribed actions, such as requiring the installation of a particular piece of pollution control equipment, this approach achieves environmental objectives by changing the economic incentives of those doing the polluting. Incentives can be changed by fees or charges, transferable entitlements, disclosure strategies, or even liability law. By changing the incentives an individual agent faces, that agent can be encouraged to use his or her typically superior information to select the best means of meeting his or her assigned responsibility. When it is in the interest of individuals to change to new forms of development, the transformation can be amazingly rapid.

Public policy and sustainable development must proceed in a mutually supportive relationship. In some cases that relationship takes the form of public–private partnerships that involve explicit agreements between government and the private sector regarding the provision of public services or infrastructure (see Example 12.2). In other cases, it involves government regulatory action to ensure that the market is sending the right signals to all participants so that the sustainable outcome is compatible with other business objectives. Economic-incentive approaches are a means of establishing that kind of compatibility. The experience with the various versions of this approach used in the United States, Europe, and Asia suggests that allowing business great flexibility within a regulatory framework that harmonizes private and social costs in general is both feasible and effective.

EXAMPLE 12.2

Public–Private Partnerships: The Kalundborg Experience

Located on an island 75 miles off the coast of Copenhagen, the city of Kalundborg has achieved a remarkable symbiosis among the various industries that provide the employment base for the city. The four main industries, along with small businesses and the municipal government, began developing cooperative relationships in the 1970s designed to lower disposal costs, attain less expensive input materials, and receive income from their waste products.

A coal-fired power plant (Asnaes) transports its residual steam to a refinery (Statoil). In exchange, Statoil gives Asnaes refinery gas that Asnaes burns to generate electricity. Asnaes sells excess steam to a local fish farm, to a heating system for the city, and to a pharmaceuticals and enzyme producer (Novo Nordisk). Continuing the cycle, the fish farm and Novo Nordisk send their sludge to farms to be used as fertilizer. Produced fly ash is sold to a cement plant and gypsum produced by its desulfurization process is sold to a wallboard manufacturer. Statoil, the refinery, sells the sulfur removed from its natural gas to a sulfuric acid manufacturer, Kemira.

This entire process resulted not from centralized planning, but simply because it was in the individual best interests of the public and private entities involved. Although the motives were purely financial, this synergetic situation has clear environmental benefits. It is therefore likely to be economically, as well as environmentally, sustainable.

Sources: Desroches, P. (2000) Eco-industrial parks: The case for private planning, *Report # RS 00-1*. Political Economy Research Center, Bozeman, MT 59718; Kalundborg Symbiosis website: www.symbiosis.dk/en (accessed December 23, 2016).

How about global environmental problems? Economic-incentives approaches could be helpful here as well. Pollution pricing facilitates cost sharing among participants while ensuring cost-effective responses to the need for additional control. By separating the question of what control is undertaken from the question of who ultimately pays for it, the government significantly widens the control possibilities and lowers compliance costs. Conferring property rights for biological populations on local communities can provide an incentive for those communities to protect the populations. Strategies for reducing debt can diminish the pressure on natural resources that might otherwise be "cashed in" to pay off the debt.

Europe, British Columbia, and parts of Asia have more experience with effluent or emissions charges. This approach places a per-unit fee on each unit of pollution discharged. Faced with the responsibility for paying for the damage caused by their pollution, firms recognize it as a controllable cost of doing business. This recognition triggers a search for possible ways to reduce the damage, including changing inputs, changing the production process, transforming the residuals to less-harmful substances, and recycling by-products. The experience in the Netherlands, Sweden, and Japan, countries where the fees are higher than in most other countries, suggests that the effects can be dramatic.

Fees and auctioned allowances also raise revenue. Successful development, particularly sustainable development, requires a symbiotic partnership between the public and private sectors. To function as an equal partner, the public sector must be adequately funded. If it fails to raise adequate revenue, the public sector becomes a drag on the transformation process, but if it raises revenue in ways that distort incentives that, too, can act as a drag. Effluent or emissions charges and auctioned allowances offer the realistic opportunity to raise revenue for the public sector, while reducing the drag from more distortionary taxes. Whereas other types of taxation discourage growth by penalizing legitimate development incentives (such as taxing wages), emissions or effluent charges provide both incentives and revenue to support sustainable development. Some work from the United States suggests that the drag on development avoided by substituting carbon pricing for more traditional revenue-raising mechanisms, such as capital gains, income, and sales taxes, could be significant.

Incentives for forward-looking public action are as important as those for private action. The current national income accounting system provides a perverse economic signal. Though national income accounts were never intended to function as a device for measuring the welfare of a nation, in practice that is how they are used. National income per capita is a common metric for evaluating how well-off a nation's people are. Yet the current construction of those accounts produces information that can be highly misleading.

Rather than recognizing oil spills for what they are, namely a source of decline in the value of the endowment of natural resources in the area, under current accounting procedures cleanup expenditures increase measured national income; spills actually boost GDP! But the reason, of course, is that no account is taken of the consequent depreciation of the natural environment. The traditional system of accounts makes no distinction between growth that is based upon drawing down or degrading its natural resource endowment, with a consequent irreversible decline in its value, and sustainable development, where the value of the natural endowment remains intact. Only when suitable corrections are made to these accounts will governments be judged by the appropriate standards.

The power of economic incentives is certainly not inevitably channeled toward the achievement of sustainable development. They can be misapplied as well as appropriately applied. Tax subsidies to promote cattle ranching on the fragile soil in the Brazilian rain forest not only stimulated an unsustainable activity, but also imposed irreparable damage on an ecologically significant area. Incentive approaches must be used with care.

A Concluding Comment

Our society is evolving. When a complementary relationship among the economic system, the court system, and the legislative and executive branches of government can be maintained, we can make progress. As the high degree of partisanship in the US illustrates, however, we are not yet out of the woods. Significantly, not only must politicians learn to work together to produce bipartisan or nonpartisan solutions to our most pressing problems, but we the public must learn that part of the responsibility is ours. Solutions are unlikely to prevail without our significant participation and support.

Not all behavior can be regulated. It costs too much to catch every offender. Our law enforcement system works because most people obey the law, whether anyone is watching or not. A high degree of voluntary compliance is essential for the system to work smoothly.

The best resolution of the toxic substance problem, for example, is undoubtedly for all makers of potentially toxic substances to be genuinely concerned about the safety of their products and to bite the bullet whenever their research raises questions. The ultimate responsibility for developing an acceptable level of risk must rest on the integrity of those who make, use, transport, and dispose of the substances. The government can assist by penalizing and controlling those few who fail to exhibit this integrity, but regulation can never completely substitute for integrity. We cannot and should not depend purely upon altruism to solve these problems, but we should not underestimate its importance either.

We also need to recognize that markets serve our preferences as consumers. Making sure our purchases and investments reflect environmental values will help markets move in the right direction. Zero-emission automobiles will enter the market much faster if many consumers demand them. Sustainably harvested fisheries will proliferate once consumers shun fish from those fisheries that are managed unsustainably. It is easy to see large corporations as villains, but it is tougher to notice the villains in our mirrors.

The notion that we are at the end of an era may well be true. But we are also at the beginning of a new one. With foresight the decline of civilization can be avoided, but success will require its transformation. The road may be strewn with obstacles and our social institutions may deal with those obstacles with less grace and less finesse than we might have hoped, but we can make progress.

Discussion Questions

1. Are you optimistic or pessimistic about the future? Why?
2. In thinking about the appropriate balance between the market and the government in achieving sustainability, do you think the government needs to take a stronger role or would you favor reducing government influence over the market? Why?

Further Reading

Anderson, Terry, and Leal, Donald (Eds.). (2015). *Free Market Environmentalism for the Next Generation*. London: Palgrave Macmillan. This book provides a free-market vision for environmentalism's future, based on the success of environmental entrepreneurs around the world. It explores the next generation of environmental market ideas.

Hawken, P. (2010). *The Ecology of Commerce Revised Edition: A Declaration of Sustainability.* New York: Harper Collins. A classic in the field, this book makes the case for why business success and sustainable environmental practices need not—and, for the sake of our planet, must not—be mutually exclusive any longer.

Speth, James Gustave. (2012) *America the Possible: Manifesto for a New Economy.* New Haven, CT: Yale University Press. Speth presents a vison of the future from the progressive point of view. He finds that we have let conditions of life in America deteriorate across a broad front and are headed straight to a place we would not want for our children and grandchildren. He presents a vison of how we could chart a better course.

Answers to Self-Test Exercises

Chapter 1

1. A shortage would promote higher prices, thereby lowering demand until it equaled the new smaller supply. Since this acts to reduce rather than intensify the shortage, it is a negative feedback loop.

    If consumers anticipate these higher prices, however, thereby buying and hoarding extra amounts before the prices rise, this is an example of a positive feedback loop because it intensifies the shortage.

Chapter 2

1. a. This is a public good, so add the 100 demand curves vertically. This yields $P = 1,000 - 100q$. This demand curve would intersect the marginal-cost curve when $P = 500$, which occurs when $q = 5$ miles.
    b. The economic surplus is represented by a right triangle, where the height of the triangle is $500 ($1,000, the point where the demand curve crosses the vertical axis, minus $500, the marginal cost) and the base is 5 miles. The area of a right triangle is $1/2 \times$ base $\times$ height $= 1/2 \times \$500 \times 5 = \$1,250$.

2. a. Set $MC = P$, so $80 - 1q = 1q$. Solving for q finds that $q = 40$ and $P = 40$.
    b. Consumer surplus = $800. Producer surplus = $800. Consumer surplus plus producer surplus = $1,600 = economic surplus.
    c. The marginal revenue curve has twice the slope of the demand curve, so $MR = 80 - 2q$. Setting $MR = MC$, yields $q = 80/3$ and $P = 160/3$. Using Figure 2.8, producer surplus is the area under the price line (FE) and over the marginal-cost line (DH). This can be computed as the sum of a rectangle (formed by FED and a horizontal line drawn from D to the vertical axis) and a triangle (formed by DH and the point created by the intersection of the horizontal line drawn from D with the vertical axis).
    The area of any rectangle is base $\times$ height. The base = 80/3 and the

    $$\text{Height} = P - MC = \frac{160}{3} - \frac{80}{3} = \frac{80}{3}.$$

    Therefore, the area of the rectangle is 6400/9. The area of the right triangle is

    $$\frac{1}{2} \times \frac{80}{3} \times \frac{80}{3} = \frac{3,200}{9}.$$

$$\text{Producer surplus} = \frac{3{,}200}{9} + \frac{6{,}400}{9}$$

$$= \frac{\$9{,}600}{9}.$$

$$\text{Consumer surplus} = \frac{1}{2} \times \frac{80}{3} \times \frac{80}{3}$$

$$= \frac{\$3{,}200}{9}.$$

d. 1. $\dfrac{\$9{,}600}{9} > \$800$

2. $\dfrac{\$3{,}200}{9} < \$800$

3. $\dfrac{\$12{,}800}{9} < \$1{,}600$

3. The policy would not be consistent with efficiency. As the firm considers measures to reduce the magnitude of any spill, it would compare the marginal costs of those measures with the expected marginal reduction in its liability from reducing the magnitude of the spill. Yet the expected marginal reduction in liability from a smaller spill would be zero. Firms would pay $X regardless of the size of the spill. Since the amount paid cannot be reduced by controlling the size of the spill, the incentive to take precautions that reduce the size of the spill will be inefficiently low.

4. If "better" means efficient, this common belief is not necessarily true. Damage awards are efficient when they equal the damage caused. Ensuring that the award reflects the actual damage will appropriately internalize the external cost. Larger damage awards are more efficient only to the extent that they more closely approximate the actual damage. Whenever they promote an excessive level of precaution that cannot be justified by the damages, awards that exceed actual cost are inefficient. Bigger is not always better.

5. a. Descriptive. It is possible to estimate this linkage empirically.
   b. Normative. A descriptive analysis could estimate the impacts of expenditures on endangered species, but moving from that analysis to a conclusion that expenditures would be wasted requires injecting values into the analysis.
   c. Normative. A descriptive analysis could compare the effects of privatized and nonprivatized fisheries, but moving from these results to a conclusion that the fisheries must be privatized to survive normally requires an injection of values. If the data revealed that all privatized fisheries survived and none of the others did, the move to "must" would have a very strong descriptive underpinning.
   d. Descriptive. This linkage could be estimated empirically directly from the data.
   e. Normative. This statement could be descriptive if it was stated as "birth control programs actually contribute to a rise in population" since this is an empirical relationship that could be investigated.
      However, as stated, it allows a much wider scope of aspects to enter the debate and weighing the importance of those aspects will normally require value judgments.

6.   a.   A pod of whales is a common-pool resource to whale hunters. It is characterized by nonexclusivity and divisibility.

   b.   A pod of whales is a public good to whale watchers since it is characterized by both nondivisibility and nonexclusivity.

   c.   The benefits from reductions of greenhouse gas emissions are public goods because they are both nondivisible and nonexclusive.

   d.   For residents, a town water supply is a common-pool resource because it is both divisible and nonexclusive to town residents. It is not a common-pool resource for nonresidents since they can be excluded.

   e.   Bottled water is neither; it is both divisible and exclusive. In fact it is a private good.

Chapter 3

1.   With risk neutrality, the policy should be pursued because the expected net benefits (0.85 × $4,000,000 + 0.10 × $1,000,000 + 0.05 × –$10,000,000 = $3,000,000) are positive. Related Discussion Question: Looking at these numbers, do you think risk neutrality is how you would actually think about this situation? Or would you be more risk averse and weigh the third outcome more heavily than its expected likelihood?

2.   a.   Cost-effectiveness in this case (according to the second equimarginal principle) requires that that target be met (10 fish removed) and the marginal costs of each method be equal. We know that $q_1 + q_2 + q_3 = 10$ and that $MC_1 = MC_2 = MC_3$. The key is to reduce this to one equation with one unknown. Since $MC_1 = MC_2$ we know that $\$10q_1$ will equal $\$5q_2$, or $q_1 = .5q_2$. Similarly, $MC_2 = MC_3$, so $\$5q_2 = \$2.5q_3$ or $q_3 = 2q_2$. Substituting these values into the first equation yields $.5q_2 + 1q_2 + 2q_2 = 10$. So $q_2 = 10/3.5 = 2.86$ (to two decimal places.) That means $q_1 = 1.43$ and $q_3 = 5.72$. (The fact that this adds to 10.01 rather than 10.00 is due to rounding.)

   b.   All three of these methods have a marginal cost that increases with the amount removed. Thus the cost of removing the first fish for each is cheaper than removing the second fish with that method, and so on. Consider the marginal cost of removing the last fish if all fish are removed by method three. In that case the marginal cost would be $2.5 × 10 or $25. Notice that the cost-effective allocation, the cost of removing the last fish when the marginal costs are equal (using q_1 for the calculation) is $10 × $1.43 = $14.30. In the case of increasing marginal costs using a combination is much cheaper.

   c.   In this case you would only use method three because the marginal cost of removing each fish would be $2.5. This is lower than the MC for method 1 ($10) and lower than the MC for method 2 ($5). Note that the marginal costs only have to be equal for the methods that are actually used. The marginal costs for unused methods will be higher.

3.   Since the benefit cost test requires that the present value of benefits be greater than the present value of the costs, we can find the maximum allowable current cost by calculating the present value of the benefits. This can be calculated as $\$500,000,000,000/(1 + r)^{50}$ where r is either 0.10 or 0.02. Whereas with a 10 percent discount rate the present value is approximately $4.3 billion, with a 2 percent discount rate it is approximately $185.8 billion. Clearly the size of the discount rate matters a lot in determining efficient current expenditures to resolve a long-range problem.

Chapter 4

1. In order to maximize net benefits, Coast Guard oil-spill prevention enforcement activity should be increased until the marginal benefit of the last unit equals the marginal cost of providing that unit. Efficiency requires that the level of the activity be chosen so as to equate marginal benefit with marginal cost. When marginal benefits exceed marginal cost (as in this example), the activity should be expanded.

2. a. According to the figures given, the per-life cost of the standard for unvented space heaters lies well under the implied value of life estimates given in the chapter, while per-life cost implied by the proposed standard for formaldehyde lies well over those estimates. In benefit-cost terms, the allocation of resources to fixing unvented space heaters should be increased, while the formaldehyde standard should be relaxed somewhat to bring the costs back into line with the benefits.

   b. Efficiency requires that the marginal benefit of a life saved in government programs (as determined by the implied value of a human life in that context) should be equal to the marginal cost of saving that life. Marginal costs should be equal only if the marginal benefits are equal and, as we saw in the chapter, risk valuations (and hence the implied value of human life) depend on the risk context, so it is unlikely they are equal across all government programs.

3. a. The total willingness to pay for this risk reduction is $200 million ($50 per person × 4 million exposed people.) The expected number of lives saved would be 40 (1/100,000 risk of premature death × 4,000,000 exposed population). The implied value of a statistical life would be $5,000,000 ($200,000,000 total willingness to pay/40 lives saved).

   b. The program is expected to save 160 lives ((6/100,000 – 2/100,000) × 4,000,000). According to the value of a statistical life in (a), the program will have more benefits than costs as long as it costs no more than $800,000,000 ($5,000,000 value per life × 160 lives saved).

Chapter 5

1. In a cost-effective allocation of emissions reduction, the marginal control costs should be equal. So $200q_1 = \$100q_2$. Furthermore, the total reduction is 21 units, so $q_1 + q_2 = 21$. Solving the first of these equations for q_1 yields $q_1 - 0.5q_2$. Substituting this into the second yields $0.5q_2 + q_2 = 21$. Solving this for q_2 results in $q_2 = 14$ and $q_1 = 7$.

2. a. From the text we know $T = MC_1 = MC_2$. From Problem 1(a) we know $MC_1 = MC_2 = \$1,400$. Therefore, $T = \$1,400$.

   b. Revenue = $T(20 - q_1) + T(20 - q_2) = \$1,400(13) \times \$1,400(6) = \$26,600$.

3. a. The control authority would auction off 16 allowances (30, which is the current level of emissions, minus 14, which is the required reduction).

   b. The market-clearing price would be $4. Since demand would equal supply and marginal abatement costs would be equal for all firms, a $4 marginal abatement cost produces the required 14 units of reduction.

   c. With a $4 price, Firm 1 would reduce emissions by 7 units so it would need to buy 3 allowances. Firm 2 would reduce emissions by 4 units and hence would need to buy 6 allowances, and Firm 3 would reduce 3 units of emissions and therefore it would need to buy 7 allowances. Note that this produces the required 14 units of reduction and accounts for the 16 allowances that were made available by the control authority.

d. We know that the cost-effective allocation is achieved when the $MC_1 = MC_2 = MC_3 = \$4$. This allocation will be achieved with an emissions charge if the firms set their MCs equal to $4. Hence the required tax rate is $4.

Chapter 6

1. Imposing the same tax rate on every unit of emissions would normally be expected to yield a cost-effective allocation of pollution-control responsibility if the environmental target were specified in terms of aggregate emissions. In that case, cost-effectiveness requires the marginal cost of emissions reduction to be equalized across emitters, and that can be achieved with a uniform tax rate. A uniform tax rate would not, however, be compatible with a cost-effective allocation of each control responsibility if the environmental target were an ambient standard. In this case, you want the marginal costs of concentration reduction (not emissions reduction) to be equalized across emitters. Since the location of emissions matters in this case (not merely the amount of emissions), a uniform tax rate will not be cost-effective.

2. Permitting the allowances to be traded after the allocation occurs is the process that achieves cost-effectiveness, so this allocation (and any others that allocated the correct number of total allowances) would be compatible with cost-effectiveness. Any cost-ineffectiveness remaining after the initial allocation would be removed by the trading. However, if firms have advance knowledge that more permits will be allocated to those with higher emissions, this creates a cost-ineffective incentive to emit more during this interim period in order to qualify for additional allowances once the system begins. Since these additional emissions make the goal harder and more expensive to meet, costs are raised above the minimum.

Chapter 7

1. Taxes do have two advantages in achieving aggregate emissions reductions. First, by lowering the cost per mile traveled fuel economy standards can encourage more miles traveled. Gasoline taxes *increase* the cost per mile traveled. Second, fuel economy standards apply only to new vehicles, while gasoline taxes apply to the whole fleet of vehicles. Since new vehicles are only a small proportion of the fleet, taxes will likely produce a quicker result.

    Obviously, however, this advantage accrues to taxes only if implementing them is politically feasible and the tax rates are high enough to produce the desired change.

2. a. Labeling has the virtue that it seems to be politically feasible, and it can encourage a more fuel-efficient new vehicle fleet. However, it only affects new cars and it has no effect on how many miles the cars are driven. Furthermore, as we have noted in earlier chapters, labeling works best when it affects attributes that directly affect consumers. Saving energy certainly directly affects consumers, but some of the benefits of this approach, particularly those relating to national security and climate change, are externalities and are therefore probably not likely to be completely internalized by prospective purchasers. These disadvantages would compromise its effectiveness.

    b. Older fuel-inefficient vehicles do typically disproportionately contribute to the problem, and therefore they are a useful target of opportunity, but they are still only part of the problem. By itself, this strategy does not internalize the large number of other externalities associated with the purchase of new automobiles or reducing emissions from the fleet of automobiles that are not old enough to be affected by this program. Furthermore, many of these older automobiles are owned by lower-income households. Depending on how these vehicles are retired (not compensating owners, for example), taking away their transportation could impose a considerable burden on the poor (particularly the rural poor who have no mass transit option).

    c.   Pay-as-you-drive insurance *could* probably be a useful complement because, unlike the others, it focuses on internalizing some of the externalities associated with miles driven. Thus it addresses a component that would not otherwise be addressed.

3.   a.   From a social point of view, efficiency would require that the marginal premium per mile driven include all costs that are specifically related to miles driven. These would include potential accident damage, contributions to climate change (greenhouse gas emissions), and national security damages (stemming from import dependence).

    b.   A private company would be concerned about recovering the costs related to the claims it will have to pay out—accident damages, not the others. Internalizing the other damages would require the participation of the government.

Chapter 8

1.   The emissions charge equalizes marginal cost, a required condition for cost-effectiveness. The subsidies induce utilities to choose options with a higher marginal cost. By equalizing their after-subsidy marginal costs, utilities will minimize their outlays. This will not minimize total costs of control, since a greater reliance on carbon-capture technologies will result than would be cost-effective.

2.   High revenues in this context arise from a combination of high charges and large amounts of uncontrolled emissions. This circumstance arises when the marginal cost of control function rises steeply at relatively low levels of control. Since the charge is equal to the marginal cost of control, high marginal control costs imply a high charge rate. Furthermore, if the function rises steeply at relatively low levels of control, then there are large amounts of emissions to which this high rate of charge is applied. Multiplying a high charge times a large amount of uncontrolled emissions yields high revenues.

3.   a.   *Uncertain.* Although in most circumstances being discussed this would be true (since a tax would internalize the external costs associated with the damages caused by greenhouse gases), it does depend on the level of the tax. It is possible to set a tax rate so high as to force the benefits from its imposition to be lower than the costs.

    b.   *True.* Regional systems control only emitters in their jurisdictions, so unless all possible regions have control systems in place some emitters will remain uncontrolled. Leakage results from the flow of business from controlled entities to uncontrolled entities (because they can produce at lower cost and, hence, charge lower prices). This flow of business from controlled to uncontrolled emitters results in an increase in emissions that at least partially offsets the reductions achieved within the region. A truly global system that included all emitters in the same emissions trading system or facing the same greenhouse gas emissions tax would exempt no one and hence eliminate the problem of leakage.

4.   a.   Since $P_A = MC_A$ and $P_B = MC_B$ at the level of reduction where each domestic cap is met, the price would be $10 in Country A and $40 in Country B. Each country would be reducing 40 tons.

b. In the linked case $P = MC_A = MC_B$ because allowance can flow from one market to the other until the prices are equalized. Because Country A can abate at a fixed marginal cost of $10, that will be the MC and the price for both markets. (Can you see why?) Achieving the desired 60 tons overall reduction implies that Country B will abate 10 tons ($MC_B = \$1 \times 10 = \$10$) and Country A will abate 50 ($MC_A = \$10$) tons. Thus Country A would use 20 tons of its 50 ton abatement to satisfy its cap and export the remaining 30 tons of allowances to Country B. Country B would apply its 10 ton reduction to its cap and import 30 tons of abatement allowances from Country A.

5. Although the cooperative outcome would be collectively preferred, it is not the most likely outcome due to the free-rider effect. Although collectively nations would be better off if everyone cooperated, individual nations can well be better off if they choose not to join the agreement. This paradox about the divergence between individual and collective incentives can arise because nonjoiners can still obtain any of the benefits of the agreement and avoid the abatement cost obligations that accrue to those who join.

Chapter 9

1. a. The price would be $1,400. In the final allocation, the first source would control 7 units and would hold 13 permits, whereas the second source would control 14 units and hold 6 permits. The first source would have to purchase 4 permits—the 13 it needs to minimize cost minus the 9 it was initially given—at a total cost of $5,600. The second source would sell 4 permits, thereby moving from the 10 held initially to the 6 it needs to minimize costs, so it would gain $5,600 from the sale.

b. We know that in the final equilibrium, the marginal control cost will be equal. Since for the third source the marginal control cost is constant at $1,600, this will determine the final marginal control cost. The final permit price will be $1,600. The control allocation can be found for the first and second sources by choosing the level of control that yields a marginal control cost equal to $1,600. Thus $\$1,600 = \$200q_1$, so $q_1 = 8$ and $\$1,600 = \$100q_2$, so $q_2 = 16$.

The third source will have to clean up sufficient additional emissions to meet the target. Uncontrolled emissions were stated to be equal to 50. The first two sources would clean up 24 units, leaving 26 units uncontrolled. Since the target emissions level is stated as 19 units, the third source would have to clean up the remaining 7 units ($q_3 = 7$). The third source would have to purchase three permits since it received no initial allocation. Two would be purchased from the second source, and one would be purchased from the first.

2. a. With these *constant* marginal cost functions, cost-effectiveness is achieved by securing as much reduction as possible from the facility or facilities with the lowest marginal cost. In this case, that means securing the first 10 units of reduction from the first facility and the next 5 from the second facility.

b. The total variable cost in this case is simply the sum of the marginal costs for each unit of reduction. Therefore, the cost from reducing at the first facility would be $30 (10 units × $3) and the cost of the reductions at the second unit would be $20 (5 units × $4), so the total variable cost would be $50.

c. The total variable cost if all 3 facilities were forced to reduce 5 units would be $15 (5 units × $3) + $20 (5 units × $4) + $25 (5 units × $5) = $60. The extra $10 over the cost-effective allocation results from the fact that this allocation of responsibility substitutes 5 units at $5 for the 5 units at $3. The extra $20 per unit reduced accounts for the additional $10.

Chapter 10

1. One main difference in practice between an approach relying on performance bonds and one imposing strict liability for cleanup costs on any firm for a toxic substance spill is that the former requires money to be deposited in an escrow account before the operation commences. For the firm, the performance bond ties up capital for the period the bond is in effect, a cost it does not incur with strict liability. For the government, a performance bond assures the availability of funds to clean up the toxic substance immediately should the need arise. This availability can make a significant difference if the firm responsible for the spill turns out to not have sufficient funds to be able to fund the cleanup (this is known as the "judgment-proof firm" problem). In that case imposing strict liability would have little effect since the firm would be unable to fulfill its legal obligations.

2. Informing the consumer about any toxic substances used in the manufacture of a product is likely to represent a move toward efficiency for those risks actually borne by consumers. However, risks borne by the workers making the product or the workers recycling or disposing of the product after its useful life are externalities to the consumer, and informing the consumer is not likely to internalize those risks sufficiently to produce an efficient outcome.

Chapter 11

1. Export taxes will only be completely passed forward to the consumer if the demand is perfectly inelastic. In that case the consumer will simply pay the higher price (including the tax). If it is less than perfectly elastic, however, demand for that product will be reduced and the domestic producer will bear some of the burden in the form of lower sales.

   In world food markets it is unlikely that demand will be perfectly inelastic. Not only can consumers choose to consume less as the price rises, but they can switch to other suppliers or even to different food products.

2. A natural disaster, such as the 2010 drought in Russia, would shift the supply curve to the left and raise prices. Consumers would be unambiguously worse off as their net benefits would be reduced. Suppliers who lost their entire crop would be unambiguously worse off, but the effects on other suppliers could actually be positive. All of those suppliers (foreign suppliers, for example) whose crops were completely unaffected would be better off as the higher prices for their crops would raise their producer surplus. For suppliers that lost some, but not all, of their crops, it would depend on how the magnitude of the losses from the destroyed crops compared to the magnitude of the gain from selling the remainder at a higher price.

3. The US tariff on imported sugar would raise the domestic cost of sugar to domestic consumers, would cause a relative increase in their consumption of domestically raised sugar, and, it follows from that, a reduction in the amount of sugar imported from abroad. The increased profitability of the domestic sugar industry would allow it to compete for more land and other local resources. (To follow up on a specific example of this phenomenon, examine the controversies surrounding the effects of the Florida Sugar industry on the Everglades.)

Glossary

Absorptive Capacity—The ability of the environment to absorb pollutants without incurring damage.

Acid Rain—The atmospheric deposition of acidic substances.

Acute Toxicity—The degree of harm caused to living organisms as a result of short-term exposure to a substance.

Adjusted Net Savings—An indicator that attempts to measure whether an economy is acting sustainably when judged by the weak sustainability criterion. (Formerly called genuine savings.)

Aerobic—Water containing sufficient dissolved oxygen concentrations to sustain organisms requiring oxygen.

Age Structure Effect—Changes in the age distribution induced by the rate of population growth.

Agglomeration Bonus—A voluntary incentive mechanism that is designed to protect endangered species and biodiversity by reuniting fragmented habitat across private land in a manner that minimizes landowner resistance.

Alternative Fuels—Unconventional fuels such as ethanol and methanol.

Ambient Allowance System—A type of transferable permit system in which allowances are defined in terms of the right to affect the concentration at a receptor site by a given amount. This design can achieve a cost-effective allocation of control responsibility when the objective is to achieve a prespecified concentration objective at a specific number of receptor locations.

Ambient Standards—Legal ceilings placed on the concentration level of specific pollutants in the air, soil, or water.

Anaerobic—Water containing insufficient dissolved oxygen concentrations to sustain life.

Anthropocentric—Human-centered.

Aquaculture—The controlled raising and harvesting of fish. (Called "mariculture" when, as is the case with some salmon fisheries, the facilities are in the ocean.) Aquaculture can provide the opportunity to create a private-property regime for affected fisheries.

Asset—An entity that has value and forms part of the wealth of the owner.

Assigned Amount Obligations—The level of greenhouse gas emissions that ratifying nations are permitted under the Kyoto Protocol.

Asymmetric Information—A source of market failure that can arise when all of the economic agents involved in a transaction do not have the same level of information.

Automobile Certification Program—The testing of automobiles at the factory for conformity to federal emissions standards.

Average-Cost Pricing—When prices charged for resource use are based on average costs. (Sometimes used by regulatory agencies to ensure that regulated firms make zero economic profits, but it is not normally efficient.)

Base-Load Plants—Electric generators that produce virtually all the time. (They generally have high fixed costs, but low variable costs.)

Benefit-Cost Analysis—An analysis of the quantified gains (benefits) and losses (costs) of an action.

Benefits Transfer—Transferring benefits estimates developed in one context to another context as a substitute for developing entirely new estimates.

Best Available Technology Economically Achievable—A more stringent effluent standard than best practicable control technology, which has been defined by the EPA as "the very best control and treatment measures that have been or are capable of being achieved."

Bid Rent Function—This function relates the maximum price per unit of land as a function of distance from the urban center that would be offered for a type of land use such as residential or agricultural.

Biochemical Oxygen Demand—The measure of the oxygen demand placed on a stream by any particular volume of effluent.

Block Pricing—A form of pricing in which the charge per unit consumption is held fixed until a threshold is reached where a new per-unit charge is imposed for all consumption beyond the threshold. For increasing block pricing, the per-unit charge after the threshold is higher.

Bycatch—Untargeted fish that are unintentionally caught as part of the harvest of targeted species.

Cap-and-Trade System—A form of emissions trading where the government specifies a cap on emissions and allocates allowances to emission sources, either by gifting or auctioning, based upon this cap. These allowances are freely transferable among sources. Distinguished from the earlier credit form of emissions trading.

Carbon Tax—A policy that would control climate modification by placing a per-unit emissions tax on the carbon content of carbon-emitting sources.

Carrying Capacity—The level of population a given habitat can sustain indefinitely.

Cartel—A collusive agreement among producers to restrict production and raise prices. In this case the group tends to act like a monopolist and to share the gains from collusive behavior.

Chapter 11—A provision in the North American Free Trade Agreement that protects investors from government regulations that decrease the value of their investments.

Choke Price—The maximum price anyone would be willing to pay for a unit of the resource. At prices higher than the choke price, the demand for that resource would be zero.

Chronic Toxicity—The degree of harm caused to living organisms as a result of continued or prolonged exposure to a substance.

Clean Development Mechanism—An emissions trading mechanism set up under the Kyoto Protocol that allows industrialized countries to invest in greenhouse-gas-reducing strategies in developing countries and to use the resulting certified reductions to meet their assigned amount obligations.

Closed System—No inputs enter the system, and no outputs leave the system.

Coase Theorem—A remarkable proposition, named after Nobel Laureate Ronald Coase, that suggests that in the absence of transaction costs, an efficient allocation will result regardless of the property rule chosen by the court.

Cobweb Model—A theory in which long lags between planting decisions and harvest can influence farmers' production decisions in such a way as to intensify or dampen price fluctuations.

Command and Control—Controlling pollution via a system of government-mandated legal restrictions. Under this approach the government has the responsibility not only for setting the environmental targets, but also for allocating the source-specific responsibilities for meeting those targets.

Common-Pool Resource—A resource that is shared among several users.

Common-Property Regimes—A property rights system in which resources are managed collectively by a group.

Community Land Trust—An organization set up to acquire and hold land for the benefit of a community. Frequently used to provide affordable access to land for members of the community.

Comparative Advantage—In trade theory a comparative advantage prevails for products that have the lowest opportunity cost of production.

Compensating Variation—A method for evaluating the welfare effects of a price increase. It is the increase in income it would take to make the consumer as well off as he or she was before the price increase.

Competitive Equilibrium—The resource allocation at which supply and demand are equal when all agents are price takers.

Composite Asset—An asset made up of many interrelated parts.

Composition of Demand Effect—Shifts in demand brought about by changes in the relative cost of inputs. (For example, rising costs of ores coupled with stable prices for recycled inputs could make the products of firms relying more heavily on recycled inputs relatively less expensive and hence more attractive to consumers.)

Congestion Externalities—Higher costs imposed on others resulting from an attempt to use resources at a higher-than-optimal capacity. Commonly used with reference to traffic flows.

Congestion Pricing—Charging higher tolls during peak hours to discourage vehicle traffic (and the resulting air pollution) and encourage public transit ridership.

Conjoint Analysis—A survey-based technique that derives willingness to pay by having respondents choose between alternate states of the world where each state of the world has a specified set of attributes and a price.

Conjunctive Use—The combined management of surface and groundwater to optimize their joint use and to minimize the adverse effects of excessive reliance on a single source.

Conservation Easements—Legal agreements between landowners and land trusts or government agencies that permanently limit uses of land in specifically defined ways in order to protect its conservation value.

Constant Dollar—Output measures that have been purged of increases due to price rises.

Consumer Surplus—The value of a good or service to consumers above the price they have to pay for it. Calculated as the area under the demand curve that lies above the price.

Consumption—The amount of goods and services consumed by households.

Consumptive Use—In water law this refers to water that is removed from the source without any return.

Contingent Ranking—A valuation technique that asks respondents to rank alternative situations involving different levels of environmental amenity (or risk). These rankings can then be used to establish trade-offs between more of the environmental amenity (or risk) and less (or more) of other goods that can be expressed in monetary terms.

Contingent Valuation—A survey method used to ascertain willingness to pay for services or environmental amenities.

Conventional Pollutants—Relatively common substances found in most parts of the country, and presumed to be dangerous only in high concentrations.

Corporate Average Fuel Economy (CAFE) Standards—Minimum average miles-per-gallon standards imposed on each auto manufacturer for new vehicles sold in a specific vehicle class. Autos are in one class and SUVs and light trucks in another.

Criteria Pollutants—Conventional air pollutants with ambient standards set by the Environmental Protection Agency (includes sulfur oxides, particulate matter, carbon monoxide, ozone, nitrogen dioxide, and lead).

Current Reserves—Known resources that can profitably be extracted at current prices.

Damped Oscillation—In the absence of further supply shocks, the amplitude of price and quantity fluctuations decreases to the point of equilibrium.

Debt–Nature Swap—The purchase and cancellation of developing-country debt in exchange for environmentally related action on the part of the debtor nation.

Deep Ecology—The view that the environment has an intrinsic value, a value that is independent of human interests.

Degradable—Pollutants that are capable of being decomposed chemically or biologically.

Demand Curve—A function that relates the quantity of a commodity or service consumers wish to purchase to the price of that commodity.

Deposition—Pollution that transfers from the air to the earth's surface (land or water).

Development Impact Fees—One-time charges designed to cover the additional public service costs of new development.

Differentiated Regulation—Imposing more stringent regulations on one class of sources (such as new vehicles) than on others (such as used vehicles).

Discount Rate—The rate used to convert a stream of benefits and/or costs into its present value.

Dissolved Oxygen—Oxygen that naturally occurs in water and is usable by living organisms.

Divisible Consumption—One person's consumption of a good diminishes the amount available for others. (For example, if I use some timber to build my house, you receive no benefits from that timber.)

Double Dividend—A second welfare advantage that accrues to revenue-raising pollution control policy instruments (over and above the welfare gain due to pollution reduction) when the revenue is used to reduce distortionary taxes (thereby reducing the welfare losses associated with those taxes).

Downward Spiral Hypothesis—A positive feedback loop in which increasing population triggers a cycle of sustained, reinforced environmental degradation.

Dry Deposition—Occurs when air pollutants get heavy and fall to the earth's surface (land or water) as dry particles.

Dynamic Efficiency—The chief normative economic criterion for choosing among various allocations occurring at different points in time. An allocation satisfies the dynamic efficiency criterion if it maximizes the present value of net benefits that could be received from all possible ways of allocating those resources over time.

Dynamic Efficient Sustained Yield—The sustained yield that produces the highest present value of net benefits.

Ecological Footprint—A sustainability indicator that attempts to measure the amount of ecologically productive land that is required to support the resource demands and absorb the wastes of a given population and their economic activities.

Economies of Scale—The percentage increase in output exceeds the percentage increase in all inputs. Equivalently, average cost falls as output expands.

Ecosystem Services—Services supplied by nature that directly benefit at least one person.

Ecotourism—A form of tourism that appeals to ecologically minded travelers. It can serve as a source of revenue to protect the local ecosystem.

Efficient Pricing—A system of prices that supports an efficient allocation of resources. Generally, efficient pricing is achieved when prices are equal to total marginal cost.

Emission Charge—A charge levied on emitters for each unit of a pollutant emitted into the air or water.

Emission Standard—A legal limit placed on the amount of a pollutant an individual source may emit.

Emissions Allowance System—A type of transferable permit system in which the permits are defined in terms of the right to emit a stipulated amount of emissions. This design can be used to achieve a cost-effective allocation of control responsibility for uniformly mixed pollutants.

Emissions Banking—Firms are allowed to store emissions reduction credits or allowances for subsequent use or sale.

Emissions Reduction Credit (ERC)—Part of a transferable permits system. Any source reducing emissions beyond required levels can receive a credit for excess reductions. These can be banked for future use or sold to other sources.

Emissions Trading—An economic incentive-based alternative to the command-and-control approach to pollution control. Under emissions trading, a regulatory agency specifies an allowable level of pollution that will be tolerated and allocates emission authorizations among sources of pollution. Total emissions authorized by these allowances cannot exceed the allowable level. Pollution sources are free to buy, sell, or otherwise trade allowances.

Energy Efficiency Investment—An investment that is designed to reduce the amount of energy input required to supply a given amount of useful energy services such as lighting or heating.

Enforceability—Property rights should be secure from involuntary seizure or encroachment from others.

Entropy—Amount of energy not available for work.

Environmental Kuznets Curve—An empirical relationship that shows environmental degradation first increasing, then decreasing, as per capita income increases.

Environmental Sustainability—This definition of sustainability is fulfilled if the physical stocks of designated resources do not decline over time.

Equivalent Variation—A method for evaluating the welfare effects of a price increase. It is the reduction in income that would leave a consumer indifferent between accepting the income reduction or accepting the price increase.

Estate Tax—A tax paid on the fair market value of property after the owner's death.

Eutrophic—A body of water containing an excess of nutrients.

E-Waste—Waste involving used electronics such as TVs, tablets, or mobile phones.

Exclusivity—All benefits and costs accrued as a result of owning and using the resources should accrue to the owner, and only the owner, either directly or indirectly by sale to others.

Expected Present Value of Net Benefits—The sum over possible outcomes of the present value of net benefits for a policy, where each future outcome is weighted by its probability of occurrence.

Expected Value—In situations where the value of a resource depends on which of several outcomes might prevail, the expected value of a resource is the sum over all outcomes of the likelihood of each outcome multiplied by the value that would prevail in that outcome.

Extended Producer Responsibility—The belief that manufacturers of products should have the responsibility to take the packaging and the products back at the end of their useful lives in order to promote efficient packaging and recycling. (Also called the "take-back" principle.)

External Diseconomy—The affected party is damaged by an externality. (For example, my well is polluted by chemicals from a factory next door.)

External Economy—The affected party is benefited by an externality. (For example, my neighbor decides not to develop a wetland that serves as a recharge area for my water supply.)

Externality—The welfare of some agent, either a firm or household, depends on the activities of some other agent. The externality can take the form of either an external economy or external diseconomy.

Feebates—A system that combines taxes on purchases of new high-emitting vehicles with subsidies for new purchases of low-emitting vehicles. The revenue from the taxes is supposed to serve as the primary source of funding for the subsidies.

Feedback Loop—A closed path that connects an action to its effect on the surrounding conditions that, in turn, can influence further action.

First Law of Thermodynamics—Neither energy nor matter can be created or destroyed.

Fixed Cost—Costs that do not vary with output.

Fleet Average Standard—Used in the Corporate Average Fuel Economy Standards, this standard is imposed on the sales weighted average of vehicles sold rather than forcing every vehicle to meet it.

Free-Rider Effect—When a good exhibits both the consumptive indivisibility and non-excludability properties, consumers may enjoy the benefits of goods purchased by others without paying anything themselves. (For example, countries that decide not to take any steps to control global warming can "free ride" on the steps taken by others.)

Fuel-Economy Standards—A government program that mandates how many miles per gallon a manufacturer's new cars must achieve by specific deadlines.

Full-Cost Pricing—In water management this pricing system seeks to recover not only all of the costs of providing water and sewer services but also the cost of replacing the depreciated capital in older water systems.

Fund Pollutants—Pollutants for which the environment has some absorptive capacity; if the rate of emission exceeds this capacity, then fund pollutants accumulate.

Gaia Hypothesis—An example of a negative feedback loop suggesting that, within limits, the world is a living organism with a complex feedback system that seeks an optimal physical and chemical environment.

Genetically Modified Organisms—A term that designates crops that carry new traits that have been inserted through advanced genetic engineering methods involving the manipulation of DNA.

Genuine Progress Indicator—A sustainability indicator that attempts to establish the trend of well-being over time by taking into account the effects of development on resource depletion, pollution damage, and distribution of income.

Global Environmental Facility—An international organization, loosely connected to the World Bank, that provides loans and grants to developing countries to facilitate projects that contribute to solving such global problems as protecting the oceans, preserving biodiversity, protecting the ozone layer, and controlling climate modification. The fund uses the "marginal external cost" rule to allocate funds.

Government Failure—An inefficiency produced by some government action.

Greenhouse Gases—Global pollutants that contribute to climate modification by absorbing the long-wave (infrared) radiation, thereby trapping heat that would otherwise radiate into space. (Includes carbon dioxide, methane, and chlorofluorocarbons, among others.)

Green Paradox—An effect that occurs when a program which is designed to reduce emissions, paradoxically either speeds up the flow of emissions or increases the total amount of emissions.

Groundwater—Subsurface water that occurs beneath a water table in soils, rocks, or fully saturated geological formations.

Groundwater Contamination—Pollution that leaches into a water-saturated region.

Hartwick Rule—The weak sustainability criterion can be fulfilled if all scarcity rent from depletable resources is invested in capital.

Health Threshold—A standard to be defined with a margin of safety sufficiently high that no adverse health effects would be suffered by any member of the population as long as the pollutant concentration is no higher than the standard.

Hedonic Property Values—The values of environmental amenities (or risks) that are determined from differences in the values of property exposed to different levels of the amenities (or risks).

Hedonic Wage Studies—A valuation technique that allows the value of an environmental amenity (or risk) to be determined from differences in the values of wages paid to workers exposed to different levels of the amenity (or risk).

High-Grading—Discarding low-value fish such as juveniles in favor of high-value fish in order to increase the income derived from a harvest quota.

Host Fees—Fees collected from disposers that are used to compensate a community hosting a regional landfill. Designed to increase the willingness of communities to host these facilities.

Human Development Index—A socioeconomic indicator constructed by the United Nations Development Program that is based upon longevity, knowledge, and income.

Hypothetical Bias—Ill-considered responses that may arise in surveys based on contrived rather than actual situations or choices.

Impact Analysis—An analysis that attempts to make explicit, to the extent possible, the consequences of proposed actions. May mix quantitative with qualitative information and monetized with nonmonetized information.

Income Elasticity—Measures the percentage change in demand for commodities or services in response to a 1 percent change in income.

Individual Transferable Quotas (ITQs)—A means of protecting a fishery and the income derived from it by limiting the number of fish caught. Individual fishermen are allocated quotas that entitle them to portions of the authorized total allowable catch. These quotas can be transferred to other fishermen or used to legalize their harvest.

Indivisible Consumption—One person's consumption of a good does not diminish the amount available for others. (For example, the benefits I receive from controlling greenhouse gases do not diminish the benefits you receive.)

Information Bias—Arises when contingent valuation survey respondents are forced to value attributes with which they have little or no experience.

Intangible Benefits—Benefits that cannot be easily assigned a monetary value.

Interactive Resources—The size of the resource stock is determined jointly by biological considerations and actions taken by humans.

Isoquant—A curve showing possible combinations of two inputs that produce the same output level.

Joint Implementation—A project-based emission trading mechanism set up under the Kyoto Protocol in which an investor from one industrialized country can get emission reduction credits for certified greenhouse gas reductions resulting from investments in a project in another industrialized country.

Junior Claims—Used in water management, this class of rights for specified amounts of water is subordinate to senior claims. In times of water scarcity, these rights become valid once the senior claims have been fulfilled.

Kyoto Protocol—An international agreement to control greenhouse gases that went into effect in February 2005.

Land Trust—An organization specifically established to hold conservation easements and to ensure that the use of land conforms to the terms of the easements.

Latency—The period between exposure to a toxic substance and the detection of harm caused by that substance.

Law of Comparative Advantage—A country or region should specialize in the production of those commodities for which it has a comparative advantage.

Law of Diminishing Marginal Productivity—In the presence of a fixed factor, successively larger additions of variable factors will eventually lead to a decline in the marginal productivity of the variable factors.

Law of Diminishing Returns—The relationship between inputs and outputs when some inputs are increased and others are fixed, eventually leading to the decreased productivity of the variable inputs.

Lead Phaseout Program—A transferable permit program designed to lower the costs of phasing out lead in gasoline as well as to eliminate lead earlier than otherwise would have been possible. It allocated transferable rights to use lead in refining gasoline to refiners. The number of rights declined over time until at the end of the program they expired.

Leapfrogging—Refers to a situation where new development takes place not at the edge of current development, but further out, skipping over tracts of land that are closer in.

Liability Rules—Rules used in courts that award monetary compensation from an injurer to an injured party after damage has occurred.

Low-Emission Vehicles—A class of vehicles that emit fewer emissions per mile driven than conventional vehicles.

Marginal Cost of Exploration—The marginal cost of finding additional units of the resource.

Marginal-Cost Pricing—Basing the prices charged for resource use upon marginal costs. (This pricing scheme is generally consistent with efficiency.)

Marginal External Cost Rule—Used by the Global Environmental Facility to disperse funds. According to this rule, the facility will fund additional expenses associated with investments that contribute to the global environment (produce positive *global* net benefits), but cannot be justified domestically (since the *domestic* marginal costs exceed *domestic* marginal benefits). Countries are expected to pick up that portion of the expenses that can be justified domestically (where the domestic marginal benefits exceed domestic marginal costs).

Marginal Extraction Cost—The cost of mining an additional unit of resource.

Marginal Opportunity Cost—The additional cost of providing the last unit of a good as measured by what is given up.

Marginal User Cost—Present value of forgone future opportunity costs at the margin.

Marginal Willingness to Pay—The amount of money an individual is willing to pay for the last unit of a good or service.

Marine Reserve—A specific geographic area that prohibits harvesting of fish and enjoys a high level of protection from other threats such as pollution.

Market Economy—An economic system in which resource allocation decisions are guided by prices that result from the voluntary production and purchasing decisions by private consumers and producers.

Market Failure—An inefficient allocation produced by a market economy.

Maximum Sustainable Yield—The maximum harvest that could be sustained forever.

Microgrid—A group of interconnected electrical loads and distributed energy resources with clearly defined boundaries that acts as a single controllable entity. Depending on the situation microgrids may be either connected to a larger electrical grid or operate completely independently.

Minimum Viable Population—The level of population below which regeneration is negative, leading ultimately to extinction.

Model—Formal or informal framework for analysis that highlights some areas of the problem in order to better understand complex relationships.

Monopoly—A situation in which the seller side of the market is dominated by a single producer.

Montreal Protocol—An international agreement to control ozone-depleting gases.

Multilateral Fund—A fund set up by the parties to the Montreal Protocol to help developing countries meet the phaseout requirements for ozone-depleting gases.

Myopia—Nearsightedness; excessive concern for the present.

Natural Capital—The endowment of environmental and natural resources.

Natural Equilibrium—Stock levels of biological populations that persist in the absence of outside influences.

Natural Resource Curse Hypothesis—Suggests that countries with abundant natural resources are likely to grow more slowly than their lesser endowed counterparts.

Negative Feedback Loop—A closed path of action and reaction that is self-limiting rather than self-reinforcing.

Negligence—A doctrine in tort law suggesting that the party responsible for a tortious act owes a duty to the affected party to exercise due care. Failure to fulfill that duty can lead to a requirement for the injurer to pay compensation to the victim.

Net Benefit—The excess of benefits over costs resulting from some allocation.

New Scrap—Waste composed of the residual materials generated during production. (Also called preconsumer scrap.)

New Source Review Process—All large new or expanding sources are subject to preconstruction review and permitting. These firms are typically subjected to more stringent requirements. The specific requirements depend on whether the source is attempting to locate in an attainment or a nonattainment area.

Nonattainment Region—A region in which the pollution concentrations exceed the ambient standards, so more stringent environmental regulations are in effect.

Noncompliance Penalty—A charge used to reduce the profitability of noncompliance with pollution control requirements. It is designed to eliminate all the economic advantage gained from noncompliance.

Nonconsumptive Use—In water law this refers to a use that does not involve diverting the water from the source or that does not diminish its availability. (Swimming, for example.)

Nonexcludability—No individual or group can be excluded from enjoying the benefits a resource may confer, whether they contribute to its provision or not.

Nonpoint Sources—Diffuse sources such as runoff from agricultural or developed land.

Nonrenewable Resources—Resources that cannot be reproduced during a human timescale, so their supply is considered finite and limited.

Nonuniformly Mixed Pollutants—For these pollutants, the damage they cause is a function not only of the amount of emissions but also the location of the emissions sources. (Examples include particulates and lead.)

Nonuse (Passive-Use) Values—Resource values that arise from motivations other than personal use.

Normative Economics—The branch of economics that is concerned with evaluating the desirability of alternative resource allocations. It is concerned with "what ought to be."

Nutrient Sensitive Waters—Water bodies that have excessive levels of nutrients causing algal blooms, low oxygen levels, and increased fish kills.

Occupational Hazards—Risks undertaken during the course of a job.

Old Scrap—Waste recovered from products used by consumers. (Also called postconsumer scrap.)

Open-Access Resources—Common-pool resources with unrestricted access.

Open System—A system that imports and exports matter or energy.

Opportunity Cost—The net benefit forgone because the resource providing the service can no longer be used in its next-most-beneficial use.

Optimal—Best or most favorable option.

Optimization Procedure—A systematic method for finding the optimal means of accomplishing an objective.

Option Value—The value people place on having the option to use a resource in the future.

Output Measure—A measure currently used in national income accounting to indicate how many goods and services have been produced.

Overallocation—More than the optimal level of a resource is dedicated to a given use or time period.

Overshoot and Collapse—A forecast that involves exceeding the natural carrying capacity of the environment, with the consequence that society collapses.

Oxygen Sag—A point of low dissolved oxygen concentration generally located around effluent injection points.

Ozone-Depleting Gases—Global pollutants that destroy the stratospheric ozone layer. (Includes chlorofluorocarbons and halons, among others.)

Pareto Optimality—An allocation such that no reallocation of resources could benefit any person without lowering the net benefits for at least one other person. (Named after economist Vilfredo Pareto.)

Pay-as-You-Drive (PAYD) Insurance—A system in which an individual's annual premium for automobile insurance is calculated by multiplying a rating factor times the number of miles driven. It is designed to reduce inefficiency by internalizing those costs of accidents that are related to the amount of driving.

Peaking Units—Those electricity-producing facilities used only during peak periods. (They generally have low fixed costs, but high variable costs.)

Peak-Load Pricing—Charging resource users during the peak period the higher cost of supplying resources during that period. The surcharge during the peak period is designed to cover the cost of expansion since the need to expand is triggered by increased demands during the peak period.

Peak Periods—Times of especially high resource demand. (For example, the demand for electricity during the hottest part of the summer when air-conditioning is in heavy use.)

Pecuniary Externalities—External effects that are transmitted through higher prices. (For example, the value of my land increases because surrounding employers expand their operations, thereby creating a scarcity of housing in the immediate area.) Unlike most externalities, pecuniary externalities do not generally result in inefficient allocations.

Performance Bond—An amount of money required to be placed into a trust fund by those initiating risky projects to cover the costs of any anticipated damages.

Persistent Pollutants—Inorganic synthetic pollutants with complex molecular structures that are not effectively broken down in water.

Planning Horizon—The time period over which the benefits and costs are considered in time-related decisions. For a specific investment such as a power plant, for example, the planning horizon might correspond to the useful life of the project. For forestry, it could either correspond to the age of the stand of trees when harvested (the finite planning horizon) or extend forever (the infinite planning horizon).

Point Sources—Sources of pollution that discharge effluent through a readily identifiable emission point such as an outfall or discharge pipe. (Most industrial and municipal sources are point sources.)

Pollution Havens Hypothesis—Stricter environmental regulations in one country either encourage domestic production facilities to locate in countries with less stringent regulations or encourage increased imports from those countries.

Porter Induced Innovation Hypothesis—Firms facing stringent environmental regulations derive a competitive advantage because they are forced to innovate. Innovation typically increases productivity.

Positive Economics—The branch of economics that is concerned with describing alternative resource allocations without forming a judgment as to their desirability. Concerned with "what is."

Positive Feedback Loop—A closed path of action and reaction that is self-reinforcing rather than self-limiting.

Potential Reserves—The amount of resource reserves potentially available at different price levels.

Present Value—The current discounted value of a stream of benefits and/or costs over time.

Present Value Criterion—Resources should be allocated to those uses that maximize the present value of the net benefits received from all possible uses of those resources.

Price Controls—The establishment of maximum or minimum prices by the government.

Primary Effects—The direct, measurable effects of an action.

Primary Standard—An ambient air pollution standard designed to protect human health.

Prior Appropriation Doctrine—Entitlements for water are allocated to the agent who diverts and first puts water to a beneficial use.

Private Marginal Cost—The cost of producing an additional unit of the resource that is borne by the producer.

Producer Surplus—The value of a good or service to producers above the cost to them of producing it. Calculated as the area below the demand curve that is above marginal cost.

Product Charges—A charge imposed on a product that is associated with emissions (such as a gasoline tax). This indirect form of controlling emissions is used when placing the charge directly on emissions proves difficult.

Property Rights—A bundle of entitlements defining the owner's rights, privileges, and limitations for use of the resource.

Property Rules—Legal rules that govern the initial allocation of entitlements. Valuation of the entitlements is left to the market.

Property Tax—A tax on the value of land and the improvements on it.

Proposition 65—A California law that requires companies producing, using, or transporting one or more of the specified substances in amounts over the "safe harbor" threshold to notify those who are potentially impacted.

Public Good—A resource characterized by nonexclusivity and indivisibility.

Real Consumption Per Capita—Constant-dollar consumption divided by population.

Real-Resource Costs—As opposed to transfer costs, these are costs borne by both private parties and society as a whole because they involve the loss of net benefits, not merely their transfer.

Rebound Effect—An increase in consumption that results from an energy efficiency investment (i.e. lowers the amount of input energy necessary to product a given level of useful energy services). Examples including driving more miles after acquiring a fuel-efficient car or turning up the target temperature after making your house more energy efficient.

Receiving Areas—Those areas under a transferable development rights system where rights acquired from owners in the sending area can be used.

Recycling Surcharge—Imposed at the time of commodity purchase, this charge attempts to recover from the consumer the cost of recycling and/or disposal of the commodity after its useful life.

Regional Pollutants—Pollutants that can cause damage some distance from the emission source. (Examples include the precursors for acid rain and tropospheric ozone.)

Regressive Distribution—Net benefits from a policy received by various income groups represent a larger portion of the income of the rich than of the poor.

Renewable Energy Credit—An official record granted to producers of qualified renewable energy that can be sold separately from the energy to allow the recovery of the extra costs associated with renewable power. It can be used to prove compliance with a renewable portfolio standard.

Renewable Portfolio Standards—These standards specify enforceable targets and deadlines for producing specific proportions of electricity from renewable resources.

Renewable Resources—Resources that can be naturally regenerated over time on a human timescale.

Rent Seeking—The use of resources in lobbying and other activities directed at securing increased profits through protective regulation or legislation.

Res Nullius Regime—A property rights system in which no one owns or exercises control over resources. Resources covered by this regime can usually be exploited on a first-come, first-served basis.

Resource Endowment—The natural occurrence of resources in the earth's crust and atmosphere.

Resource Taxonomy—A classification system used to characterize the nature of natural resource stocks in terms of the certainty of the stock estimates and the economic likelihood of their recovery.

Return Flow—A term used in water management that refers to the unconsumed portion from an upstream user's water allocation that will eventually return to the watercourse (and, hence, be available to a downstream user).

Revenue-Neutral Tax or Fee—A government charge that does not add to the total government revenue. This can be achieved by such means as rebating the revenue back to households or lowering the rates on existing charges such that the decrease in revenue from those sources equals the increase in revenue from the revenue-neutral source, leaving total revenue unchanged.

Riparian Rights—Allocates the right to use water to the owner of the land adjacent to the water, as long as no adverse effects are imposed on other rights holders.

Risk-Free Cost of Capital—Rate of return earned on an investment when the risk of earning more or less than expected returns is zero.

Risk-Neutrality—An agent who has no preference between options that produce the same expected value.

Risk Premium—Additional rate of return required to compensate the owners of the capital when the expected and actual returns may differ. It represents compensation for a willingness to undertake some risk.

Scale Effects—How the size of an operation affects average costs.

Scarcity Rent—Producer's surplus that persists in long-run equilibrium due to fixed supply or increasing costs.

Secondary Effects—Indirect consequences of an action; beyond primary effects.

Secondary Standard—An ambient standard designed to protect those aspects of human welfare other than health.

Second Law of Thermodynamics—Entropy, the energy not available for work, increases.

Sending Areas—Areas where the owners of land can sell rights in a transferable development rights system that can be used in receiving areas, but not the sending areas.

Senior Claims—Used in water management, this class of claims entitles the holder to a priority for specified amounts of water. These rights have a higher priority in times of low water availability than junior claims.

Social Cost of Carbon—The additional economic damage that would accrue from emitting one more ton of CO_2 or CO_2-equivalent into the atmosphere.

Socialist Economy—A centrally planned economy where the means of production are controlled by the government.

Social Marginal Cost—The cost of producing an additional unit of the resource that is borne by society at large. Generally includes private marginal costs plus external marginal costs.

Sprawl—An inefficient land use pattern where the uses are excessively dispersed.

Stable Equilibrium—A level of stock that will be restored following temporary shocks.

Starting-Point Bias—Arises when a contingent valuation survey respondent is asked to check off his or her answer from a predetermined range of possibilities and the answers depend on the range specified by the survey instrument.

Static Efficiency—The chief normative economic criterion for choosing among various allocations when time is not an important consideration. An allocation satisfies the static efficiency criterion if it maximizes the net benefits from all possible uses of the resource.

Static Efficient Sustained Yield—The sustained catch level in a fishery that produces the largest annual recurring net benefit.

Stationary Source—An immobile pollution source. (Factories, for example, as opposed to automobiles.)

Statistically Significant—Observed differences are unlikely to result from pure chance.

Stock Pollutants—Pollutants that accumulate in the environment because the environment has little or no absorptive capacity for them.

Strategic Bias—A respondent provides a biased answer to a contingent valuation survey in order to influence a particular outcome.

Strategic Petroleum Reserve—A petroleum stockpile established by an importing nation to minimize the damage that could be done by an embargo imposed by a foreign supplier. It would serve as an alternative source of supply for a short period.

Stratosphere—The atmosphere that lies above the troposphere. It extends to about 31 miles above the earth's surface.

Strict Liability—A tort law doctrine requiring that the party responsible for pollution contamination compensate victims for damage caused. Differs from negligence in that the victim does not have to prove that the injurer was negligent.

Strong Sustainability—This definition of sustainability is fulfilled if the value of the natural capital stock does not decline.

Suboptimal Allocation—An allocation that could be rearranged so that one or more people could be made better off while no one was made worse off. (Also called an inefficient allocation.)

Subsidies—Payments or tax breaks from the government that make the cost to the buyer lower than the marginal cost of production.

Substitution—Replacing one resource with another. May occur, for example, when the original resource is no longer cost-effective or is diminishing in quantity or quality.

Sulfur Allowance Auction—Run by the Chicago Board of Trade, this annual auction requires utilities to place a proportion of these allowances up for sale each year. The proceeds are returned to the utilities. (This is called a "zero revenue auction" since the government derives no revenue from it.) It ensures the continual availability of permits and provides good public information on prices.

Sulfur Allowance Program—A transferable permit program targeted at electric utilities that was designed to reduce sulfur emissions from 1980 levels by 10 million tons. Involves an auction and an emissions cap.

Surface Water—The freshwater in rivers, lakes, and reservoirs that collects and flows on the earth's surface.

Sustainability Criterion—A criterion for judging the fairness of allocations of resources among generations. Generally requires that resource use by any generation should not exceed a level that would prevent future generations from achieving a level of well-being at least as great.

Sustainable Forestry—Forestry practices that are consistent with one of the definitions of sustainability, though most commonly this term refers to compatibility with the environmental sustainability criterion.

Sustainable Yield—Harvest levels that can be maintained indefinitely, achieved by setting the annual harvest equal to the annual net growth of the population.

Synergistic—The dose-response relationship is dependent upon several interrelated factors.

"Take-Back" Principle—The belief that manufacturers of products should have the responsibility to take the packaging and the products back at the end of their useful lives in order to promote efficient packaging and recycling. (Also called extended producer responsibility.)

Tangible Benefits—Benefits that can reasonably be assigned a monetary value.

Technological Progress—An innovation in process or technique that allows more output or services to be derived from a given set of inputs.

Thermal Pollution—Pollution caused by the injection of heat into a watercourse.

Third Parties—Victims who have no contractual relationship to a pollution source. (They are neither consumers of the product produced by the source nor employed by the source.)

Total Cost—The sum of fixed and variable costs.

Toxicity—The degree of harm caused to living organisms as a result of exposure to the substance.

Toxic Release Inventory—A system for reporting toxic emissions releases from individual facilities in the United States. By making the data public, it was designed to warn communities of the risks they face and to encourage reductions prior to regulation.

Transactions Costs—Costs incurred in attempting to complete transactions. (For example, in buying a home, these might include payments to the broker for arranging the sale, to the bank for onetime special fees, and to the government for the required forms. The value of the time expended in negotiating would also be a transactions cost.)

Transferability—Property rights can be exchanged among owners on a voluntary basis.

Transfer Coefficient—A coefficient used in simulating pollutant flows. It relates the degree to which pollution concentrations at a specific receptor site are increased by a one-unit increase in emissions from a specific source.

Transfer Cost—A cost to a private party that is not a cost to society as a whole, because it involves a transfer of net benefits from one private party to another.

Troposphere—The atmosphere that is closest to the earth. Its depth ranges from about 10 miles over the equator to about 5 miles over the poles.

Two-Part Charge—As used in water management, this type of charge combines volume pricing with a monthly fee that doesn't vary with the amount used. The monthly fee is designed to help cover fixed costs.

Underallocation—Less-than-optimal levels of a resource are dedicated to a given use or time period.

Uniform Emission Charge—A charge on effluent that applies the same per-unit rate to all sources regardless of their size or location.

Uniform Treatment—A strategy to reduce effluent levels by the same specified percentage at each emissions level.

Uniformly Mixed Pollutants—For these pollutants, the damage done to the environment depends on the amount of emissions that enters the atmosphere. The location of emissions is not a matter of policy concern. (Examples include ozone-depleting gases and greenhouse gases.)

User Cost—Opportunity cost created by scarcity. It represents the value of an opportunity forgone when the resource can no longer be used in its next-best use. (For example, for a unit of a depletable resource used now, the user cost is the net benefits that would have been received by saving it and using it during the next time period.)

Usufruct Right—Holders of this right may use a resource (normally subject to restrictions), but do not have full ownership rights, such as the privilege of being able to sell it to someone else.

Variable Cost—Production costs that vary with output.

Volume Pricing—Making the cost of the service a function of the volume used. Used in both trash disposal and water distribution.

Weak Sustainability—Resource use by previous generations should not exceed a level that would prevent future generations from achieving a level of well-being at least as great. This definition of sustainability is fulfilled if the total capital stock (natural capital plus physical capital) does not decline over time.

Welfare Measure—A measure that reflects whether economic activity increases or decreases society's well-being.

Wet Deposition—Occurs when air pollutants fall to land or water during rain or snow events.

Zero Discharge—No emissions of the targeted pollutant are allowed.

Zero Emission Vehicle—Automobiles that directly emit no air pollutants. (Examples include vehicles powered by solar energy and fuel cells.)

Zoned Effluent Charge—A charge on effluent that applies different per-unit rates to sources depending on their location. Generally sources closer to, and upstream from, locations with more serious pollution problems face higher rates.

Index

Note: **Bold** page numbers refer to tables; *italic* page numbers refer to figures and page numbers followed by "n" denote endnotes.

absorptive capacity 108, 198–9, 291
accelerated retirement strategies 165, 168
accounting stance 56
acid rain 109, 112, 139–40, 144, 277, 291
Ackerman, F. 100–1
acute toxicity 230, 291
adaptation 176, 189–91, 192
Africa 4–5, 153, **197**, 218, 255, 267
aggregation 56, 93
air quality: atmospheric deposition of pollution 215; Clean Air Act 52–3; conventional pollutants 132–4, 135; Geographic Information Systems (GIS) 93; market-based approaches 138, 142–3; Mexico 259; policy toward mobile source air pollution 160, 165, 168–9
Alaska 73, 84, **197**
allowance auctions 121, 123, 126, 140, 280
alternative fuels 159–60, 291
alternative measures of development 266–8
alternative vehicles 160
ambient standards: cost-effective pollution control 130; definition 291; mobile-source air pollution 168–9; stationary-source air pollution 132, 133–6, 138–9, 143; water pollution 202–3, 204, 206–8, 215, 224n2
America *see* United States
American bison 28–30, 29
Anas, A. 162
anthropocentrism 46, 291
aqueducts 4

assimilative capacity 110, 198, 214, 266
asymmetric information 34, 39, 42, 188, 291
atmospheric deposition of pollution 195, 215
auctioned allowances 121, 123, 126, 140, 280
Austin, D. 156
Australia **159**, 210, 242, 267
averting (avoidance) expenditures **79**, 93, 95, 102, 110–11, 124

Barbier, E. B. 27
Barrett analysis 178
BAT (best available technology economically achievable) 203, 204, 292
Bateman, I. *et al.* 96–7
benefit-cost analysis: applying the concepts 51–3, 54–5, 56–7, 58–63; defining the concepts 46, 47–8, 48–9, 49–51
benefit estimation issues 56–7
benefit transfers 80, 91–2, 98–9, 102
Bennett, L. L. *et al.* 207, 212
best available technology economically achievable (BAT) 203, 204, 292
biases *see* hypothetical bias; information bias; payment vehicle bias (protest bids); starting-point bias; strategic bias
bike sharing programs 164
Bilmes, L. 88
biochemical oxygen demand (BOD) 198, 202, 215, 218, 222, 292
biodiversity 5, 18, 31, 47, 274
biological diversity 30–1, 33
bison 28–30, 29
Bisphenol A (BPA) 230–1
BOD (biochemical oxygen demand) 198, 202, 215, 218, 222, 292

Boyle, K. 94, 95
BP (British Petroleum) 73–4, 102, 197, 220–1, 223, 228
British Columbia carbon tax **182–3**, 280
British Petroleum (BP) 73–4, 102, 197, 220–1, 223, 228
Brundtland Report 249

CAFE (Corporate Average Fuel Economy) standards 154–7, 159, 165, 294
California Air Resources Board (CARB) 153, 160
Canada: climate change 173, **182**–3; discount rates 61; mobile-source air pollution 161, 165, 167; sustainable development quest 259, 266, 269; toxic substances and environmental justice 229, 241; valuing the environment 94, 98–9; water pollution **197**, 210, 219
cancer 19, 77, 181, 229–30, 237, 244–5, 251
cap-and-trade: climate change 182, 185, 186; definition 292; pollution control policies 118–19, 120–1, 123, 124, 125, 126; stationary-source air pollution 133, 137, 139, 142; water pollution 198
capital accumulation 6, 254
Car Allowance Rebate System (CARS) 167
car insurance 165, 166
car-sharing 158–9
CARB (California Air Resources Board) 153, 160
carbon dioxide (CO_2) emissions: climate change 174, 176, 181–2; evaluating trade-offs 54, **54**–5, 57; mobile-source air pollution 157, 159, 167; pollutant taxonomies 108; sustainable development quest 266
carbon markets and taxes 183–4
carbon monoxide 76, **138**, 148, 151, 163
carbon pricing programs 182–3, 184–7, 192
carbon reduction 54–5, 142, 274
carbon sequestration 18, 177
carrying capacity 3, 11, 13, 268, 278, 292
CARS (Car Allowance Rebate System) 167
Carson, R. T. 84, 220
cartels 33, 252, 292
Cash for Clunkers 167
CBO (Congressional Budget Office) 139–40, 209
CERCLA (Comprehensive Environmental Response, Compensation, and Liability Act) 241
certification 40–1, 139, 152–3
CFCs (chlorofluorocarbons) 174, 180–1, 251

China: climate change 179, **182**; contingent valuation method 80; fuel economy standards 159; population growth 274; toxic substances 246; water accessibility 4; water pollution 217, 219
chlorine manufacturing 143–4
chlorofluorocarbons (CFCs) 174, 180–1, 251
choice experiments 78–9, 83–8, **85–6**, 98, 102
chronic toxicity 230, 292
CITES (Convention on International Trade in Endangered Species) 255–6
Clean Air Act: evaluating trade-offs 51–**3**; mobile-source air pollution 151, 153, 159; stationary-source air pollution 131–2, 134–6, 139–40, 144; valuing the environment 74
Clean Water Act (CWA) 74, 202, 204, 205, 208, 213
climate change 173–93; adaptation policy 189–91; introduction 173–4; mitigation policy choice **182–7**; mitigation policy timing 188–9; policy negotiations 176–80; reducing ozone-depleting gases 180–1; the science 174–5; summary 191–2; visions of the future 2–4, 5
climate engineering 176
climate science 174–5
closed systems 19, 292
clustered emissions 40, 149
co-benefits 179–80
Coase, R. 37
Coase theorem 36–9, 292
coffee production 40–1
collective net benefits 178
Colombia 218
combined approaches 58, 221
command-and-control approach: cost-effective pollution control policies 116; definition 292; developing countries 216, 218; stationary-source air pollution 132, 133–6, 136–8, 143
common-pool resources 28, 112, 293
common-property regimes 27, 28, 293
compensating variation 81–2, 97, 293
compensation and risk acceptance 243
compensation as policy instrument 242
composition effect 256–7
Comprehensive Environmental Response, Compensation, and Liability Act (CERCLA) 241

concentration levels: air pollution 132–3, 136, 149; pollution control 129; toxic substances 228; water pollution 199, 204

concentration versus exposure 136

congestion externalities 162, 293

congestion inefficiency *150*

congestion pricing 161–4, 169, 293

Congressional Budget Office (CBO) 139–40, 209

consumer surplus *21*–2, 23, 31, 89, 293

contamination sources: air pollution 160; toxic substances 228, 231, 236; water pollution 196–8, 199, 206

contingent valuation method 78–9, *79–85*, 91–2, 96, 98, 102

control authorities: pollution control policies 114, 115, 117–19, 120, 124, 125–6; water pollution 202, 206, 222

Convention on International Trade in Endangered Species (CITES) 255–6

conventional measures of development 264–6

conventional pollutants 131–2, 147, 203, 223, 293

Copenhagen Consensus Center 11

coping expenditures *93*, 95

Corporate Average Fuel Economy (CAFE) standards 154–7, *159*, 165, 294

cost-effectiveness: allocations 107, 114–*15*, *116–19*, 126; analysis 66–7; equimarginal principle 67, *115*; policies for uniformly mixed fund pollutants *114–20, 118*; pollution control 129

cost estimation approaches 58

cost-minimizing choices 113, *116*–18, 220

cost savings 183–4

Costa Rica 41

Council on Environmental Quality 68

counterproductive policy design 109, 133, 168, 232, 258, 277

criteria pollutants 131–2, 135, 148, 167, 294

Cropper, M. 100

Cross-State Air Pollution Rule (CSAPR) 141

CWA (Clean Water Act) 74, 203–4, 205, 208, 213

deadweight loss 26, 35, 44n3

deep ecology 75, 294

Deepwater Horizon oil spill 73–4, 102, 103n5, 205, 220–1, 223

demand pressure 274–5

Denmark 80, **182**, 267

Department of Energy (DOE) 55

depletable resources 109–10, 252–4, 274, 275

depleted fisheries 47

developing countries: air quality 138; certification 41; climate change 4, 179–81, 186, 191; discount rates 64; economics of pollution control 119, 120; mobile-source air pollution 169; sustainable development quest 256–7, 258, 267; toxic substances and environmental justice 233, 245–6; valuing the environment 95, 104n11; water pollution 216–19

differential treatment 260–1

dilution 108, 111, 136, 139, 144, 197

Dinan, T. 156

discount rates 60–3, *63*–4, 155–6, 253–4, 294

discounting over long time horizons 62–3

dissolved oxygen (DO) 198, 211, 213, 294

distance decay 96–7

DO (dissolved oxygen) 198, 211, 213, 294

DOE (Department of Energy) 55

dominant policies 59

dry deposition 214, 215, 294

dynamic efficiency 51, 69, 109, 110, 294 *see also* static efficiency

Earth Summit (United Nations Conference on Environment and Development) 11, 249

Easter Island 2, 3

eco-certification 40–1

ecological economics 7–8

Ecological Footprint 251, 266–7, 268, 271n4, 278, 294

ecological sensitivity 112

econometrics 9, 10

economic analysis: climate change 188, 189, 192; emissions trading 139; evaluating trade-offs 45, 48, 60, 65–7, 69; positive and normative economics 19; role of 7, 9, 12; water pollution 209

economic approach 17–44; efficient role for government 40–1; environmental problems and economic efficiency 21–2; externalities and market failure 25–6, 26–7, 27–30, 30–1, 31–4, 34–6; human-environment relationship 18–19, 19–21; introduction 17; property rights 23–4; pursuit of efficiency 36–9, 39–40; summary 42

economic efficiency: air pollution 136; definition 303; and environmental problems 21–2; evaluating trade-offs 48, 51, 69; and property rights 23; and public goods 31; pursuit of 36–40; water pollution *207*, 216, 223
economic impact analysis 20, 60
economic incentives: air pollution 143, 169; climate change 185; ecological and environmental economics 7; efficiency and sustainability 253, 270, 278–80; pollution control 116, 120, 122; water pollution 201, 208–9, 215–16, 218, 222
economic surplus: efficiency criterion 36, 42; environmental problems 21–2; optimality and efficiency 48; property rights 23, 28, 30; public goods 31, 33
economic system and the environment *18–19*
economics of site location 237–40
economies of scale 165, 195, 213, 248n2, 294
ecosystems: climate change 174; environmental valuation methods 94; evaluating trade-offs 46, 52; goods and services *18–19*, 31; stationary-source air pollution 134, 141; visions of the future 2–4, 5, 11, 274
efficiency and cost-effectiveness, US water policy 206–15
efficiency and sustainability 252–4
efficiency criterion: economic approach 21, 42; evaluating trade-offs 48, 51, 69; pollution control 113; sustainable development quest 254
efficiency equimarginal principle 49, 67
Efficiency Maine (EM) 123
efficient allocations: economic approach 23, 25–6, 30–1, 37, 42; evaluating trade-offs 48–9, 62, 67, 69; and institutional responses 275; pollution control 109–12; stationary-source air pollution 134; sustainable development quest 252, 253–4, 268; water pollution 206
efficient output with pollution damage *37*
efficient provision of public goods *32*
efficient role for government 40–1
effluent trading 211–12
EKC (Environmental Kuznets Curve) 257–9, 295
elephant populations 255–6
EM (Efficiency Maine) 123
Emerson, Ralph Waldo 17, 30
emissions allowance system 126, 295

emissions charges: pollution control *116–18*, 120, 126; public and private sectors 280; stationary-source air pollution 138–9, 140; water pollution 198, 215, 223
emissions load *108*
emissions standards: mobile-source air pollution 151, 152, 153, 168–9; pollution control policies 115–17, 123–4, 126; stationary-source air pollution 132; toxic substances 228; water pollution 215, 222
emissions trading: climate change **182**, 183–4, 185, 186, 187; definition 295; pollution control policies 116, 118–*19*, 126; stationary-source air pollution 139–42
emotional well-being 269
energy production 64, 122
enforceability 23, 295
enforcement: climate change 177; command-and-control approach 132–3; developing countries 120; enforcement 247; mobile-source air pollution 148, 152–3; sustainable development quest 255–6, 281; toxic substances and environmental justice 239, 240, 244–5; water pollution 202, 208, 213, 217–19
engineering approach 58
entropy law 19
environmental challenges 2–5, 5–6, 6–9
environmental damage *see* natural resource damages
environmental economics: climate change 173–93; economic approach 17–44; evaluating trade-offs 45–70; mobile-source air pollution 147–71; pollution control 107–30; stationary-source air pollution 131–45; sustainable development quest 249–71; toxic substances and environmental justice 227–48; valuing the environment 73–104; visions of the future 1–13, 273–81; water pollution 195–225
environmental justice 9, *95*, 201, 228, 236, 237–40, 240–6
Environmental Kuznets Curve (EKC) 257–9, 295
Environmental Protection Agency (EPA): economic approach 20; evaluating trade-offs 51–2, 55, 60, 63, 67; mobile-source air pollution 151, 152, 153–5, 163, 171n8; stationary-source air pollution 131–2, 134–5, 138, 140–1; toxic substances and

environmental justice 230, 236, 237, 240, 242, 244; water pollution policy 203–4, 204–5, 208–9, 210–11, 213, 215; water pollution problems 200

Environmental Protection and Community Right to Know Act (EPCRA) 242

environmental regulations 6, 65, 256–8

environmental taxes 121

Environmental Valuation Reference Inventory (EVRI) 92, 104n12

EOs (Executive Orders) 65

EPA (Environmental Protection Agency) *see* Environmental Protection Agency (EPA)

EPCRA (Environmental Protection and Community Right to Know Act) 242

equimarginal principles 49, 67

equity analysis 60

equivalent variation 81–2, 97, 295

Essay on the Principle of Population, An (Malthus) 2

estimating benefits of carbon dioxide emission reductions **54**–5

ethanol 159–60, 291

ethical concerns 49, 62, 76, 187, 188, 233–4

EU ETS (European Union Emissions Trading Scheme) 183, 186

EU (European Union) *see* European Union (EU)

European Union Emissions Trading Scheme (EU ETS) 183, 186

European Union (EU): climate change 173, **182**, 183, 183–4; legislative and executive regulation 40, 44n4; mobile-source air pollution 152–3, 157–9, 168–9; sustainable development 279–80; toxic substances and environmental justice 228, 241; water pollution 201, 215–16, 223

European Water Framework Directive 216, 223

evaluating trade-offs 45–70; applying the concepts 51–3, **54**–5, 56–7, 58–60; discount rates 60–3, 63–6; normative criteria for decision-making 45, 46, 47–8, 48–9, 49–51; other decision-making metrics 66–8; summary 68–9

EVRI (Environmental Valuation Reference Inventory) 92, 104n12

exclusivity 23, 25, 295

Executive Orders (EOs) 65

expected present value of net benefits 59–60, 295

experimental economics 9, 10

external benefits 26, 159, 164–5, 215

external costs: air pollution 144, 149, 150, 161; climate change 173; economic approach 25, 26, 38; social costs 55, 57; toxic substances and environmental justice 236, 246; water pollution 220

externalities: evaluating trade-offs 63; institutional responses to resource scarcity 275; and market failure 25–6, 26–7, 27–30, 30–1, 31–4, 34–6; mobile-source air pollution 149–50, 157, 159, 161–2; pollution control 112; sustainable development quest 254–5, 257–8, 260, 265, 268; toxic substances and environmental justice 237, 251–2; valuing the environment 93 *see also* congestion externalities; pecuniary externalities

extrapolations 59, 76

Exxon Valdez oil spill 73–4, 84, 102, 104n9, **197**, 220–1

FDA (Food and Drug Administration) 200, 231

Federal Energy Regulatory Commission 74

feebates 165, 169, 296

feedback loops *see* negative feedback loops; positive feedback loops

first equimarginal principle 49, 67

first law of thermodynamics 19, 296

Fish and Wildlife Service 74

Flint River Drought Protection Act 10

flood insurance 261, 262

Food and Drug Administration (FDA) 200, 231

France: contingent valuation method 80; discount rates 63; environmental justice 241; sustainable development quest 266; water pollution **197**, 216, 220

free-access resources 112, 275

free-rider effect: climate change 177–9, 181, 191–2; definition 296; economic approach 31, 35, 38; occupational hazards 233

Frey, B. S. 243

fuel economy standards 154–7, 157–9, 169, 296

fuel prices 156–7

fuel taxes 149, 155–6, 157, *161*–2, 183

fund pollutants: definition 296; economics of pollution control 110–12, *111*, 114–20, *115*, 125–6; water pollution 198–9, 208

Gaia hypothesis 7, 296
Gallagher, K. P. 259
game theory 176–80, 192
gas guzzler taxes 149, 157, 165, 171n10
GATT (General Agreement on Tariffs and Trade) 259–61
GDP (Gross Domestic Product) 5, 264–6, 266–7, 280
GEMS (Global Environmental Monitoring System) 138, 145n4
General Agreement on Tariffs and Trade (GATT) 259–61
genetic diversity 30, 251
Genuine Progress Indicator (GPI) 266–7, 296
Geographic Information Systems (GIS) 92–3, 94, 104n13, 214–15, 237, 239
geographic scope (social cost of carbon) 57
Germany 137, 157–9, 186, 215–16, 228, 266
GHGs (greenhouse gases) see greenhouse gases (GHGs)
Gibbon, E. 1–2
gifting allowances 118, 121, 126
global climate negotiations 176–80
Global Environmental Facility 179
Global Environmental Monitoring System (GEMS) 138, 145n4
global environmental problems 6, 249, 280 see also Global Environmental Facility; Global Environmental Monitoring System (GEMS)
global pollutants 108, 174, 176–7, 180, 191
government failure 34–6, 296
GPI (Genuine Progress Indicator) 266–7, 296
Great Britain see United Kingdom
greenhouse gases (GHGs): climate change policy negotiations 176, 179–80; definition 296; economic approach 21; estimating benefits of carbon dioxide emission reductions 55; market allocations 252; mitigation policies **182–3**, 185, 187, 188–9; mobile-source air pollution 147–8, 150, 155, 165; pollution control 109, 121, 123, 125; reduction 181, 191; science of climate change 174; sustainable development quest 276; visions of the future 2–4, 6
Gross Domestic Product (GDP) 5, 264–6, 266–7, 280
Gross National Happiness 267–8
groundwater: definition 297; and methyl tertiary butyl ether (MTBE) 160, 169; toxic substances and environmental justice 235; water accessibility 4; water pollution 196–7, 199, 215, 223
growth-development relationship 264–8
Gulf of Mexico 73, 197, 220–1, 223, 228

Haagen-Smit, A. J. 151
Haefele, M. et al. 85, 87–8
Hanley, N. et al. 97
Hanna, B. G. 238
Harrington, W. 70n7, 166
Hartwick Rule 253, 297
Haveman, R. 64–6
hazardous waste siting decisions 236–46
hazardous workplaces 231–5, 232
HDI (Human Development Index) 267–8, 270, 297
health effects 92, 134–6, 153, 181, 229, 244
health threshold 134, 135, 297
hedonic property values: definition 297; nonmarket valuation 102; valuation methods **79**, 89, 91, 92, 93, 94
hedonic wage methods **79**, 89, 91, 101, 297
Heinzerling, L. 100–1
Hicks, J. 265–6
high occupancy vehicle (HOV) lanes 162
History of the Decline and Fall of the Roman Empire, The (Gibbon) 1–2
Hooker Chemical 227
Horowitz, J. K. 82
housing values 238
HOV (high occupancy vehicle) lanes 162
human capital 251
Human Development Index (HDI) 267–8, 270, 297
human-environment relationship 18–21
Hungary 215–16, 241
hydrogen fuel cells 160, 169, 174
hypothetical bias 79, 80, 87, 297

impact analysis 68
impending scarcity 2, 3, 113
imperfect market structures 31–4
implicit subsidies 149
India: carbon markets and taxes **182**; mobile-source air pollution 169; rising consumption levels 274; sustainable development quest 267; toxic substances and environmental justice 228, 242, 246; water accessibility 4

Industrial Revolution 2
industrialized countries 6, 64, 119–20, 181,
    237, 278
inefficiencies: discount rates 64; economic
    approach 31, 33–4, 34–5, 38–9, 40, 42;
    market allocation of pollution 113; mobile-
    source air pollution *150*, 166; stationary-
    source air pollution 136, 138, 143; sustainable
    development quest 258, 276
information bias 79, 297
inorganic chemicals 199
institutional responses (to resource scarcity) 275–8
instrument choice 124–5, 163
intangible benefits 56–7, 70n5, 297
Integrated Pollution and Prevention Control
    (IPPC) 215
Interagency Working Group on Social Cost of
    Greenhouse Gases 55
Interface Corporation 276
intergenerational context 5, 63, 73, 110,
    250, 268
Intergovernmental Panel on Climate Change
    (IPCC) 174
international agreements 176–8, 180, 191–2,
    244–6, 259–60
international cooperation 5–6, 173, 179
intrinsic value of environment 75
IPCC (Intergovernmental Panel on Climate
    Change) 174
IPPC (Integrated Pollution and Prevention
    Control) 215
Ireland 217
iron and steel *see* steel production
ivory trading 255–6

Japan: air pollution 139, 159, 170n5; carbon
    markets and taxes **182**; sustainable
    development 266, 280; toxic substances and
    environmental justice 242, 243, 246; water
    pollution 199–200

Kahneman, D. 269
Kathmandu Valley, Nepal 95
Kibler, V. 214
Kling, C. 82
Kousky, C. 262
Krupnick, A. 65
Kuznets, S. 257
Kyoto Protocol 179, 182, 298

labeling 39–40, 260, 274
latency 229, 230, 235, 298
lead and Proposition 65 245
Lead Phaseout Program 153–4, 298
Leard, B. *et al.* 156–7
legislative and executive regulation 39–40
level of the ambient standard 134
liability laws 219, 236, 246, 279
liability rules 37–9, 298
life evaluations 269
Lindsey, R. 162
local pollutants 108, 139, 179
Lomborg, B. 11, 13
Long Island Sound **211**–13
long time horizons, discounting over 62–3
Loomis, J. B. 96
Love Canal 127n5, 227–8
Lovelock, J. 7
Lyme disease 2

Malthus, T. 2, 3
managing toxic risk 230–1
mandatory disclosure 245
marginal benefits: air pollution 133, 150; climate
    change 178; evaluating trade-offs 49, 61, 67;
    and externalities 26; sustainable development
    quest 264; water pollution 222
marginal control costs 67, 111–12, 113, 117,
    125, 214
marginal cost curve: economic approach *22*,
    30–1, 35, 38–9; evaluating trade-offs 46, 48;
    pollution control 112, 114–*15*, 117, 124–5;
    toxic substances and environmental justice
    232–3; water pollution 213
marginal damages: adaptation policy 189; nonpoint
    source pollution 209; occupational hazards 233;
    pollution control 110, 112, 113–14, 124–5;
    stationary-source air pollution 134
marginal net benefits 206
marginal opportunity costs 46, 298
marginal social damage 113
Marine Mammal Protection Act (MMPA) 260
market allocations 112–13, 231–6, 251–2
markets: equilibrium *24*, 119; failures 25–6, 35,
    191, 239, 258, 298; imperfections 26, 251–2,
    268, 275; incentives 6, 232; market-based
    approaches 138–42; market-based instruments
    119, 120, 138–42, 143, 183–4, 213; processes
    34, 275

Mayan civilisation 2, 3
McConnell, K. E. 82
measures of development 264–6, 266–8
meta-analysis 91–2, 98, 101, 102
methane 6, 174, 182
methyl mercury 200
methyl tertiary butyl ether (MTBE) 35, 159–60,
    169, 205, 277
Mexico 164, 168, 173, 259, 261
microwave oven rule 55
Middle East 5
Minorca, Spain 90–1
minority neighborhoods 239
Mitchell, R. C. 220
mitigation 122, 176, 182–7, 188–9, 189–90,
    261–2
MMPA (Marine Mammal Protection Act) 260
mobile-source air pollution 147–71; introduction
    147–9; policy toward mobile sources 151,
    152–3, 153–4, 154–7, 157–9, 159–60, 161–8;
    subsidies and externalities 149–50, 151;
    summary 168–9
models, use of: air pollution 136, 152–3; climate
    change 179, 188; pollution control 109;
    sustainable development quest 252–3; valuing
    the environment 79, 89, 91, 92–4, 97, 102;
    visions of the future 6, 8–9
monetary values 56, 76–7, 85, 99, 102, 221
monitoring: certification 41; climate change
    177; developing countries 120; mobile-
    source air pollution 152–3; stationary-source
    air pollution 138, 141; toxic substances
    and environmental justice 240, 244; water
    pollution 198–9, 209
monopolies 31, 33–4, 42, 44n3, 299
Montreal Protocol 180–1, 299
morality 100, 187, 244
mortality risk valuation 100
MTBE (methyl tertiary butyl ether) 35, 159–60,
    169, 205, 277
municipal wastewater treatment subsidies
    208–9

NAAQS (National Ambient Air Quality
    Standards) 132, 135
Naess, A. 75
NAFTA (North American Free Trade
    Agreement) 259
nation-states 4, 5

National Ambient Air Quality Standards
    (NAAQS) 132, 135
national effluent standards 204, 208, 223
National Environmental Policy Act 68
National Flood Insurance Program (NFIP) 262
National Highway Traffic Safety Administration
    (NHTSA) 155
National Oceanic and Atmospheric
    Administration (NOAA) 74, 83, 84, 91, 102
National Parks 85, 87–8, 89, 112
National Pollutant Discharge Elimination System
    (NPDES) 211–12
nationally determined contribution (NDC) 180
natural disasters 261–2
natural resource curse hypothesis 263, 299
natural resource damages: air pollution 149;
    institutional responses 275, 277; valuing the
    environment 73–4, 78, 84; water pollution
    219, 221, 223n3
natural resource economics 9, 12, 47
Nature Conservancy 33
NDC (nationally determined contribution) 180
NDP (Net Domestic Product) 264
negative feedback loops 7, 9, 11, 299
negotiations 36–9, 176–80
Nepal 93, 95
net benefits: air pollution 134, 155, 168; benefit-
    cost analysis 52–3, 55, 59–61; climate
    change 178, 180; definition 299; discount
    rates 63–4, 66–7; dynamic efficiency 69;
    economic approach 26–7, 35; efficiency and
    sustainability 252; institutional responses 275;
    normative criteria for decision-making 46–7,
    48–9, 49–51; pollution control 109–10, 121,
    127n1; water pollution 206, 220, 222 see also
    collective net benefits; marginal net benefits;
    private net benefits; social net benefits
Net Domestic Product (NDP) 264
New Source Review (NSR) Program 132,
    133, 299
New Zealand 182, 210, 269
NFIP (National Flood Insurance Program) 262
NHTSA (National Highway Traffic Safety
    Administration) 155
NIMBY (Not in My Backyard) 238, 241
nitrogen 108, 122, 132, 151, 211–12
Nixon, Richard M. (37th US President) 68
NOAA (National Oceanic and Atmospheric
    Administration) 74, 83, 84, 91, 102

nonexclusivity 28

nonmarket valuations 74, 93–7, 98, 102

nonpoint sources: benefit-cost analysis 222; contamination sources 196–7; definition 299; European legislation 215–16; toxic substances and environmental justice 228, 236; US legislation 203–4, 206, 209–10, 213–14

nonrenewable resources 253, 299

nonuse (passive-use) values: definition 299; how to value the environment 77–8, 83–5, 91–2, 97–8, 102; oil spills 220–1

normative economics 19–21, 45–51, 59, 60, 62, 69, 300

North American Free Trade Agreement (NAFTA) 259

Not in My Backyard (NIMBY) 238, 241

NPDES (National Pollutant Discharge Elimination System) **211**–12

NSR (New Source Review) Program 132, 133, 299

Oberholzer-Gee, F. 243

occupational hazards 231–5, 232

ocean pollution 197, 205–6

OECD (Organisation for Economic Co-operation and Development) 122, 188, 245

off-shore drilling 197, 219–20

Office of Management and Budget (OMB) 20, 62–3

offsets: carbon pricing programs 181, 184, 185–7, 191–2; efficiency and sustainability 253; emissions standards 168; environmental regulations 65; fuel economy standards 155, 157–8; imperfect market structures 33; sustainable development quest 278; water pollution controls 210, **211**, 214, 217

OFPA (Organic Foods Production Act) 40

oil spills: environmental regulations 65; liability law 39; sustainable development quest 280; toxic substances and environmental justice 228, 235; valuing the environment 73–4, 77–8, 83–4, 89–90; water pollution 196–7, 205, 218, 219–21, 223

OMB (Office of Management and Budget) 20, 62–3

open-access (res nullius) regimes: definition 300, 302; improperly defined property rights systems 27–8, 30, 42; pollution control 113; sustainability of development 251, 255

open systems 19, 300

opportunity costs 46, 58, 89, 102, 300 see also marginal opportunity costs; social opportunity costs

optimal levels of pollution 111–12

optimal outcomes 47–8, 48–9

optimization procedure 67, 300

option values 77, 102, 300

organic certification 41

Organic Foods Production Act (OFPA) 40

Organisation for Economic Co-operation and Development (OECD) 122, 188, 245

overexploitation 6, 28, 30, 112, 275, 277

ozone-depleting gases 176, 180–1, 191, 300

Pareto optimality 49, 300

Pareto, V. 49

Paris Accord 180–1, 188, 193n1

parking cash-outs 164, 169

Parry, I. et al. 161, 166

partial values 94

passive-use (nonuse) values see nonuse (passive-use) values

Pastor, M. Jr. 239

Paterson, R. 94

Pay-as-You-Drive (PAYD) Insurance 165, 166, 300

payment vehicle bias (protest bids) 79, 80

pecuniary externalities 26, 300

percentage change in US emissions, 1980–2015 **139**

persistent pollutants 49, 199, 201, 300

perverse incentives 27–30, 151

point-nonpoint trading 211, 213–14

point sources: definition 301; toxic substances and environmental justice 228; water pollution 196–7, 209, 210, 213–14, 218, 223

polar bears 94, 98–9

policy instruments 113–14, 115–16, 120, 125, 129, 228

policy issues and toxic substances 229–31, 240–2

policy toward mobile sources of air pollution: alternative fuels and vehicles 159–60; Lead Phaseout Program 153–4; other countries 157–9, 159; transportation pricing 161–8; United States 151, 154–7; United States and EU 152–3

political processes 34–5, 66

pollutant damages 112

Pollutant Release and Transfer Registers
(PRTR) 242
pollutant types 108–9, 110–12, 125, 198–201
pollution control 107–26; cost-effective policies
for uniformly mixed fund pollutants 114–*15*,
115–20, *116*, *118*, *119*; developing countries
216–18; efficient allocation of pollution
109–12; efficient policy responses 113–14;
evaluating trade-offs 51–3, 66–7; introduction
107; iron and steel industries 20; legislative
and executive regulation 39; market allocation
of pollution 112–13; other policy dimensions
120–1, 121–2, 124–5; pollutant taxonomy
108–9; summary 125–6; valuing the
environment 76
pollution costs 109, 113
pollution damage *37*, 52, 77, *108*, 127n2, 139
pollution externalities 26
pollution havens 256–7, 259
Porter Induced Innovation Hypothesis 257, 301
Porter, M. 257
positive economics 19–21, 301
positive feedback loops 6, 9, 11, 301
present value: definition 301; evaluating
trade-offs 49–**51**, *50*, 52–5, 59–61, 63, 69;
mitigation policy 188; pollution control 109,
121; toxic substances and environmental
justice 241; water pollution 222
pretreatment standards 203, 209, 228
price volatility 142, 186–7
pricing public transport 164
primary standards 132, 204, 301
primary versus secondary effects 56
private costs 65, 149–50, 220, 275
private discount rates 63–4
private incentives 276
private net benefits 27
private toll roads 164
producer surplus: definition 301; discount rates
63; economic efficiency *22*, *23*; markets 26,
31, 33; resolution through negotiation 36, 38
product safety 235
promoting resilience 260–1, 262
property rights: climate change 191; definition
301; discount rates 63; economic approach
23–4, 25–6, 27–30, 31, 36–8, 42; institutional
responses 275, 277; pollution control policies
123; sustainable development quest 253, 255,
257–8, 280; WTP versus WTA 82

property rules 37–8, 301
Proposition 65 244, 245, 301
PRTR (Pollutant Release and Transfer
Registers) 242
public goods: climate change 177, 180, 191;
definition 301; economic approach 38, 42;
externalities and market failure 28, 30–1, *32*,
33, 35; occupational hazards 233; social cost
of carbon 57; valuing the environment 80, *97*
public-private partnerships 279

rebates: carbon pricing programs 183, 184–5;
mobile-source air pollution 160, 165, 167;
pollution control 122, 126
Rechtschaffen, C. 245
recreation benefits 70n5, 195
recreational value estimation 90–1
recycling: definition 302; evaluating trade-offs
48; externalities 26; hazardous waste siting
decisions 242, 244–6; institutional responses
275, 276; Irish bag levy 217; pollution control
109–10, 112, 125; sustainable development
quest 280; transportation pricing 165
reducing emissions: air pollution 140, 144,
166; carbon pricing programs 184;
cost-effectiveness analysis 67; definition
295; iron and steel industries 20–1; RGGI
revenues 123
Refuse Act 201, 203
Regional Greenhouse Gas Initiative (RGGI) 121,
123, 142, **182**, 184, 186
regional pollutants 108, 139, 302
regulatory environment, responses to changes
124, 258
renewable energy 185, 271n1, 275, 302
renewable resources 49, 183–4, 251–4,
273–5, 302
rent-seeking 35, 41, 42, 302
reproductive effects 229, 244, 245
res nullius (open-access) regimes *see* open-access
(*res nullius*) regimes
resource policies 10, 39, 278
resource scarcity 2, 3, 113, 125, 274–5
return flows 206–7, 224n5, 302
revealed preference methods 78–**9**, 89–91, 102
revenue effects 121–3
RGGI (Regional Greenhouse Gas Initiative) 121,
123, 142, **182**, 184, 186
Ricardo, D. 24

rising sea levels 2, 174, 274
risk-free cost of capital 62, 63–4, 302
risk-neutrality 59–60, 302
risk perception 241
risk premiums 62, 63–4, 232–3, 302
risk treatment 58–60
road congestion *150*
Rome, fall of 1–2
runoff 195, 196, 204, 214
Russia 153–4

Safe Drinking Water Act 204–5
Safe Drinking Water and Toxic Enforcement
    Act 244
Sathirathai, S. 27
scale effects 256–7, 259
scarcity rents 24, 28, 30, 253, 303
Schaafsma, M. *et al.* 97
Schmalensee, R. 142
second equimarginal principle 67, 115
second law of thermodynamics 19, 278, 303
secondary standards 132, 134, 204, 303
self-enforcing agreements 176–7
self-extinction premise 1–2
Shabman, L. A. 262
Shiller, R. 65
Shimshack, J. P. *et al.* 200
shrimp farming 27
side effects of social policies 35
Singapore 162, 163
site location economics 237–40
Skeptical Environmentalist, The (Lomborg) 11
small particulates 132
SO_2 emissions 137
social cost of capital 55, 62
social cost of carbon 54–5, 56, 57, 155, 303
social costs of driving 150, 163
social discount rates 63–4
social marginal benefits 49, 178
social marginal costs 25, 29–30, 49, 169, 303
social net benefits 27, 49
social opportunity costs 62, 63
South Korea 159, **182, 197**
Spain 89, 90–1, **197**, 220, 241
spatial data 94
Sport Utility Vehicles (SUVs) 149, *155*
Sri Lanka 28
starting-point bias 79–80, 303
state-property regimes 27–8

stated preference methods: choice experiments
    83, 87; estimating oil spill damages 221;
    nonmarket valuation 102; valuation methods
    78–**9**, 92, 96; valuing life 98
static efficiency 21–3, 31, 48, 51, 69, 303 *see also*
    dynamic efficiency
stationary-source air pollution 131–45;
    command-and-control (CAC) approach 132,
    133–6, 136–8; conventional pollutants 131–2;
    introduction 131; market-based approaches
    138–9, 139–42; summary 142–4
Stavins, R. N. 142
steel production 20, *25–6*, 35–8, *39*, 222, 259–60
stock pollutants: definition 303; pollution control
    108, 109–10, 113, 125; toxic substances
    and environmental justice 228, 242; water
    pollution 199–201
strategic bias 79, 303
Sulfur Allowance Program 140, 141–2
sulfur oxides 132, 140, 145n4
survey approach 58
susceptible populations 2, 196, 234
sustainable development 249–71; aspects of
    250–1, 251–2, 252–4, 254–9, 259–61, 261–2,
    263; car-sharing 158–9; growth-development
    relationship 264–6, 266–8; introduction
    249–50; summary 268–70; visions of the
    future 6, 9, 11–12, 275, 276, 278–80
SUVs (Sport Utility Vehicles) 149, *155*
Sweden 122, 157–8, **182**, 216, 280
Switzerland 28, 158, **182**, 228, 243, 267

tangible benefits 56–7, 70n5, 77, 304
tankers *196*–7, 219–20
Tata Motors 169
tax credits for electric vehicles 165
technique effect 256–7
technological progress: definition 304; efficiency
    and sustainability 253–4; pollution control
    110, 117–*18*, 124, 126; visions of the future
    13, 277, 278; water pollution 222, 223
technology diffusion 143–4
TEV (total economic value) 87–**8**
Thailand 27
thermal pollution 198, 304
third parties 82, 231, 235–6, 246, 304
threshold concept 133, 134
time factor (benefits and costs) 49–51
time preferences 64, 82

timing of emissions flows 134, 135–6, 143
TMDL (Total Maximum Daily Load) program 204, 212
total economic value (TEV) 87–**8**
Total Maximum Daily Load (TMDL) program 204, 212
total willingness to pay (TWP) 22, 77–8
Toxic Release Inventory (TRI) data 237–8, 242–4, 304
toxic storage and disposal facilities (TSDFs) 239
toxic substances and environmental justice 227–48; hazardous waste siting decisions 236–7, 237–40, 240–2, 242–3, 243–6; health effects 229; introduction 227–8; market allocations 231–4, 235–6; policy issues 229–31; summary 246–7
trade and the environment 254–63
trade restrictions 258, 260–1, 271n3
transaction costs 39, 40–1, 209–10
transferability 23, 304
transport subsidies 149
transportation pricing 161–8
travel-cost methods 89, 90–1
TRI (Toxic Release Inventory) data 237–8, 242–4, 304
tropospheric ozone depletion 181
Trump, Donald J. (45th US President) 55, 65, 180, 193n1, 274
TSDFs (toxic storage and disposal facilities) 239
Twain, Mark 207
TWP (total willingness to pay) 22, 77–8

UK *see* United Kingdom
uncertainty: air pollution 134, 159; climate change 173, 177–8, 186–7, 188–9; contingent valuation method 79; evaluating trade-offs 53nn1–3, 60, 63; pollution control 124–5, 126; toxic substances and scientific evidence 229, 230–1; visions of the future 10, 12; water pollution 213, 220
UNDP (United Nations Development Program) 267
UNFCCC (United Nations Framework Convention on Climate Change) 180
uniform ambient standards 134–5
uniformly mixed fund pollutants 114–20, *115*, *116*, *118*, *119*, 126
United Kingdom 63, 158, 159, **182**, **197**, 242
United Nations 4, 138, 180, 218, 249, 267

United Nations Conference on Environment and Development (Earth Summit) 11, 249
United Nations Development Program (UNDP) 267
United Nations Framework Convention on Climate Change (UNFCCC) 180
United Nations Millennium Development Goal 218
United States: climate change 173, 180; economic approach 28, 40; evaluating trade-offs 51–3, *55*, *57*, 60–1, 63; mobile-source air pollution 147–8, 149, 151, 152–3, 154–7, 157–8; pollution control 107, 114; stationary-source air pollution 131, 132, 134–6, 137, **139**, 144; sustainable development quest 259, 260–1, 261–2, 264, 265, 269; toxic substances and environmental justice 227, 229, 230–1, 233, 241; transportation pricing 161–2, 165, 168, 170n3; valuing the environment 76, 87–8, 93, 99, 101–2, 103n5; visions of the future 2, 4, 274, 279–80; water pollution 199, 205, *207*, 210, 218–21
US emissions, 1980–2015 **139**
US EPA *see* Environmental Protection Agency (EPA)
US Global Change Research Program (USGCRP) 2
use values 77, 97, 102, 220
USGCRP (US Global Change Research Program) 2
using the revenue from carbon pricing 184–5

value categories 99
value of statistical life (VSL) 100–2, 104n16
value transfers 92
valuing human life 97–102
valuing the environment 73–104; benefit transfer and meta-analysis 91–2; challenges 93–7; choice experiments 83–8; contingent valuation method 79–83; Geographic Information Systems (GIS) 92–4; introduction 73–4; revealed preference methods 89–91; stated preference methods 78–9; summary 102; types of values 77–8; valuation techniques 75–7; valuing human life 97–102; why do it? 74–5
vehicle emissions 147, 151, 168
vehicle miles traveled (VMT) 147, 156, 163, 166, 170n3
vehicle pollution 35, 163

visions of the future 1–13; environmental challenges 2–4, 4–5; meeting environmental challenges 5–6; overview 12–13; the road ahead 9–12; self-extinction premise 1–2; societal response to challenges 6–7, 7–8, 8–9

visions of the future revisited 273–81; conceptualizing the problem 274–5; conclusion 281; institutional responses 275–8; the issues 273; sustainable development 278–80

VMT (vehicle miles traveled) 147, 156, 163, 166, 170n3

Volkswagen 152–3

VSL (value of statistical life) 100–2, 104n16

waste flows 19, 107, 110

waste products *18*, 37, 107, *108*, 112, 279

waste-receiving water 196–201

water accessibility 4–5

Water Framework Directive (WFD) 216, 223

water pollution 195–225; control policy assessment 220–2; developing country control policy 216–19; European control policy 215–16; externalities 26–7, 35; introduction 195; nature of problems 196–8, 198–201; oil spills 219–20; summary 223; US control policy 201–6, 206–10, 210–15

Water Pollution Control Act 201–2, 206

Water Quality Act 202

water quality trading 213–15

water supplies 4–5, 93, 95, 218, 236, 277

watershed-based trading 210–15, **211**, *214*

Wätzold, F. F. 137

wealth effects 38

welfare levels 250–1, 268, 275

wet deposition 215

WFD (Water Framework Directive) 216, 223

WHO (World Health Organization) 138, 145n4, 163, 218, 246

willingness to accept (WTA) 79–82

willingness to pay (WTP) 79–82, 96–7, 101, 221 *see also* total willingness to pay (TWP)

with and without principle 56

World Bank 5, 120, 153, 168, 190

World Health Organization (WHO) 138, 145n4, 163, 218, 246

World Trade Organization (WTO) 259–61

Worldwatch Institute 11, 13

WTA (willingness to accept) 79–82

WTO (World Trade Organization) 259–61

WTP (willingness to pay) 79–82, 96–7, 101, 221 *see also* total willingness to pay (TWP)

zero-discharge goals 206–8

zero emission vehicles (ZEVs) 160, 281, 305

ZEVs (zero emission vehicles) 160, 281, 305

Zhao, J. 82

Zipcar 158–9

zone of influence 108, 144